Gramm...
Happy Mother's Day
1983 —
Love Always —

Jill
xox

by
KITTY KELLEY

ELIZABETH TAYLOR

The

Last Star

SIMON AND SCHUSTER • NEW YORK

1 2 3 4 5 6 7 8 9 10

LIBRARY OF CONGRESS CATALOGING IN PUBLICATION DATA

KELLEY, KITTY.
ELIZABETH TAYLOR, THE LAST STAR.
BIBLIOGRAPHY: P.
INCLUDES INDEX.
I.   TAYLOR, ELIZABETH, 1932–
2.   MOVING-PICTURE ACTORS AND ACTRESSES—
UNITED STATES—BIOGRAPHY.   I.   TITLE.
PN2287.T18K44   791.43'028'0924   [B]   81-9306
AACR2
ISBN 0-671-25543-6

A Niño de su osita rubia—siempre.

"Your heart knows when you meet the right man. There is no doubt that Nicky is the one I want to spend my life with."
—*Elizabeth Taylor*
Wedding to Conrad Nicholson Hilton, May 6, 1950

🙣

"I just want to be with Michael, to be his wife. This is, for me, the beginning of a happy end."
—*Elizabeth Taylor*
Wedding to Michael Wilding, February 21, 1952

🙣

"I have given him my eternal love. . . . This marriage will last forever. For me it will be third time lucky."
—*Elizabeth Taylor*
Wedding to Mike Todd, February 2, 1957

🙣

"I have never been happier in my life. . . . We will be on our honeymoon for thirty or forty years."
—*Elizabeth Taylor*
Wedding to Eddie Fisher, May 12, 1959

🙣

"I'm so happy you can't believe it. . . . I love him enough to stand by him, no matter what he might do, and I would wait."
—*Elizabeth Taylor*
Wedding to Richard Burton, March 15, 1964

🙣

"There will be bloody no more marriages or divorces. We are stuck like chicken feathers to tar—for lovely always."
—*Elizabeth Taylor*
Second wedding to Richard Burton, October 10, 1975

🙣

"John is the best lover I've ever had. . . . I want to spend the rest of my life with him and I want to be buried with him."
—*Elizabeth Taylor*
Wedding to John Warner, December 4, 1976

🙣

SHIMMERING in blue sequins and periwinkle eye shadow, Elizabeth Taylor strode onto the stage of the Mark Hellinger Theater to present the 1981 Antoinette Perry Award for Broadway's best musical. Her diamond necklace with its sapphire pendant bobbed against her bosom as the television cameras zoomed in on her imposing cleavage. Viewers were mesmerized.

As she started to speak, the entire audience suddenly rose to give her a standing ovation. Wildly cheering, the crowd paid homage to the woman whose beauty had for so long enchanted America. Now ripe and opulent at forty-nine, she no longer looked like the little girl who had ridden to glory in *National Velvet;* but the audience did not care. She could still bestow a touch of magic.

For years they had watched her suffer through illnesses, injuries, and heartbreaks, plus the scandals of her many marriages and divorces. They had witnessed her plummeting box-office appeal and gasped as she ate and drank to excess, ballooning into obesity. Seeing her glamour fade and her star falter, they had expected her to capsize, but somehow she had managed to survive—and now here she was dazzling them again, fresh from the triumph of her Broadway debut in *The Little Foxes.*

As she gushed her thanks, rambled on in her presentation, and even giggled as she mispronounced the names of the people she was supposed to honor, the audience whistled and stomped and screamed its approval. People knew that there would never be another star like this violet-eyed beauty. Her life had been extraordinary. She was the last of her kind. She had earned this resounding tribute.

CHAPTER 1

SARA TAYLOR WAS FRANTIC. She did not want Elizabeth to waste any film in this movie because her role was simply too small to justify such an extravagance. So as the lights dimmed on the *Jane Eyre* sound stage, she hid behind the director and started signaling to her daughter. Crossing her pudgy arms on her breast, Sara fluttered her eyes and lifted her head to heaven. The little girl in front of the camera strained to see her mother, who quickly put a finger to her neck; a signal that meant "You're overdoing it."

Earlier, Elizabeth saw her mother touch her stomach; that meant her voice was too shrill. A finger to the cheek was a secret signal to smile more. Now, seeing Sara plop her hands on her heart, Elizabeth knew she needed to put more emotion into her performance.

The scene called for the little girl to die of pneumonia, and the stage mother was determined that it be a perfect death and in one take. Still, Sara Taylor might have risked a few extra takes if she had thought her precious little angel was being upstaged by Margaret O'Brien and Peggy Ann Garner, the leading child stars in 1944.

Elizabeth Taylor was merely a featured player under contract to Metro-Goldwyn-Mayer studios and on loan to 20th Century–Fox. She had yet to reach star status. The difference between "featured player" and "star" was the difference between obscurity and celebrity—between $150 a week and $5,000 a week.

MGM beauticians styled hair for featured players. The stars were coiffed by Sidney Guilaroff, studio hairdresser *extraordinaire*. Wardrobe girls fitted featured players. The stars were dressed by Helen Rose, the studio designer. Clearly, there was a substantial difference between a featured player and a star—but it was a difference that Sara Taylor would soon overcome.

Like an antebellum lady with a swansdown fan, Sara Taylor hid her driving ambition behind a soft-spoken facade. A diminutive woman, she spoke with honey-dripping sweetness. She called her husband "Daddy," her daughter "my angel," and her son "my sweet lambie pie." Everyone else was simply "my dear." She understood the importance of meeting the right people, and tried always to be in the right place at the right time. She demonstrated her shrewd sense of timing by arriving in the film capital of the world with a spellbindingly beautiful daughter just when child stars were reigning supreme.

The year was 1939. The war devastating Europe had found Francis and Sara Taylor, both American nationals, running an art gallery in England for Francis' multimillionaire uncle, Howard Young, a well-known dealer with an important gallery in New York. To avoid the growing conflict, Francis Taylor sent his wife and two children home to America while he remained behind to close out his uncle's business. In a few weeks he joined his family in Los Angeles and opened his own art gallery.

Sara immediately identified with the glamour and excitement of the movie industry. By Christmas she was completely bewitched by the bright lights of Hollywood's dream factories. Like so many prospectors before her, she saw southern California as a gold-bearing mother lode to be mined for great fortune. With indefatigable energy she began making social contacts with anyone prosperous who might be associated with movies or interested in buying art from her husband.

She took her seven-year-old daughter with her everywhere and relished the reactions of people getting their first look at Elizabeth. Often there would be an audible intake of breath when someone saw the porcelain face haloed by its wreath of coal-black curls. The most arresting feature of this child's flawless face was the pair of sapphire-blue eyes framed with a double set of long black lashes. So blue were those eyes that in certain lights, they would seem violet. The first gasp would usually be followed by an exclamation: "What a beautiful child!" "Why, she's just exquisite!" "Absolutely gorgeous!"

Sara would smile proudly and look at her daughter. "Say 'Thank you,' my angel," she would purr, and little Elizabeth would smile, say "Thank you," and curtsy just as her mother had taught her. It was a charming performance, designed to impress.

No traces remained of the ugly baby Sara had given birth to on February 27, 1932. She sometimes winced when she remembered the strange little bundle the nurse had placed in her arms that day. Her reaction had been one almost of revulsion. The baby's eyes were squeezed shut and remained so for ten days, while her splotchy red face was crinkled and covered with black fuzz. Elizabeth Rosamund Taylor's mother was heartsick, especially when she thought of the Botticelli-beautiful boy she had borne two years before. But Sara turned her mind over to the Christian Science religion of Mary Baker Eddy, fully believing that her baby would be healed of its defects if only she willed it so.

Soon after moving to California, Sara joined a Christian Science church and enrolled her children in Sunday school. Although the Taylors could not afford to send their youngsters to private schools, Sara insisted that Elizabeth be given dancing lessons in a class with the daughters of many movie executives.

What Sara had anticipated soon happened. Through the parents of a child in her dancing class Elizabeth was asked to screen-test for Metro-Goldwyn-Mayer, and one of the patrons of Francis Taylor's art gallery asked her to test for Universal Studios. Convinced that her abiding faith had paid off, Sara told her gleeful eight-year-old that if God wanted her to be in movies, she would most certainly be in movies. "Divine love always has met and always will meet every human need," she said, with Christian Science confidence.

Over her husband's objections, Sara spent hours preening Elizabeth for both these studio introductions. She ran scales on the piano, drilled Elizabeth in her manners, and had her curtsying around every corner of the house. Too passive to voice real objections to his wife, Francis Taylor worried about the effect of all this activity on his daughter, but Elizabeth quickly assured him that she wanted to be an actress "just like Mommy."

Mommy never tired of telling her daughter about her years on the stage when she performed in stock companies under the name of Sara Sothern. Hating her maiden name of Warmbrodt because it sounded so guttural and unglamorous, Sara had it officially changed before departing Arkansas City, Kansas. With a new name but no money, she left home before finishing high school and made her way to the stage. She worked as an actress until 1926, when she married Francis Taylor. "I gave up my career when I married Daddy," she said, "and all the king's horses and all the king's men couldn't have made me take it up again."

Possibly true, say skeptical friends; but all the king's horses were not thirty years old when they married, either. "Sara, who was four years older than Francis, was almost an old maid in 1926," recalled a family friend. "She was thirty years old, and the prospect of finally landing a husband, and such a gorgeous one, too, was worth giving up a less-than-stellar career."

Still, Sara never forgot that she had once been an actress who had received rave notices in England. Elizabeth was enthralled by her mother's glamorous past and told her classmates she wanted to be an actress when she grew up.

"I knew . . . there would come a time when she would want to follow in my footsteps," said Sara Taylor. "I could still hear the applause of that wonderful night . . . when *The Fool* had opened in London at the Apollo Theater and I, playing the part of the little crippled girl, had stood alone in the middle of the stage and taken a dozen curtain calls, while a reputedly staid British audience called, 'Bravo, bravo, bravo!' "

For the audition at MGM, Sara dressed Elizabeth in a ruffled pinafore and patent-leather Mary Janes. She also carefully dressed herself. To simulate the silk stockings she could not afford, she rubbed suntan lotion on her legs and drew a dark seam with an eyebrow pencil. Before leaving the house, she sat Elizabeth down with her Christian Science prayer book and instructed her to think good thoughts. They repeated this routine a week later when Elizabeth auditioned at Universal.

When both studios made offers, the child begged her mother to sign with Metro, where Clark Gable was king and twenty-year-old Mickey Rooney was the number one box-office star in the business. But Sara, playing power broker, decided to pit one studio against the other. She told Universal that MGM had offered Elizabeth $100 a week. Universal promptly offered a contract of $200 a week, and Sara grabbed it. She told her daughter she would be much better off at the smaller studio because she would be given more time and attention.

Universal Studios gave Elizabeth Taylor three days' work in a movie called *There's One Born Every Minute*. Then, a year later, it declined to renew her option. Universal felt she didn't look as if she could ever be a star. She didn't have dimples like Shirley Temple. She couldn't sing like Judy Garland. She couldn't dance like Jane Powell. She couldn't cry on command like Margaret O'Brien. The final blow was delivered by Universal's casting director. "Her eyes are too old," he said.

Sara Taylor was devastated. Losing Elizabeth's salary in June of 1942 did not bankrupt the family, but the loss was felt. Francis and Sara had put aside half the Universal money to be held in trust until Elizabeth was twenty-one, as they were required to do by law. The other half—approximately $4,000—had allowed them to live less close to the edge in the flats of Beverly Hills.

The overseas war had now reached America—and this meant rationing and coupons at home. There was little surplus money available, especially in the art business, and Francis Taylor began spending long idle hours in his gallery.

The effort to defeat Hitler and Mussolini united America and

England. This Allied front aroused pro-British sentiments throughout the country, but nowhere to a greater degree than in Hollywood, where Louis B. Mayer of Metro-Goldwyn-Mayer worshiped all things English. Vivien Leigh and Laurence Olivier were lionized as the golden lovers of the era. Greer Garson emerged as MGM's first lady when her movie *Mrs. Miniver* won seven Academy Awards and swept the boards as the most popular motion picture of 1942.

During that year MGM had to recast the part of a little girl with a British accent to play opposite Roddy McDowall in *Lassie Come Home*. The child originally selected had grown too tall by the time her scenes were to be filmed, so the studio started searching for short girls with British accents. The producer, Sam Marx, knew Francis Taylor and had noticed that his British-born daughter was small for her age and very pretty. He called the art gallery to see if Elizabeth might be interested in trying out for the small role.

Francis called his wife. Within minutes Sara and ten-year-old Elizabeth were speeding to MGM, nearly blowing the gaskets out of the family's secondhand Chevrolet.

"Oh, Mommy, Mommy, Mommy," Elizabeth chanted, "I'm going to be in movies, I'm going to be in movies."

Sara remembered what had happened at Universal and how disappointed Elizabeth had been.

"If it's right for you to have it, my precious, you will," she said. "But if it's not God's design for you, it won't be right."

Elizabeth got the part of the little girl who sets Lassie free and was paid $100 a week as a free-lance player. *Variety* mentioned her in passing as a pretty moppet who showed up to good advantage. *The New York Times* ignored Elizabeth and hailed the collie as "the most remarkable performer in this film." Still, MGM seemed satisfied enough to offer her a long-term contract at $75 a week. This time Sara did not even try to negotiate. She signed without an argument, figuring she would get an agent and renegotiate later. Elizabeth jumped up and down with excitement and raced out to tell her thirteen-year-old brother, Howard, who remained unimpressed.

Her gentle father was happy for her, but apprehensive. Sara, of course, was enraptured, and from this point on the career of her daughter became the passion of her life.

She rolled Elizabeth's thick black hair in rags every night so the stovepipe curls would hang perfectly. She starched and ironed the hand-me-down dresses her daughter received from their neighbor Anne Westmore. She accompanied Elizabeth to the studio every morning and made sure she learned how to hit a mark on the floor without looking and how to work within the nimbus of her key light. She shepherded her to the studio acting classes, dancing classes, singing classes, makeup sessions, and costume fittings. And she was always on the set, delivering subtle signals behind the director's back. Sara also saw to it that Elizabeth read her Scripture lessons every day on the set and attended Christian Science Sunday school every week. For these relentless efforts in her daughter's behalf, MGM designated Sara legal guardian and chaperone and paid her from Elizabeth's salary for every week that the child worked.

For aspiring stars and starlets, Metro-Goldwyn-Mayer was then the mecca of movie studios—the richest, the biggest, the best. Producing one full-length feature film every week, this fantasy factory boasted as its motto "More stars than there are in the heavens." By the time Elizabeth Taylor walked onto the lot, the crowns of Joan Crawford, Greta Garbo, Norma Shearer, and Myrna Loy had been passed to Greer Garson, Judy Garland, Katharine Hepburn, and Lana Turner. Other studios produced stars like Rita Hayworth and Betty Grable, but MGM remained the studio renowned for its glamorous movie queens.

Acclaimed internationally for assembling the greatest aggregate of creative manpower, MGM was the world's biggest entertainment enterprise—with the largest number of famous people ever controlled by one organization.

Sprawling over 167 acres in Culver City, this magic kingdom consisted of parks and lakes and a private zoo. There were a red brick schoolhouse, a playground, a hospital, and a commissary where Louis B. Mayer put his mother's chicken soup on the menu and placed matzohs on every table. There were an avenue of cardboard building fronts straight out of New York, a Paris boulevard, and a street of houses with white picket fences where Andy Hardy lived. Cavalry units in full-dress uniform shot blank cartridges and charged through paper jungles on one lot while three-ring circuses jumped through plastic hoops on another.

This fantasy world was the exclusive domain of Louis B. Mayer, a short Russian immigrant who loathed homosexuals, Communists, and intellectuals but loved children, especially little children under contract to MGM. They provided the magic that brought millions of people stampeding into theaters every week for movies of laughter and music and patriotism. It was the children who wove the spell of innocence and hope. They were the good, clean, wholesome elements of the folksy entertainment that was MGM's specialty.

In order to keep his stars shining, Mr. Mayer, as he was fearfully addressed, instituted the Department of Special Services, better known as the publicity department. From this area flowed the real power of the studio, for it was the efficient and thorough publicists who created and packaged the stars.

"Publicity people formed us in those days," recalled Peggy Lynch, a Metro featured player. "They really shaped our persona, our psyche, our selves. They chose the image they felt would be best for us; then they would fine us and take the money from our paychecks if we did not live up to that studio image. I was supposed to be the girl-next-door type and act as a wedge against June Allyson not to let her get out of line, the same way Kim Novak was later supposed to keep Rita Hayworth in check. If I went to the store in a man's shirt hanging out of a pair of jeans, like we did in those days, I'd be fined. That was considered detrimental to the star system. As a pretty princess type, Elizabeth was never once fined by Publicity because her mother kept her dressed perfectly at all times."

Not content with merely creating its stars, the studio manipulated their lives—arranging dates, orchestrating courtships and engagements, planning marriages, even announcing divorces. Along the way, it took care of anything that might threaten the star system—an arrest, adultery, or an occasional abortion.

"We did everything for them," said Howard Strickling, former MGM publicity head. "There were no agents, no personal press agents, business managers, or answering services in those days. All these services were furnished by the MGM publicity department. No other studio did it quite the way we did. We told the stars what they could say and what they couldn't, and they did what we said because they knew that we knew best. When things went wrong, we had a way of covering up for that, too."

Homosexual male stars posed a problem for the studio publicity department because of Mr. Mayer's frenzy on the subject. So all single men were required to publicly date studio starlets and be photographed looking brawny and tough. Naturally, MGM men were encouraged to marry so that Louis B. Mayer would be reassured of their masculinity. He was rabidly suspicious of any unmarried male star who did not chase women.

Metro-Goldwyn-Mayer guarded its female stars even more carefully. "They had to stay as pure as the driven snow," said Ann Straus, head of the studio portrait gallery. "Metro girls didn't smoke or drink or swear, and Metro girls never ever had sex before marriage. Our girls could never have done that."

Understandably, the MGM publicity department was the perfect vehicle for a stage mother like Sara Taylor. She now had an entire staff of people who were paid to help her make her daughter a star. She knew that the studio publicists would be as obsessively possessive of Elizabeth as she was and just as enterprising in her behalf. Still, Sara took no chances.

On her own, she began cultivating friendships with the most powerful columnists in Hollywood. With Elizabeth in tow, she visited Louella Parsons to gush over her cocker spaniel, "Jimmie." Then she called Hedda Hopper to say that Elizabeth was begging to see "Wolfie," Miss Hopper's beloved mutt, and ask whether she might bring her over. Miss Hopper, of course, was charmed. Sheilah Graham, who was British, was regularly invited to tea. When the studio arranged a luncheon interview for Elizabeth with Adela Rogers St. John, Sara bought a pink rosebush for her daughter to take as a gift, knowing that the famous Hearst columnist was inordinately proud of her rose garden.

Craving affection and approval, Elizabeth was eager to please her mother by cooperating with the MGM publicity department. She loved posing for photographs and could sit for hours while someone curled her hair. But more cooperative was Sara Taylor, who took great liberties in spinning tales of Elizabeth growing up in England. Catering to MGM's pro-British sentiments, Sara waxed eloquent about an upper-class world of nannies and chauffeurs and elegant estates in the English countryside. She alluded to garden parties at Buckingham Palace and royal dancing classes with the little princesses, Elizabeth and Margaret Rose. MGM publicity dutifully ground out stories about its new contract player incorporating all of these fantasies.

"The years we lived in London were such wonderful years of grandeur, pomp, and ceremony," Sara said. "There was the wedding of the Duke of Kent and the beautiful Princess Marina . . ."

Sara was nothing if not upwardly mobile. Her breathless recitation of the Silver Jubilee of King George V made it sound as if she had actually shared crumpets with Queen Mary in the royal box instead of merely watching from the sidelines like everyone else. Still, Louella and Hedda loved it. So did Sheilah and Adela. Soon short items appeared in their syndicated columns about "the beautiful little British-born Elizabeth Taylor." By shrewdly exploiting the dual citizenship which linked Elizabeth to England and America, Sara ensured that her daughter would be considered for any movie needing an English child.

After a bit part in *Lassie Come Home* and another bit part in *The White Cliffs of Dover,* Elizabeth was "loaned" to 20th Century–Fox to die of pneumonia in *Jane Eyre.* Still, she was merely a featured player, unheralded and unbilled. The stars were Margaret O'Brien, hailed as "extraordinary," and Peggy Ann Garner, a blond wisp who was reviewed as "desperately appealing." Elizabeth Taylor did not merit a notice. In fact, she did not even get a screen credit. But Sara was not concerned. Her precious angel was already in training for her next role, which her mother was convinced would lift her to stardom.

CHAPTER 2

HAVING ONCE SEEN ELIZABETH TAYLOR on a horse, Pandro S. Berman considered her for the lead in *National Velvet*. He looked again and reconsidered. "Pretty enough, but just too small," said the MGM producer.

That was in the fall of 1943, when Elizabeth was eleven years old but only as tall as a first-grader. She would not have been convincing then as Velvet Brown, the British youngster who disguises herself as a boy, sneaks into the jockeys' weighing room, and rides her horse to victory in the Grand National Sweepstakes.

But Berman decided to wait for her to grow. He sent his assistant, Billy Grady, to tell Elizabeth and her mother the story of *National Velvet,* the best-selling novel by Enid Bagnold about a little girl who fantasizes about winning a horse named The Pi in a village lottery. She wins the horse and has another fantasy about entering The Pi in the Grand National. Then Velvet Brown fantasizes about winning the world's most prestigious and demanding steeplechase. Her mother, who once swam the English Channel, encourages her. "Everyone should have a chance at a breathtaking piece of folly at least once in his life," she says.

So, with the help of a failed jockey to be played by Mickey Rooney, Velvet begins to train her horse. Then, disguised as a boy, she rides it to victory. When her sex is discovered, Velvet is disqualified, but she doesn't care: she has fulfilled her dreams by pulling off a magnificent ruse that any little girl on earth would have loved to call her own.

Elizabeth wanted the part of Velvet because Berman promised that the studio would pay for her riding lessons at the Dupee stables, where she would learn how to steeplechase and jump horses. Sara, of course, wanted her to have the part because it was a major star-making role. She convinced her daughter that she was indeed Velvet Brown, and Elizabeth, so very impressionable, was transformed into the young English girl. She turned her bedroom into a horsey boudoir of bridles, saddles, and statues of horses, and began calling herself Velvet.

"National Velvet was really me," she said years later, still believing her childhood fantasy.

Each day Sara would pray with her daughter from the Christian Science prayer book before going into Berman's office at MGM, where he would measure Elizabeth against his office door. When she was tall enough to play opposite Mickey Rooney, he planned to schedule shooting. "Considering that Mickey was only titty-high, she really didn't have to grow that much," said the producer.

Later Sara and MGM decided, for publicity purposes, that this account was not dramatic enough; they put forward another story claiming that Elizabeth, to win the coveted role, had actually willed herself into growing three inches in three months. Sara was quoted as saying that when she took her daughter into Mr. Berman's office, he told her Elizabeth was just too short for the role. She said that Elizabeth, with great conviction, answered, "I will grow, Mr. Berman—I will grow into the part." And, said Sara, whispering at the wonder of it all, she did grow. "She promised that she would, and I think she started growing from that very minute."

Elizabeth too preferred the more arresting version. In an early demonstration of blending fantasy with reality, she always parroted the MGM story as if it had really happened that way.

National Velvet took seven months to shoot and gave Elizabeth her first lesson in how excruciating moviemaking could be. "I worked so hard on that movie," she recalled. "I worked harder on that film than in any other movie in my life."

She got up every morning before school and rode for an hour, practicing on a skittish horse by the name of King Charles who would be The Pi in the movie. All the difficult jumps on the racecourse were performed by a professional jockey, but Elizabeth did the rest of her own riding. While none of the scenes in which she rode was particularly dangerous, she still had to spend long hours developing her horsemanship.

The role of Velvet Brown called for Elizabeth to wear orthodontic braces. The studio initially sent her to a dentist who made a set of gold braces for $120 and a set of silver braces for $86. Both sets were tested in Technicolor, but neither was photogenic. So a new wire brace with a false palate was custom-designed, and Elizabeth was called in to test it. Two of her baby teeth were pulled and two temporary teeth inserted in the raw sockets so that the appliance would fit properly.

Watching his daughter suffer so for this role made Francis Taylor angry. When MGM wanted to cut Elizabeth's hair so that she would look like a male jockey, he balked. The studio checked with its lawyers to see if Elizabeth could legally be made to cut her hair.

After several conferences, the legal department stated this conclusion in an in-house memorandum: "This is an unreasonable request and we do not have a contractual right to require her to disfigure herself or alter her appearance to this extent." Thus, Elizabeth kept her hair and wore a wig.

This was the first and last time Francis Taylor ever took such a stand. In fact, his position as husband, father, and head of the household was slowly eroding. That year Elizabeth bought two Valentines. One she gave to her father, and forgot to sign it. The other went to her movie father, Donald Crisp. On it she wrote: *"From your littlest daughter with love, Velvet."*

Making that movie became the focus of Elizabeth's days and her mother's as well. Sara accompanied her every minute she was on the set and continued the secret signaling whenever she felt her daughter's performance was lagging. "The California state law is that any child working in a studio must be accompanied at all times by a parent or guardian until he or she is eighteen,'' Sara explained. ''I would have been with her anyway. It was the only way we could have allowed her to be in pictures.''

More than parental protection motivated Sara. She was as entranced as her daughter by the glamorous movie stars she saw daily in the MGM commissary. Elizabeth satisfied her infatuation by carrying an autograph book and begging for the signatures of Spencer Tracy, Katharine Hepburn, and Hedy Lamarr. At the same time, Sara was pestering studio publicists for an introduction to Clark Gable.

''I was Elizabeth's camera double in *National Velvet*,'' said Margaret Kerry, ''and about the only thing I remember is cringing every time I heard her mother speak. I can still hear her say, 'Oh, Elizabeth' in that voice of hers.'' Miss Kerry's impersonation of Sara's high-pitched tone skitters up the scale, growing shriller with each succeeding note.

'' 'Oh, Elizabeth,' her mother would call out after every scene. 'Oh, Elizabeth, darling. Come along.' '' recalled Miss Kerry. ''And Elizabeth, who was very well behaved in those days, would obediently respond, cooing, 'Coming, Mother dear.' ''

Elizabeth's own speaking voice was never properly developed for range or dimension by the MGM drama coach. ''We'd all go to Lucille Ryman for our daily lessons,'' said Margaret Kerry, ''and Miss Ryman coached all of us—Susan Peters, Donna Reed, Kathryn Grayson, Elizabeth, and me—to come out sounding identical.''

Margaret Kerry also recalled that Elizabeth had a flair for the melodramatic not unlike her mother's. ''I was standing in for Elizabeth in scenes where you'd just see her back,'' she said. ''During one part I was next to Angela Lansbury when a man kicked her in the leg so hard I could hear the thwack on her bone. It nearly killed her. And as soon as it happened, Elizabeth ran over to Angela, threw her arms around her, and said, 'Oh, Angela, Angela. Are you all right? Are you hurt?' She screamed and cried and wept and moaned and it was all very theatrical, but still I think she cared.

''Originally, Mona Freeman was cast as Elizabeth's older sister in the movie," continued Margaret Kerry, "but one day she was suddenly replaced with Angela. Elizabeth and I found Mona outside the sound stage dissolved in tears. That really shook up Liz. She never knew until that very moment that anyone could be replaced. It frightened her."

It also prompted her to work hard, going to great lengths to endear herself to the director, Clarence Brown, who became quite paternal toward his young player. One day, after watching the rushes, someone put a gold star on Elizabeth's dressing room door and "MISS TAYLOR" on the sign. Brown insisted that the star be removed and "ELIZABETH" put on the sign instead.

"He was afraid I would be hurt about it," said Elizabeth, "and he explained that he was afraid it might go to my head, or wherever it does go that makes people change—and he wanted me always to stay the same. I knew what he meant because Mummie and I had talked it over before, and I promised him with all my heart that I would never, never change. . . ."

That vow was inevitably broken once *National Velvet* was released. The movie was a smash hit. Critics hailed Elizabeth's "burning eagerness tempered with sweet fragile charm." When the Academy Awards were presented, Anne Revere won the Oscar for best supporting actress as Velvet Brown's mother and Robert J. Kern received an Oscar for film editing. But it was Elizabeth Taylor who became a star.

"Elizabeth Taylor is as natural and excellent a little actress as you would ever hope to see," said the *New York Post*.

"It makes a star of 12-year-old Elizabeth Taylor," claimed *Pic* magazine.

"She really did a wonderful job in that movie," recalled producer Pandro Berman. "Afterwards she came to me and said, 'I never cared so much about anything in all my life as I do about that horse, King Charles.' So I went to Louis Mayer and said I thought it would be a wise gesture and a good business investment to give Elizabeth the horse. It was the only thing she cared about, and she had done a splendid job in the movie."

Again the studio lawyers were consulted. They discussed the

possibility of giving away a property purchased for $800 and now worth $500. Finally, according to a 1945 legal memo, they decided on a conditional gift. Elizabeth would get the horse "with the understanding that if we need him in future retakes he will be available to us at any time and without cost."

On her thirteenth birthday she received a call from Benny Thau, the studio personnel chief, informing her that King Charles would be hers. A few weeks later she received another surprise present from MGM. In appreciation of her performance in *National Velvet,* the studio awarded her a bonus of $15,000.

The chasm between featured player and star had finally been bridged. It had taken MGM five years of small roles and bit parts to make Judy Garland a star. The big studio and the stage mother had accomplished the same feat for Elizabeth Taylor in half that time.

With her daughter now established as one of MGM's outstanding assets, Sara Taylor wasted no time. Her suggestion that Elizabeth get a new contract produced a quick raise in her weekly salary—from $200 to $750. For forty weeks' guaranteed work, thirteen-year-old Elizabeth Taylor now earned $30,000 a year. Also included in the new contract was a clause directing $250 a week to Mrs. Taylor. Thus Sara earned $10,000 a year for acting as her daughter's chaperone—compensation that was deducted from Elizabeth's salary.

Although she tried to have it deleted, Sara could do nothing about a clause stipulating that ten percent of Elizabeth's gross salary had to be used to purchase U.S. war bonds and stamps. She did, however, manage to steer her daughter into the lucrative realm of commercial tie-ups, or CTU's, as they were called in the forties.

The first commercial agreement paid $3,000 for the use of Elizabeth's photograph in an endorsement of Lux soap. Next came CTU's with Woodbury soap and Max Factor cosmetics; then a greeting-card company which promised to pay thousands for one of Elizabeth's drawings, followed by Elizabeth Taylor paper dolls and Elizabeth Taylor coloring books. She also received

$3,000 for every radio appearance, half of which went to Sara Taylor as a fee for coaching her daughter.

One of the most effective commercial agreements was with Duell, Sloan and Pearce for a book titled *Nibbles and Me*. For her first effort as an author, celebrating her trained chipmunk Nibbles, Elizabeth received $1,000. The seventy-seven-page book, with "illustrations by the author," was submitted to "Dear Mr. Editor" by Elizabeth in her penciled longhand. The deft touch of MGM publicity surfaced in the letter Elizabeth wrote the publisher: *"The lady at the studio said she didn't want us to have this typed because she thought you would rather have it as it is."*

First there was Lassie, then The Pi, and now Nibbles. The book put the finishing touches on the studio image of Elizabeth Taylor as a sort of little-girl reincarnation of St. Francis of Assisi. The publicity department arranged for pictures of her to appear in fan magazines surrounded by her pets—a golden retriever, a cocker spaniel, a black cat named Jeepers Creepers, her horse, eight chipmunks, and a squirrel. Quite predictably, her next picture was *Courage of Lassie,* in which she received top billing over the famed MGM collie. Still, some critics were more impressed with the dog. Wrote the *New York Herald Tribune:* "Lassie walks off with all the acting honors, which is as it should be."

That film was released in 1946, the year more people went to the movies than at any other time in history. For the flood of veterans returning from the war with high hopes and little money, movies provided cheap entertainment. Young GI's and their wives flocked to see the films of Van Johnson, Gary Cooper, Bob Hope, Humphrey Bogart, Greer Garson, Betty Grable, Roy Rogers, Bing Crosby, Ingrid Bergman, and Margaret O'Brien, the top ten stars in the world.

Elizabeth had been insulated from the war. Her father had been too old to enlist and her brother too young. Mickey Rooney was one of the few persons she knew to actually go into the armed services. Living on Elm Street in Beverly Hills and attending school in the single classroom at Metro-Goldwyn-Mayer also shielded Elizabeth from the reality of the outside world. Although she was thirteen years old when President Roosevelt died, his death had little impact on her, partly because her parents were such staunch Republicans that they totally ignored the nation's intense grief.

Nor were the Taylors impressed by Roosevelt's successor. "Why, he's just a merchant, a haberdasher," Sara told friends when Harry Truman took office. But Sara's distaste for Truman was quickly forgotten in January of 1946, when she was invited to accompany Elizabeth to the White House for a radio broadcast with Bess Truman. Elizabeth later told her mother that President Truman looked exactly like Louis B. Mayer, the head of MGM.

Elizabeth's only vivid recollection of the war years is celebrating V-J Day with her family in Chicago during a train layover. Those memories do not revolve around the mass celebration of the war's end as much as around herself as a newly minted movie star.

"We were so surprised to find in all the excitement that crowds of people recognized me as Velvet and wanted my autograph," she said at the time. "It made me feel very happy. I felt dazed by all the noise."

Such moments of elation were often followed by periods of brooding depression when Elizabeth called in sick and took to her bed for days at a time. The studio chose to consider these layoffs instead of sick days, so Elizabeth still was paid—as was Sara.

Elizabeth's first illnesses seemed a reaction to changes taking place within the family which she was too young to comprehend. These changes began when Elizabeth was "loaned" to Warner Brothers to do *Life with Father*. The movie took five months to shoot. By the middle of it, Sara was in love with the director, Michael Curtiz, a fifty-eight-year-old Hungarian who is best remembered for directing *Casablanca* and discovering Doris Day. To the lusty Curtiz, Elizabeth's fifty-year-old mother represented merely another romance—one that would end as soon as the film was completed.

That brief affair ruptured the Taylors' marriage for a time. In the fall, Francis left with his son for Wisconsin to stay with his uncle, Howard Young. Elizabeth remained in Hollywood with her mother. During the separation her times of sickness increased. Although the studio's legal files show at least two absences a month through the year, she was officially charged with only five days of illness and so had to forgo only five days of pay. Most of her 1946 absences occurred in November, the month her parents separated.

"I think that is more coincidence than anything else," said a friend. "She really wasn't that upset when her father moved out of the house. I don't think it bothered her very much at all."

Elizabeth admitted as much herself. "It was no special loss," she said. "I had felt fatherless for years anyway. I looked upon my agent, Jules Goldstone, and Benny Thau of MGM as my two fathers. I went to them for help and advice."

At the time, Elizabeth was filming *Cynthia,* a movie that cast her as a sickly teen-ager whose physical frailties were intensified by her overprotective parents. "I think she might have carried her ill and ailing on-camera role into real life," said a co-worker.

Off camera, MGM was hovering anxiously. When Elizabeth's face sprouted a small blemish, the studio doctor was summoned and she was dismissed from work to consult a top dermatologist in Los Angeles. When she stepped on a nail, she was rushed to the studio hospital in an ambulance. A minor cough demanded thoracic examination. In the beginning it was the attentive studio that reacted to any physical ailment or cosmetic affliction, but soon the juvenile star was alerting the studio. A production memo from one of Elizabeth's early movies shows the type of attention she came to expect as a teen-ager:

> At approximately 9 A.M. today Elizabeth Taylor phoned to the set from the makeup department to advise that one of her eyes was bloodshot and wanted to know whether she should have it checked at the studio hospital. She was advised to see the director first, whereupon she came to the set. The director said it would not interfere with shooting. Dr. Blanc was called. He arrived at approximately 11 A.M.,

gave her an eyewash lotion, and advised that it was nothing serious. . . .

Earlier in the week there had been another production memo:

On Tuesday, July 6, Elizabeth Taylor complained of a slight irritation on her nose when she was in makeup. Dr. Blanc was called; he examined her and advised that she could be made up. . . .

Besides the fretting over her health, there were other changes. As the little girl of *National Velvet* suddenly grew up, co-workers like Mary Astor, who played her mother in *Cynthia,* saw Elizabeth's childish shyness and sweetness disappearing.

"I had seen Elizabeth from a distance in the MGM commissary during the making of *National Velvet,*" said Miss Astor, "and she had at that time a serious, dedicated look. That was gone; she was no longer quite as shy, and she was beginning to be conscious in a very normal, teen-age way of her own beauty. She was also bright. Very bright. Head-of-the-class type of brightness. For a kid, she concentrated very well on the work—and I liked her. But I liked another 'daughter' better—Judy Garland. Judy was warm and affectionate and exuberant. Elizabeth was cool and slightly superior. More than slightly. There was a look in those violet eyes that was somewhat calculating, as though she knew exactly what she wanted and was quite sure of getting it."

By this time Elizabeth definitely knew that she wanted to be a movie star. She had a row with her mother one day at the studio, and Sara, waspish because of her marital problems, snapped at her daughter for doing her work badly.

"Elizabeth, if you aren't interested in doing well whatever you have to do—then quit," she said. "It's up to you."

That night Elizabeth wrote her mother a "sorry" note. *"I've done a lot of thinking,"* she said, *"and I realize that my whole life is being in motion pictures. For me to quit would be like cutting away the roots of a tree—I'd soon wilt and become dead and useless."*

Elizabeth thrived on her studio life. She loved going on location trips and making movies. She enjoyed receiving fan mail. She was thrilled to see herself on the cover of *Life*. She relished her special status as an MGM celebrity, especially her proximity to other movie stars.

"It was tremendously thrilling to go into the commissary for lunch," she recalled. "They were all there—Judy Garland, Lana Turner, Spencer Tracy, Hedy Lamarr. And there was the lovely sweet smell of the Pancake makeup the women wore. . . ."

There was also the indescribable scent of sex in the air whenever women like Ava Gardner glided by. Fourteen-year-old Elizabeth was especially intrigued by glamorous stars like Lana Turner. She saw the looks they got when they walked into a room. All heads turned. And there was something more than admiration in the reactions of men. She wanted to stimulate the same kind of response. So she painted her fingernails and toenails scarlet; splashed toilet water all over herself; wore earrings the size of bracelets, and full skirts and peasant blouses with plunging necklines. She cinched in her waist as tightly as she could and stood straight, thrusting her breasts forward as if offering the world two huge dollops of freshly whipped cream.

"I was constantly having to watch Elizabeth in those off-the-shoulder blouses," recalled Ann Straus. "She'd just discovered how much attention she could get when she wore one, and when she discovered that, she was impossible. She'd have herself paged during lunch and then she would pull her shoulders down and walk through the commissary—the entire length—so everyone could see her. I'd always pull those shoulders up whenever I could, but she was too fast for me sometimes."

But apparently not fast enough for Sara, who did nothing to discourage her daughter from trying to look older. In fact, she promoted the effort, pushing her headlong into womanhood.

"I still remember when Elizabeth was only thirteen years old and went to Washington to launch the March of Dimes campaign with Mrs. Truman in the White House," recalled a friend. "Sara dressed that little girl in a black velvet dress, a white fur coat, and a pair of seamless nylon stockings. Of course, Sara dressed herself in pastel frills befitting an ingenue, but she had Elizabeth looking like a Joan Crawford hussy.''

Like a hothouse flower artificially forced to spread its petals, Elizabeth bloomed before her season. At fifteen she had blossomed into a staggeringly beautiful woman whose looks suggested dark, seductive secrets. The writer J. D. Salinger was overwhelmed when he first saw her. "She is the most beautiful creature I have ever seen in my life," he said.

One day Elizabeth was sitting idly at the children's table in the commissary, wearing one of her provocative off-the-shoulder blouses, when a magazine photographer approached and asked if he might take pictures of her in a bathing suit. Elizabeth turned to her mother for approval.

"Oh, I think that would be lovely, darling," said Sara, who proceeded to arrange a session at the beach for the next day. Elizabeth posed in a one-piece white bathing suit and the photographer snapped hundreds of pictures, each one exquisite.

"You have no bad angles," he informed her. "In fact, I think you are the most beautiful woman I have ever photographed, and I've photographed every one in the world."

"Oh, golly," squealed Elizabeth. "Did you hear that, Mother? Did you hear what he said? He said I was the most—"

"Yes, my angel, I heard him," said Sara, and quickly repeated his words to her good friend Hedda Hopper. The next day Miss Hopper's column proclaimed fifteen-year-old Elizabeth Taylor the most beautiful woman in the world.

Sara was in regular communication with all the leading Hollywood columnists by this time, but Hedda was her favorite—the one she always called first. (Shortly before Elizabeth's fifteenth birthday, Sara became ill and contacted her estranged husband, begging him to come home and try to make a go of their marriage. Francis Taylor dutifully went to his wife's bedside to comfort her and then agreed to try a reconciliation. The next day he read about it in the newspaper. The item was headlined, "ELIZABETH TAYLOR'S PARENTS REUNITED." The by-line: Hedda Hopper.)

Capitalizing on the newest bloom in its garden, MGM tossed

the flowering starlet into *A Date with Judy,* a glossy musical designed to promote a pretty blond singer by the name of Jane Powell. Elizabeth had the secondary role of a beautiful young girl from an affluent background who was spoiled and sophisticated. It was a rich-girl role she would play to perfection for years.

Sara Taylor remembers *A Date with Judy* as the movie that launched her daughter from child stardom to screen seductress. "That was the beginning of the glamour buildup," she said.

Sara was right. The *New York Herald Tribune* said that the erstwhile child of *National Velvet* had disappeared and in her place was "a real 14-carat, 100-proof siren with a whole new career opening in front of her."

Despite the reviews, the most beautiful fifteen-year-old in the world could not get a date. She continued pulling down her shoulders, hiking up her skirts, and belting in her waist to show off her perfect figure. Her determined mother bought her a black strapless evening gown and let her wear lipstick every day, but no one asked her out. Finally, in desperation, Sara asked her seventeen-year-old son, Howard, who was attending Beverly Hills High, to bring his friends home to meet his sister. Howard replied that his friends wouldn't be interested in a movie star. Sara insisted. She even staged cookouts and beach parties to attract Howard's friends. Sara's efforts still did no good. The boys simply ignored Elizabeth.

"Elizabeth would come to my house weekends and she would spend hours telling dreamy stories about handsome Prince Charmings," recalled girlhood friend Gaylen McClure. "She was pretty idealistic and childish. When I took her to parties, she didn't know how to act with boys."

During this time Elizabeth spent hours by herself lying on her bed daydreaming. She played games of make-believe with her animals, making chirping sounds like a squirrel and tweeting like a bird. Comfortable in her fantasy world, she felt unsure of herself away from it. She read *Archie* comic books and devoured stories in fan magazines about movie stars, their mansions, their gowns, their furs, and their priceless jewels. The "fannies," as

they were called, became the cornerstone of her formal education while movies formed her ideas of love and romance and the
ways of the world. She confided to her neighborhood chum that
after getting her first screen kiss in *Cynthia,* she "practiced kissing" with a pillow every night.

She also "practiced looks"—sitting in front of a mirror for
hours trying out expressions, posing and puckering her lips. She
once startled a photographer by posing in a tight sweater and
inquiring, "What sort of a look do you want now—one that says
I'm waiting for time to go by?"

Elizabeth became fixated on romance, drawing pictures of herself wrapped in a man's arms and writing dreamy poems and
rhymes. Sara destroyed the morbid poetry that reflected her
daughter's adolescent depressions, but she allowed selected writers to see some of Elizabeth's happier rhymes. One was entitled
"My First Kiss." Another was called "Loving You":

> *Loving you*
> *Loving you*
> *Could be such heavenly bliss,*
> *And as our hearts would tenderly kiss,*
> *I would know how happy I could be . . .*
> *Happier still, if only you'd love me.*
> *If only you'd love me.*

"I did a lot of reading, painting, drawing in those days," Elizabeth later recalled. "Anything that was escapism, I suppose. I
went to the movies all the time. Horseback riding meant everything to me—the friendly isolation, the solitude, the companionship with the animal."

Sara remained her daughter's best friend and constant companion. "Elizabeth and I are so close we think as one person," she
said.

"I told her every kind of inside fear I had," said Elizabeth.

And her biggest fear in 1947 was that she would never get a
date. She was heartsick about it—and her mother was almost
panic-stricken.

CHAPTER 3

"MOTION PICTURES ARE NOTHING MORE than beautiful photographs," Louis B. Mayer was fond of saying. And it was on that premise that Metro-Goldwyn-Mayer built its empire, giving its beautiful women as much screen exposure as they needed to become box-office sensations. Beauties like Ava Gardner and Lana Turner were cast in movie after movie; such unrelenting exposure created millions of loyal fans who would flock to whatever film they were in. In 1948, MGM executives estimated that a maximum investment of $150,000 in a female star would eventually make the Metro lady worth at least $2.5 million to the studio.

By her sixteenth birthday, MGM considered Elizabeth Taylor a wise investment. After eight movies in five years she was not yet getting star billing, but she was well beyond the featured-player stage. Unlike Margaret O'Brien and Shirley Temple, she had made the transition from child star to ingenue without awkwardness. With stardom only a few steps away, the studio raised her salary to $1,000 a week and increased her exposure.

During the filming of *Julia Misbehaves,* the director, Jack Conway, stopped production to throw a surprise birthday party for the young starlet. MGM, knowing of her near-obsession with clothes, gave her the sophisticated wardrobe she wore in the movie. Her parents presented her with a solid-gold key to a baby-blue Cadillac—but refused to give her driving lessons. Yet all

Elizabeth Taylor really wanted for her birthday was a date with a young man. The studio soon took care of that too, by producing as an escort an All-American football player from West Point by the name of Glenn Davis.

"I had come home from the Army in the summer of 1949 to play an exhibition game for Army against the Los Angeles Rams," Davis recalled, "and Hubie and Doris Kearns took me out to Malibu to meet Elizabeth. Doris worked in the publicity department of MGM, and Elizabeth was a famous young girl at the time."

Davis was known throughout the country as "Mr. Outside," the halfback who made football history at the U.S. Military Academy with his running partner, Doc Blanchard, nicknamed "Mr. Inside." Formerly co-captain of the West Point football team, Davis also was the star of the basketball team and captain of the baseball team.

Matching America's hero with the most beautiful teen-ager in the world seemed inspired, especially to Sara Taylor. "When I saw that frank, wonderful face, I thought, 'This is the boy.' I felt such a sense of relief. My worries were over," she said.

Elizabeth was filming MGM's remake of *Little Women* at the time. When not needed at the studio, she would race to the Malibu beach house her family had rented for the summer. A frequent companion was her stand-in, Marjorie Dillon.

"Elizabeth never wanted to be alone, and so I would always go along with her," said Miss Dillon. "She did not feel secure by herself. She needed someone with her all the time, even to go for a soda, or to go shopping.

"Although everyone was always telling her how great she was, how beautiful she was, how spectacular she was, she needed even more reassurance. She was constantly asking, 'How do I look?' 'Do you like my hair this way or should I set it again?' 'Do you think I should wear this color or would I look better in that color?' She worried constantly about how she looked and was always looking in the mirror for blemishes. She once said, 'If I don't feel I look really good, I feel just awful physically.' She showered three times a day and changed her clothes all the time. Her mother had impressed on her the importance of good grooming, and it's about all she thought about.''

In *Little Women* MGM once again typecast Elizabeth, putting her in the role of the pretty but spoiled Amy March. The movie was designed to spotlight June Allyson, MGM's reigning sweetheart, with Elizabeth, Janet Leigh, and Margaret O'Brien as co-stars. Always standing by was Sara Taylor, ready to tell anyone who would listen that it was her own appearance as Amy in an Arkansas City presentation of *Little Women* that had inspired her theatrical career.

Elizabeth's summer romance with Glenn Davis, meanwhile, was as prim and proper as any in Louisa May Alcott's novel. Recalled Davis: "We didn't drink or smoke, and I never laid a hand on her. We kissed and stuff like that, but we certainly didn't sleep together."

"Elizabeth felt Glenn's epaulets and that was about it," said a man who knew them both during the summer of 1948.

Their dates included family barbecues at Malibu; playing touch football on the beach with Elizabeth's brother, Howard, and his friends; and going to the movies with Janet Leigh and her date. One of the most memorable dates occurred on August 26, when Glenn took Elizabeth to a Los Angeles Rams intersquad game where he set a record of 10.8 seconds for the 100-yard dash wearing full football equipment and carrying a football. Elizabeth did not understand the significance of the accomplishment, but she was dazzled by the swarms of reporters chasing Glenn and the photographs that appeared in the newspapers the next day.

In the fall of that year, Movietone News recorded Elizabeth flinging her arms around Davis at the airport as he was leaving for Korea. She was inconsolable, especially since she had tried so hard to keep him home.

Months before Davis was scheduled to ship out, Elizabeth called newspaper columnist Frank Farrell when she was in New York. "I was a close friend of her great-uncle, Howard Young, and so I too was called 'Uncle,'" recalled Farrell. "Elizabeth asked me to pick her up at eight P.M. at the Plaza. When I arrived, she informed me we were going to Mamma Leone's on Forty-eighth Street.

" 'Christ sakes,' I said, 'We'll be mobbed.' But she insisted, saying, 'Oh, no, we won't. Please, Uncle Frank. I want to go there. I just must go there.' So, of course, we went there. Little did I know that the West Point officers were having dinner at Mamma Leone's that particular evening. She'd already called the restaurant and made a reservation in my name. We arrived and were led to a table surrounded by fifty damn Army officers. As a Marine I wasn't exactly in seventh heaven, but Elizabeth didn't care. She knew that the West Point football coach, Red Blaik, would descend on us to say hello, and her primary purpose for being there was to talk to Red. She was determined to get Glenn Davis out of the Army and onto a pro football team so he wouldn't have to go to Korea."

The coach came to the table and Elizabeth pounced on him with her project. Rather taken aback by her boldness, Red Blaik said he couldn't do much to help her, but he jokingly suggested that she talk to her Uncle Howard, who was a good personal friend of General Eisenhower.

"Elizabeth cornered Howard the next day," said Farrell, "and I told him if he had the balls to actually go to Ike with this one, he'd be a bigger man than I was."

As Francis Taylor's rich uncle, Howard Young had enabled the Taylors to enjoy a life-style they otherwise could never have afforded. They vacationed with him at his ranch in Wisconsin, at his winter home in Florida, and at his country estate in Connecticut. The multimillionaire art dealer lived in a New York penthouse overlooking Central Park with his alcoholic wife, Mabel, who spent her days with round-the-clock nursing care. Mumps at the age of twenty-two had deprived Howard of the ability to have children, so he took special pleasure in his namesake, Howard Taylor, and Elizabeth, whom he spoiled outrageously. When she begged him to talk to his friend Dwight D. Eisenhower to keep Glenn Davis at home, Howard Young did not want to disappoint her, so he approached the General with the request—and was promptly turned down.

"Ike said that Glenn Davis was an Army officer first and a football player second and that if he was summoned to Korea he would, by God, go to Korea, and that was the end of that," recalled Frank Farrell.

Before leaving, Glenn Davis gave Elizabeth his gold All-American football and she put it on a chain around her neck. "This football means I'm engaged to Glenn," she said. With tears in her eyes, she kissed Davis goodbye. "I'm going to wait for Glenn and we'll marry when I'm eighteen or nineteen. As soon as I finish my picture, I'm going to Korea to see him," she announced. "I love Glenn and want to be with him."

In October, MGM shipped her to England to make *The Conspirator* with Robert Taylor. Sara accompanied her, of course, but Francis Taylor could not afford to join them. "I don't see how I can, as I am not doing much business right now and it costs such a lot to travel that distance," he told his gallery assistant.*

As Elizabeth's star rose, so did her life-style and that of her mother. For the London trip they had a bedroom–and–living-room suite at Claridge's and a personal studio representative to handle all press relations. A private teacher supplied by the Los Angeles Board of Education made sure that Elizabeth spent three hours a day at her lessons as required by California law. During their stay Sara and Elizabeth insisted on a side trip to Paris,

---

* The year before, Sara had insisted on a return trip to England to visit her friends and show off her movie-star daughter. The studio made all the arrangements for their trip, including limousine service at every stop, but refused to pay for the transportation. Sara suggested that the cost be deducted from Elizabeth's salary, but MGM sent the $2,641.01 bill to Francis. "There is no way in which this sum can be deducted from Elizabeth's salary without the approval of the court, which procedure would be lengthy and costly," the studio said, "and we are wondering if it would be convenient for you to send us a check to cover the above amount at this time." Francis paid the bill, but nearly bankrupted himself in the process. So there was no way he could consider making the trip with his wife and daughter in the fall of 1948.

demanding luxurious accommodations plus a car and driver to take them sight-seeing and shopping. The studio paid for everything. In addition, it had a basket of twenty-four white orchids waiting in their suite when they arrived in London. What most impressed Elizabeth, though, was a much smaller bouquet—a dozen red roses that cost Glenn Davis, who was still in Korea, a month's pay and a lot of trouble to have sent.

"We're engaged to be engaged," she said, confiding that the twenty-three-year-old Army lieutenant had proposed and that she had accepted.

"She was so in love," recalled her mother. "She wrote Glenn every night and never went out on a date the five months we were there."

In one of her nightly letters, Elizabeth said that when she had to give her screen kiss to Robert Taylor she merely closed her eyes and pretended it was Glenn. Of course it wasn't as good as kissing Glenn, she said, but it helped her get through the scene.

"They told her to kiss," recalled Robert Taylor, "and she kissed. The only thing I had to teach her was to powder down her lips." The powder was necessary so that Elizabeth's enthusiastic kissing would not smear her co-star's makeup.

Playing the screen wife of Robert Taylor was her first adult role, but the movie was so uninspired that MGM refused to release it until her career was more secure. Studio officials were pushing their Elizabeth Taylor investment toward stardom, but there was a growing concern about the dividends.

"Elizabeth was a bit of a worry then to all of us," said Pandro Berman, the MGM producer who made her a star in *National Velvet*. "We recognized her beauty, but she didn't have the strength of voice at sixteen or the personality to go with her face. . . . She was half child, half adult, and she was actually not as good an actress as she had been at the beginning, making *Courage of Lassie* or *Life with Father*."

Actually, Elizabeth cared more about getting married than about making movies. After *The Conspirator* was finished, she and her mother met Francis Taylor in Florida, where Uncle

Howard was planning a huge party to celebrate Elizabeth's seventeenth birthday. Her best present was a telephone call from Glenn to say that he would be furloughed on March 1 and would meet her at her uncle's home.

Before Glenn arrived, Elizabeth was introduced to a handsome twenty-eight-year-old man by the name of William D. Pawley, Jr., who took her to a few parties. His multimillionaire father had been ambassador to Brazil and Peru, and when Sara saw how wealthy and socially prominent his family was, she began having second thoughts about Glenn Davis.

Accompanying her daughter to the Miami airport a few days later, Sara tried to divert the photographers from recording the passionate kiss Elizabeth planted on her returning hero's lips. Despite her efforts, pictures of the handsome returning Army officer being embraced by the famous movie star appeared around the world.

"I flew to Uncle Howard's place straight from Korea," recalled Glenn Davis. "I was wearing my uniform and that was about it. I had no civilian clothes with me, and not very much money."

However, Davis was carrying a cultured-pearl necklace with sixty-nine graduated pearls for Elizabeth's seventeenth-birthday present, plus a ruby-and-diamond ring—a miniature of his crested West Point ring—in a blue velvet box, which he planned to give her before the formal announcement of their engagement. She got the pearls, but she never received the engagement ring.

"It just never happened," said Davis. "She had started dating that rich guy, Pawley, and—let's face it—he showed her a better time than I did. The guy was real slick. He gave a party for us when I arrived. I stayed there for about a week or ten days of high-stepping and then I took off. I just said 'Screw it' and left.

"I wasn't exactly broke at the time—I had twenty thousand dollars from starring in *The Spirit of West Point*—but I sure as hell couldn't compete with Pawley's millions. Liz's family didn't have any money at all and that concerned her mother a lot, so Sara really pushed this Pawley deal."

The very ambitious mother was also concerned about appearances, and that was where the young lieutenant blundered.

"When Glenn Davis showed up in his T-shirt and Army trousers at Howard Young's formal dinner table, that did it for Sara," recalled Frank Farrell. "Yet Sara was no one to talk about good manners. Her biggest preoccupations in life were her Christian Science religion and her blocked bowels, which she would discuss *ad nauseam.*"

Glenn Davis left Florida carrying the engagement ring he had bought for Elizabeth, but not the gold football she had worn for seven months. "I suppose I'll give it back," she told a reporter, "but he did say I could keep it." She also kept the cultured-pearl necklace with the sixty-nine graduated pearls.

"Liz called me a few weeks later and said, 'Please do me one last favor and take me to the Academy Awards,' so I did, because I didn't want to embarrass her," Davis recalled, "but I didn't hang around after that. That was the last time we ever really saw each other."

Shortly after the Oscar presentations, the MGM publicity department announced the end of the romance between the All-American football hero and the most beautiful teen-ager in the world.

"Afterwards I felt pretty bad for a while," Glenn Davis recalled, "but I'm glad now that I didn't marry her."*

Francis Taylor also felt bad. "We thought sixteen too young for marriage, but we never forbade it," he said. "There would have been no point in playing the heavy-handed parent, especially when the boy in question was a splendid one."

Elizabeth felt bad too, but for different reasons. She was concerned about the negative publicity generated by her split with Davis. "Maybe I should have fallen for a busboy or something,"

---

* After being discharged from the Army, Davis played professional football for the Los Angeles Rams. In 1951 he married Hollywood starlet Terry Moore, was divorced a year later, then married a woman from Louisiana. In 1960 he was appointed director of special events for the *Los Angeles Times.*

she said. "Then the whole thing wouldn't cause so much attention."

Sara shrewdly responded to the sudden rash of bad press by calling Louella Parsons to ask her advice. During the conversation she told the Hollywood columnist that Elizabeth was still making fudge in the kitchen on rainy days and getting down on her knees every night to say her prayers.

Actually, Sara felt quite good about the split, because with Glenn Davis out of the way Elizabeth could now concentrate on the splendidly rich Bill Pawley, whose socially prominent family owned a yacht and a mansion with servants and a swimming pool. Young Pawley seemed to Sara so much more sophisticated than the young Army officer.

"Bill was twenty-eight and Elizabeth was seventeen," Sara said. "He had been everywhere. He was tall, dark, and handsome, with deep blue eyes that matched her own. He fascinated her—and all of us—with his tales of India, China, and South America. . . ."

As soon as Bill Pawley read about the breakup, he wrote Elizabeth a romantic letter declaring his love and proposing marriage. He offered to fly to California to present her with a diamond engagement ring. She called him to accept, telling him how much she loved him, but at her mother's insistence she asked him to keep the news private until they could make a formal announcement.

Elizabeth and Sara flew to Florida in May to spend three weeks with the Pawleys at their home on Sunset Island. "They became engaged the day after we arrived," recalled Sara, "and Elizabeth begged me to announce the engagement so she could wear her lovely diamond ring in public."

Bill Pawley had given Elizabeth her first diamond—a 3.5-carat emerald-cut solitaire flanked by two half-carat diamonds on either side.

To announce the engagement, Sara called a press conference and for forty-five minutes did all the talking. Bill Pawley did not say a word. Neither did Elizabeth, except to instruct photographers to take pictures of her engagement ring. "Nice piece of ice," she said. "That's what Bill calls it."

"Elizabeth won't be graduated from the Metro-Goldwyn-Mayer high school until next February," said Sara Taylor. "That's why we'd like to wait until spring for the wedding. Elizabeth will be returning to Hollywood in two weeks to start work on a new picture.

"Yes, she will continue her career, but we aren't talking much about that right now," added Sara. "We're going to let it work out."

From the very beginning Bill Pawley had made it clear that he expected his bride to be a wife, not a movie star, and Elizabeth eagerly agreed to give up her career. It was no sacrifice, she assured her fiancé, because she was bored to death making movies. "I'd much rather make babies," she said.

A few days later Elizabeth received a call from Sam Marx, the MGM producer who had cast her in *Courage of Lassie.* Marx was in Miami filming a movie, and he invited Elizabeth and her mother to tea. The Taylors accepted.

When Sam Marx arrived at the Pawley mansion, Bill answered the door and asked him what he wanted.

"I'm taking Elizabeth to tea," he said.

"The hell you are!" roared Bill Pawley. "She's coming fishing with me."

Elizabeth settled the matter by saying, "Mr. Marx gave me my first chance in movies, and I told him I would come for tea and I'm going to tea."

Bill Pawley slammed out of the house without saying a word. Elizabeth went to tea, but was tearful all afternoon. Once again Sara Taylor reassessed the situation. That night she told Bill that Elizabeth was truly in love with him and wanted to marry him, but perhaps they should let a little time and distance test their commitment to each other.

Still wearing her diamond engagement ring, Elizabeth returned to Hollywood to begin work on *The Big Hangover,* a romantic comedy starring Van Johnson. She spent hours every night talking long-distance to her fiancé in Florida. But tension grew as Bill pressed her to give up her career and her mother warned her against it.

Unable to make up her mind, she asked everyone around her what she should do. At times she became depressed.

"She was still going to school, getting ready for her high school exams, when we were making the picture," recalled Van Johnson. "One day I passed her dressing room; there she was with a schoolbook in her hand, gazing at the ceiling with a tragic look.

" 'Hey, sugar,' I said. 'What's wrong?'

" 'Oh, Van, I'm so depressed,' she sighed. 'I just feel as if I'd like to die today.'

"One couldn't laugh," said Johnson. "You remembered too well how it was when you were having growing pains yourself."

But it was more than growing pains. A very immature teenager found herself in the awful position of wanting to marry her handsome rich fiancé but having to give up her movie-star career to do so. "She would have done it, too, if only her mother hadn't made her feel so guilty about it," said her stand-in, Marjorie Dillon. "Mrs. Taylor made Elizabeth feel that she was the sole support of the entire family and that she would be throwing away all their love and faith in her if she quit the movies."

There was also another consideration. If Elizabeth gave up her career, Sara would automatically be off the MGM payroll. With Francis Taylor virtually retired, Sara could not afford to lose the money she was earning as her daughter's guardian. She shrewdly proposed that Elizabeth and Bill get married, live in Miami, and stay in Hollywood only when Elizabeth was working. Bill Pawley tentatively agreed, and Elizabeth was ecstatic. "In Hollywood I would not be anything but Elizabeth Taylor," she told *Photoplay* magazine. "In Miami I'll be Elizabeth Pawley—and I'll like it."

Sara's solution held things together while Elizabeth began another rich-girl role in *Father of the Bride* with Spencer Tracy and Joan Bennett. She announced to the press that she felt "positively drooly" playing the part of a bride-to-be on camera while looking forward to the same role in real life.

The solution fell apart on December 15, 1949, when MGM announced that Elizabeth Taylor had been "loaned" to Paramount for a highly dramatic role in *A Place in the Sun*, a movie based on Theodore Dreiser's *An American Tragedy*. The release went on to say that Elizabeth would be appearing opposite Montgomery Clift and Shelley Winters under the direction of the legendary George Stevens.

"Oh, Mother, can you possibly believe it?" Elizabeth cried when told the news.

"Oh, my precious. I always knew you'd make the top. With the best director in Hollywood instructing you. . . ."

Bill Pawley was not so thrilled. He phoned Elizabeth demanding to know the exact date they would marry and the exact date she would give up her career.

"Bill, just as soon as I get this picture finished, then we'll get married," she promised.

"I thought you wanted to give up your career for me."

"Oh, Bill, I do, I do—the moment I finish this picture."

"I thought you were bored with your career."

"Bill, I am. I truly am. But you don't know what it is to work for somebody like George Stevens. . . ."

"No, I don't. I thought you loved me."

"Bill, I do. I love you more than anything in the world. Oh, Bill, wait. Mother wants to talk to you."

Sara took the phone.

"Bill, dear, listen," she said. "It won't take Elizabeth any time to make this picture—not more than five or six months at the most. And after all, she is only seventeen, and to make a picture with George Stevens—well, you wouldn't want her to miss out on such an opportunity, and . . ."

That evening Bill Pawley flew to California for a showdown with his fiancée and her family. He told Elizabeth that everything would be over between them if she didn't give up her career that instant. He said that he had waited for her to do the Van Johnson movie and then the Spencer Tracy movie, but he wasn't going to wait for her to do one more movie, even if it was for George Stevens, whoever the hell he was.

Elizabeth sobbed and Sara pleaded and begged, but Bill Pawley remained unyielding. He left California the next day and made the announcement to the press that his engagement to Elizabeth Taylor was broken. He admitted that her motion-picture commitments "had something to do with it."

CHAPTER

W‍HEN THE EXECUTIVES AT P‍ARAMOUNT P‍ICTURES told Montgomery Clift that he was taking Elizabeth Taylor to the premiere of *The Heiress* at Grauman's Chinese Theater, he refused. He hated dressing up in a tuxedo to attend what was in his opinion merely a tawdry spectacle that produced only flashbulb blindness and aching cheeks from smiling at the hysterical fans pressing against police barricades. He felt that he was a serious actor who shouldn't have to play these "cheap movie-star games." Besides, he had never even met the bosomy starlet he was to be paired with. "Who the hell is this Elizabeth Taylor, anyway?" he asked.

She was a gorgeous seventeen-year-old MGM princess, Clift was told, and she had recently been on the cover of *Time*. He remained unimpressed. He did not want to go to the premiere. The thought of having to sit in a theater with hundreds of strangers watching him watch himself on the screen seemed the worst sort of voyeurism. But Paramount insisted that he attend and that he escort Elizabeth. After all, the studio reminded him, he was now the hottest male property in Hollywood, and she was going to be his romantic co-star in *A Place in the Sun*. Since the movie would pivot around the affair of the young lovers portrayed by Clift and Taylor, it made perfect sense to the Paramount publicity department that the two of them make a splashy public appearance together. Montgomery Clift had no choice: Paramount had produced his last movie, *The Heiress,* and Paramount was producing his next movie, *A Place in the Sun.*

At the prospect of going out with the twenty-nine-year-old Broadway actor, Elizabeth raced to Helen Rose in the MGM wardrobe department to plan her outfit for the evening. She begged the designer for something "sexy and sophisticated," and waltzed out with a strapless net gown and a white fur cape.

Sara Taylor greeted Clift at the front door when he arrived to pick up her daughter. She was as curious as Elizabeth about this "Method" actor from New York who everyone said was so talented. Monty Clift's sensitive good looks and charming manner left Sara gushing—so much so that Elizabeth was embarrassed. In the car she turned to Clift and said, "Sorry about Mother. She can be a real pain in the ass."

That earthy apology, coming as it did from the lips of what appeared to be the most beautiful and virtuous young woman on earth, so startled Clift that he laughed out loud and immediately relaxed. The press agent accompanying them later told Clift's biographer Patricia Bosworth that Elizabeth had looked ravishing that evening but had been so foul-mouthed and unconcerned about going to the premiere that she had made everyone feel at ease. Monty had dragged along his drama coach, Mira Rostova; a block before they reached the theater, Mira and the press agent leaped out of the limousine so that Monty and Elizabeth could be photographed making their romantic entrance unencumbered by chaperones.

Having braved the gantlet of shrieking fans and exploding flashbulbs, they took their seats. As the house lights dimmed, Monty slouched in his seat and began moaning as his image appeared on the screen. "Oh, God, I'm so awful, Bessie Mae," he said to Elizabeth. "I'm so awful."

"You're wonderful," whispered Elizabeth, who was mesmerized by Clift's performance. "Really, you're wonderful, just wonderful."

When the movie was over, the audience shouted its approval with lusty cheering and clapping. People made their way through the crowd to congratulate Monty, telling him what a spectacular performance he'd given. He nodded and smiled and said "Thank you." Then, laughing his strange, wild cackle, he grabbed Elizabeth's hand and pulled her out in the aisle. "Let's get out of here, Bessie Mae," he said. "Let's get out of here right now."

Back in the limousine, Elizabeth asked in her twangy voice why he called her "Bessie Mae." He told her he didn't want to call her by her movie-star name. "The whole world calls you Elizabeth Taylor," he said. "Only I can call you Bessie Mae."

After the premiere, Elizabeth and Monty attended a party at the Hollywood mansion of William Wyler, director of *The Heiress*. They were among the last to leave, and it was nearly two in the morning before Clift took Elizabeth home. He walked her to the door, kissed her lightly on the forehead, and turned to go.

"Sleep well, little Bessie Mae," he said.

Elizabeth watched him walk backward to the limousine and waited until he was in the back seat before going inside the house. Later she told her mother that Montgomery Clift was the strangest man she had ever met. Complicated, intense, and wound up, he was unlike anyone she had ever known. He took his "craft," as he called it, seriously, and had even spent a night in the San Quentin death house to prepare for his electric-chair scene in *A Place in the Sun*.

This movie was based on Theodore Dreiser's novel *An American Tragedy*. The author's blunt indictment of "the American dream" and its corrupting influences had caused quite a stir when it was published in 1925. Elizabeth had no idea who Theodore Dreiser was, nor did she know why George Stevens had altered Dreiser's characters and renamed the movie. All she knew was that she was going to play the part of a beautiful, rich socialite named Angela Vickers who falls in love with Monty in the role of George Eastman, a young, poor employee in her father's factory. She also knew that Shelley Winters, an actress from Universal Studios, was playing the pathetic factory girl who, after becoming pregnant by Eastman, insists he marry her and give up Angela. When she persists, Eastman takes her boating, knowing she cannot swim. When the boat capsizes, he does nothing to save her.

Elizabeth had no concept of the psychological implications of the story, nor did she understand its powerful nuances of characterization. She wasn't too concerned about her part. To her it was quite obvious what the role of Angela Vickers personified. "It's another rich-girl role," she said. All she really cared about was her bathing-suit scene and the flattering evening gowns Edith Head was designing for her.

George Stevens was extremely concerned about everything pertaining to the film. He had to be very careful that this movie would not be construed as un-American. He also had to convince Theodore Dreiser that the film wouldn't cheapen the author's condemnation of a particularly ugly facet of American life. Dreiser despised the earlier movie version made by Paramount in 1931, which depicted the George Eastman character as a homicidal sexual deviate.

Elizabeth was unaware of the blacklist. She knew nothing of the House Un-American Activities Committee and was oblivious to the vicious witch-hunting taking place in Hollywood at the time. "She was not one to read the newspaper," said her stand-in, "and she never listened to the news on the radio. Her whole life was making movies, having fun, and wearing pretty clothes. She was too young to know what a Communist was. All she knew about was cashmere sweaters."

To pacify the studio, Stevens discarded the negative title of the book for the more upbeat *A Place in the Sun*. He also renamed the characters, hoping this would increase the distance between the novel and the movie. Despite changing the title and the names of the characters, Stevens convinced Theodore Dreiser that he would remain faithful to the plot and tell the story without melodramatic contrivances. In the end, although Stevens strayed from the original story, he produced a cinematic masterpiece that reflected the American obsession with money, sex, and social standing and showed what striving to achieve them can do to a person's character.

George Stevens needed Elizabeth Taylor in this film because of her extraordinary, almost surrealistic beauty. "The part calls for not so much a real girl," he said, "as the girl on the candy-box cover, the beautiful girl in the yellow Cadillac convertible that every American boy sometime or other thinks he can marry."

And Elizabeth Taylor in 1949 personified the outer reaches of male fantasy. She was breathtakingly exquisite. Her velvet skin and black sable eyebrows framed eyes so deceptively blue they frequently looked violet. Her nose was perfectly chiseled and set above the sort of full and sensuous lips that produced the fantasies of adolescence in mature men and the soppiest of verse from serious poets. There was not one flaw on her face—the only mark was a charming mole on her right cheek. Weighing 110 pounds, she claimed measurements of 37-19-36 and lied about her height, saying she was 5 feet 4 inches tall when she was barely 5 feet 2. On the screen she looked tall and willowy, so her actual height made little difference. Spilling over with sex appeal, she was indeed the kind of girl American boys dreamed of marrying. Elizabeth Taylor was the ideal woman. She had the kind of beauty that would bring all a man ever dreamed of—wealth, fame, position. George Stevens knew that with Elizabeth Taylor as his star, the audience would understand why George Eastman would kill for a place in the sun with her.

The fact that Elizabeth Taylor had so far demonstrated little acting ability was something George Stevens would worry about later. In Montgomery Clift and Shelley Winters he had two colossal talents eager to work under his renowned direction.

Shooting began in October at Lake Tahoe, a clear mountain lake with water the color of an emerald, straddling the border between California and Nevada high in the Sierra Nevada mountains. Elizabeth arrived by train from San Francisco, accompanied by her stand-in, Marjorie Dillon; her MGM schoolteacher; and her ever-vigilant mother. Montgomery Clift arrived with his drama coach, a tiny but imposing woman, and Shelley Winters was accompanied by her sister, Blanche.

The first scene on the schedule was Elizabeth and Monty making love by the side of a lake and then splashing around in the water together like playful kids having a water fight. The mountains at that time of year were so cold that patches of snow had to be hosed off the ground and smudge pots kept constantly burning.

The script called for Monty and Elizabeth to throw off their outer clothes and rush into the lake in their bathing suits, but Monty refused to disrobe. Stevens then rewrote the scene with only Elizabeth wearing a bathing suit. With the cameras ready to roll, Sara Taylor refused to let Elizabeth do the scene. She told Stevens that her daughter was menstruating and had terrible cramps and could not risk the "grave danger."

"What's the matter?" asked the director. "Can't she swim?"

"Of course she can swim," replied Sara, explaining that the "grave danger" was not drowning but exacerbating Elizabeth's menstrual cramps and imperiling any future pregnancies.

Over Sara's objections, Stevens insisted that Elizabeth do the scene. When she didn't do it right, he made her do it over and over and over. Sara watched as Elizabeth ran into and out of the freezing water. At the end of the day she took Elizabeth back to the hotel and would not allow her to resume shooting for three days. Shelley Winters recalls Sara spending the rest of the time at Tahoe complaining that Elizabeth would never be able to have children because Stevens had made her go into the frigid lake in a bathing suit. For the next twenty years Elizabeth refused to work during her period and had the stipulation written into her contracts.

George Stevens was a demanding man who gave painstaking attention to every detail of his films. "I'm one of those directors who believe every element that goes into a picture affects the viewer," he once said, "although the viewer may not realize the impact of the tiny minor things."

Stevens' obsession with minutiae included the installation of a Stutz Bomber motor in a boat that skims the lake while George Eastman rows the pregnant factory worker to the spot where he intends to leave her drowning. The noise generated by the Stutz motor is ominous, creating a mood of impending disaster.

In a lecture to the American Film Institute, Stevens said that what interested him most in making *A Place in the Sun* was the relationship of opposing images. "Shelley Winters busting at the seams with sloppy melted ice cream . . . as against Elizabeth Taylor in a white gown with blue ribbons floating down from the sky. . . . Automatically there's an imbalance of images which creates drama."

So effective was Stevens in establishing these opposing images that Shelley Winters literally got sick when she saw herself as the drab, pregnant, and unwed Alice Tripp looking at a newspaper photograph of her lover motorboating with the beautiful Angela. Although this was one of the best parts she would ever play and one that was to earn her a nomination for an Academy Award, she resented having to look so ugly alongside Elizabeth Taylor's beauty. At one point she asked Stevens if Elizabeth had to look quite so gorgeous in the movie.

"I was kidding, but I wasn't," Shelley Winters said. "I mean, with that beautiful black curly hair, enormous violet eyes, tiny waist, and gorgeous bosom. . . . Besides that, she kept driving an enormous white convertible Cadillac through the picture."

Shelley admitted that for the rest of her life she drove a succession of white convertible Cadillacs simply to make up for her feelings of deprivation during *A Place in the Sun* and Elizabeth's overwhelming beauty in the picture.

As beautiful as she was, Elizabeth still wasn't much of an actress. Stevens was aware of her basic shortcomings and spent most of his time working with her to get the performance he wanted. Elizabeth was accustomed to the adulation of MGM directors who were delighted to have her merely appear in front of their cameras looking pretty. She had never worked with anyone like Stevens, who demanded take after take of her scenes and called for physical gestures and vocal inflections she had never thought of. Stevens constantly talked to her about her role, telling her over and over again the type of girl she was portraying. When he couldn't get the results he wanted, he sometimes baited her. Other times he ignored her and concentrated on Clift. Once, in exasperation, he reminded her that this movie was not entitled *Lassie Comes Home to a Place in the Sun.* Humiliated by the insult, Elizabeth burst into tears and ran off the set. Stevens kept on working as if nothing had happened. He later accused the MGM princess of fits of "distemper," saying, "If we had a little something that would disappoint her, if she thought I was more severe in my aim than the scene needed to be in a make-believe thing like a movie, she'd spit fire."

Years later, when he was directing her in *Giant* and wanted her to wince in pain, he tried the same baiting technique, but by then she had grown much tougher and refused to respond to him. Finally, he instructed the wardrobe lady to ram Elizabeth's size-8 feet into a pair of size-5 shoes so she would have to do the scene in real pain and thus give him the genuine wince he wanted on film.

When it came time for the very intimate scenes with Monty, which Stevens knew would be difficult for Elizabeth, he closed the set and worked with the two of them alone. "Everyone had to get off the set," recalled Marjorie Dillon, "and if you were caught peeking, you'd really get it from Stevens. He kept all of us away so that Liz and Monty could say what they wanted to say and he could make suggestions and not humiliate them in front of anyone.

"He would then play mood music softly and quietly to help them get into character. He changed the volume by hand control, and with that music he showed them what he wanted them to do, and he finally got the performance out of them."

Monty also tried to help Elizabeth. When they were together off the set, he would ask her questions about her character that made her think about the woman she was playing. He probed her psyche and showed her how to go inside herself for characterization. He was never impatient or harsh. She was awed by his highly charged concentration before the camera and, stimulated by his intensity, transcended her own rudimentary talent and began responding to him in kind.

The greatest demands on Elizabeth came during the first love scene with Monty, which Stevens shot entirely in close-up, the camera going in so tight that it records the fuzz on the nape of Elizabeth's neck and the mole on her right cheek. Stevens wanted the dialogue in that scene to be a rushed and staccato torrent of words. "Monty had to let loose—he was so enormously moved by her," said the director. "Elizabeth must be compelled to tell him how wonderful and exciting and interesting he is all in the space of a few seconds. . . . It had to be like nothing they had ever said to anyone before."

Stevens worked on the dialogue until two in the morning. He presented it to Elizabeth the next day. She looked at the slip of paper which said, *"Tell mama . . . Tell mama all."*

"Forgive me, but what the hell is this?" she asked.

"This is what you're going to say when you pull Monty's head toward you," said Stevens.

Elizabeth balked at the line, but Stevens insisted. He tried to explain to the seventeen-year-old virgin the primitive sexual urgency he wanted to wring from her.

"Elizabeth dissolved when she had to say 'Tell mama,' " Stevens recalled. "She thought it was outrageous she had to say that—she was jumping into a sophistication beyond her time."

Every night Stevens would show the rushes in the projection tent and patiently explain why one particular print of a scene was better than another. For the first time since she had gone before the cameras, Elizabeth was learning the art of motion pictures. She was thrilled seeing herself on film with Monty. The chemistry between them on the screen was so intense that it made her squirm in her seat. Never before had she been so aroused. It was unsettling to watch what George Stevens had captured.

Excited by her daughter's performance, Sara Taylor invited Hedda Hopper to the set to watch Elizabeth and Monty rehearse. Hedda was wide-eyed watching the little girl from *National Velvet* seduce Montgomery Clift in front of the camera. "Elizabeth, where on earth did you ever learn how to make love like that?" she asked before racing off to her typewriter to tell the world about "the magnificent lovebirds."

Monty was enraged that Stevens had allowed Hedda Hopper on the set, and he criticized Elizabeth for playing up to "an old gobbler." It had never occurred to Elizabeth not to cooperate. She knew the Hollywood rules and tried to explain them to Monty as she had learned them from her mother and MGM. She urged him to cooperate with the media by giving interviews and posing for pictures. "If you did," she told him, "you'd not only be the biggest superstar in the world, you'd win an Oscar too."

Later, George Stevens moved the cast back to the Paramount sound stages in Hollywood to complete the interior scenes and again allowed reporters on the set. Dick Williams, the entertainment editor for the *Los Angeles Mirror,* appeared as Elizabeth and Monty were waiting to shoot the dancing sequence in which she appears in a billowing strapless white tulle gown. The columnist stared at Elizabeth in the dress, and her mother called her over to talk to him.

"Show him the petticoats," said Sara Taylor.

Elizabeth lifted the skirt and the transparent petticoats up to her panties.

"Dear, now, not too much," cautioned Sara, who proceeded to answer all the reporter's questions about Elizabeth and her role in the film.

"Elizabeth was never allowed to speak for herself," Stevens recalled. "When we had lunch in the studio commissary, Mrs. Taylor would preface most of her remarks with 'Elizabeth thinks' or 'Elizabeth says' until I finally felt like shouting, 'Why don't you let Elizabeth say it for herself?' "

Ivan Moffat, the associate producer of *A Place in the Sun,* remembers walking over to Elizabeth one day at the studio to say hello. "I said, 'How are you, Elizabeth?' and Mrs. Taylor popped up and said, 'Oh, hello, Mr. Moffat. Elizabeth is fine. She's having a wonderful time.' "

Men like George Stevens and Ivan Moffat felt that Sara's protectiveness of her daughter was mixed with a frustrated desire to be in the limelight herself. Women, however, felt that Elizabeth was simply stupid and consequently had little to say. Shelley

Winters recalled sitting in the dressing room with her one day writing a letter. "I asked Elizabeth for the date," she said. "She answered that she didn't know. I noticed the *Hollywood Reporter* on a chair next to her and asked her to look. She did and said, 'It's no good, it's yesterday's *Reporter*'!"

Another woman remembers standing in a buffet line with Elizabeth, who was puzzled by a platter of pink fish. "What's that?" she asked. When told it was smoked salmon, Elizabeth said, "Oh. It looks like lox."

Blissfully unaware of her ignorance in those days, Elizabeth did not know enough to resent the inadequate education she was receiving at the studio. The little red MGM schoolhouse barely taught her the essentials of reading and writing. But then, she never was a student, nor was she encouraged by her mother. Indeed, when someone suggested to Sara Taylor that Elizabeth should develop her mind and go to college, her mother scoffed: "I'm sure all those college girls would give anything to be Elizabeth Taylor."

Elizabeth's formal education consisted of three hours a day of tutoring on the set. No matter how deplorable her marks were, at the end of the year she was automatically promoted to the next-higher grade. As a result, she never learned the basics of mathematics. Instead, she developed a habit of counting on her fingers. Her spelling was embarrassing. Her reading ability was as bad as her math, a shortcoming that made her ignore books in favor of movie magazines. "I know they're full of baloney," she said. "They make up things about everybody, even me. But I still read every one I can scrape up."

"You could not carry on a conversation with Elizabeth about books or current events or anything like that," said her stand-in, "but she knew who was starring in what movie, what they were wearing, if their sweater was cashmere, and how much they paid for their clothes."

At seventeen, Elizabeth was absorbed in becoming a movie star. She concentrated on her spectacular looks and on improving her appearance in front of the camera. Edith Head, who won an

Oscar for her costume designing in *A Place in the Sun,* recalled
fitting her for the evening gowns she wore in various scenes. "I'll
always remember Elizabeth saying, 'You can make the waist a
little smaller.' I'd tell her I'd already made it smaller, but she'd
say, 'You can make it even smaller.' She had a nineteen-inch
waist at the time, and she was always trying to get us to make
the waists as small as possible."

When Elizabeth walked on the set wearing the white strapless
evening gown, Montgomery Clift whispered in her ear, "Your
tits are fantastic, Bessie Mae, just fantastic." Then he teased
her, saying if he weren't such an old man he'd make her run
away with him. It was obvious to everyone that Elizabeth was
arousing the bisexual Clift in a way no other woman ever had.
She flirted with him and teased him and spent as many hours with
him as she could, but there was no sex between them during that
time at all. Instead, they laid the foundation for a complicated,
intensely close relationship that would develop through letters
and telephone calls after the movie was completed and they went
their separate ways. It was to last until the day Montgomery Clift
died.

Elizabeth idolized Monty; in the years ahead, her feelings of
love for him were to become so intertwined with guilt, recrimi-
nation, and regret that even years after his death she would not
be able to talk about him without crying.

At the time of making *A Place in the Sun,* Elizabeth considered
Monty the most talented person she had ever met. She had no
idea then about the hidden homosexual part of his life or the
terrible self-destructiveness that would later surface. She only
knew that here was someone who seemed to see inside her, to
understand her, and to accept her as she was.

In many ways she felt as if she had found her male counterpart.
Monty was as darkly beautiful a male as she was a darkly beautiful female. Both of them had hair all over their bodies, and in
some hirsute, androgynous way they looked alike. Emotionally
and psychologically, they felt they were as much alike as any
unrelated man and woman could possibly be. Both child actors

with driving, ambitious mothers, they were narcissistic and totally self-involved. In later years they were to share similar neuroses and develop a perverse predilection for exotic illnesses and assorted infirmities that would lead them to a total preoccupation with medicine.

At the time, however, all Elizabeth knew was that Monty genuinely cared about her, and so she told him all her girlish secrets. Later she would unburden herself completely, making him her closest confidant. "I've told him everything—even the things I'm most ashamed of," she said.

In Montgomery Clift she knew she had finally met someone who was not judgmental. Unlike her mother and her employer—both of whom cared only that she turn a profit for them—Clift was concerned about her personal happiness. Monty knew how much Elizabeth wanted to get married, and he told her, "Marry a monkey, if it will make you happy, Bessie Mae, but make damn sure it's a monkey worthy of you."

That was his first gentle caution when she started dating the hotel heir Nicky Hilton, whom she met during the shooting of *A Place in the Sun*. After the movie was wrapped Monty returned to New York, and Elizabeth called him regularly. When she told him she was going to become the hotel heir's fiancée, Monty said, "Oh, Bessie Mae, are you sure Nicky Hilton is the right man for you?"

Elizabeth swore that she was as sure as sure could ever be.

CHAPTER 5

SARA TAYLOR COULD NOT BELIEVE HER EYES as she walked through Conrad Hilton's sixty-four-room mansion in Bel Air. Tuxedoed servants seemed to pop up like dandelions after a spring rain. Butlers bowed at every corner, and uniformed maids whipped in and out of the sixteen bedroom suites. There were twenty-six bathrooms, four dumbwaiters, five kitchens, five wet bars, and twelve fireplaces in twelve different colors of marble. "And every single fixture in the place is plated in fourteen-carat gold," Sara told a friend.

Francis Taylor was equally awed by the fourteenth-century bronze statues of Devi and Siva from India in the entrance hall, the Ming vases from China in the foyer, and the eighteenth-century panels painted by the French artist Jean-Baptiste Hult in the drawing room.

Elizabeth gasped when she saw the master bedroom with its gold silk walls and bedspreads and draperies, the gold cashmere carpeting, and the green Italian marble fireplace. "Oh, Nicky," she whispered. "I can't believe that it's all so beautiful."

Conrad Nicholson Hilton, the twenty-three-year-old son of the chairman of the Hilton Hotel corporation, had invited his fiancée and her parents to his father's house for dinner. He had driven them along Bellagio Road; through the iron gates of the estate; up the sweeping driveway past the bronze fountains, the lofty pines, and the Doric pillars. It was too dark to see the rose garden with its five hundred rosebushes, but he pointed out the badminton court, the swimming pool, and the tennis courts, which were illuminated for night play. He explained that it would take him at least two hours to give them a full tour of the house and its eight and a quarter acres, so as Sara said later, he just "hit the highlights."

Conrad Hilton, Sr., whose wealth was conservatively estimated at $125 million when even a million dollars was considered a fortune, had purchased this sprawling three-story showplace in 1949 for $250,000. In 1980 it was to sell for $15 million, confirming the hotel magnate's claim that it was a good investment as well as a nice place to live and entertain. Only William Randolph Hearst in his castle at San Simeon, two hundred miles up the California coast, could afford to entertain as well.

Nicky had dated Elizabeth through the fall of 1949 after being introduced to her by Pete Freeman at Paramount Studios. "We liked each other right away, but it was not love at first sight," she said. "Nick invited me to the movies. Then we discovered we liked to dance. We saw each other pretty often—afternoons on the beach, parties with our gang. Well, then I knew it was the first time I was really in love."

As heir to the Hilton hotel fortune, Nicky was everything Sara Taylor fantasized in a son-in-law. She lived for the invitations to "Connie's house," as she now referred to the Bel Air palace, and luxuriated in the evenings the Taylors spent nightclubbing with Conrad Hilton at the Mocambo.

The hotel tycoon was not an American aristocrat, whose quiet money moves through family generations in the form of sturdy trust funds and solid securities. Conrad Hilton was a scrambling, self-made, dirt-scratching millionaire from Texas who believed money was a commodity to be spent lavishly and loudly. Sara appreciated Conrad's extravagance, and Elizabeth reveled in Nicky's presents. First there were diamond-and-pearl earrings for Christmas. Then came record albums, cashmere sweaters, a matched set of golf clubs, a trip to Lake Arrowhead for her family, and—finally—a five-carat diamond engagement ring and a $10,000 platinum-and-diamond wedding band.

"When Nicky and Elizabeth became engaged, there was no happier person than Sara Taylor," recalled Helen Rose, the MGM designer. "Francis was not so sure. Elizabeth was still in her teens and very unsophisticated. Nicky, who was in his early twenties, had been reared by a wealthy, indulgent father and was considerably spoiled."

The wealthy, indulgent father was particularly impressed by the moneymaking ability of the bride. "Connie bragged all the time that Elizabeth was making two thousand dollars a week at MGM and three thousand dollars for every radio broadcast she made," said Zsa Zsa Gabor, Conrad Hilton's second wife. "Of course, that's all he cared about—making money."

After his divorce from Zsa Zsa, Conrad Hilton began dating Ann Miller, the MGM dancer. She was with him the night Nicky told his father he was going to marry Elizabeth. "Connie, of course, was delighted at the prospect of having such a beautiful daughter-in-law," said Ann Miller. "He was probably a little jealous, too. Knowing how he loved beautiful young girls, I'm sure the thought must have crossed his mind that he'd like to be in his son's shoes."

Conrad Hilton was proud that his son was marrying such a world-famous movie star. He felt that Elizabeth Taylor's fame enhanced his own family name, and he encouraged her to continue her career after her marriage. So did Nicky. This, of course, was a huge relief to Sara, whose MGM salary was secure only as long as her daughter remained under contract.

"Nick is a wonderful boy," she said. "He likes Elizabeth's work and is very proud of her, and there will be no complications because he wants to live out here."

Elizabeth was also relieved. "Nicky is not only willing for me to continue my career, he wants me to," she told reporters. "The thing I am proudest of is that Nick is proud of me!"

"Elizabeth told me that her career meant everything in the world to her," recalled Mrs. Barron Hilton, Nicky's sister-in-law. "She said, 'One of these days I'm going to be so good that I'm going to win an Academy Award.' She was so sweet then, so beautiful, and so very much in love with Nicky."

Entranced with the idea of being Nicky Hilton's mother-in-law, Sara Taylor refused to believe his reputation as a playboy. She ignored reports of his drinking and gambling. "He couldn't have been nicer or more charming," she said. "We couldn't have liked Nick more."

Several people tried to warn Sara that Connie Hilton's oldest son was too spoiled to be responsible. "I told her myself that all Nicky ever did was drink until he was drunk and shoot craps with Glen McCarthy," said former newspaper columnist Frank Farrell, referring to an oilman from Houston, Texas. "And Bob Considine tried to tell her too; but Sara wouldn't listen to anyone. Nicky was heir to all those millions and therefore he was perfect."

Sara knew nothing of Nicky's other proclivities—his violent temper, his addiction to drugs, his compulsive gambling. She only saw a handsome young man whose Texas drawl made him sound polite and gentle. He didn't smoke or drink in front of her, and unlike Bill Pawley, he didn't make a fuss about Elizabeth's wearing bright colors and revealing necklines in public. He also seemed to care a great deal about his religion—so much so that Sara encouraged her daughter to convert to Catholicism in order to marry him in the Church.

"She did more than encourage her," recalled Marjorie Dillon. "She pushed her. She actually sat down and drilled Elizabeth out loud in the Catechism to get her ready to take instruction. Sara had no problems with Liz signing the papers you had to sign in those days if you were going to marry a Roman Catholic in the Catholic Church. In fact, she wanted her to sign her life away, swearing she would bring up her children as Catholics, that she would never practice birth control, and that she would never get a divorce.

"It was kind of surprising because Sara always had that Mary Baker Eddy book out on the set with Elizabeth whenever we were filming. She pushed Christian Science real hard, and Elizabeth enjoyed her religion. But when Nicky Hilton came along, Sara suddenly decided that it would be okay for Elizabeth to believe in both religions."

Despite the divorce of his parents, Nicky remained a devout
Catholic all his life. He had attended Loyola College, but left at
nineteen to join the Navy. From that point on he slept with numerous women, but insisted on marrying a virgin who was a
Roman Catholic. He rarely went to church, but he would never
have considered marrying outside his religion. He kept a rosary
on his bedside table next to his pornographic books and pill bottles. Joan Collins, a lover in later years, remembers a crucifix
lying on that table alongside his gun.

Francis Taylor worried about the reports of Nicky's instability
and opposed Elizabeth's becoming a Catholic, but there was
nothing much he could do. He finally persuaded her to wait until
her high school graduation and eighteenth birthday to announce
her engagement. But she insisted on setting a date, saying she
was in love and would do anything to become Nicky Hilton's
wife.

"There is no doubt in my mind that Nick is the one I want to
spend my life with," she said. "I met him last October and in all
that time we have never had one quarrel, one moment of misun-
derstanding. Every day I love him better. If this were not true, I
would not be marrying him in the church of his faith which rec-
ognizes one marriage in a lifetime in the eyes of God."

Metro-Goldwyn-Mayer turned corporate somersaults the day
the Taylors announced Elizabeth's engagement. With the wedding date set for May 6, 1950, the studio decided to release *Father of the Bride* on June 6, capitalizing on the nuptials to boost
box-office sales. Its executives immediately wired Loew's, Inc.,
in New York: "Under no circumstances can any photographs of
Elizabeth Taylor in any wedding clothes or trousseau be exclusive to any publication because this matter is a news event." And
they made sure this wedding would indeed become the most
newsworthy event in Hollywood's social history.

They began by announcing that as their gift to their prized
starlet, MGM would present her with a dream gown in which to
float down the aisle. They awarded Helen Rose the honor of
designing this phantasmagoric wedding dress, which would cost
$3,500. The studio also announced that Mrs. Rose would design

daffodil-yellow dresses for the seven attendants and Sara Taylor's bronze chiffon mother-of-the-bride outfit. Once that news was released, Edith Head called to say that Paramount Studios wanted her to design and donate the going-away costume. Ceil Chapman called from New York and offered a complete trousseau. The Gorham Silver Company offered to give the bride a forty-five-piece silver service if she would pose pouring tea from a Gorham pot. Elizabeth gleefully accepted everything that came her way, including full-length mink coats for herself and her mother. But Nicky Hilton was chagrined. "When we're married, my wife won't be allowed to accept such stuff," he said.

Still, the expensive wedding presents rolled in. MGM announced the more spectacular ones, such as the $65,000 pearl ring from Uncle Howard Young and the one hundred shares of Hilton Hotel stock from Conrad Hilton.* All furniture was removed from the Taylor living room to provide space for the flood of gifts.

"I just love everything about getting married," said Elizabeth, "and every little detail seems terribly important to me. Helen Rose is designing my wedding dress and I start each morning talking with her about every seam!"

The bride-to-be badgered the designer to create a low-cut gown for her, but Helen Rose insisted on decorum. "It's a church wedding," she said. "You've got to be ladylike." Finally they compromised. The neckline was cut to cleavage but covered with a flesh-revealing transparent white chiffon.

Studio publicity trumpeted the wedding as Hollywood's most extravagant ever. Everyone in the film colony recognized the worldwide coverage the event would receive and clamored to be included. Each invitation carried a small white card to be shown by guests crossing the police lines that would surround the church. A week before the wedding, the invitation list exceeded

---

* A share of Hilton Hotel stock cost $13.50 in April of 1950, making Conrad Hilton's wedding gift worth a mere $1,350. However, thirty years later the stock had split several times and with dividends was worth well over $150,000.

six hundred. Everyone from Metro-Goldwyn-Mayer was invited as well as the executives of all the Hilton hotels.

"I remember Patricia Neal wanted to be invited so badly," said Marjorie Dillon. "She told her stand-in to call me, and the stand-in did, practically begging me for an invitation. So I went to Liz and asked her. She said, 'It's okay with me as long as she brings a present.' "

The highly publicized bridal showers kept pumping excitement throughout Hollywood. Each present received a handwritten acknowledgment from Elizabeth. To her stand-in, she wrote:

> *That was such a wonderful shower last night and that was so sweet of you to go to all that trouble. You shouldn't have but gee I'm so glad you did. We had such a good time and I got such a nice lot of loot.*
>
> *I just love the darling half slip you gave me. The lace trim is so pretty and matches the pants you gave me. I'm getting the most wonderful presents.*
>
> *Thanks again, Margie. I'll do the same for you someday. All love from your ex fellow slob.*
>
> *Liz*

A few days later, she again wrote Margie Dillon thanking her for "real Saxy" lingerie. "You really are fixing me up with a wonderful set," she wrote. "First panties and now that beautiful slip." She signed the note *"Love, Liz (deserter of SLOB)."*

"The S.L.O.B. club was something Liz and Betty Sullivan, daughter of Ed Sullivan, started when they were really desperate about getting dates," recalled a childhood friend. "The initials stood for Single Lonely Obliging Babes."

"She thought of herself then as a SLOB," said Marjorie Dillon. "And when I became her stand-in she automatically made me a member of the club."

The fairy-tale wedding was scheduled for Saturday, May 6, in the Church of the Good Shepherd in Beverly Hills. Liz had signed all the papers necessary to marry a Catholic, but since she had yet to be baptized, there could be no nuptial Mass on the altar. Instead, the 5 P.M. ceremony would have to be performed outside the altar rail.

The morning of the wedding, police estimated that more than three thousand fans were gathered outside the church. Little old ladies brought collapsible chairs. Youngsters climbed the trees lining Santa Monica Boulevard to get a better view. Metro-Goldwyn-Mayer dispatched its security force, headed by Whitey Hendry, to work with the Beverly Hills police in holding back the crowds.

Unable to cope with all the excitement, the bride-to-be got a cold the night before her wedding and took to her bed with a prescription for penicillin. The next morning telegrams of good wishes began arriving, along with more presents—six silver coffee services, three sets of silverware, and 472 pieces of crystal.

By noon, fans swarmed around the Taylors' white stucco house on Elm Drive in Beverly Hills, hoping to catch a glimpse of Elizabeth on her way to the church. Two hours before the ceremony they saw Sidney Guilaroff, the MGM hairstylist, arrive with his little brown bag of equipment to comb out the bride's hair. He was followed by Mrs. J. A. Ryan, the studio's fitter, who would arrange the Juliet cap of seed pearls and the veil, which was ten yards of shimmering silk illusion net. Soon Helen Rose arrived to help Elizabeth step into her MGM dream gown —twenty-five yards of shell-white satin sprinkled with bugle beads and tiny seed pearls, trailed by fifteen yards of satin chiffon train. The gown commanded the attention of fifteen MGM seamstresses, stitching and sewing full time for two months before the wedding.

Across the street the six bridesmaids were dressing at Anne Westmore's house, and throngs of fans got their first look at the bridal party when Jane Powell came running in late. An hour later the bridesmaids left the house in buttercup-yellow organdy gowns, carrying huge bouquets of yellow tulips and daffodils. The fans cheered as they watched Marilyn Hilton walk with Mara Reagan, who later married Elizabeth's brother, Howard. Jane Powell received a big hand when she appeared with Marjorie

Dillon, followed by Betty Sullivan and Barbara Thompson, the wife of actor Marshall Thompson. Anne Westmore, Elizabeth's best friend and maid of honor, hurried out later alone.

By the time the motorcycle police arrived to escort the bridal limousine to the church, the crowd was hushed, waiting for Elizabeth to appear. Her seventeen steamer trunks, packed with her free trousseau, had already been loaded to go aboard the *Queen Mary* for the European honeymoon voyage, another gift from Conrad Hilton. Her personal stationery was engraved with her married initials, as was her monogrammed luggage. The wedding-night outfit, a white satin negligée trimmed with rose-point lace—also designed by Helen Rose and a gift from MGM—was packed separately in an overnight bag. She had already given her bridal attendants their initialed wedding bells designed by Philip Paval. So, with a lucky penny stuck in her white satin platform heel and a blue garter wrapped around her left thigh, Elizabeth grabbed her mother's ancient lace handkerchief and descended the staircase like a traditional bride with something old, something new, something borrowed, something blue.

On the arm of her handsome silver-haired father she walked out the door and into the spring sunshine. Flashbulbs exploded, and the people now standing four deep on the street clapped their affection and approval as the most beautiful bride in movieland made her way toward the limousine. Alighting at the church, she snagged the hem of her gown and ripped away part of the satin lining, but with true movie-queen aplomb remained unflustered, graciously acknowledging the thunderous applause. She stood patiently holding her huge white orchid bouquet while photographers snapped her picture.

Waiting inside the church were several hundred guests, including Van and Eve Johnson, Janet Leigh and Arthur Loew, Jr., Spencer Tracy, Freddie Brisson and Rosalind Russell, Zsa Zsa Gabor, Fred Astaire, Ginger Rogers, Esther Williams, Greer Garson, Terry Moore, Roddy McDowall, Phil Harris and Alice Faye, June Allyson and Dick Powell, George Murphy, Margaret O'Brien, Joan Bennett, Walter Wanger, Gene Kelly, Debbie

Reynolds, and Mrs. Ida Koverman, top assistant to Louis B. Mayer. Gloria DeHaven arrived just before the doors were closed and sat down in the rear of the church. Hedda Hopper, Louella Parsons, and Sheilah Graham each had her own special perch on the aisle. Yet none of them seemed to notice the tall, dark, angry young man who stood at the edge of the crowd glaring at the bride.

Bill Pawley refused to step inside the church to watch Elizabeth Taylor become another man's wife. He had already had his final say an hour before when he stormed the Taylor house, commanding Sara to let him in. Marching straight into Elizabeth's room, he confronted her with her past promises of eternal love and a marriage forever. She burst into tears. Fifteen minutes after he arrived, he departed. Bill Pawley, in love with his former fiancée for two decades, did not marry until 1974.

The ceremony opened with organ music and MGM actress Mary Jane Smith singing the "Ave Maria." On the last stanza the bridesmaids started down the yellow-carpeted aisle, followed by the maid of honor in green organdy. Then came the bride on the arm of her father.

The double-ring ceremony lasted twenty minutes; then Monsignor Patrick J. Cancannon pronounced the twenty-three-year-old groom and his eighteen-year-old bride man and wife. Nicky gave Elizabeth a loud smack which lasted "a little too long," according to one guest; but Elizabeth kept kissing her husband until laughter rippled along the pews. Finally, the priest leaned over and said, "I think that's long enough, dear." Flushed with embarrassment, Nicky steered his bride up the aisle. She stopped to give her parents a hug and walked on, clutching the arm of her new husband. At the church door she turned her face up to him, closed her eyes, and said, "Kiss me, Nicky. Please kiss me."

The crowds lining Santa Monica Boulevard roared their approval of this public intimacy and had to be held back by police as the young couple headed for the limousine that would carry them to their immense MGM-financed reception at the Bel Air

Country Club. Elizabeth leaned forward to wave to the fans and then turned to kiss her husband again.

Violins played softly in the lobby. The reception line seemed endless as six hundred people waited to kiss the bride and congratulate the groom. "I'm just so happy," Liz said to everyone. "I'm so very happy." Nicky shifted from one foot to the other as the couple stood in line for two hours before breaking away to cut their elaborate five-tier wedding cake. By that time the four-foot-high ice statue of kissing doves had melted and the anchovy canapés were soggy. Still, the dewy-eyed bride, fortified by champagne, was sparkling.

Clutching her husband, she spotted Hedda Hopper and whispered, "I'm so glad I waited for Nicky." Walking across the room, she hugged Louella Parsons and said, "I cried for joy when Monsignor Cancannon pronounced us Mr. and Mrs." Then she tossed her bouquet and dashed upstairs to change into her blue gabardine Edith Head going-away costume. Carrying a blue-gray mink stole, she reappeared for more photographs and a shower of confetti and rice. Barron Hilton escorted his brother and the bride to their "getaway" car. As Elizabeth was leaving, she gave her mother a quick kiss and said, "Oh, Mother! Nick and I are one now for ever and ever."

CHAPTER 6

THE DUKE AND DUCHESS OF WINDSOR were aboard when the *Queen Mary* sailed on May 24, 1950. So were Mr. and Mrs. Conrad Nicholson Hilton, Jr. The royal couple insisted on meeting the famous newlyweds and sent a note inviting the young couple for dinner.

"It was sailing day," recalled a former Cunard Line employee. "Poor Nicky was so terribly unsophisticated. He had to call me to ask if he was supposed to dress for dinner."

The assumption here is that everyone should know one doesn't "dress" on the first or last night out, because one's personal valet is too busy unpacking on the first day to press one's "dress" clothes, and too harried repacking them on the last day.

"I was quite surprised that Nicky Hilton, the hotel heir, was so uninformed," continued the former employee, "and I nearly died when I saw Elizabeth Taylor. I couldn't believe my eyes. She had black hair all over her arms and was as hairy as a little ape."

Everywhere Elizabeth Taylor went, heads turned and crowds gathered. "Even on the ship people rushed up to Liz begging for her autograph and practically knocked over poor Nicky in the process," recalled Melissa Wesson, a woman honeymooning at the same time. "It got to be awful for him after a while. And for her too. In the end, the honeymoon was hell."

The Hiltons and Wessons honeymooned together in Monte

Carlo and Cannes and Cap d'Antibes. Wherever they went, crowds swarmed toward Elizabeth, screaming to take her picture and begging for her autograph. In true MGM movie-star style, she accommodated her fans by posing patiently and spending up to two hours signing her name.

"Nicky was enraged by all this," said Mrs. Wesson. "He just got madder and madder. Liz, who truly adored him—oh, she was so in love with Nicky Hilton—was hurt and confused by his rage. She'd start sobbing to me and say, 'Why is he acting like this? He knew I was a famous star when we got married. He knew I was Liz Taylor. Why is he so mad now?' "

Overwhelmed by the public adulation of his wife, Nicky became surly and argumentative. He stayed out late to drink and gamble in the casinos. In the beginning Elizabeth would accompany him, but when he refused to leave with her she would burst into tears and run out by herself. Then, as she told a friend, she would take a taxi back to the ship and wait hours for Nicky to return "so we could make love to each other."

For Elizabeth, sex was something new and wonderful, and she regarded Nicky as a very gentle, very exciting lover. But sex also was a weapon he used against her. Often, when she made an overture by snuggling up to him or putting her arms around him, he would drunkenly hurl her aside, cursing and telling her how she bored him and ordering her to let him alone. "I'm so goddamned sick and tired of looking at your face!" he once yelled at her.

"She was so affectionate, always wanting to hug and kiss Nicky, but he was so angry," said Melissa Wesson. "The thing that hurt her most was when he began refusing to go to bed with her. She loved sex with him so much. It was not just sex—it was also coziness and warmth—and he just cut her off. She would beg him, but he would refuse. Then she'd be in tears and come running to our room, where she would crawl into our bed and spend the night sleeping with my husband and me."

Betty Sullivan, a bridesmaid from the wedding, met the couple in France and was appalled by the way Nicky treated his bride.

"He had a belligerent attitude," she said. "He was very, very cold to Elizabeth. It was like he was trying to show her how unimportant she was to him. We met three boys from Princeton that I knew at the time and we all went water skiing together. Nicky would always sleep late. He became annoyed that she went with us.

"He would stay up all night gambling. Once I saw him come downstairs after he had gotten up in the afternoon, and Liz skipped across the whole lobby to throw her arms about him. He shrugged her off. It was a very difficult atmosphere. It left her with a scar."

Nicky's hostile behavior and Elizabeth's hysterics naturally attracted attention. Soon reporters were filing stories on the couple's matrimonial problems. Nicky blamed his famous wife for the unfavorable publicity, touching off more fights. Elizabeth became more upset knowing that her mother would see the stories. Soon she was so miserable she stopped eating and started smoking cigarettes.

"Liz was so terrified to tell her mother the marriage wasn't working, she almost made herself sick," said her friend. "Liz said her mother would blame her for the breakup."

By the time the fourteen-week honeymoon ended, Elizabeth was so agitated about facing her mother that she collapsed on the boat as it approached New York. As expected, Sara Taylor, who had every intention of remaining a Hilton in-law, was waiting for her at the pier.

"I met the mother in New York then," said a shipmate. "She was terrible—real cold and hard. Liz and I had talked about it a lot, and Liz said she felt her mother set her up for things and used her in an inhuman way."

Sara suggested that Elizabeth "grow up." Even though Nick was "a bit spoiled," Sara said, he would in time become an ideal husband. "You're never going to do any better than Nicky Hilton," Sara told Elizabeth, who was so distressed that she entered a hospital.

Harassed by the press and the continual public appearances that Elizabeth felt she had to make, Nicky frequently regretted marrying a movie star. "He hated being known as Elizabeth Taylor's husband," said his sister-in-law Mrs. Barron Hilton. "He did not like being called Mr. Taylor. He was the I'm-the-boss-and-you-do-as-I-say type. He had a terrible temper and could be a real bastard, but he also could be sweet and gentle and really wonderful.

"But Liz, who was terribly naive in those days, would come to me and say, 'Marilyn, how can he be so sweet and then yell and scream at me like a madman?' I'd tell her to be patient with Nicky. He was raised by his father with no mother and was rather difficult at times, but she couldn't be patient because she needed one-hundred-percent total attention all the time and Nicky just wouldn't give her that."

Despite their problems, Elizabeth remained very much in love with her husband and said she would return to California to give her marriage a fair chance. Stung by the bad press reports that had haunted their honeymoon, she insisted that Nicky accompany her to Louella Parsons' house and assure the columnist that all was well between them. Nicky went, but under duress. He despised the roly-poly reporter who had chastised him on the radio and in her syndicated column. Even so, he made the effort for Elizabeth and promised to be charming.

By this time the studio had decided to capitalize on *Father of the Bride,* a big MGM money-maker, by releasing a sequel. It recycled the same cast in *Father's Little Dividend,* making Spencer Tracy a grandfather and Elizabeth an expectant mother. Elizabeth began shooting when she returned from her honeymoon. Midway through the film, in which she was having a baby in front of the cameras, she discovered that she was actually pregnant.

"It was an early pregnancy—she wasn't very far along at all," said her stand-in, "and one day she fainted on the set and had to be rushed home. Nicky's uncle was an obstetrician and he came to the house, but Liz had already miscarried. She was in bed and wanted Nicky to stay with her, but he had already made plans to go deep-sea fishing. He gave her a kiss and said, 'I'll be back in a couple of days. Marge will spend the night with you.' I did, of course, and that's when she cried and cried and told me all the terrible things that happened on the honeymoon."

After the movie was completed, Elizabeth and Nicky decided to try to have a "little honeymoon," as Elizabeth called it, and fly to New York. Their plane lost the power of its right inboard engine shortly after takeoff and made an emergency landing. The passengers were terrified, but no one was injured. "I just held tight to Nicky's hand and prayed," Elizabeth said. "I prayed every minute."

Elizabeth apparently also promised Nicky that if they got out of the crash alive, she would try again to get pregnant and have his baby. "They did get out alive, but she didn't keep her promise," said Betsy Von Furstenberg, the next woman in Nicky Hilton's life. "He said he caught her douching a week later, and he was so disappointed. Nicky later told me that their final breakup came because of two things. He said Liz let the dogs mess all over the house and she would sit there all day and do nothing about it. He couldn't believe that she never cleaned up after them. Also, she did not have a baby, and he wanted one desperately."

Nicky Hilton was a husband who wanted a traditional house-wife, while his wife wanted an attentive lover. Both were spoiled, self-centered, and frustrated over not getting their way. "Every time Liz would get mad she'd stomp out," recalled Marilyn Hilton. "She left Nick three or four times in Europe on their honeymoon. One day Barron told Nicky that if he didn't shape up he'd lose her for good, but Nick said, 'Oh, she'll come back. She always does.' "

The night of December 6, 1950—exactly seven months from the day she floated down the aisle—Elizabeth once again stormed out of the house they were renting in Pacific Palisades. Another fight had erupted, with Nicky calling her "a fucking bore" and saying if she didn't like things, she could "get the hell out." Convulsed with tears, she ran to her car and drove to Marjorie Dillon's house. She knew she could never go home and confront her mother, because no matter what Nicky Hilton did or said, she felt Sara would force her to return to him.

"She was broken up and hysterical when she finally split,'' said Marjorie Dillon. "She left in the middle of the night and came to my house in Hollywood to stay with me and my father. She screamed and sobbed and cried, 'I can't take it anymore. I just can't take it!' She stayed for three weeks and left her car in my dad's backyard so the press wouldn't find out.''

Elizabeth refused to call her parents. Instead, they learned of the breakup by discovering in the *Los Angeles Examiner* a statement prepared by MGM publicity quoting Elizabeth as saying: "I am sorry that Nicky and I are unable to adjust our differences and that we have come to a final parting of the ways. We both regret this decision but after personal discussion we realize there is no possibility of a reconciliation.''

Sara immediately called her daughter and pleaded with her to return to her husband and make the marriage work. She said she could not bear even the remotest suggestion of a divorce. "We've never had a divorce in our family,'' she said.

"Liz was just hysterical during this time,'' said Marjorie Dillon. "We were shooting *Love Is Better than Ever* and she broke down and bawled on the set every day. She was in tears constantly. She was getting no help from her family, and she was so young at the time.

"On top of that, Liz said the Hiltons were real ugly about everything, too. She said the house and linens and towels all had Hilton Hotel monograms. 'There is nothing in there that is mine,' she said. 'All owned and operated by the Hiltons.' She said it was unbelievable. They even counted the sheets so they got everything that was theirs. Liz had put all her wedding presents in storage and never did take them out. Afterwards, she said she couldn't bear to look at them.''

The fairy-tale wedding turned completely to ashes when MGM demanded return of the $3,500 wedding dress. The bridesmaids, too, had to turn in their yellow organdy gowns. "They measured each of us at the time of the wedding and promised we could keep those gorgeous dresses,'' said one bridesmaid. "And of course, we were all thrilled. Then later they made us give them back, if you can believe it. They didn't even send someone to pick them up. We all had to take them back to the studio ourselves.''

When the pressure from her mother and the Hiltons became too much, Elizabeth collapsed again and was admitted to Cedars of Lebanon Hospital for a week under the name Rebecca Jones. This collapse started a pattern she would follow the rest of her life whenever emotional strain became too much for her to handle. She would escape into a hospital where she was totally removed from whatever stressful situation was tormenting her, all the while satisfying her craving for constant care and attention.

A few days after her release from Cedars of Lebanon, Elizabeth, pale, trembling, and wearing white gloves, walked into Judge Thurmond Clarke's Los Angeles courtroom and asked for an interlocutory divorce on the grounds of extreme mental cruelty. Nicky Hilton, represented by his lawyer, was not present. Nor did he contest her action.

In a barely audible voice Elizabeth testified that her husband had been indifferent to her, used abusive language, and left her alone on their honeymoon. She tried to keep speaking, but broke into gasping sobs and covered her face with her hands. Her lawyer asked the judge to waive alimony and requested that her maiden name be restored to her. The judge agreed, with the stipulation that she could not remarry for a year. It took no more than twenty minutes—the same amount of time it had taken Monsignor Cancannon to pronounce her Nicky Hilton's wife eight months before in the Church of the Good Shepherd.*

---

* The waiver of alimony did not let Nicky off scot-free. Elizabeth instructed her lawyer to fight the Hiltons for a private property settlement—which she eventually received, in addition to all the wedding presents and the 100 shares of Hilton Hotel stock. Embittered for years by the failed marriage, she later retaliated by refusing to sign papers that would have entitled Nicky to remarry in the Catholic Church. ''Nicky did not want the stigma of a divorce,'' said his sister-in-law. ''When he wanted to remarry in the Church, he asked Elizabeth to sign a statement that would have annulled their marriage. She refused because she was up for an Academy Award at the time, and she thought it would be adverse publicity for her.''

Some press reports on Elizabeth's divorce mentioned the name of Stanley Donen, suggesting that the director of *Love Is Better than Ever* might become her next husband. Their affair had been no secret to anyone on the set.

"Liz desperately needed someone to lean on, and Stanley was there," said Marjorie Dillon. "He was overwhelmingly attentive and ended up giving her more time than the picture."

The short, swarthy twenty-seven-year-old director was hardly the man Sara Taylor envisioned to replace Nicky Hilton. She sneered at Donen's background as a chorus boy and harangued her daughter about the fact that he was still married, though separated from his wife. Added to Donen's Jewish heritage and marital status was the fact that he had no money—a combination which made Sara absolutely splenetic.

One night during shooting Donen visited Elizabeth at her parents' home and stayed until two in the morning, prompting the disapproving Sara to ask him to leave.

"If he goes, I go," screamed Elizabeth as she followed her lover out the front door.

The next morning Elizabeth asked Marjorie Dillon to move into an apartment with her, but Margie was getting married. So Elizabeth appealed to her agent, Jules Goldstone, who in turn introduced her to Peggy Rutledge, a former secretary to Mrs. Bob Hope. Peggy agreed to become Elizabeth's secretary and roommate in an apartment she rented on Wilshire Boulevard.

"I never want to see my parents again," Liz announced, informing the studio that if Sara Taylor stepped foot on the lot she would leave and never return. To appease its moneymaking starlet, MGM decided to quietly keep Sara on the payroll in exchange for relinquishing her chaperone duties to Margie Dillon and Peggy Rutledge.

"When the big break with her mother came, Liz did not speak to her for a long time," said Marjorie Dillon. "I was there at the studio to be responsible for her. Although Sara didn't come around, she called me at least five times a day. 'Now, Margie,' she'd say, 'be sure Elizabeth eats, and make sure she brushes her hair and takes off her makeup before leaving the studio.'

Then she would start in on Stanley. 'Did she see that awful Stanley Donen last night? What time? Where did they go? How long were they together? What did they say? How did she look?' She was constantly telling me, 'Elizabeth should not get involved with that Donen or his religion.' "

Still troubled by her divorce, Elizabeth kept wondering why Nicky Hilton had been so indifferent to her. She often asked Donen why he thought Nicky had ignored her and found her boring. To compensate for Hilton's disregard and to demonstrate his own commitment, Donen became Elizabeth's twenty-four-hour lover, giving her the tender care and affection she craved.

Despite Donen's lavish attentions, Elizabeth was not passionately in love with him as she had been with Nicky Hilton. In fact, her physical attraction to her husband persisted, and two months after her tearful divorce hearing she secretly met him in Palm Springs and spent the night with him at the Thunderbird Hotel. Months later, when Nicky announced plans to marry Betsy Von Furstenberg, a nineteen-year-old actress and German countess, Elizabeth broke down and sobbed.

Under the guise of completing final details on their property settlement, she called Nicky and begged to see him. They got together in New York, while publicly denying any possibility of a reconciliation. Privately, though, they decided to sneak away to Howard Young's baronial estate in Connecticut. En route to their romantic hideaway, their car broke down.

An auxiliary state policeman stopped to see what had happened and, recognizing Elizabeth, offered to drive them to their destination. When they arrived at Howard Young's estate in the Branchville section of Ridgefield, the grateful couple invited the policeman inside for a drink. The policeman later said he couldn't help noticing that Nicky and Elizabeth seemed to be more than just good friends.

"When we first went into the house they sat in different chairs," he recalled. "But after a few drinks they sat together, and Nicky kissed her several times and had his arms around her.

She called him 'Honey.' It looked to me as if she was still in love with him.''

Still, Nicky Hilton was never as tolerant as Stanley Donen, who cheerfully put up with Elizabeth's changing moods, her tearful outbursts and fatiguing depressions. He tried to succor and comfort her. But he could not eradicate her terrible insecurity. She questioned herself constantly and turned to everyone around her for counsel.

"Liz was always asking what to do," said her stand-in. "She asked advice of everyone. 'Should I go out with Stanley Donen?' 'What do you think of him?' 'Should I be seen here or there?' 'What should I wear?' 'Should I do this?' 'Should I do that?' ''

Publicly recognized as a couple, Stanley and Elizabeth became part of a trendy social group called "The Fox and Lox Club," which included Janet Leigh, Tony Curtis, Colleen Gray, Diana Lynn, Barry Sullivan, and Martin Ragaway.

"In order to get in you had to throw a brunch, and then we all would go from house to house every Sunday, eating and partying," recalled comedy writer Marty Ragaway. "One Sunday, Elizabeth and Stanley gave the brunch at Liz's apartment. We were all there waiting for Stanley Roberts [a screenwriter] to deliver the silver and plates so we could start. After an hour Elizabeth got very annoyed. 'I'm so mad at Stanley for keeping us waiting I'd like to smash that in his face,' she said, pointing to a big chocolate cake with light blue frosting. I laughed and didn't think any more about it. But then Stanley walked in a few minutes later and Elizabeth tore across the room, grabbed the cake, and smashed him full in the face with it. He was covered with frosting and absolutely furious. The rest of us were so stunned we couldn't believe it. Poor Liz realized it wasn't funny and burst into tears because she had done something wrong. That was the end of the Fox and Lox Club, but Stanley later sent her flowers and apologized for making her cry.''

On April 5, 1951, Elizabeth, in plunging décolletage, pranced into the benefit premiere of *Father's Little Dividend* on the arm of Stanley Donen. The movie did not match the entertainment value of *Father of the Bride,* but *Variety* congratulated Elizabeth for beautifying her scenes. Very conspicuously beautifying the Egyptian Theater in Hollywood that evening, Elizabeth posed for every photographer on hand. Many of their pictures showed her possessively clinging to her escort, Stanley Donen.

Four days later, Jeanne Donen filed for divorce, claiming alienation of affections and citing but not naming "another woman" as the cause of her marital breakup. At nineteen years of age, Elizabeth suddenly was notorious as "the other woman."

Now ostracized from her family and involved in an affair criticized by everyone, she defensively tried to explain herself to the world. "I know I have been spoiled," she said, "but I think people are unfairly severe. I'm just a normal girl with the average faults and virtues, but being a movie actress I wasn't allowed to develop on normal lines. I've been able to wear a plunging neckline since I was fourteen years old, and ever since then people have expected me to act as old as I look. My troubles all started because I have a woman's body and a child's emotions."

CHAPTER 7

ELIZABETH CONTINUED TO IDOLIZE MONTGOMERY CLIFT. She wrote him girlish, giggly letters from one place after another and called him regularly. Even while honeymooning with Nicky Hilton, she thought of Monty. "She told me she was crazy about him," recalled Melissa Wesson. "She talked about him with awe."

In February of 1951, after the breakup of her marriage, she flew to New York to see him. The studio reserved a room for her at the Waldorf-Astoria, but she went uptown to stay at Clift's town house on East Sixty-first.

"When Liz came to New York, she and Monty spent all their time together," recalled photographer Blaine Waller. "They had a weird relationship and a closeness that was not to be believed. I think they were really in love, but . . .

"Monty kept Liz totally separate from the gang that saw him regularly, but once in a while he'd bring her into Gregory's, which is where I met her. He was very protective of her then. I remember him saying, 'Christ, it's a big thing for her to be here after her marriage bust-up.' Just talking to Monty then, I knew they were in love. But Monty lived twelve different lives, and he was such a mess—drinking too much—and such a loner. And she was too young. But God Almighty, was she beautiful! It was like a punch in the stomach to see her for the first time.

"The fun thing about her was that dirty, filthy, foul mouth of hers. The things she said were so shocking because you just didn't expect any kind of coarseness to pass those gorgeous lips.''

Many acquaintances were not amused by Elizabeth's language, considering it crude and common. Eventually, Peggy Rutledge was approached by a studio executive about the problem. "Somebody at Metro said to me, 'You've got to clean up her language,' " recalled Elizabeth's roommate. " 'Out of that beautiful face comes this language.' I don't know where she got the habit of swearing—I think from Stanley Donen, or maybe Montgomery Clift; he swore a lot.''

Monty and Liz spent hours together telling each other everything. They went shopping one afternoon and Elizabeth bought him a miniature French chair that he admired. With people she loved she was exceedingly generous, showering them with expensive gifts.

Marjorie Dillon remembers Elizabeth sweeping into a store one day and seeing a piece of jewelry. " 'That looks just like you, Margie,' she said. 'I want to get it for you.' And she promptly wrote out a check on the spot.'' She also gave her stand-in a silk shantung suit to get married in, a monogrammed set of luggage, and a peignoir for her wedding night.

"She was always buying things for other people,'' said Margie Dillon. "I remember when she was sixteen years old, she wanted to buy her mother a Cadillac. Peter Lawford sent her to some place on Wilshire Boulevard and Liz had her agent buy the automobile with her money. It didn't occur to her to even ask for a deal on it. She just said, 'Oh, Mother is going to be so excited. She's never had a brand-new car before.' ''

In later years she would finance around-the-world trips with first-class accommodations for her friends, bestow trunks of hand-me-down couturier clothes on her maids and lavish fur coats on her secretaries, hairdressers, and press agents. Frequently, her generosity embarrassed recipients who could not afford to reciprocate in kind. But even that excess was characteristic of someone who felt so insecure she always had to overcompensate.

"Subconsciously," said a friend, "it may have been Liz's way of binding someone to her in gratitude, or perhaps it was the only way she knew how to show her love."

To Montgomery Clift, whom she termed her "dearest, most devoted friend," she would eventually give the most precious gift of all—a reason to go on living. But that would come later, when she was in a position of power and he was in need.

During her New York visit, Elizabeth told Monty how much she loved him; but although he adored her and proclaimed, "I'll never love another woman like I do you, Bessie Mae," he said he could not possibly marry her. She begged him to change his mind, but she slowly came to understand that he had a secret homosexual life which would always restrain him from giving her the kind of total commitment she so desperately wanted.

Elizabeth later told the writer Thomas Thompson that she "never made it" sexually with Monty. As she later said to Truman Capote, "Well, one doesn't always fry the fish one wants to fry. Some of the men I've really liked really didn't like women." Elizabeth also confided her feelings about Monty to the director Richard Brooks, who said, "She thought he was God. I think he loved her as much as he loved any woman. It was a tragic situation. It reminds me of *The Sun Also Rises*."

Years later Elizabeth told Max Lerner, the syndicated columnist, that she had been deeply involved with Monty romantically and that he was desperately in love with her. "She told me they had an affair," recalled Lerner, "but you've got to remember with Elizabeth that a homosexual is a prime sexual target—a challenge to be met. After all, that represents the unattainable, and how better to demonstrate your sexual power than to possess the unattainable? In Monty's case she wanted to make him straight. But she couldn't do it."

Instead, she settled for the only relationship possible—one that was to become extremely involved and convoluted until Clift's lonely death in 1966. During her first visit with him in 1951, his terrifying self-destructiveness had yet to take over his life, and he was able to give her the support and comfort she needed after her divorce. But he knew he wasn't the kind of man who could ever marry, especially someone like Elizabeth Taylor.

She was desperately in need of a man at that time, and out of loneliness dated people like associate producer Ivan Moffat, Betty Hutton's ex-husband Ted Briskin, theater-chain heir Arthur Loew, Jr., and George Stevens, Jr., son of the director. One of her dates, the eccentric billionaire Howard Hughes, offered her $1 million to marry him.

"He was such an out-and-out bore I wouldn't have married him for all his money," Elizabeth said years later. "The few times I went out with him, he was always staring into space and never answered any of my questions. And he often looked like he needed a bath. Whenever I saw him, his pants were wrinkled and hanging on him like a tent, and sometimes he wore dirty sneakers with no socks and his toes sticking out of holes."

Watching his estranged wife date a series of men, Nicky Hilton commented caustically: "Every man should have the opportunity of sleeping with Elizabeth Taylor, and at the rate she's going every man will."

Elizabeth frankly admitted she wanted to marry again, saying, "I'm happier married than single." She naturally responded to the attentions of Stanley Donen, but when their affair became too public and controversial, the studio worried about its star's being tarnished by notoriety. Finally, MGM decided to ship Elizabeth and her traveling chaperone, Peggy Rutledge, to England to make *Ivanhoe* with Robert Taylor, Joan Fontaine, and George Sanders.

MGM envisioned Sir Walter Scott's literary classic as a spectacular Technicolor production with elaborate sets, medieval costumes, and one of the largest casts ever assembled.

Elizabeth did not want to make the movie or go to England. Everyone there now hated her, she said, and without Stanley Donen she would be all alone. She was unaware that the studio and Sara were desperately trying to break up their affair.

The producer of *Ivanhoe* was Pandro Berman, who had produced *National Velvet, Father's Little Dividend,* and *Father of the Bride.* He recalled that Elizabeth stamped her feet and shook her curls in an effort to stay home. "Then she had her doctor contact us, saying she had colitis and an incipient ulcer and was just recovering from a nervous breakdown," he said. "We assured him that we would take very good care of her and that we would not work her too hard.

"Once in London the picture was going well enough, but Elizabeth was not giving a good performance. She was not in tune with the director, Richard Thorpe. He was terribly good on size and spectacle, but he didn't cater to Liz and massage her ego to get the performance out of her.

"He came to me and said he was having difficulty getting anything good out of her—which was quite evident in the rushes—but I immediately made the decision to go ahead. I told him to just do the scenes the best he could. Then, when the film was finished and we came to the United States, I had to go to Lillian Burns, the MGM drama coach, and tell her to do something with Liz. I said we didn't want to have one word she spoke in London on the sound track. So poor Lillian had to spend days coaching her and coaching her. Then we had to loop everything—which means we had to have Elizabeth say all her lines over again in a Hollywood studio and dub in every single word.

"She was not a good enough actress to do it right the first time. Maybe a woman's director like George Cukor could have got it out of her, but that's the point. A director has to get it out of her. She can't give it spontaneously and naturally like a fine actress can. She can't do it alone."

During the *Ivanhoe* filming, Elizabeth seemed to care less about her acting than about dressing up every night for Michael Wilding, the thirty-nine-year-old British matinee idol who quickly became more than just her guide to London's restaurants and nighteries. She had met him three years earlier when she was wearing Glenn Davis' gold football and filming *The Conspirator.* She developed a wild crush on him at the time. "All we heard about after she got back was 'Michael Wilding this' and 'Michael Wilding that,' " recalled her stand-in. The elegant and sophisticated Wilding was amused by her efforts then to get his attention. He told Stewart Granger: "Rather than ask the waitress for some salt, that Taylor chit will walk clear through the commissary to get it from the kitchen, wiggling her hips. Then she wiggles her way back again, past my table."

When she arrived in London for *Ivanhoe,* Michael Wilding called and invited Liz and Peggy to dinner their first night in town. "I honestly thought she might be lonely," he said later. They began going out every night. Within six weeks Elizabeth declared herself madly in love. Michael Wilding, like Stanley Donen, was still married but not living with his wife at the time. Elizabeth begged him to get a divorce and marry her. Anticipating agreement, she bought herself a huge sapphire ring surrounded by diamonds, plopped it on her left hand, and announced to the world that she was engaged to the British actor.

"I finally proposed to him," she admitted. "He was everything I admired in a man, and I thought him remarkable. We'd already said we loved each other earlier. But he said I was too young, I'd change my mind. When I objected, he said we should wait."

Wilding stalled Elizabeth while continuing to see his idol, Marlene Dietrich, who was eight years his senior. "Michael used to take Marlene to the beauty parlor and wait for her to be washed and set and combed out and manicured and pedicured," said Sheilah Graham. "He was mad for her and completely devoted to her, but she was not the marrying kind."*

Elizabeth was nothing but the marrying kind, and extremely determined to make this charming, whimsical man her next husband. But he still resisted. Herbert Wilcox, the British producer, recalled finding Michael in a painful dilemma. "He was in love with both Marlene Dietrich and Elizabeth Taylor," he said. " 'If you can't make up your own mind, Michael, I'm afraid I can't help,' I told him."

Elizabeth kept making the point that at nineteen she could give

---

* Or perhaps not the remarrying kind. Marlene Dietrich had been married to Rudolph Sieber, a chicken farmer, since 1924.

Michael the children he had never had—something her forty-seven-year-old rival could not do. She also noted that she needed him more.

"Michael was the one who needed Marlene emotionally and was charged by the exciting chemistry between them," said a friend, "but the fact that Liz needed *him* gave him a feeling of protectiveness he had never known before."

"Elizabeth is affectionate and kind," said Wilding. "People forget she has been through a very trying year. She wants to be married to someone who will love and protect her, and that someone, by some heaven-sent luck, turns out to be me."

When *Ivanhoe* was wrapped in September, Elizabeth flew to New York wearing the sapphire engagement ring she had bought for herself. She immediately phoned Montgomery Clift, and they began seeing each other all day every day. They beamed as photographers recorded their presence at Le Pavillon, the "21" Club, and Voisin. "Ain't it great being famous, Bessie Mae?" howled Monty.

They celebrated reviews of *A Place in the Sun* that praised Monty for being "almost too good, too sensitive," and credited Elizabeth with "the top effort of her career." *Variety* wrote that "For Miss Taylor, at least, the histrionics are of a quality so far beyond anything she has done previously that Stevens' skilled hands on the reins must be credited with a minor miracle."

Said Al Hine in *Holiday:* "Stevens has placed Elizabeth Taylor in a part where all the uncomfortable, preening mannerisms that have brought a touch of nausea to her recent screen portrayals are valid. The conceit, artificiality, and awkwardness which mar her playing in most ingenue roles are not only acceptable but essential to her rendition of Miss Rich Bitch of 1951."

Shelley Winters received her first Academy Award nomination and Monty his second. But it was George Stevens who won for Best Director, Edith Head for Best Costumes, Michael Wilson and Harry Brown for Best Screenplay, William C. Mellor for Best Cinematography, Franz Waxman for Best Score, and William Hornbeck for Best Editing. *A Place in the Sun* lost the

Academy Award for Best Picture to *An American in Paris,* but it
was named the outstanding film of the year by the National Motion Picture Board of Review.

Despite the reviews, Elizabeth felt self-conscious. "I've never
considered I could act," she told Herbert Wilcox at the time. "I
don't like acting enough, so I guess that's why I'm not a good
actress. . . ."

She still craved constant companionship and most days got it.
She charged around New York City drinking with Montgomery
Clift, partying with newspaper columnist Frank Farrell, eating
pasta with comedian Merv Griffin, ice skating with actor Roddy
McDowall. She enjoyed a luxurious suite at the Plaza Hotel—
compliments, she said, of the management. She was so accustomed now to having everything come her way that she expected
it as her due as an internationally famous movie star. Weeks
later, she inquired about her room service charges and was told
that her total bill was $2,500.

"I thought this was all free!" she screamed.

"No, Miss Taylor," said the desk clerk. "We show only the
first four days as being complimentary from the management."

Elizabeth cursed and swore and acted spoiled, informing the
clerk that she was leaving the hotel immediately and would never
return. Then she called Monty to complain. "We were both so
mad we decided to get revenge before leaving," she said.

Within minutes Monty arrived with Roddy McDowall, and the
three of them ordered a pitcher of martinis and proceeded to get
very drunk as they packed Elizabeth to move to the St. Regis.

They vandalized the suite, ripping curtains from the walls,
turning pictures upside down, unscrewing bathroom fixtures, and
stealing the embossed towels and bath mats as well as the shower
nozzle and the martini pitcher. They dueled with the giant chrysanthemums that had been sent to Elizabeth by a fan and littered
the suite with hundreds of yellow petals and broken stems.

"Elizabeth was prankish in a blunt sort of way," recalled
Frank Farrell. "While she was in New York I took her to a very
important party preceding a ball of some kind which was hosted

by a member of the Rockefeller family. We were having drinks at the door and carrying them in. The hostess came up to us and asked Elizabeth what she would like to drink.

" 'Oh, I don't drink,' Elizabeth said, 'but I'd love some bubble gum.'

" 'I'm terribly sorry, Miss Taylor, but I don't allow bubble gum in my house,' said the hostess.

"Liz thought things like that were funny," said Farrell. "She was always trying to embarrass me by playing those kinds of pranks."

Unfazed by the broad strokes of her humor, Merv Griffin remembers taking Elizabeth to dinner: "She loved to belch just loud enough for the fans to hear but discreetly enough for them to whisper, 'That couldn't have been her.' "

"Liz has a very heavy-handed concept of fun," said one friend. "That business at the Plaza Hotel with Monty and Roddy, the cake-in-the-face incident—all that stuff. She likes to hit and slug and sock and get it in return. Maybe it's tied up with her huge sex drive—who knows?"

The dutiful daughter of Sara Taylor, so easily led and influenced as a child, indeed did seem to have developed aggressive instincts by the time she was nineteen. She pursued Michael Wilding with the single-minded intensity of a hunter stalking prey, and she ignored skeptics when they pointed out their twenty-year age difference.

"No matter what you or anybody else thinks," she told Hedda Hopper, "I love this man and I'm going to marry him. I love him, I love him, I love him."

For much of her life she was attracted to passive, gentle men like Michael Wilding. "I don't know why," said a friend, "but Liz always gravitated to men like Michael and Monty Clift, which was strange for such a robust, passionate woman. Or else she went for flawed men like Eddie Fisher with his drug addiction or Richard Burton with his alcoholism. I guess those are the kind of men she could manage and control the way her mother did her father."

Both Michael Wilding and Montgomery Clift were attracted to older, glamorous, extremely formidable women. In Monty's case, it was a torch singer by the name of Libby Holman. With Michael it was Marlene Dietrich. In fact, when Michael Wilding finally joined Elizabeth in New York in the fall of 1951, he told the press he didn't consider himself engaged to her. Nor was his trip to America solely for the purpose of seeing Liz. "It was because of Herbert Wilcox and Anna Neagle that I visited. . . . They asked me to accompany them for personal appearances in behalf of *The Lady with the Lamp,* in which Anna plays Florence Nightingale." And he continued to see Marlene Dietrich. The producer Sam Marx remembers making the rounds one night in Manhattan and seeing evidence that Wilding might still prefer the older woman.

"I saw Elizabeth at the St. Regis," Marx recalled. "She and Montgomery Clift were together, slugging vodka. I joined them and the atmosphere was very tense. Later that evening I saw Elizabeth with Wilding. He looked so bored. And later that same night I was in '21' and I saw Wilding with Marlene Dietrich. And he was so alive. The difference was astonishing. I wondered then what Elizabeth was getting into."

Elizabeth followed the reluctant Wilding to California, where he stayed with his best friend, Stewart Granger, and his wife, Jean Simmons. Liz stayed with them too, and continued badgering Michael to marry her. His strongest argument against the marriage was money. He said he would be unable to support her in Hollywood. At that time he was under contract to Herbert Wilcox and Anna Neagle as a romantic young lover and on top of the British box-office standings. As a British subject leaving England, he said, he would lose everything that his first wife didn't take in the divorce.

Elizabeth went to Benny Thau at MGM with her problem. She told him that she wanted to marry Michael Wilding and live in Hollywood but that Michael could not afford to leave England. Unless Metro offered him a handsome movie contract, she said, she would leave the studio and give up her career and live abroad with her husband. Thau began negotiating with Wilding at once. Wilding accepted the Metro offer just as fast. Then he nonchalantly informed Herbert Wilcox and Anna Neagle that their partnership was over. He told them that he was sure they would not want him to stay in Britain if he would not be happy.

Wilcox was stunned. "And so ended one of the happiest and most successful associations in the British film industry in a way that was sad, unnecessary, tragic," he said.

The handsome offer from MGM enabled Elizabeth to break Michael's resistance, and he agreed to "think about" marrying her. During this time Nicky Hilton announced his engagement to Betsy Von Furstenberg, and Elizabeth tortured herself with jealous imaginings about the blond, blue-eyed countess. Knowing that Nicky would be attending a particular premiere with his fiancée, she appeared with Wilding. Afterward they waited in the lobby for hundreds of people to pass, ostensibly so that she could say hello to her former husband.

Nicky Hilton was not fooled. "He told me later that the only reason she was waiting there for us in the theater was to see what I looked like," said Betsy Von Furstenberg. " 'Do you believe that bitch?' he said. 'She was checking you out.' I could never understand why Michael Wilding allowed himself to be put through that; but then, maybe he didn't realize what she was up to at the time."

Wilding was a gentle, placid man whose charm prevented him from ever giving offense. It would never have occurred to him to say no to Elizabeth. He was too passive to argue with anyone. "I'm the type who just can't stand a row of any kind," he said. "I never could stand them. They're just too demanding." Years later he confessed that when Liz had tried to start quarreling, he would just let her get on with it. "I'd say, 'Yes, darling,' and 'Certainly, my love,' and 'All right, dear,' but that never seemed to work. It just made her even more furious."

Only a man as agreeable as Michael Wilding would have allowed himself to be subjected to the Hollywood game as Elizabeth and her mother played it. No sooner had the British actor arrived than Sara Taylor was on the phone calling Louella Parsons and inviting Hedda Hopper for tea. Having given up all hope for a reconciliation between Elizabeth and Nicky Hilton, Sara now resigned herself to the inevitable—that her daughter was determined to marry a man exactly like her father. That was preferable to her marrying Stanley Donen, but she fretted about Michael Wilding. The weak-chinned British matinee idol was going bald and had to wear a toupee. Worse, he did not have any money. In fact, he owed British Inland Revenue $100,000 in taxes. Without great wealth to brag about, she decided to focus on his aristocratic background, telling Louella and Hedda that he was a descendant of the Archbishop of Canterbury who had crowned Queen Victoria. The columnists remained unimpressed and publicly cautioned Elizabeth to remind her fiancé to wear his hairpiece.

Michael Wilding had freely admitted that his great ambition in life was "to be rich and not have to work too hard." Basically lazy, he enjoyed the money his acting brought him, but his career was not his life. "I've never considered myself a good actor," he said. "I do the best I can for the paycheck. I just don't get excited about things, particularly my work."

"He enjoys sitting home, smoking his pipe, reading, painting —and that's what I intend doing," said Elizabeth. "I just want to be with him, to be his wife, and to have a baby right away."

Having shamelessly chased the man, proposed to him, purchased her own engagement ring, and then secured a lucrative movie contract for him, Elizabeth now announced that she and Wilding would marry the minute their divorces became final. Back in England, Wilding was astonished to hear her statement. "Elizabeth's announcement came as a surprise to me," he said. "I had thought we would wait a few weeks and . . . well . . . and . . ." He recovered gallantly by saying their plans were so vague he didn't know when or where the wedding would take place.

Already Elizabeth was conferring with Helen Rose on the design for her second wedding dress. The day after her divorce from Nicky Hilton was final, she started packing for London. Sara Taylor, wild that her daughter was leaving without a firmer commitment from her fiancé, voiced strong disapproval of his intentions. Elizabeth told her to go to hell. She arrived in England on February 11, 1952. Ten days later she persuaded Michael Wilding to marry her. The ceremony took place in Westminster's Caxton Hall. She wore a dove-gray suit. He wore an air of surprise.

CHAPTER 8

"WHAT A CIRCUS IT TURNED OUT TO BE," recalled Herbert Wilcox, who ushered Michael Wilding into the airport VIP lounge to greet his fiancée. "When Liz entered she took one look at Michael and in a flash she was in his arms and they were embracing madly. The reporters and I were completely forgotten. The embrace lasted so long and was so passionate that we all moved to the bar and left them to it."

Elizabeth had arrived with three cabin trunks and thirty suitcases and was determined to stay as long as it took to get Wilding to marry her. It was only a matter of days before the lovebirds set the date. Knowing Michael's tenuous financial situation, Anna Neagle and Herbert Wilcox offered to attend to the wedding arrangements. They paid for everything, including the champagne reception at Claridge's. Elizabeth agreed to pay for the honeymoon.

During the wedding rehearsal Elizabeth gazed so steadily at her fiancé that it became uncomfortable for everyone in the room. When the registrar of Caxton Hall told Michael to kiss the bride, Elizabeth grabbed him and would not let go.

"They fell into a clinch which had to be seen to be believed," said Herbert Wilcox.

The day of the wedding, Elizabeth arrived alone at Caxton Hall in a chauffeured Rolls-Royce. She had refused to invite her mother, and Francis Taylor certainly would not have come without Sara. Her brother, Howard, was in a combat unit in Korea, leaving Elizabeth on the brink of her second marriage without any family beside her. Ben Goetz, the head of MGM in Great Britain, was there with his wife as surrogate father and mother.

Michael Wilding, fortified by a bottle of champagne, waited inside the hall with his disapproving parents, along with Anna Neagle and Herbert Wilcox. The ceremony lasted ten minutes. When the registrar pronounced them man and wife, Elizabeth said, "Please, may I kiss the groom now?" Once again she hurled herself at Wilding. The couple then walked outside and were besieged by a clamoring horde of bobby-soxers shouting congratulations.

As thousands of people surged toward them, Elizabeth shouted to her new husband, "Hold me tighter, Michael. Hold me tighter." Wilding looked alarmed as burly policemen broke through the crush and carried Elizabeth to the waiting limousine.

"Good God, but marriage is a tiring affair," he said.

Reporters shoved in to ask him how he and his new bride intended to spend their honeymoon. "Together, I hope," he replied.

"Can you give us the formula, Mr. Wilding, for a successful marriage?"

"I haven't a bloody clue," he shrugged.

"Tell us, why did you marry Miss Taylor, eh?"

"She's a nice kid and she has a nice sense of humor."

"Carried away, ain't ya, mate?"

Breaking loose from the pawing throng, the groom finally made it to the limousine, climbed inside, and straightened his twisted clothes. Liz turned to the panting crowds and called, "I hope you will all be as happy some day as I am right this moment. This is to me the beginning of a happy end."

When Sara Taylor was informed in Hollywood that her daughter had completed her marriage vows in London, she said, "That's very nice. I think it is wonderful that Liz married someone older than she. An older man is more considerate, thoughtful, and understanding, and he'll make her more considerate and understanding too." Francis Taylor, who never disagreed with his wife, remained silent.

After an eight-day honeymoon in the French Alps, where Elizabeth celebrated her twentieth birthday, the Wildings returned to London so Michael could begin work on *Derby Day*, his sixth film with Anna Neagle. Meanwhile, Elizabeth's seven-year contract with MGM, signed in 1945, was expiring, and the studio was campaigning strenuously to keep the most magnificent face in films from turning elsewhere.

Corporate anxiety, always high in the motion-picture business, skyrocketed in the early fifties. The paranoid search for Communists in Hollywood, led by Joe McCarthy and his witch-hunting posse, was destroying the industry by stifling creativity and turning friend against friend. Compounding the problems was the consent decree the major studios had entered into with the U.S. Department of Justice. Under terms of this agreement, the studios were forced to divest themselves of their distribution companies and the theaters they owned. In effect, this marked the end of studio dominion, which had allowed studios to control their product and its profits every step of the way. To exacerbate the crisis, the era of television had arrived, biting sharply into movie profits. Weekly theater attendance dropped from an all-time high of 125 million in 1945 to 60 million in 1952. Unquestionably, the colossal studio system was teetering on the edge of obsolescence.

Loew's, Inc., the corporate parent of Metro-Goldwyn-Mayer, panicked. With profits $3 million below the preceding year—the lowest since the Depression year of 1933—it cut back on everything. MGM was no longer sweeping the Academy Awards, and its contract stars were leaving in droves to form their own production companies. Louis B. Mayer, for years the MGM production czar and highest-paid executive in the country, was forced to resign and was replaced by Dore Schary. Others, like Clark Gable, Spencer Tracy, Mickey Rooney, Jane Powell, Greer Garson, and Esther Williams, were unconditionally released; but Metro wanted to keep Elizabeth Taylor.

Elizabeth's agent, Jules Goldstone, recommended that she too leave MGM and form her own production company. He explained that by free-lancing she could bargain for better scripts, pick and choose the parts she wanted to play, control the production, and earn much more money, which, thanks to capital gains, would be taxed at a lower rate. But Elizabeth wanted the security of the studio. She also knew that as an independent she would no longer have access to the MGM wardrobe department. "She was so in love with clothes," said Jules Goldstone, "that frequently when I had Metro ready seriously to reconsider increases for her she would go in and ask for some of the clothes she wore in a recent picture. That would satisfy her."

MGM further enticed Elizabeth by offering her a five-year contract at $5,000 a week, forty weeks guaranteed, with $300 a week to Sara Taylor, who managed to stay on the payroll as long as her daughter. Wilding received a three-year contract at $3,000 a week with an option of two years at $4,000 a week. As part of the new contract Elizabeth negotiated a $50,000 loan from the studio to buy a house with a swimming pool for herself, her new husband, and the baby they were now expecting. Later she collected $47,000 in bonds which had accumulated from her required savings as a child star. This money furnished the new house.

While Wilding remained in London to sell his apartment, Elizabeth returned to Hollywood in June to begin work on another rich-girl role in *The Girl Who Had Everything*. Because of her patrician beauty she was called upon by MGM to play this role in every picture the studio produced. In a succession of films that in effect were a single saga, she waltzed across the screen in sumptuous gowns and jewels and furs.

By the time the movie was wrapped, she was luxuriating in her pregnancy. She ballooned from 112 pounds to 155 pounds, and MGM placed her on reduced-pay suspension at $2,000 a week. The change in her physical appearance made it impossible to film or photograph her.

Her first baby, Michael Howard Wilding, named after her husband and her brother, was born by cesarean section on January 6, 1953. A month later Elizabeth was still too heavy to work, but Metro continued paying her $2,000 a week until she lost all her excess weight. When she lost the starring roles in *All the Brothers Were Valiant* and *Young Bess* because she was too fat, she finally agreed to diet and to present herself for inspection.

"She is to come to the studio to see Mr. Thau, who will look at her and then decide at that time as to whether or not her physical appearance is such that her contract should be resumed at full compensation," stated an office memorandum.

By crash dieting, Elizabeth managed to get down to 117 pounds in time to be "loaned" to Paramount for *Elephant Walk,* replacing Vivien Leigh, who had suffered a mental collapse. Internationally famous as Scarlett O'Hara in *Gone with the Wind* and Blanche DuBois in *A Streetcar Named Desire,* Miss Leigh was a victim of manic depression. She slipped into and out of madness during her marriage to Laurence Olivier, and during location shooting in Ceylon she began hallucinating. By the time she returned to Hollywood to complete *Elephant Walk* in the studio's sound stages, she was unable to continue.

Because of her resemblance to the fabled actress, Elizabeth was selected to replace her so that the movie would not have to be completely scrapped. The replacement later caused *Time* magazine to comment: "Elizabeth Taylor, though very beautiful, is too young and inexperienced an actress to fill a role designed for Vivien Leigh."

When Elizabeth arrived on the set, the producer was still reeling from the havoc caused by Leigh's breakdown. "Even after Vivien left I had problems," recalled Irving Asher. "Peter Finch continued to carry on about his tremendous romance and love affair with her, which had been going on in Ceylon, and Dana Andrews was drinking so heavily that sometimes we couldn't shoot his scenes. Elizabeth was a dream to work with. She arrived on time, knew her lines, and was really quite patient and helpful with Dana. Sometimes he was in such bad shape that we had to shoot him from behind, and in their scenes together Elizabeth led him. She was thoroughly professional."

While doing publicity stills for *Elephant Walk,* Elizabeth experienced the first in a series of freakish accidents that would haunt her for years. She was sitting in a Jeep with Peter Finch and Dana Andrews while a wind machine blowing full blast to simulate a hurricane was directed at them. As she threw back her head, a rusty splinter was driven into her eye. A doctor removed the splinter and bandaged the eye, but an ulcer later developed which required surgery.

"Every time I blinked, there would be the most awful scratching sensation," she wrote. "Later, when the eye got goopy and stuff was coming out, I went to a doctor who probed around and said, 'My dear, you have a foreign object in your eye.' And I said, 'Anybody I know?' Another doctor put my head in a little vise and operated to get out my foreign object. It had shot deep into the eyeball and had rusted. They can't knock you out because you have to keep your eye open and stare at a certain spot on the wall. They have a needle with a tiny knife at the end and you can hear them cutting your eye. It sounds rather like eating watermelon on a minor scale."

Elizabeth wrote this description ten years after the accident occurred. She enjoyed telling about her sicknesses and surgeries and took great pleasure in discussing the most graphic aspects of each operation. She soon became fixated by her own physical melodramas and later would boast of having had more than thirty operations. Her interests were bounded by her ailments, and she described each in excruciating detail for anyone who would listen.

Montgomery Clift, himself a dour hypochondriac, relished her ghoulish recitations. "Bessie Mae is the only person I know who has more wrong with her than I have," he said.

As soon as Elizabeth recuperated from her ulcerated eye, she began yet another spoiled-rich-girl role in *Rhapsody,* a glossy romantic drama with Vittorio Gassman. According to the *New York Herald Tribune,* the movie was merely a vehicle "to show off Miss Taylor wearing attractive gowns, sobbing in loneliness or radiant at a concert. . . . Her animation is only the animation of a doll with the strings being pulled behind the scenes. Under these difficult circumstances, without flair in either script or direction, even her evident and genuine beauty seems at times to be a fake.''

Michael Wilding was filming *Torch Song* with Joan Crawford at the same time Elizabeth was doing *Rhapsody;* they regularly met for lunch in the MGM commissary, and she frequently visited him on the set. Crawford, returning to Metro at the age of forty-eight after an absence of ten years, still expected star treatment.

"One time Liz came on the set and she snubbed Joan and hurt her feelings by not saying hello," recalled Dore Freeman, a longtime MGM employee. "Joan called me over and said, 'You tell that little bitch never to walk in here again without acknowledging me. I want you to teach her some manners.' I never said anything to Liz, of course, but I never forgot the incident.''

Neither Elizabeth nor Michael Wilding could fathom Joan Crawford's intensity about her work. They were shocked to learn that she actually spent twenty-four hours a day at the studio. "My God! She even sleeps here!" Michael told his wife. It was hard for him to understand such compulsion for work. He much preferred staying at home, painting portraits and lolling beside the pool. Suspended frequently by the studio, he had to forfeit his weekly salary of $3,000 whenever he refused a role, and he refused several, including a small part in *Latin Lovers* with Lana Turner. He also refused to make a screen test for *The Swan* to play opposite Grace Kelly.

This lackadaisical attitude didn't bother Elizabeth—until bills piled up and debts mounted. When Michael refused to take Rex Harrison's role in the national company of *My Fair Lady,* she called Hedda Hopper and pleaded with her to do something. "Talk with Mike, Hedda. Reason with him," she begged. "It's such a wonderful part." But Wilding refused the role and continued refusing others. "I was just too lazy to do them," he admitted later.

By the time Elizabeth was pregnant with her second child, she gave the studio an extra year on her contract rather than face another reduced-pay suspension. "I simply couldn't afford it," she said. Now her husband had to go to work. "Since we want a larger family, it behooves me to bestir myself," he said. "As it is, frankly, we live on a scale which involves both our incomes." The Wildings had abandoned themselves to luxury, buying and shopping and spending to the hilt. They regularly presented each other with new cars. Elizabeth announced that her favorite hobbies were "clothes and jewels." Wilding tried to accommodate his wife by presenting her with the diamond necklaces and sapphire bracelets and emerald rings that she picked out; but since he had no money, Elizabeth usually paid for them. She complained to Montgomery Clift that she had dreamed of finding a "big strong guy" to take care of her and buy her jewels and furs and now found herself paying all the bills.

When Elizabeth was sent to England in the fall of 1953 to star in *Beau Brummell,* the studio financed an extra six weeks in Europe to give the Wildings a second honeymoon abroad before Elizabeth started work. While traveling, she enthusiastically pursued her jewelry hobby and had to be bailed out by the studio. "PLEASE BE SWEET ENOUGH TO WIRE PERMISSION TO NEW YORK ALLOWING ME $1,600 EXTRA FOR STOCKHOLM FOR JEWELRY I HAVE WITH ME," she telegraphed MGM. "I WOULD JUST DIE OF EMBARRASSMENT IF JEWELERS COME TO COPENHAGEN TO RECLAIM IT. FORGIVE MY TROUBLING YOU BUT DESPERATELY URGENT. FONDEST LOVE, ELIZABETH."

Two months later, pursuing her clothes hobby, she had to wire Metro again. "DEAREST BENNY," she telegraphed Benjamin Thau, "I HATE TO BOTHER YOU BUT IT IS TERRIBLY IMPORTANT. I NEED SOME OF MY CLOTHES FROM *RHAPSODY* RIGHT AWAY AS IT IS DREADFULLY COLD HERE. I CAN MAKE OUT LIST TO HELEN [Rose] AFTER YOUR OKAY SO THEY CAN BE FLOWN OVER IMMEDIATELY. PLEASE LET ME KNOW AS SOON AS POSSIBLE. FONDEST LOVE AND THANKS, ELIZABETH."

Together the Wildings earned more than $350,000 a year, but their expenses nearly capsized them. In addition to Elizabeth's "hobbies," there were the monthly mortgage, the interest and payments on the MGM house loan, and salaries for Elizabeth's personal secretary, Peggy Rutledge; a gardener; a cook; a maid; and a nurse for the newborn baby, Christopher.

Four unhousebroken dogs, five cats, and two ducks romped through the house. The cats clawed the woven grass-cloth wallpaper to shreds, the ducks chomped on the furniture, and the dogs dropped their daily deposits on the thick white rug in the living room. Elizabeth kept her poodle, Gee Gee, and all her puppies in the nursery with the baby. That enraged the nurse, who frequently stumbled upon heaps of hardened droppings near the crib.

The menagerie shocked even Sara Taylor, who was now allowed one weekly visit. "I couldn't keep from saying, 'Oh, Elizabeth, don't let Gee Gee lick the baby,' " said Sara. "She looked at me in amazement. 'Why, how can you feel that way, Mother? You know a dog's saliva is the purest thing in the world—it's a disinfectant. That's nature's way of taking care of animals and their babies.' "

Elizabeth did not know how to cook or clean or grocery-shop, nor did she care. "She hangs things up on the floor," said her husband. "Any floor. She can make a room look more like a typhoon hit it than a typhoon would."

Wilding tolerated Elizabeth's sloppiness, but he could never understand her tardiness. "The thing I find difficult is her lack of any sense of time," he said. "She was born without it."

Persistently late, Elizabeth would keep people waiting for hours as she casually applied her makeup, combed her hair, or polished her nails. It was her defiant way of saying, "I will do what I want when I want." She never apologized for this arrogance, and if criticized she lashed out. "You must not rub her the wrong way," warned Wilding. "She upsets very easily."

Loathing confrontations of any kind, Michael Wilding indulged his wife in the beginning of their marriage. He catered to her vanity by painting portraits of her and posing her for hundreds of photographs which crowded the walls of their home. Stacks of movie magazines with Elizabeth on the cover were always piled high on their coffee table. Yet this obeisance was not enough.

"Actors require love on many levels, and Elizabeth needed more than the love of her husband and child and even her parents," said the director Richard Brooks. "She needed the love of critical approval, and I made up my mind that if I could do it she would get it in *The Last Time I Saw Paris*."

At this time Elizabeth Taylor, though a star, had yet to be nominated for an Academy Award. Nor was she top box-office. The biggest names in the business were John Wayne, Dean Martin and Jerry Lewis, Gary Cooper, James Stewart, Marilyn Monroe, Alan Ladd, William Holden, Bing Crosby, Jane Wyman, and Marlon Brando.

After finishing *Beau Brummell* in London, Elizabeth returned to Hollywood to work with Richard Brooks on his movie based on *Babylon Revisited*, F. Scott Fitzgerald's story of expatriate Americans. Her leading man was Van Johnson, her co-star from *The Big Hangover*—the 1950 movie that had prompted *The New Yorker* to say, "Miss Taylor is beautiful and cannot act. This puts her one up on Mr. Johnson."

Four years later the combination of Elizabeth Taylor and Van Johnson was still unconvincing. "Van was good, very facile, but you just couldn't believe that each of these two people was desperately in love with the other," said the director.

"Richard Brooks fell in love with Liz during this movie," said a member of the cast, "and he killed himself to get a good performance out of her."

While lavishing time and attention on the star, Brooks was brutal to her stand-in. "It's true that he liked Liz an awful lot and was very good to her," recalled Marjorie Dillon. "I wasn't an actress, so he was terrible to me. I was supposed to be there so the crew could set up lighting and arrange the cameras for the star, but Brooks made me do other things and then yelled at me, screaming that I couldn't act at all. I knew I couldn't. I wasn't an actress."

The Last Time I Saw Paris tells the story in flashbacks of a recovered-alcoholic writer—played by Van Johnson—who tries to reclaim his daughter from the custody of a sister-in-law who has never forgiven him for her sister's death. One of the flashbacks shows how during an argument the writer, while drinking, locks out his wife—played by Elizabeth—who suffers pneumonia from the bitter cold and dies.

In the lockout scene Elizabeth wears a red chiffon evening dress with the usual plunging neckline. After banging on the door and crying to get in, she begins to walk away from the house but faints in the snow. The cameras pull back to show a blotch of blood red against a pure-white background. "The effect was impressive and dramatic," said Helen Rose, the MGM costume designer.

In 1954 the studios' censorship departments still ruled Hollywood. Films were carefully scrutinized for anything "morally objectionable"—such as dialogue with a *double entendre,* kisses too passionate, skirts too short, or necklines too revealing. In her filmy red dress Elizabeth displayed more cleavage than usual, and an assistant director called in one of the studio's "bust inspectors." Mrs. Rose remembers the censor as being a young woman with horn-rimmed glasses and a no-nonsense air.

"She took one look at Elizabeth in that dress and immediately requested a tall ladder. Working her way up to the top rung, she adjusted her glasses and peered down into that gorgeous bosom. She informed all of us standing silently around that the dress would have to be changed, the décolletage filled in, or we would have to replace the dress with something more modest."

Richard Brooks exploded with curses. The bust inspector burst into tears, fled the set, and quit her job before expunging the scene. The scarlet gown remained, but it failed to salvage the movie for Bosley Crowther of *The New York Times.*

"The story is trite. The motivations are thin. The writing is glossy and pedestrian," he wrote. "The acting is pretty much forced. Mr. Johnson as the husband is too bumptious when happy and too dreary when drunk. Miss Taylor as the wife is delectable but she is also occasionally quite dull."

The reviews of *Beau Brummell,* released in the fall of 1954, were even worse for Elizabeth. "As for Miss Taylor, she is decorative but something less than useful as a heroine . . ." said the *New York Herald Tribune.*

Hurt and humiliated, Elizabeth blamed the studio for casting her in bad parts. She wanted desperately to be a top box-office star and to win an Academy Award. She tried constantly to get better roles for herself. In 1953 she begged for Ava Gardner's part in *The Barefoot Contessa*. She wired Benny Thau from London, pleading: "DEAREST, DARLING BENNY: SAW JOE MANKIEWICZ IN ROME AND ASKED HIM TO LET ME READ *BAREFOOT CONTESSA*. I WANT TO DO IT MORE THAN ANY SCRIPT I HAVE EVER READ. I KNOW WHAT HAPPENED BETWEEN AVA AND SCHENCK BUT IF METRO HAS NOTHING IMPORTANT FOR ME, PLEASE HELP ME WITH THIS BECAUSE AS YOU KNOW IT WOULD DO ME MORE GOOD PERHAPS THAN ANYTHING I HAVE EVER DONE. PLEASE, PLEASE, PLEASE BENNY AND LET ME KNOW AS SOON AS POSSIBLE DORCHESTER. FONDEST LOVE, ELIZABETH."

Benny Thau wired back that Ava Gardner still had the role. Elizabeth did not give up. After the birth of her second baby on February 27, 1955, she instructed her agent to send Thau a letter that said: "When you visited with Liz at the hospital yesterday she intended to discuss *I'll Cry Tomorrow* with you but forgot to. From what she knows of the story, she feels it would be something she would very much like to do, and in view of the stories in the press about the production she wonders whether the picture might not be held back long enough so that she could do it." Again the answer was no. Susan Hayward got the part and was nominated for an Academy Award.

Elizabeth then heard that George Stevens was directing *Giant* and that his first choice for the female lead, Grace Kelly, would not be available. She felt that this role, in which her life would span thirty years from young bride to grandmother, would be the kind of part to win her critical acclaim, especially with Stevens directing. She didn't care that she would be a second choice. She approached Benny Thau and begged to be "loaned" to Warner Brothers for the role. This time MGM agreed.

CHAPTER 9

ON THE EVENING OF SEPTEMBER 30, 1955, George Stevens and members of the cast were screening rushes in the projection room of Warner Brothers. Suddenly the phone rang and the director answered.

"No—my God!" he cried. "When? Are you sure?" George Stevens replaced the receiver, stopped the film, and turned on the lights.

"I've just been given the news that Jimmy Dean has been killed," he said.

There was an audible intake of breath, but the news didn't register. No one believed that the twenty-four-year-old actor who had ricocheted to stardom in *East of Eden* was actually dead.

"I can't believe it, George; I can't believe it," said Elizabeth.

"I believe it," replied the director. "He had it coming to him. The way he drove, he had it coming."

James Dean, the most dynamic screen discovery since Marlon Brando, had slammed his silver Porsche Spyder into the side of another car on a road near Paso Robles, California. Four days before, he had finished his final scenes in *Giant* and Elizabeth had given him a Siamese kitten as a farewell gift.

"I just can't believe this awful thing has happened," she sobbed. "Not to Jimmy—he was so young, so full of life."

The next morning George Stevens called her to come back to the studio and finish her final scene in the movie. She said her eyes were swollen from crying all night. He said he didn't care. She was still expected to work. He said James Dean was not worth the self-indulgent tears that had sent her spinning into hysteria.

"George was not very kind to her," said Rock Hudson. "Elizabeth is very extreme in her likes and dislikes. If she likes, she loves. If she doesn't like, she loathes. And she has a temper, an incredible temper which she loses at any injustice. George forced her to come to work after Dean's death. He hadn't finished the film. And she could not stop crying. Remember that scene in my office? She kept sobbing and sobbing, so he photographed me over the back of her head. But she let him have it."

"You are a callous bastard!" Elizabeth screamed at Stevens as she stormed off the set. "I hope you rot in hell!" The next day she collapsed with abdominal pains and was rushed to the hospital. "If I hadn't had that blowup with George Stevens, hysterical and crying, and if I hadn't eaten, it wouldn't have happened," she asserted later.

Determined to punish the director, she remained in the hospital for two weeks, stalling completion of the film while keeping the entire company waiting for her. She did not attend Dean's funeral in Indiana, but she wired flowers. When she learned that the Academy of Motion Picture Arts and Sciences refused to posthumously award the actor a special Oscar for his work in *Rebel Without a Cause,* she again became enraged.

"I won't go to the Awards," she said. "I won't honor any group of people who refuse to bestow the recognition due Jimmy —an Oscar for one of the brightest talents ever to come into our industry."

By the time *Giant* was released, James Dean was a hero with a cult reaching beyond the grave. His shrug of rebellion became a totem for teenagers in the fifties. His performance as the surly ranch hand who becomes a drunken oil king in Edna Ferber's Texas saga mesmerized critics. "It is James Dean who gives the most striking performance and creates in Jett Rink the most memorable character in *Giant,*" said *The New York Times.*

Dean did not get all the praise. Elizabeth received the kind of reviews she long had craved for her portrayal of Leslie Benedict, the young Maryland woman who marries an incredibly rich Texan and becomes mistress of his Reata Ranch. ". . . She grows old with a grace and sweetness that can arouse only admiration and envy," said the *New York Herald Tribune*.

"Miss Taylor, whose talent and emotional ranges have usually seemed limited, turns in a surprisingly clever performance that registers up and down the line," said *Variety*. "She is tender and yet stubborn. Curiously enough, she's far better in the second half of the film, when her hair begins to show some gray, than in the earlier sequences. Portraying a woman of maturity, who has learned to adjust to a different social pattern, Miss Taylor is both engaging and beautiful."

But Elizabeth's best performance to date was not good enough for an Academy Award nomination. That honor went instead to her co-stars Rock Hudson, James Dean, and Mercedes McCambridge. In all, *Giant* attracted ten Academy Award nominations. But only George Stevens won, for best director.

Filming was rigorous work for Elizabeth, especially during location shooting in Marfa, Texas, where the temperature rose as high as 120 degrees. Stevens insisted that she watch the daily rushes every night, and he carefully critiqued every intonation and gesture and asked her the motivation of her actions. Unable to accept any kind of criticism, Elizabeth frequently clashed with the director. "She has every qualification necessary for stardom —except the ability to concentrate," Stevens said. Elizabeth retaliated by getting sick and incapacitating herself.

"She would be sitting on the set in a wheelchair, attended by a nurse, because she said she was in such excruciating pain from her sciatic nerve," said one eyewitness. "She would cry when she tried to walk. But at the end of the day's work she'd yell to Rock Hudson, 'Hey, wait for me!' and she'd run off the set as gaily as if nothing were wrong. Physically, I don't think anything was wrong."

Emotionally, Elizabeth was distraught. Her marriage to Michael Wilding was crumbling, and she was traumatized by the thought of another divorce. She anguished about the future of her children and sobbed hysterically when she thought of herself alone again without a man. Throughout the filming of *Giant* she clung to Rock Hudson for support. She said that next to Montgomery Clift, Rock was her best friend.

"I feel sorry for her and the kids," he said. "She loves them, but she never seems to know what she wants or where to go."

Michael Wilding visited his wife only once on location and left after a few days because of their quarreling. Later he flew to Morocco to film *Zarak Khan* with Anita Ekberg, and Elizabeth visited him there. Again they quarreled, and she soon left.

"It was horrible, filthy and smelly," she said. "The streets were narrow, winding passages, crowded with unwashed Arabs and Spaniards, and with about three inches of sewage floating between the cobblestones. Everything was dirty, and the food was awful. I came home and went into a hospital for a month."

Wilding joked about his wife's using hospitals like resort hotels. She claimed in turn that he didn't take her sicknesses seriously enough. Friends noticed the growing friction. Once when Wilding was sitting by their swimming pool, Elizabeth summoned him over the house intercom.

"Could you please come look at my new dress, dear?" she said.

"I'm busy, darling," he replied.

"Michael, will you come here immediately!" she snapped.

Muttering in exasperation to his friends, Wilding went to see his wife and her new clothes. When asked why he always capitulated, Wilding shrugged his shoulders. "Liz is kind and gracious to me," he said, "so why not?"

During a trip to New York, Elizabeth called Frank Farrell and asked him to take her to dinner. He agreed to pick her up at the St. Regis, where she was staying in the suite of her great-uncle Howard Young.

"I rang and Michael Wilding answered the door," recalled Frank Farrell. "He was there with Montgomery Clift and Roddy McDowall.

" 'I thought I had a date with Elizabeth,' I said.

" 'You do,' he replied. 'You're taking her to dinner, right?'

" 'That's what I thought, but I didn't know you were in town too.' I was quite puzzled, but Elizabeth came into the room then all dressed to go and the two of us went out, leaving those three men to themselves. It was a weird scene."

By 1956, Elizabeth was openly cavalier toward her husband, and he no longer tried to hide his impatience. Both stopped trying to deny rumors about their marital problems. Around the time of Christopher's first birthday a reporter arrived at their house with a photographer to do a story on Elizabeth, who answered the door wearing nothing but a white bath towel. She then began setting her hair in curlers.

"I bet you started doing that when you heard my car coming up the hill," said the reporter, aware of her tardiness.

"Of course," she said. "Talk to Mike—I'll be right with you."

"You're naked as a jaybird," observed the reporter.

"I won't be a moment," Liz said. "Have Mike show you my portraits."

Wilding was humiliated by his wife's careless disregard. "The happiest years of my marriage were when you were so dependent on me," he told her. "I hate it now. Now *I* follow *you* around. Now I'm left in a corner."

Years later he summed up his downfall by saying, "I went to Hollywood for Metro-Goldwyn-Mayer, married Elizabeth Taylor, and watched my career turn to ashes."

At the same time Elizabeth said, "I am afraid that after five years my marriage to Michael Wilding had become the relationship for which we were much more suited—brother and sister."

Montgomery Clift had rented a house in Hollywood during this period to prepare for *Raintree County,* in which he was starring with Elizabeth. He spent many evenings with the Wildings in their home near the top of Benedict Canyon, and soon became their emotional referee. Daytime hours found him listening to Elizabeth berate her passionless forty-four-year-old husband, who she said now treated her like a child. In the evenings, Wilding privately told him his side of the story. "Poor Monty was put in the terrible position of trying to help Liz and Mike decide whether or not they should get a divorce," said a friend. "It was really awfully selfish of them, but they both needed an outlet. Monty, when he was half stoned, was a good listener."

So close were Elizabeth Taylor, Michael Wilding, and Montgomery Clift in those days that many in Hollywood assumed a *ménage à trois* existed. The arrangement was extremely intimate, but it was not in the least sexual. Monty was the shield that Elizabeth and Michael used to battle each other. He also was their diversion from boring each other.

On May 12, 1956, the Wildings invited a few people for a Saturday dinner, including Eddie Dmytryk, the director of *Raintree County,* and his wife, Jean; Rock Hudson and Phyllis Gates; Kevin McCarthy; and Monty. At first Monty refused to come, saying he was too tired. Elizabeth kept calling him and begging him to change his mind. She said the party was for a young priest who admired him. "Father is so hip. He says 'fuck' all the time," Elizabeth said. "You've just got to meet him."

Finally, Michael Wilding called Monty and insisted he come. Both Michael and Elizabeth put his refusal on such a personal basis that Monty gave in and said he would be there.

Principal photography on *Raintree County* had been going on for six weeks at MGM, which had budgeted $5 million for this Civil War saga centering on the romance between an idealistic Yankee schoolteacher (Monty) and a schizophrenic Southern belle (Elizabeth). During the dinner, Liz and Monty kidded each other about how gorgeous the cameraman was making them look in the first rushes. Liz talked about her elaborate antebellum costume and the fact that only the finest materials were used even for her concealed hoopskirts. Monty said no one would look at her petticoats. "All they'll see is your tits." Later he said, "I knew Liz probably would steal this pic, but it was worth running that risk in order to work with her again." Conversation centered on the film because there wasn't much else to talk about.

The party was subdued to the point of being uncomfortable. Michael lay stretched out on the couch most of the evening, suffering a back spasm. Monty was obviously nursing a hang-over, and Elizabeth's modern priest never appeared. The food was uninspired and served with gallons of warm rosé. Elizabeth, who was crazy about Frank Sinatra at the time, kept jumping up to play his records. By 11 P.M. everyone had stayed too late. Monty wanted to leave, but he had given his chauffeur the night off and was nervous about driving down the canyon road. "Kevin has to help me down that mountain or I'll drive around in circles all night," he said.

When Kevin McCarthy left, Monty followed him on a zigzag route down the treacherously steep canyon. The warm red wine combined with two "downers" he had taken earlier in the evening slowed his reflexes, and he began weaving his car from one side of the road to the other. Suddenly there was a terrible crash, and Kevin saw a cloud of dust in the rearview mirror. He rushed back and found Monty's car crumpled against a utility pole with the motor still running and gas leaking. There was no sign of life inside.

Kevin ran back to his car, sped to the Wildings', and banged on the door. "Monty's had a terrible accident!" he screamed. "I think he's dead!"

Michael Wilding thought he was playing a sick joke and said, "Oh, shut up, Kevin!" Elizabeth came to the door and found Kevin trembling so much his words did not make sense at first. But she heard him say, "Monty. He's . . . accident. . . . Oh, God. I think he's dead. . . ."

Pushing past her husband, Elizabeth ran out the door and raced down the hill. "I've got to go to Monty!" she screamed. "I've got to go to Monty!" Michael Wilding called the police and Dr. Rex Kennamer; then he followed his wife and Kevin McCarthy and Rock Hudson down the hill.

"Oh, God, oh, God, oh, God!" Elizabeth screamed when she saw the wreck. She heard Monty's moans from inside and climbed through the back door, crawled over the seat, and cra-dled his head in her lap. The windshield was shattered and the dashboard smashed in, pinning Monty under the steering wheel.

"He was bleeding from the head so much that it looked like his face had been halved," Elizabeth said.

Monty's teeth had been knocked out and were lodged in his throat, causing him to choke. Elizabeth rammed her hand into his mouth and pulled them out so he could breathe. (He later gave them to her as a macabre souvenir of the evening.)

"It took forever for the doctor to come—forever," recalled Rock Hudson.

Monty, although in shock, recognized Dr. Kennamer as soon as he showed up. "Dr. Kennamer," he mumbled, "meet Elizabeth Taylor."

Moments later, a horde of photographers arrived. "Elizabeth prevented the photographers from taking Monty's picture by the foulest language I have ever heard," recalled Rock Hudson. "She shocked them out of taking it. 'You son of a bitch!' she said. 'I'll kick you in the nuts. If you dare take a picture of him like this, I'll never let you near me again. Get out of here, you fucking bastards.'"

The photographers, flabbergasted at the obscenities flying from Elizabeth's mouth, backed off.

"Miss Taylor, you shouldn't be talking like that," said one.

Then Michael Wilding, Kevin McCarthy, and Rock Hudson formed a line to hide Monty. Baring their teeth in skeletal grins, they looked straight at the cameras. "Take a picture of us," they said. "We'll smile for you."

After an interminable wait the ambulance arrived. Elizabeth rode with Monty to the hospital, trying not to vomit from the smell of his blood all over her silk dress. Afterward, she had to be sedated. "His head was so swollen it was almost as wide as his shoulders," she said. "His eyes had disappeared. His cheeks were level with his nose . . . and his upper lip—it was like a spoon had gouged a great big chunk out of his mouth and teeth."

Racked with guilt, Elizabeth knew this accident would never have happened had she not insisted that Monty come to her house for dinner. The next day she told MGM executives that they must hold up production on *Raintree County* and wait for

Monty to recuperate. If they did not allow him to continue in the film, she said she would risk suspension and quit. Metro closed down the company and waited eight weeks for Montgomery Clift to recover.

Ordinarily, such a halt in the production of a multimillion-dollar film would have bankrupted the studio. But MGM executives had taken out an insurance policy to cover such a freakish accident—the first time Metro had such protection against the sickness or injury of a star during a film. The policy saved the studio over half a million dollars.

Elizabeth visited Monty almost every day in the hospital and then accompanied him to his rented house in Hollywood to get him settled. On May 22 she wrote to his friend Bert Padell saying, *"We brought Monty home from the hospital today and he is remarkably improved. Because of a fracture just above his upper teeth, it will be at least two and a half weeks before he'll be completely well."* Actually, it was two and a half months before Monty returned to work. By then he was so addicted to pills and alcohol that he could barely function.

Worn out from worrying about their friend, the Wildings leaped at a last-minute invitation from Kevin McClory to spend the weekend of June 30 cruising with Mike Todd and his fiancée, Evelyn Keyes. Saddled with the weight of their lifeless marriage, they needed this kind of diversion from each other.

The invitation had originally been extended to producer Pandro Berman and his wife, but they had turned it down. "I wasn't much of a sailor," Berman said, "and I didn't want to spend four days on the water. So the Wildings were invited instead."

The chartered yacht had sleeping accommodations for ten people. In addition to his fiancée, Mike Todd had invited his biographer, Art Cohn; Cohn's wife, Marta; his secretary, Richard Hanley; his assistant film director, Kevin McClory; the Wildings; and the agent Kurt Frings and his wife, Ketti.

Famous as the cigar-chomping producer of peep shows, Mike Todd was then fifty-two years old and in the process of filming *Around the World in 80 Days*. He was trying to recoup a lifetime fortune and simultaneously write motion-picture history by presenting a film spectacular with fifty stars and 68,894 extras in thirteen different countries wearing 74,685 costumes. By means of a special camera system known as Todd A-O, this movie would unfold on a widened screen stretching into optical infinity and give audiences their most innovative cinema vision to date. The purpose of the weekend cruise was to finish filming with shots of a magnificent Japanese schooner scheduled to arrive under full sail thirty miles off the Santa Barbara coast.

"Might as well make a party out of it at the same time and write it off to the production," said one guest. "That was the way Mike operated."

The host had never met Michael Wilding and had only a passing acquaintance with Elizabeth. But he greeted them both warmly and started the champagne flowing as soon as they arrived. Though abstemious by nature, he was a gracious host and provided his guests with an unlimited supply of Piper-Heidsieck.

Immediately after boarding, Elizabeth remembered leaving her purse behind and started fretting out loud because it contained a gold Fabergé cigarette case and a gold Cartier compact. She whined so much that Todd became slightly irritated. "Don't make a Dreyfus case out of it," he said. "We'll get it back."

Later in the weekend Elizabeth complained of a severe headache but continued swilling champagne. "Go as far as you like," said Todd, filling her glass. "It's your head."

"Elizabeth was everything Mike professed not to care for," recalled Evelyn Keyes. "She was the epitome of movie star in dress, attitude, and demands. And she never stopped drinking champagne from the moment she stepped on the boat until she got off two days later. Besides actresses, Mike didn't like women who drank a great deal."

Elizabeth sensed the hostility and later mentioned it to her husband. "I know Mike was upset aboard the yacht. It all added up that he was extremely displeased," she said. "Why, he hadn't said ten words to me the entire weekend."

A few days later, Todd hosted a lavish dinner party for a

hundred guests, honoring the distinguished television journalist Edward R. Murrow and his wife. The Wildings arrived late after a nasty quarrel. Elizabeth, striking in a white satin gown with plunging décolletage, barely ate. Instead, she began drinking champagne. Michael Wilding, charming and debonair as always, pleaded an early studio call and departed after an hour, leaving his wife behind with Kevin McClory, one of Todd's assistants, whom she had been quietly dating.

Elizabeth knew she was headed for another divorce, and the thought of it traumatized her. Fearful and lonely and filled with self-pity, she sought comfort from anyone who would fill her champagne glass and try to make her laugh. She confided her unhappiness with Michael Wilding that night, saying that her life was over.

"I was dead, old at twenty-four," she said. "It was just smog and no sunshine. We would wake up in the morning without hope, with nothing to do or talk about, with no reason for living out the day."

Then she burst into tears and ran out of the room, causing everyone to look up.

"What's with her?" Mike Todd asked. When told about the conversation, he immediately felt protective. "Poor kid," he said. "She needs someone to look after her."

A few days later, he invited the Wildings to a barbecue he and Evelyn Keyes were hosting at their rented house overlooking the Sunset Strip. Among the other guests were Shelley Winters, Vittorio Gassman, Debbie Reynolds, and Eddie Fisher. After dinner Todd, a compulsive gambler, started a serious poker game with the men. As the game went on, Wilding and Fisher were losing between $25,000 and $30,000.

"Mike Todd was the big winner," recalled Shelley Winters. "Debbie looked distressed, but her friend Elizabeth was really upset. Then, when the betting was at its most furious, I saw Todd glance at the distressed faces of his friends' wives; then, accidentally on purpose, he upset the table. Cards and chips and money went flying, and consequently nobody owed anybody anything. Vittorio was slightly annoyed. I saw Elizabeth's expression as she looked at Mike Todd and I thought to myself, 'I wonder if Evelyn knows Elizabeth is planning to marry him. . . .' "

Evelyn Keyes, with Todd's engagement ring on her finger, had no such knowledge. Like her fiancé, she felt only sympathy for Elizabeth, who was so obviously miserable in her marriage.

Talking to Pandro Berman, Miss Keyes said, "That poor Liz Taylor. I'm so sad for her. She's so unhappy."

"Don't worry about Liz," said the producer. "Don't let it concern you. If she's unhappy, she will find her way out of it very quickly. She always has."

The next week a *Look* magazine story by Eleanor Harris mentioned the lengths to which Elizabeth would go to get what she was after. "Using a small sweet tone of voice, she can make an infinitely varied series of birdlike sounds when she is trying to tease an agreement out of someone," stated the article. "She coos, gurgles, chirps, laughs liltingly, gives expectant trills."

After reading the article, Todd called Elizabeth and said that every time he had seen her lately she had been in tears. "So lemme hear ya coo and gurgle and chirp like a bird, will ya?"

Elizabeth laughed. That started Todd on a series of cheer-up calls. Then he invited the Wildings to a special screening of *Around the World in 80 Days*. "The next day he called and asked how I liked it," said Elizabeth. "In fact, he called five times and asked how I liked it."

"Liz told me then that Mike Todd fell in love with her after reading my article," said Eleanor Harris. "She said that he was just fascinated by her little bird sounds."

On July 19, 1956, MGM announced that Elizabeth Taylor and Michael Wilding were separating. "It is being done so that we will have an opportunity to thoroughly work out our personal situation."

The next day Todd called Elizabeth again. He said he had something important to discuss with her. This time she didn't laugh. She met him at MGM. "He told me that he loved me, that he had been thinking of me constantly, and he said he was going to marry me," she said. "We had never touched hands."

CHAPTER *10*

"I KNOW ELIZABETH AND MONTY HAD A SEXUAL RELATIONSHIP during *Raintree County,*" said the assistant director, "because Whitey Henry, chief of studio security, came to me and said, 'I wish those kids would be more discreet, leaving their towels all over the room like they do.' "

MGM had rented separate houses for its stars on location in Danville, Kentucky. Montgomery Clift often left his quarters in the middle of the night and showed up on Elizabeth's doorstep without a stitch of clothing on. Occasionally she tried to sober up her naked friend by throwing him into the shower, toweling him dry, and putting him to bed. Other times she simply refused to open the door.

While many people assumed an affair was going on between Elizabeth and Monty, Metro executives couldn't have cared less if they were sexually involved. Their only concern was keeping Monty reasonably sober so that MGM's first film in Panavision could be completed without throwing the studio into bankruptcy. They relied on Elizabeth to keep Monty off his pills and alcohol as much as possible during shooting.

"Elizabeth was totally supportive," recalled Dore Schary, MGM production chief. "She nursed him, aided and covered for him. On the very bad days she called me for help. . . ."

Raintree County was then the most ambitious and expensive

production ever mounted by MGM. Clift headed a cast of 119 speaking roles which included Elizabeth, Eva Marie Saint, Lee Marvin, Rod Taylor, Agnes Moorehead, and Nigel Patrick.

Occasionally the pressures of ministering to Monty became overwhelming for Elizabeth. Her problem was compounded by an exhausting shooting schedule that required her to wear heavily corseted costumes in unbearable heat and humidity.

"I'm so sick of all this I feel like screaming half the time," she told Eva Marie Saint. The next day she collapsed with an acute attack of hyperventilation, complicated by tachycardia, and was tranquilized with sodium amytal on a continuing basis. It was a week before her nerves were steady enough for her to resume work.

During her convalescence she either dined alone with Monty or invited crew members to her house for all-night drinking sprees. "One night Liz had a party where you had to drink yourself to death," recalled Ridgeway Callow, the assistant director, "and I passed out on the toilet seat. She had Bob Surtes, the cameraman, take a picture of me, develop and enlarge it, and said, 'Okay, you son of a bitch, if you say anything about me again, I'll publish this photograph.' Liz was carrying on hot and heavy with Mike Todd then, and she'd get real mad whenever we reminded her she was still married to Michael Wilding."

By the end of location shooting, Elizabeth's rented house was a shambles. It was such a wreck that the studio demanded she make restitution. A September 17, 1956, studio memorandum set the damage at $800 and described the scene: "Liquor is spilled all over the house. The walls are full of grease. Her makeup is all over the bedspreads, etc. Imprints of her hands on the window-sills, on a door, and during a party the back end of the couch was broken. While we are entitled to wear and tear, I believe this is a little bit beyond that, and all of it should be charged to her. . . ."

In the end, Elizabeth paid for fixing four lamps, repainting the living-room and dining-room and staircase walls, cleaning rugs throughout the house, cleaning all the furniture and draperies, reupholstering a sofa with nine yards of satin, refinishing tables, refilling seat cushions in the living-room chairs, and replacing broken crystal and china.

Not everyone associated with the film remembers Elizabeth for her partying alone. The director, Edward Dmytryk, recalled her as easy to work with. "On the set she is quite untemperamental—almost phlegmatic at times—but she does have fire and can achieve a fine anger at some stupidity, though I've never seen this anger directed at a co-worker on the set. She also has great inner strength, and she needed a lot of that on *Raintree County*."

Every weekend a chartered plane arrived on location to whisk Elizabeth to New York for a stay with Mike Todd in his Park Avenue penthouse. During the week he sent flowers and called her five or more times a day. Titillated by the romance, the two telephone operators in Danville took turns eavesdropping on the nightly conversations, which sometimes lasted five hours. The next day everyone in the small town knew that the fifty-two-year-old producer could hardly wait to get Elizabeth back to New York and back to bed.

On one return trip Monty waited for Elizabeth at the Louisville airport in a battered sedan—battered so that reporters wouldn't be tipped off that they were movie stars. When she got into the car, he gave her a $30,000 pearl ring, a prearranged gift from Mike Todd. *"This is for weekdays,"* said the card. Monty, serving as go-between for Elizabeth and Todd in much the same way as he had for Elizabeth and Wilding, looked at his friend and added, "You'll get your real engagement ring later."

Elizabeth immediately put the mammoth pearl on her ring finger. When reporters asked how she could possibly accept an engagement ring from Todd while still married to Wilding, she said, "But this isn't an engagement ring. It's only a friendship ring."

The "friendship" made news around the world in the fall of 1956. The headlines got especially bigger when Elizabeth announced, "I love Mike Todd. I love him passionately, absolutely passionately." Wilding, filming in Sweden at the time, was nonplussed. "It isn't this romance that hurt him," said a friend. "It's the one before it."*

Gracious to the very end, Michael Wilding did nothing to stand in his wife's way. "It wouldn't have done any good to try to keep her," he said. "And it's not true that Mike Todd stole her away from me. He didn't have to. Our marriage had been finished months before she took up with Mike."

Faced with its star's blatant extramarital affair, MGM announced that Elizabeth Taylor and Michael Wilding would seek a divorce. Todd placed a transatlantic call to Evelyn Keyes, whom he had sent to Caracas to scout movie theaters big enough for *Around the World in 80 Days*.

"Listen," he said, "I have to tell you . . . I've fallen in love with Elizabeth."

"Elizabeth who?" asked Miss Keyes innocently. At first she thought he was joking, but when she finally realized it was not one of his miserable jokes, she went to pieces.

"I felt doubly wretched because I knew I should have known better," she said.

After finishing her final scenes in *Raintree County*, Elizabeth flew to New York, leaving her two parentless children in California with a nurse. Her lover was now her first priority, and it seemed as if nothing else, including her children and her career, mattered as much. She wanted to prove to Mike Todd that she was a woman before she was an actress.

"I'll never marry an actress," he had said. "To live with an actress, ya gotta be able to worry about her hair. And when their bosoms start to drop they get panicky and run to headshrinkers."

So to prove her eternal love, Elizabeth decided to announce her retirement from motion pictures. "I may never work again," she said. "I want to be a woman to Mike's man. That is why I want to retire, why I must retire. A home, a husband, a real family means so much more to me."

---

* Friends felt that Wilding had been referring to the love affair his wife told people she had had with Frank Sinatra.

Later, when she was questioned about her retirement plans, Elizabeth said, "A career wasn't my idea. I am far more interested in being Mrs. Michael Todd than in being an actress."

Sara Taylor's heart almost stopped beating when she heard this news. Elizabeth's retirement would automatically end her weekly $250 paychecks—which had become vital, since Francis Taylor had closed his art gallery in February and gone into early retirement. But that wasn't to be the worst blow Sara received from her daughter.

"I still remember when Liz told her mother she was going to marry Mike Todd," recalled his secretary. "Her mother said, 'Oh, darling, I think that is so wonderful. A nice Italian man like Mike will make a very good husband for you.' Sara thought that Mike Todd of Todd A-O was Italian. Boy, was she upset to find out that his real name was Avrom Hirsch Goldbogen! Elizabeth told me that she just loved laying that one on her mother."

Todd enjoyed the story too. "Mike helped convince Elizabeth that her mother didn't own her," said his secretary. "Although Sara Taylor was the most prejudiced woman in the world, Mike did not dislike her. He simply ignored her. She was inconsequential in his scheme of things."

Sara winced every time she heard Mike Todd introduce Elizabeth as "my fat little Jewish broad, Lizzie Schwartzkopf." She cringed whenever he put his hand down the front of Elizabeth's dress and declared for all to hear, "Boy, these little Jewish gals sure have big tits, don't they?" Yet Sara forgave Mike Todd his brash manner and coarse humor because, after all, he was very, very rich.

Sara might not have been so deferential had she known that at the age of seven Avrumele, as his poor but pious parents called him, was running the streets of Minneapolis shining shoes for a nickel and stealing cigars to sell for three cents. At the age of eight he went to work for a carnival pitchman, peddling worthless watches for $5. As he got older his cons grew bigger.

Later his parents moved their eight children from Minneapolis to Chicago, where his father, a Hasidic rabbi, joined a small synagogue. Avrom, restless for action, quit Tulle High School after the first year. Leaving his immigrant family behind, he hit the streets again to hustle his fortune.

"I can't spell good, but I know what I want," he said, changing his name to Mike Todd and becoming a producer. "I believe in giving customers a meat-and-potatoes show. Dames and comedy. High dames and low comedy—that's my message." To underscore his common touch, he advertised one of his shows as "Guaranteed not to win the Pulitzer Prize. It's not Shakespeare but it's Laffs."

By the time Mike Todd entered Elizabeth Taylor's life, he had produced more than twenty musicals, strip shows, and burlesque revues. He had undergone bankruptcy twice and married twice. His first wife, Bertha, refused for years to give him the divorce he wanted. "I brought him up and wiped his nose for him and now he's not going to throw me out like an old shoe," she stated publicly.

After twenty years of marriage, Todd sued her for divorce on grounds of mental cruelty. A few days later, she cut herself with a knife in the kitchen and Mike suggested that her wound required surgery. He drove her to a hospital. There, under anesthesia, she died. An investigation cleared Todd of any involvement in the bizarre death, but suspicion that he had bribed the anesthesiologist created a scandal which followed him for years. He then married his lover, Joan Blondell. She divorced him after two years of a volatile relationship during which he gambled away her money and was again forced into bankruptcy.

Years later she was still bitter. "I have blotted Mike Todd out of my mind," she said. "It was not easy. It took a long time. I had a breakdown. But I triumphed! I now remember nothing about him. Nothing."

"The Todd A-O Corporation and *Around the World in 80 Days* was Mike's way of squaring himself with the world and showing everyone," said a friend. "It was his comeback—his way of regaining all he had lost financially, socially, and professionally. And having Liz Taylor on top of it all was the real capstone."

By Labor Day, Todd had decided to give Elizabeth her "real"

engagement ring. He spent $92,000 for a 29.7-carat diamond that looked like an ice cube. Bill Doll, his publicity manager, summoned reporters to his office the day after Elizabeth received her ring. "The rock is only twenty-nine point seven carats," he said. "Mike says thirty carats would be vulgar and in bad taste."

When one naive reporter saw the diamond on Liz's finger, as big as a hard-boiled egg, he thought it was costume jewelry. "What's that?" he asked.

"What's THAT?" shrieked Elizabeth. "It's the RING."

"Oy, vey!" muttered Mike. "What's that, he says!"

The engagement was publicly announced the night of October 17 to coincide with the premiere in New York of Todd's *Around the World in 80 Days*. Lavish reviews added to the celebration. "Mike Todd's picture makes this a better world!" exclaimed the Associated Press.

"In any formal disciplined sense *Around the World* is hardly a movie at all," wrote *Holiday* magazine, "but it is a wonderfully entertaining grab bag of treats and surprises produced on a scale reminiscent of Cecil B. DeMille and the Emperor Nero."

No man in show business had ever before launched such an ambitious film, and no one familiar with the industry could figure out how Mike Todd had managed to retain sole and independent ownership of this gigantic project which cost him over $6 million. "All it takes is a little charm and a lot of chutzpah," he said. He had bamboozled colossal stars like Frank Sinatra and Marlene Dietrich and Noël Coward into playing bit parts which he called "cameos."

Whenever he could not meet his weekly $329,000 payroll, he badgered friends for money. At one point he was offered $10 million to sell the film, plus the Todd A-O process. He refused the offer but used it as a snare to borrow even more money to keep going.

"I knew someone would stake a fella who'd just turned down ten million bucks," he said. "Ya see, money is only important if you don't have it. I've been broke lotsa times in my life, but I ain't never been poor."

Rich women were always a good source of capital for Mike Todd, who rewarded Lorraine Manville with seventy-five thousand shares in Todd A-O for $150,000 in cash. There were more like her begging to lend him money. "He was a charming rogue," said the author Anita Loos, "the kind of man for whom a beautiful woman would give the diamonds off her back and not ask why."

Todd's film swept the 1956 movie honors, including the Oscar for Best Picture plus awards from the National Board of Review and the New York Film Critics Circle. It grossed $30 million its first week, and Todd bragged that it would gross $100 million before the end of a year. "I'll make bums outa everybody," he crowed. "Now I just gotta figure out a way to spend all this loot."

Always given to manias of extravagance, Todd now surpassed himself. He laid out $3,000 a month to rent a super-deluxe Lockheed Lodestar, which he christened the *Lucky Liz*. He spent $5,000 to install a phone on it and $100,000 to let Elizabeth play interior decorator. He rented a yacht. He bought a Rolls-Royce Silver Cloud and installed two phones and a bar equipped with separate "HIS" and "LIZ" trays. He commissioned his cigars custom-rolled with gold bands reading "MADE ESPECIALLY FOR MIKE TODD." He bought two theaters in Chicago and designated one "His," the other "Hers." He leased a mansion in Beverly Hills. He rented a resort home in Palm Springs and spent $36,000 to rent a twenty-acre estate in Westport, Connecticut, with a swimming pool and tennis courts.

He treated every Saturday as an anniversary to celebrate the day he had first met Elizabeth Taylor. Saturday night after Saturday night, he presented her with ruby necklaces, diamond earrings, emeralds, sapphires, mink coats, bushels of hats, designer dresses, and couturier evening gowns.

"It pleased Mike to give to Elizabeth," his secretary recalled. "She was the one who wanted and he was the one who gave."

Todd publicized every gift. "This angel-faced baby is three years the junior of my son, Mike Todd, Jr.," he told the press.

"But she is a lot of woman. Everything I have is hers—and brother, that's plenty."

"Mike is the most exciting man in the world," replied Elizabeth. "I just can't stop him giving me presents."

"I think Mike liked giving her the diamond tiara best of all," recalled a friend. "He told me that when he presented it to her she ran into the bedroom to try it on and came out totally nude to model it for him. He said she jumped around the room and then on top of him wearing nothing but that tiara."

Mike Todd and Elizabeth Taylor publicly reveled in their sexuality and occasionally flaunted it. At a dinner party hosted by Hollywood director Silvan Simon, the fifty-two-year-old producer was asked what it was like having a beautiful young movie star like Elizabeth Taylor in love with him.

"Lemme tell ya," Todd said. "Any minute this little dame spends out of bed is wasted, totally wasted."

At Tyrone Power's cocktail party in New York, Todd waved a chicken leg in the air and motioned to Elizabeth across the room. "I'm going to eat this and you too!" he yelled.

A magazine photographer recalled appearing at three o'clock one Sunday afternoon to take pictures of Todd beside his swimming pool. "Five minutes into the shooting Liz appeared on the balcony in a nightgown and in that squeaky voice of hers yelled to Mike to come back to bed with her," the photographer said. "Mike yelled up that he'd be right with her, but she said, 'You come right now. I want to fuck you this minute.' "

Titillated by this open love affair, reporters hounded the headline-happy couple with questions as to when they would marry. "I don't know, fellas," Mike joked. "Liz hasn't asked me yet."

After visiting his twenty-one-year-old son, he announced that Mike Todd, Jr., approved of Elizabeth. "And so does his kid," he said, referring to his four-month-old grandson. "So now maybe I'll think about marryin' the broad."

In November, Elizabeth's lawyers filed papers in California for her divorce from Michael Wilding. Under the law she would have to wait a year before the final decree was granted. That meant she could not marry until November of 1957. "If she's a good girl, maybe I'll hang around," said her fiancé.

A few days later, Elizabeth and Mike flew to Florida for a vacation and then to Nassau for a visit with Lord Beaverbrook aboard his yacht. On the way back, Elizabeth was walking down a stairway and talking over her shoulder when she tripped and landed on her back. Todd rushed her to an orthopedic specialist at Harkness Pavilion in New York, where tests revealed a mass of crushed spinal discs.

Elizabeth blamed her back trouble on Robert Taylor, her co-star in *The Conspirator*. She said she had wrenched her spine when he bent her over a staircase to kiss her in the movie. Sara Taylor felt the trouble had started when Elizabeth fell so often while learning how to jump horses for *National Velvet*. Later, filming *The Last Time I Saw Paris,* she was hit by a swinging door, which exacerbated her earlier injuries and required regular visits to a chiropractor. By December of 1956 she claimed that one leg was going numb and was completely without feeling.

"In a few days I couldn't feel a feather at all," Elizabeth said. "Even when they stuck pins in my right leg and drew blood I couldn't feel anything. I couldn't walk on it anymore. The leg was paralyzed. Then it started to atrophy."

After further tests, delicate back surgery was recommended. On December 8, Elizabeth underwent a four-hour operation. "Three discs were absolutely gone," she later wrote. "They cut away all the dead bone right down to the nerve center. They took bone from my hip, my pelvis, and from a bone bank and made little matchsticks and formed clusters that finally calcified and became one long column, about six inches long."

In later years she rewarded certain people by allowing them to touch her fused back. She also added the graphic recitation of this surgery to her growing repertoire of ailments.

"A lot of Elizabeth's doctoring and sickness is really babying," said Mike Todd's secretary, "but that spinal fusion was real. She was definitely sick then."

In writing about her agony, Elizabeth said that every three

hours the nurses rotated her with sheets to keep the newly con-structed spinal column from sagging. She said the pain was so excruciating that she would pass out. "It is so astronomical I can't remember it too well," she said.

Todd took a room next to hers and gave reporters regular bulletins on her progress. He ordered catered food from the Col-ony restaurant and rushed out to buy paintings for her hospital walls, presenting her with a Renoir, a Pissarro, a Franz Hals, and a Monet. "She really digs the Franz Hals," he told the press. He also reported that Elizabeth's first words upon coming out of the anesthesia were "Where's my diamond ring?"

"That really killed the doctors and nurses," he said.

The only news that Mike Todd withheld was the fact that his twenty-four-year-old fiancée was pregnant. This he kept a secret from everyone but his lawyers. He ordered them to find a way to get Elizabeth legally divorced so that he could marry her as soon as she got out of the hospital.

With a baby on the way, Todd refused to wait a year for Eliz-abeth's California divorce to become final. His lawyers contacted hers and concluded that a Mexican divorce was the quickest way to dissolve her marriage. But the divorce would be valid, they said, only with the cooperation of her husband. The lawyers suggested that the Wildings apply jointly for a divorce on the ground of mutual consent. A gentleman to the end, Wilding said he would be happy to accommodate his wife.

On January 21, 1957, Elizabeth checked out of Harkness Pa-vilion. A few days later she, Todd, and Wilding flew to Mexico City. There the Wildings applied for a divorce. The first petition was denied. "Not a court here will touch it," the judge said. "The public is against quick divorces and marriages."

Todd called the judge a "goddamn fucking hillbilly son of a bitch" and threatened to kill him. He and the Wildings then flew to Acapulco to file a second petition, and it was granted. The moment the official divorce papers arrived, Michael Wilding flew back to California. Mike Todd and Elizabeth Taylor remained in Mexico and applied for a marriage license. They announced that they would marry the next day, on February 2, 1957.

Elizabeth Taylor with mother Sara and brother How-
ard. An unlovely baby, Elizabeth by age three had
already become a stunning beauty.

Fetching Liz,
as a teenager.

Donald Crisp, Nigel Bruce, Elizabeth Taylor and Elsa Lanchester in Lassie Come Home, *1943. After playing this small role, Elizabeth was put under a long-term contract by MGM.*

A year later, Elizabeth won the star-making title role in National Velvet. *Her screen parents were played by Donald Crisp and Anne Revere.*

"National Velvet was really me," said Elizabeth. Here, in her horsey boudoir, she admires one of her many equestrian figurines.

A gathering of young stars. Left to right: Jane Powell, Arthur Hamilton, Darryl Hickman, Roddy McDowall, his sister Virginia— and Elizabeth.

Carmen Miranda, Xavier Cugat, Jane Powell, and Elizabeth Taylor as Carol Pringle in MGM's A Date with Judy (1948), the first of Elizabeth's rich-girl roles.

It was while playing the sickly teenager Cynthia that Elizabeth began indulging her own off-camera hypochondria.

Elizabeth and her animals entertaining Hollywood gossip columnist Hedda Hopper.

Much-photographed Liz would spend hours before a mirror practicing different looks and poses.

VERYBODY OVES **LITTLE WOMEN**

M-G-M's NEW TECHNICOLO ROMANCE!

Starring

JUNE ALLYSON · PETER LAWFORD
MARGARET O'BRIEN · ELIZABETH TAYLOR
JANET LEIGH · ROSSANO BRAZZI · MARY ASTOR

WITH LUCILE WATSON · SIR C. AUBREY SMITH · HARRY DAVENPORT

A MERVYN LeROY PRODUCTION

SCREEN PLAY BY ANDREW SOLT, SARAH Y. MASON AND VICTOR HEERMAN · FROM THE NOVEL BY LOUISA MAY ALCOTT

PRODUCED AND DIRECTED BY MERVYN LeROY · A METRO-GOLDWYN-MAYER PICTURE

Elizabeth played the pretty but spoiled Amy March in MGM's re-make of Little Women, *1949.*

Wiping lipstick off her first beau, All-American football player Glenn Davis.

UPI

On location for A Place in the Sun *with Montgomery Clift. Studio executives brought Liz and Monty together for an "arranged" date, the beginning of their long, intense friendship.*

Elizabeth in 1949 with her fiancé Bill Pawley, who presented Liz with her first diamond.

[ABOVE] *Spencer Tracy escorts Elizabeth Taylor down the aisle in MGM's* Father of the Bride, *released soon after Elizabeth's headline-grabbing real-life marriage to Conrad Nicholson Hilton, Jr., seen at left.*

Newlyweds Nicky Hilton and Elizabeth greet her mother, Sara Taylor.

Within eight months, the fairy-tale wedding had turned to ashes. Here, a bewildered Liz is comforted by her lawyer during her painful, first divorce in 1951. Liz was nineteen.

UPI

MEMORY SHOP

Elizabeth Taylor and director Stanley Donen. "Liz desperately needed someone to lean on," said a friend, "and Stanley was there."

A studio shot of the ever-more-alluring Liz.

Elizabeth had resisted leaving Stanley Donen to make Ivanhoe *in England—but it was there that she met her second husband, British matinee idol Michael Wilding.*

At last on the screen! BIGGEST SPECTACLE since 'Quo Vadis'

M·G·M PRESENTS SIR WALTER SCOTT'S FAMED NOVEL!

Ivanhoe

STARRING

ROBERT TAYLOR
ELIZABETH TAYLOR
JOAN FONTAINE
GEORGE SANDERS
EMLYN WILLIAMS

COLOR BY TECHNICOLOR

Greeting Monty Clift at the airport before leaving for England to make Ivanhoe *in 1952.*

Francis and Sara Taylor in California proudly displaying the first picture taken of their daughter and her new husband, Michael Wilding, after their wedding in England, February 22, 1952.

Beaming with pride, Liz and Michael present their first baby, Michael Wilding, Jr., to the Hollywood press.

With James Dean in Warner Brothers' Giant, *1956. Elizabeth collapsed in grief when Dean died in a car accident shortly after finishing his final scenes.*

MONTGOMERY CLIFT   ELIZABETH TAYLOR   EVA MARIE SAINT

M·G·M PRESENTS IN M·G·M CAMERA 65 "WINDOW OF THE WORLD"

RAINTREE COUNTY

IN THE GREAT TRADITION OF CIVIL WAR ROMANCE

Dean's death would not be the only tragedy for Liz that year. During the filming of Raintree County, *Monty Clift was to be gravely injured in a car crash following a dinner party at the Wildings' Benedict Canyon home.*

Elizabeth and Montgomery Clift take a break during the filming of
Raintree County.

*"I was dead, old at twenty-four," said Elizabeth as she felt her
second marriage falling apart. But producer Mike Todd then pursued her, and the two were married in Acapulco in February of
1957. Debbie Reynolds was matron of honor and Eddie Fisher was
best man.*

Mike Todd flashes Liz an international gesture in the London airport in 1957. Their public rows were already legendary.

In the end, Michael Wilding and Liz had parted amicably. Here Todd and a pregnant Liz welcome Wilding to Nice, France, in June of 1957.

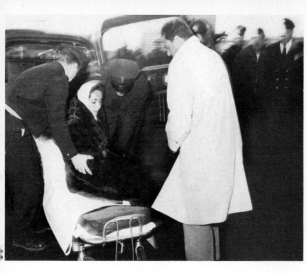

Elizabeth is lowered onto a stretcher at Idlewild Airport after the first of a series of spinal operations, as Mike Todd looks on.

Mr. and Mrs. Mike Todd with their beautiful baby, Elizabeth Frances (Liza), born August 6, 1958.

UPI

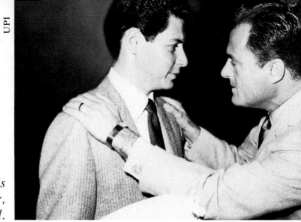

Eddie Fisher with his friend and mentor, Mike Todd.

Elizabeth is escorted by her brother Howard at Mike Todd's funeral in Chicago.

CHAPTER *11*

A CARAVAN OF TRUCKS inched toward the Acapulco villa of Fernando Hernandez, transporting fifteen thousand white gladioli that Mike Todd had had flown in for his wedding to Elizabeth Taylor. A work gang at the villa unloaded twenty-five cases of champagne and sixty bushels of white orchids. From other trucks young Mexicans lifted heavy crates of cracked crabs, barrels of baby lobsters, and tureens of caviar from Havana.

Chewing his cigar, Todd paced the terraced gardens to check on construction of the bandstands that would accommodate the mariachis he had ordered from Mexico City and the jazz musicians he was flying in from New York.

"Where are my shirts?" he barked, sending a youngster to fetch the sport shirts he had ordered for all his wedding guests. He had stipulated that each be monogrammed with "ET" and "MT." Then he hurried into the kitchen to sample the hot tamales, tortillas, and tacos being prepared for the reception. With Cantinflas, the Mexican comedian, he discussed arrangements for the fireworks display he had planned as the finale of the evening. More than $100,000 worth of pyrotechnics would rocket into the night sky and erupt in the initials "ET" and "MT."

Todd then rounded up a tribe of Indian boys to scale the giant palms for coconuts, which he wanted cut in half and filled with champagne. He ordered the violinists to wear straw gaucho hats as they strolled among the guests that evening, and he insisted on special kerosene torches to light up the night.

By early afternoon Mike Todd had still not found a rabbi willing to perform a Jewish ceremony for him and his Protestant fiancée. So he called in Mario Lepotoguí, the mayor of Acapulco, to officiate at a civil service.

While the groom was frenetically supervising every detail of the wedding and reception, the bride was sunbathing beside the swimming pool and drinking champagne with Eddie Fisher and Debbie Reynolds, Todd's best man and her matron of honor. Because of the close friendship between Mike Todd and Eddie Fisher, the two couples spent a great deal of time together, although Debbie frequently bowed out when the gambling and carousing stretched into the early morning hours. Neither Eddie nor Debbie was particularly fond of Elizabeth. Eddie, especially, felt that at times she was too demanding. "A real pain in the ass" was how he privately described her. However, they both loved Mike Todd, and having spent three years with him and Evelyn Keyes, they saw how different he was with Elizabeth.

"Mike adored her," said Debbie Reynolds. "I had known him before he ever met her and I never heard him make a fuss over a woman, but he just sweet-talked Elizabeth all the time. He was crazy about her boys. He was always telling her and everyone else what a great mother she was, and how beautiful she was, and how intelligent. She'd laugh and she'd say, 'Oh, come off it, Mike.' But she loved every word of it, because he didn't just say it, the way other people do. He bought her clothes and he gave her jewels fit for a princess, and he treated her like one. He made Elizabeth feel more beautiful than she is—if that is possible."

Though both women were under contract to MGM, apparently the only thing Debbie Reynolds and Elizabeth Taylor had in common was their friendship with the studio costume designer, Helen Rose.

"When I finally got around to meeting Elizabeth at MGM, we were friendly on a 'Hello, there' basis," said Debbie. "I was only seventeen and just beginning in show business, and Elizabeth was already a star."

By 1957, Debbie too was a star. But even as twenty-five-year-old women, she and Elizabeth could not have been less alike.

Debbie looked adorably cute and fresh-faced, with a pert pug nose. A compulsive worker and fearsomely ambitious, she sewed her own clothes. (As a teen-ager, she had embroidered her sweaters with the initials N.N., for "non-necker.") She had many girlfriends; she did not smoke, drink, or swear; and she went to church every Sunday. "What I really want is to be a Cub Scout mother or a Brownie mother, and go camping with my kids," she said.

Elizabeth was dark, sultry, voluptuous. Lazy and self-indulgent, she was careless about her career, wore only couturier designs, had no close women friends, smoked and drank to excess, swore constantly, enjoyed a bawdy sex life, and had not been inside a church since her marriage to Nicky Hilton.

Another big difference was that Elizabeth was on the brink of her third marriage while Debbie was heading toward her first divorce, from the only man she had ever loved. The Fishers were having severe marital problems at the time, and each was seeing a psychiatrist to try to hold the marriage together.

"All is not smooth at the Fishers'," Mike Todd told a reporter. "Eddie is a nighttime boy. Debbie is a home girl."

Since Mike Todd considered Eddie Fisher and his wife to be family, he naturally included them with Elizabeth's parents; her brother, Howard, and his wife, Mara; Mike Todd, Jr., and his wife, Sara; and Cantinflas to witness the private ceremony before the huge reception.

Everyone assembled in the main room of the Hernandez villa at the appointed hour, waiting for the bride and groom. An hour passed before Elizabeth, tense and tipsy from drinking champagne all day, made her entrance. She was carried in and delicately set down so she would not hurt her back. Wearing a hydrangea-blue chiffon gown designed by Helen Rose, she flashed Mike Todd's wedding present, an $80,000 diamond bracelet. Eddie Fisher serenaded the couple with the "Mexican Wedding Song," and Mayor Lepotoguí pronounced them man and wife. Then Mike Todd and Cantinflas again lifted Elizabeth up and carried her outside.

"Liz was so drunk she could barely stand up," recalled one

guest. "You could say that the bride was beautiful but *borra-cha!*"

Throughout the evening Mike Todd was constantly at his wife's side. Whenever he slipped out of whispering range, she screamed, "Mike, Mike! Don't leave me! Don't leave me!"

For the next six months Elizabeth honeymooned with her husband, fighting off morning sickness and nausea. "Mike was especially solicitous then because she was pregnant," said his secretary. "He was so proud to be having that baby at his age."

In July the Todds headed for their Connecticut estate to be near Harkness Pavilion. A month later Elizabeth felt labor pains, and her husband summoned an ambulance and, with state troopers clearing the way, rushed her to the hospital.

"She's in terrible pain," he told reporters. "She's crying all the time."

On August 6, eight doctors hovered over Elizabeth and performed cesarean surgery to deliver a girl weighing barely five pounds. The doctors told Mike Todd that his wife should not risk childbirth again and recommended a tubal ligation. Todd gave his permission for the surgery, and when Elizabeth awoke to this news she said, "It was the worst shock of my life—like being killed."

The Todds named their daughter Elizabeth Frances and called her Liza. The exuberant father could hardly contain his excitement. He called London, Paris, and Hollywood to announce her birth. He reported that the baby did not breathe for fourteen minutes after she was born. "I nearly died waiting for that first yell. Those were the longest damn fourteen minutes of my life," he said. "But the baby is so beautiful she makes her mother look like Frankenstein. Liz and I are eternally grateful for the miracle job the doctors did."

The next day Mike Todd brought a present to his new daughter, who was in an incubator. The solid-gold hairbrush from Tiffany's carried an engraved message: "DEAR LIZA, IT WOULD HAVE BEEN PLATINUM BUT YOUR MOTHER WOULD HAVE SAID I WAS SPOILING YOU."

He told reporters he was thinking of buying his wife the Taj Mahal to express his appreciation for their beautiful child. "If the joint's for sale, I might consider it," he said. "Liz has been the bravest girl through this ordeal, and I reckon she deserves a present. I'd modernize it, 'cause the plumbing probably wouldn't suit her, but I could turn it into a swell number. . . ."

Instead, he commissioned five thousand color reproductions of a Marcel Vertès painting which he and Elizabeth sent around the world to announce Liza Todd's birth. The blue parchment print showed a fat cherub floating in a lacy gold-lined bassinette with snowy-white draperies suspended from a jeweled crown encircled with garlands of flowers. The elaborate 8×12-inch painting arrived with only the engraved calling card of Elizabeth and Michael Todd. There was no mention of the baby's name or even her date of birth.

Although twenty-seven years separated the pampered actress and the flamboyant showman, they seemed ideally suited. Both needed the excitement of living close to the edge. Her dramatic illnesses and his reckless gambling had provided that exhilarating danger in the past. Now their supercharged life together, gliding through time zones, ensured the constant excitement they needed. "We don't live like ordinary people," Mike Todd declared.

Both craved an audience. They seemed to thrive on a public display of their relationship, in all its passion or violence. Announcing their love pact to the world, Elizabeth said, "We've made a deal that we'll always be together. Mike doesn't believe a husband and wife should ever be separated, and so I tell him, 'Whither thou goest, I will go too, Buster.' "

"I dress the way Mike wants," she said. "I wear my hair this way for Mike. I can't stop talking about marriage. It's because I understand it now. I know what it means."

At an official luncheon in New South Wales, the couple impulsively leaned across the Prime Minister to kiss, an act that caused Australian newspapers to condemn them for "cheap necking in public." At the Academy Awards they again kissed repeatedly after Mike Todd won the Oscar. Photographers begged for a full-face shot, but they refused to stop kissing. "Nuts to 'em," Todd said. "I want the whole world to know how much I love this little dame."

At other times their public passion for each other erupted into violent brawls. She screamed, he snarled, and each pummeled the other with headline-grabbing invective. Photographs of them howling at each other and using universal hand gestures flashed around the globe.

"Look, this gal's been cruising for trouble all her life," Todd said. "And now she's found somebody to give it to her. Trouble is, everybody was too nice to fight back. Not me. When she flies into a tantrum, I fly into a bigger one. She's been on a milk-toast diet all her life with men. But me—I'm red meat."

"Tell Ol' Flannelmouth there to stuff it," snapped Elizabeth.

Former Associated Press reporter James Bacon remembers sitting between the Todds in their Rolls-Royce and being caught in a crossfire.

"Elizabeth, absolutely gorgeous, was furious at Mike for putting Marlene Dietrich in *Around the World in 80 Days*," he said. "It was obvious that this young dream was jealous of an old dame like Marlene. Once, Mike had had a little fling with Marlene. I'll never forget the shock I felt when Elizabeth's beautiful mouth kept yelling 'Fuck you' at Mike. It shattered a dream."

Each public quarrel caused speculation about how long their marriage would last. When one columnist wagered six months at the most, Mike Todd called her a "frustrated old biddy" and said, "I'm a betting man and I'll give anyone odds on this lash-up lasting forever."

Elizabeth insisted that their fights invigorated their relationship. They had more fun feuding, she said, than most people did making love. Her husband agreed. "I wish every married couple could have fights like we do," he said. "It's great. You fight and make up and you're more in love than ever."

The Todds began their marriage by circling the globe to promote *Around the World in 80 Days*. They flew to England for a dazzling premiere in London, where they spent $126,000 hosting a party with sixteen orchestras for 2,500 people at the Battersea Amusement Park. To commemorate the event, Mike bought Elizabeth a red velvet Dior gown and a matching ruby necklace from Van Cleef and Arpels.

In the South of France they courted the judges of the Cannes Film Festival by hosting a lavish party at the casino at Nice, complete with caged lions rented just for the evening. Then they flew to Paris to throw yet another spectacular party for the French premiere, which Todd commemorated by giving Elizabeth an emerald necklace and diamond chandelier earrings.

Promoting and publicizing his film became the focus of Mike Todd's existence. To celebrate its first anniversary, he decided to rent Madison Square Garden and invite 18,000 people for an "Intimate Little Party for a Few Chums."

"This will be the biggest goddamned birthday party the world has ever seen," he vowed.

He flew set designer Vincent Korda from London to decorate the vast arena with a twenty-four-foot Oscar made of rust chrysanthemums.

He badgered Swansdown into donating $15,000 worth of mix for a cake that stood fourteen feet high and weighed almost a ton. "Blue icing," Todd stipulated. "Pale blue for the television cameras."

He cajoled CBS-TV into paying $300,000 to televise the spectacle during prime-time hours for 50 million viewers across the country.

He persuaded manufacturers to donate thousands of dollars' worth of merchandise so every guest could take home a present. He arranged a drawing which featured a Cessna airplane as the grand prize. Consolation prizes included four Oldsmobiles, six motorcycles, one hundred cameras, six typewriters, forty mink stoles, ten thousand cigars, two hundred and fifty bottles of vodka, one hundred pairs of ivory chopsticks, six pistols, and forty cats donated by the King of Siam.

He hired Arthur Fiedler to conduct the orchestra. He talked

Sir Cedric Hardwicke into riding an elephant. He careened from coast to coast, soliciting, demanding, begging, and bartering. Full-page ads promising free champagne and prizes appeared in newspapers throughout the country, making this party the most publicized event in the United States, one that completely overshadowed Queen Elizabeth's state visit to Washington.

On the evening of October 17, 1957, hundreds of celebrities swarmed into Madison Square Garden for Mike Todd's shindig. Shelley Winters, Tony Curtis, Janet Leigh, George Jessel, Emmett Kelly, Senator Hubert Humphrey, Ginger Rogers, Elsa Maxwell, Bert Lahr, Steve Allen, Jayne Meadows, and five thousand reporters gawked at one another as looters and freeloaders plundered the arena, grabbing prizes and throwing egg rolls at the Philadelphia Mummers.

Enterprising waiters took advantage of the ensuing confusion by diluting the free champagne and selling it for $10 a bottle. The men tending the hot-dog wagons threw franks and buns at mink-clad matrons screeching for food. The girls in the doughnut trucks joined in tossing sticky pastries at the guests trapped in the balcony seats. Soon a chaotic scramble began to build, reaching near-hysteria. Sleekly lacquered women and tuxedo-clad men bellowed their frustration in unison with the elephants and monkeys, which were provoked to the verge of stampeding.

"The whole thing was an unmitigated disaster," declared Elizabeth Taylor. *Life* magazine agreed, describing the affair as "a colossal hodgepodge." "The worst," said *Newsweek*. "HUGE GARDEN SOIREE RATES MIKE TODD AN O," headlined *The Chicago American*.

To escape the barrage of bad publicity, Mike took Elizabeth on another trip around the world pledging never again to give a party for more than eight people. Everywhere they went the Todds drew a full press complement, with reporters besieging them for details of their latest expenditure. In Paris the voluble producer said he had purchased three paintings from Aly Khan for $71,428.

"They'll think I'm crazy when they hear about this in Hollywood," he said. "Paying that much for pictures that don't even move."

At every stop Elizabeth modeled her newest acquisition. "I never wore hats before," she said, "but Mike said he liked them so I went out and bought fifty."

"See that dress?" said Todd, pointing to his wife's form-fitting satin Chinese sheath. "She's gonna start an epidemic—bring sex back. We bought twenty-five of 'em in Hong Kong. Wait'll the Russians get a load of Liz in the new clothes she got in Paris. It'll make them wish they never heard of Communism."

In Hong Kong Elizabeth was stricken with an abdominal pain she swore was appendicitis. She recovered within hours but decided to return to California to have the appendix removed, her third operation in less than a year. Mike Todd could not understand his wife's desire for surgery, but he acquiesced and checked her into Cedars of Lebanon. "This will be her last time in the hospital," he said. "We're going to take off for Europe first thing in January. But no more hospitals."

Years later Elizabeth admitted the appendectomy had been unnecessary but said it was the only way she could get any extended time alone with her husband. She insisted he take a hospital suite next to her own—without a telephone.

Working constantly, Mike Todd frequently ignored his wife to pursue business interests. At home he was always on the phone, barking orders into one receiver while making deals on another. He kept a third phone free to take calls from his bookie. In desperation, Elizabeth finally had several telephone extensions removed to cut down the number of incoming and outgoing calls.

"I've still got one phone on the plane and two in the car," Todd said, "but Liz can't complain anymore when I'm playing with the boys and don't call her."

On gambling binges, Todd disappeared for hours at a time without saying where he was going or when he would be back. Win or lose, though, he always returned with a present, knowing that that was the only way to appease his wife.

"While he was off gambling, Mike usually sent someone like

his assistant, Dick Hanley, to keep Elizabeth company," said his secretary, "because she couldn't stand being by herself. She needed constant company—someone with her all the time." *

Even on their round-the-world trips Todd always took along a secretary or friend or staff member to keep his wife company, run her errands, go shopping with her, and help her get dressed.

"I stuffed Liz into her bras too many times to count," said playwright Ketti Frings, whose husband, Kurt, was Liz's agent. "She was too cheap to pay for a lady's maid. Dr. Rex Kennamer was the patsy on one trip to Russia. He was put on the payroll for twenty-five thousand dollars, and he laid out her clothes at every stop along the way."

Leaving Moscow, Mike Todd talked to reporters. "What impressed the Russians most," he said, "was that a bum like me could grow up in America and become Elizabeth Taylor's husband, which is a helluva better job than being President of the United States!"

Later Todd got mad at the Russians when they turned down *Around the World in 80 Days.* "They don't want anything that doesn't show us Americans as slobs, monsters, and morons," he fumed.

From Moscow the Todds traveled to Prague, Athens, Belgrade, Nice, Madrid, New York, and Hollywood. En route they got word that Elizabeth had received her first Academy Award nomination for her performance as the schizophrenic Southern belle in *Raintree County.* As soon as Mike Todd arrived in Hollywood he started advertising the film in movie trade journals, hoping to influence members of the Motion Picture Academy of Arts and Sciences. He wanted their votes for his wife as Best Actress of the year, although he knew she was a long shot to win, the favorites being Joanne Woodward for *The Three Faces of Eve* and Anna Magnani for *Wild Is the Wind.* Deborah Kerr also was nominated for *Heaven Knows, Mr. Allison* and Lana Turner for *Peyton Place.*

---

* Once Elizabeth called Mike Todd in London from the South of France and he said, "Look, sweetheart, I'm gonna get me a plane and come and get you, 'cause I don't want you to come here alone."

Mike Todd's only concern was Elizabeth. He knew how hurt she was never to have been nominated before, especially for her performance in *Giant*. "She was robbed," he said at the time. Now he was determined to do all he could to help her. He even called Helen Rose to design a gown for her to wear to the presentations. "You do the dress and I'll take care of the diamonds," he said.

Although Elizabeth kept threatening to retire, she was still under contract to MGM. In February her husband propelled her back to work to play Maggie in *Cat on a Hot Tin Roof*.

"We got Mike to get her to do it," said producer Pandro Berman. "You had to go to Mike if you wanted anything. She was plastic in his hands. She had no thoughts of her own in those days."

"It's a great script," Todd told his wife, "and it will be a great picture. You oughta win the Oscar for *Raintree,* but just in case you don't, you'll win for sure with Maggie the Cat."

Elizabeth liked the idea of playing a woman as sexually driven as a cat on a hot tin roof. It was her first Tennessee Williams role. Playing the part of a seductive wife trying to get her homosexual husband to impregnate her, Elizabeth glided across the screen wearing a provocative shell-pink satin-and-lace slip in all the bedroom scenes. She was also scheduled to wear a skirt-and-blouse ensemble and "a simple afternoon frock" that the director, Richard Brooks, decided would be a tailored shirtwaist dress. Without consulting Elizabeth, he instructed Helen Rose to design the costume in white.

"I had misgivings about Elizabeth liking it," recalled the designer, "and though Richard said confidently, 'Don't worry, I'll handle it,' I still had my doubts about the dress being right."

The day before shooting began, Elizabeth came to the studio for her three costume fittings. She adored the sexy slip, approved the skirt and blouse, but abhorred the tailored shirtwaist dress. She took it off, threw it on a chair, changed back into the alluring slip, and called the director to her dressing room.

Richard Brooks walked through the door and saw his ravishingly beautiful star spilling out of her slip.

"Richard! Love!" she squealed.

"Darling, you look wonderful," he responded.

They kissed and hugged and kissed again. Then Elizabeth pointed to the mannish dress drooped over the side of the chair. "Love, I can't wear that," she said. "It looks awful on me."

Still enraptured by his star, the director did not even look at the discarded dress. "Darling," he said, kissing her again, "wear whatever makes you happy. I'll leave it to you and Helen. Just keep it simple."

The designer then sketched a short white chiffon dress slashed low in front and nipped in at the waist. "Elizabeth adored it," she recalled. "The bodice fit like she was poured into it, and there was not one tiny wrinkle. To point up her very small waist, we made a two-inch satin belt. When she appeared on the set in this dress, Richard was enormously pleased."

So was Mike Todd, who had moved his offices to MGM to be close to his wife. They lunched together in the commissary every day, and after shooting they reviewed the rushes. He was elated by his wife's performance in the brief unedited scenes they saw each night.

Mike Todd felt blessed with a beautiful movie-star wife, an exquisite baby daughter, and an Academy Award for the first movie he ever produced. Having made and lost millions, he was now rich again and famous throughout the world.

"I'm aware that this is the best time of my life," he told a friend. "But I'm so happy it almost scares me. Being a gambling man, I know the law of averages, and I get spooked I'll have to lose something to compensate for being so damn lucky."

In March he was selected by the Friars Club of New York as Showman of the Year, an honor he had always coveted. More than 1,200 invitations were sent out for the ceremonial roast in his honor at the Waldorf-Astoria on Sunday evening, March 24, 1958. Acceptances came from such celebrities as Governor Averill Harriman, Sir Laurence Olivier, Attorney General Herbert Brownell, Jr., and baseball star Jackie Robinson.

Todd planned to fly to New York for the gala in the *Lucky Liz,* his twin-engined twelve-passenger airplane, and to stop in Chicago for the Sugar Ray Robinson–Carmen Basilio fight before returning to Hollywood. Art Cohn, his biographer, was accompanying him on the trip, figuring that one more interview would complete his book, *The Nine Lives of Mike Todd.*

Since Elizabeth was sick in bed with a cold and unable to accompany her husband, he invited Joseph Mankiewicz.

"Ah, c'mon," Todd said. "It's a good, safe plane. I wouldn't let it crash. I'm taking along a picture of Liz, and I wouldn't let anything happen to her. Besides, I've got three million bucks' worth of insurance. You'd be covered too."

When Mankiewicz begged off, Todd called Kirk Douglas and Kurt Frings. They too turned him down. Then he called UPI reporter Vernon Scott. "Why don't you come along?" he asked. "I want somebody to play gin rummy with." Scott also declined. Finally Todd persuaded Associated Press reporter James Bacon to accompany him on the ten-hour cross-country flight. But minutes before their 10:21 P.M. departure from Burbank Airport, Bacon called Mike to cancel.

"The weather scared me," Bacon recalled. "It was one of the worst nights in Southern California history, with rain, sleet, lightning, thunder—the works. Frankly, I asked myself, 'Is this trip necessary?' "

"You son-of-a-bitch," said Todd. "You're not going because your girlfriend Liz is not going."

Unable to corral any of his card-playing cronies, Todd took off with Art Cohn and his pilot and copilot into the teeth of a torrential downpour. He had kissed his wife goodbye six times before driving to Burbank. When he got to the airport, he called her to say goodbye once more and promised to call again on a refueling stop in Tulsa, Oklahoma. It was a pledge he could not keep.

En route to Tulsa, the *Lucky Liz* hit another violent storm. The plane plummeted from the sky high over the Zuni Mountains in New Mexico and crashed to the floor of a valley ringed with pine-studded hills. The explosion incinerated everyone on board, requiring dental charts to make positive identifications. Only one belonging could be traced to any of the victims in that charred wreckage: Mike Todd's twisted gold wedding ring, which was brought to his widow.

CHAPTER 12

DR. REX KENNAMER AND DICK HANLEY raced to the house on Schuyler Road in Beverly Hills early Saturday morning bearing word of Mike Todd's death. They wanted to reach Elizabeth before she saw the front page of the newspaper or heard the grisly details on the radio. As they walked through the doorway of her bedroom, she looked up from her bed and smiled. Without saying a word, the doctor moved toward her. From the strange look on his face she knew immediately that something was wrong.

"Liz, darling . . ."

"Oh, God!" she screamed. "No! No! It can't be! No! God, I can't live without him!"

Elizabeth bolted out of bed in her sheer nightgown and tore through the house barefoot, wailing uncontrollably.

"She screamed so loud that even the neighbors heard her," said Dick Hanley. "She went completely hysterical. As she dashed for the front door and the open street, Dr. Kennamer grabbed her, and we took her up to bed. She submitted to sedatives that eventually quieted her."

The news of Mike Todd's death jolted Hollywood. The street outside Elizabeth's house soon filled with television camera crews and reporters from all over the world. MGM police arrived to bar unauthorized visitors from entering. MGM publicist Bill Lyon tried to handle press relations.

Inside the house were friends from the studio like Helen Rose and Sidney Guilaroff and Ann Straus as well as Michael Wilding and Kurt and Ketti Frings.

"There was also a little lady I didn't recognize at first who had on red slacks, a scarf over her head, and her hair up in curlers," recalled Ann Straus. "I couldn't believe my eyes, but it was Debbie Reynolds, who had come to take Elizabeth's children home with her. Poor Eddie Fisher was out of town at the time."

Everyone gathered in Elizabeth's bedroom, where she was sipping a stiff drink and pouring out her heart in spasmodic sobs.

"I begged him not to go—to wait one more day," Elizabeth said. "I don't think he wanted to go. He came upstairs to kiss me goodbye six times before he left the house. Oh, God. I can't bear to go on. I loved Mike so much, and he loved me. No one can ever know how much. If only I'd been on that plane with him. I feel like a half pair of scissors. That's what he always used to tell me when he was away from me."

Elizabeth spoke in disjointed sentences punctuated by sobs. "Why, why, why did it have to happen?" she asked. "Mike and I had so much planned . . . little things we just talked about last night."

"I remember that scene so vividly," recalled James Bacon. "Here was this girl heavily sedated and drinking and without sleeping most of the night, and how beautiful she looked."

"She had no sooner stopped crying than she'd start sobbing hysterically again," said Bill Lyon.

"I have never seen anyone so grief-stricken," said Helen Rose. "Her whole life seemed to have come apart, and there were no words of comfort."

Soon Elizabeth's brother, Howard, arrived, and her parents, who had cut short their vacation in Florida. MGM executives Benny Thau and Eddie Mannix stopped by to offer condolences. Laurence Weingarten, producer of Cat on a Hot Tin Roof, also came to the house. Midway through that visit Elizabeth became hysterical again, and Dick Hanley quickly called Richard Brooks.

"You've got to get over here right away," he said. "She's

screaming like a maniac. I think she's about to go off the deep end."

Brooks went directly to the house. As soon as Elizabeth saw him, she started shrieking again.

"You son-of-a-bitch!" she yelled. "I guess you're here like all the rest of these bastards who've been wondering when the hell I'm going back to work?"

"Elizabeth, I'm only here to see you," replied Brooks. "I'm sorry for what has happened. If you never want to come back to the movie, that's fine."

"Well, I'm never coming back!" she screamed. "Screw you and the movie and everybody else."

Elizabeth began talking about killing herself. She said she did not want to go on living another day without Mike Todd. Her first mention of suicide was not alarming; it seemed a natural reaction for someone so grief-stricken. But Elizabeth kept talking about it. "I want to die," she said. "I just want to die."

Finally her sister-in-law, Mara, could stand it no longer. "Elizabeth, you ought to be ashamed," she said. "You have three children. Two sons and Mike's own baby. It's your duty to get yourself strong and well for them, no matter how you feel. Mike would be furious with you!"

Still, Elizabeth could not pull herself together. She was so hysterical that Dick Hanley worried about getting her to the funeral, which was to be held on Tuesday—two days after Todd's death—at Jewish Waldheim Cemetery in Zurich, Illinois, outside Chicago.

Mike Todd's brother David Goldbogen announced that there would be no chapel services, just a private family burial at the graveside. His brother's grave, he said, would be marked by a massive replica of an Oscar carved out of a two-ton block of Vermont marble, standing nine feet tall and costing $8,000. Mike Todd, Jr., was appalled by his uncle's proposal, and the Academy of Motion Picture Arts and Sciences threatened legal action. The Goldbogens stemmed their initial impulse and ultimately chose a less gaudy marker for Todd's grave.

Elizabeth begged them to reserve the plot next to Mike Todd's, declaring her wish to be buried alongside her husband. The Goldbogens complied with the twenty-six-year-old widow's request and purchased an additional plot for Elizabeth.

The day of the funeral, Elizabeth was so heavily sedated that Dick Hanley and Dr. Kennamer had to hold her by the arms to keep her from toppling over. Together they left Los Angeles with Eddie Fisher, Helen Rose, Howard Taylor, and Jim Bacon on a private plane provided by Howard Hughes. Debbie Reynolds remained at home to tend Elizabeth's children, who had been with her since Saturday.

Wearing dangling diamond earrings and a black veiled hat, Elizabeth arrived in Chicago so emotionally distraught that she could barely walk from the limousine to the grave. Upon seeing the closed bronze coffin of her husband for the first time, she let out a piercing scream.

"Oh, Mike, I love you, I love you," she sobbed.

She moved forward as if to throw herself upon the casket. Her brother restrained her by grabbing her shoulders.

Only family and intimate friends were permitted entrance to the tented burial site. The cemetery itself teemed with thousands of morbid curiosity seekers who pushed and shoved one another as they scrambled to gawk at Elizabeth in her misery. Some sat atop gravestones, drinking Coca-Cola and munching potato chips as if they were on a picnic. Others sprawled on blankets and littered the normally tranquil cemetery with candy wrappers and ice cream sticks.

"He was not only a wonderful father but the greatest human being I've ever known," sobbed Mike Todd, Jr., unable to hold back his tears as he approached his father's casket.

Elizabeth trembled as she tried to restrain her sobs. Placing her hand on the coffin, she whispered goodbye to her husband and stumbled to her limousine. Then she cried out, "Mike! Mike! My darling! I can't leave you here! I can't leave you here!"

In the car she collapsed on her brother's shoulder. The mob surged forward, screaming Elizabeth's name and thrusting pieces of paper toward her for autographs.

"For God's sake, get this car moving!" she shrieked.

Montgomery Clift had flown from New York for the funeral. Although Elizabeth refused to see him, he was there at the graveside if she needed him. He too was enraged by the ghoulish horde stampeding the cemetery.

"It was noisy, vengeful," Monty said. "I saw envy in their faces, envy and hatred and bleakness."

Lulled by sedatives, Elizabeth flew back to Los Angeles and the house Mike Todd had rented on Schuyler Road. There were hundreds of telegrams awaiting her, including a wire from the White House extending the sympathy of President and Mrs. Eisenhower.

The next night Elizabeth watched the Academy Awards at home with her brother, his wife, and Bill Lyon, the MGM publicist, who was there just in case she won for *Raintree County*.

"She was wearing one of those magnificent house gowns Mike had liked to see her in," recalled Lyon. "She had on no makeup and no jewelry except Mike's own wedding ring. That was the only thing that had been saved from the plane wreck—the ring of their marriage. We turned on the show and one of the very first awards, a technical one, was to Todd A-O. Well, all that did, of course, was to remind her of the year before when Mike had won, when he had run back and kissed her.

"She just sat there with tears running down her face. She didn't make a sound, but her tears continued. Finally, as it was getting toward the top awards, she said, 'I am not going to win. Joanne Woodward is going to win. Nothing is going to go right for me now. Nothing will go right for me from now on because Mike is gone.' "

Joanne Woodward did win the Oscar for Best Actress, and Elizabeth told Lyon to send her a corsage of white orchids with a card reading, *"Best wishes and congratulations and much love from Elizabeth Taylor Todd, and Mike too."*

"Then she really broke down and we had to carry her back upstairs," said Lyon. "It was a very dramatic moment."

So precarious was Elizabeth's emotional stability that Mike

Todd, Jr., decided to send his father's secretary from New York to California to stay with her for a while.

"I've never seen such grieving and carrying on," recalled the secretary. "Liz wasn't working then, and she just sat around the house and cried hysterically all night long. She talked and talked and talked, and I listened. She felt great guilt over the accident, feeling that she should have been on the plane too. She had stayed home because she had had a cold. Dr. Kennamer was always there giving her pills—pills to sleep, pills to get up, pills to stop crying, pills to calm down. She was grieving so much that the sleeping pills didn't help, so he gave her some other pills to counteract the sleeping pills. There were just too many pills then. All she did was drink Coors beer and eat popcorn."

Elizabeth slept with the shirt Mike Todd had been wearing before he left. She put his pajamas under her pillow. She refused to change the sheets he had slept on, saying she wanted to keep his odor with her as long as she could. She vowed to wear his charred gold wedding band always. "They'll have to cut off my finger before they get it off my hand," she said.

Overcome by depression, Elizabeth remained in bed for days and let other people take care of her children, her pets, her house. The only thing that seemed to rouse her was the news that Lana Turner's young daughter, Cheryl, had stabbed Lana's lover, Johnny Stompanato.

"She turned her face to the wall and kept saying, 'Poor Lana, poor Cheryl,' " recalled Helen Rose. "Several times that day I would get Lana on the phone so Elizabeth could say some words that might comfort her. In spite of Elizabeth's own suffering, Lana was on her mind constantly."

After three weeks of catatonic stupor, Elizabeth began thinking about *Cat on a Hot Tin Roof.* She said she didn't want to go to work, but was curious about how the film was progressing. Todd's secretary called the director and asked if Elizabeth might come by. When she arrived, the set was closed and the crew jumpy, because Paul Newman, Burl Ives, and Madeleine Sherwood were shooting the scene in which Burl Ives as Big Daddy first realizes he may be dying. Elizabeth watched a few minutes of shooting and then got up to leave.

"Come over tomorrow if you feel like it," said Richard Brooks.

"If you would shoot just one small scene of mine tomorrow, I'll try to do it," she said.

Brooks was delighted. Elizabeth asked if she might come to work after lunch instead of early in the morning like everyone else, and he readily agreed.

"I knew it must be because of the sleeping pills that she asked that," he said.

Mike Todd's will was filed for probate in April. It divided his $5 million estate between his widow and his son. It stipulated that Mike Todd, Jr., receive his inheritance outright while Elizabeth's be placed in a trust paying her an income for life. However, Todd, besieged by creditors, had left his financial affairs in such disarray that it was years before the estate was settled. At the time of probate, Mike Todd, Jr., announced Elizabeth's plans to resume her acting career and to join him in distributing *Around the World in 80 Days.* What Todd, Jr., did not announce was the fact that he and Elizabeth planned to file a $5-million damage suit against the leasing company of the *Lucky Liz,* claiming that its gross negligence in the operation, maintenance, and control of the plane had caused Mike Todd's death.*

Elizabeth eased into her return to the studio, spending an hour a day the first week and frequently leaving in tears. "Several times, of course, she broke down," said Brooks. "The worst time was when in a scene we were filming Judith Anderson said, 'I guess things never turn out the way you want them to.' Liz just broke down and fell apart. She wept and couldn't work. Someone took her to her dressing room.

"In *Cat,* she was still in this transitional period between child

---

* That lawsuit, filed in New York Federal Court on August 21, 1958, was settled February 20, 1963, for $40,000. After $12,907.45 in attorney's fees was deducted, Mike Todd's daughter, Liza, received $27,-092.55, which the court ruled could be spent only under its supervision.

and woman actress. We'd rehearse a scene and Elizabeth seemed to be giving very little. Early on, Paul Newman called me aside and asked, 'Is this how it's going to be?' But directly that camera began rolling, she was at the peak of her performance. They were all left standing, including Newman. 'Now, wait a minute,' he said. 'I wasn't ready for that.' "

"Elizabeth, I think, has got a hell of a lot more talent than most people give her credit for," said Paul Newman. "And like everybody, I suppose, her biggest problem is herself, and the biggest thing that limits her efficiency as an actress and the scope of her acting is something that has to do with her own personal problems."

During shooting, those personal problems became acute. The film itself focused on death, which only heightened Elizabeth's grief, her loneliness, and her guilt. Again she started talking about suicide. On May 12, Dr. Kennamer was summoned to her home. Hours later, at 5.55 A.M., he telephoned the assistant director and said that Elizabeth had been "ill" during the night, that he had spent most of the night with her, and that she would be unable to report for work. "She lost the will to live," he admitted later.

Elizabeth had talked of suicide in the past, especially when she was depressed and drinking. One night in Cannes she had surprised British journalist Leonard Mosley by throwing an ashtray at a loudspeaker playing the French version of "Around the World in 80 Days."

"When you come to write my life story, Leonard, shall I tell you how to begin it?" she asked. "Start it this way: 'It was four o'clock in the morning in a very crummy bar on the French Riviera. The radio was playing "80 Days." And suddenly Elizabeth Taylor felt sick of everything—of films, of people, above all things, of herself.' "

"It sounds like the opening chapter of a tragedy," said Mosley.

"You're goddamn right," Elizabeth said. "And do you know what you should call it? 'I am twenty-five years old and I do not want to live.' "

In the wake of Todd's death Elizabeth seemed to be losing her grip, succumbing to the lure of self-destruction. Finally Dick Hanley called Rabbi Max Nussbaum of Temple Israel in Hollywood. Realizing how desperately Elizabeth needed help, the rabbi visited her every day.

"I have seldom seen the death of a husband make such an impact on a wife," he said. "For many weeks no one could penetrate her sorrow. It took weeks to console her. She wanted to make an end of her career. She said, 'My life has no value now.' "

Friends like Helen Rose, Sidney Guilaroff, Rex Kennamer, Joanne Woodward, and Paul Newman kept inviting Elizabeth to dinner in an effort to get her out of her melancholy. Always she arrived with Mike Todd's secretary.

"She took me so that if she broke down she'd have someone there to take care of her, and also, she didn't want to make me feel like a servant," said the secretary. "I stayed with her in California about six weeks and then I called Mike Todd, Jr., and said she was going to make it. She had planned a trip to Europe and I was supposed to go with her, but other things happened and I returned to the East Coast."

When Mike Todd's secretary left, his former assistant, Dick Hanley, agreed to move in to handle Elizabeth's business affairs and personal appointments the way he had for Todd. Hanley supervised the household help—maids, cooks, gardeners—hired and fired nurses for the children, and traveled with Elizabeth wherever she went. He also screened her phone calls, bought her clothes, and cleaned up after her dogs.

Cat on a Hot Tin Roof was wrapped in May, leaving Elizabeth with nothing to occupy her days. She began dating men like Arthur Loew, Jr., with whom she and her children vacationed in Arizona. Even while mourning Mike Todd, she soon evinced interest in meeting other men.

"I remember interviewing her at the Beverly Hills Hotel a couple of months after Mike's death," said former *Newsweek* reporter Betty Marshall, "and I mentioned that I was taking all my girlfriends to aerospace conventions to meet scientists because those men were so handsome. Liz reached across the table, patted me on the arm and said, 'Don't take them. Take me.' "

"All the people she was squiring after Todd—it was pathetic, but she was just so lonely," recalled Todd's secretary. "Then in the summer the Eddie thing started brewing."

Since the funeral, Elizabeth had become close to the singer who had been her husband's best friend. Mike Todd had been Eddie Fisher's idol—his father surrogate. Eddie had admired him to the point of trying to emulate him by smoking cigars and gambling recklessly. His son, born three weeks before Todd's death, was named for the showman. Mike Todd's death left Eddie as bereft as Elizabeth, and it was only natural that they console each other. They spent long hours alone together at the beach. In June Elizabeth accompanied Eddie and Debbie to Eddie's Las Vegas opening at the Tropicana, her first public appearance since the funeral. Eddie knew that her presence at his ringside table contributed greatly to his success that evening. Afterward he sent her a telegram saying, "YOUR GRACIOUSNESS IN COMING TO MY OPENING IS ONLY EXCEEDED BY MY GRATITUDE."

On August 10, Eddie's thirtieth birthday, Elizabeth called him to say that she had a present for him—something that had belonged to Mike. It was the money clip she had given Todd, engraved with one of his favorite sayings: "BEING POOR IS A STATE OF MIND. I'VE BEEN BROKE LOTS OF TIMES BUT I'VE NEVER BEEN POOR."

Eddie later recalled how he felt upon seeing his best friend's widow that day: ". . . Elizabeth's eyes . . . I can't ever forget how they burned into my heart that day. I felt her need for me from the depths of my soul. My feelings were identical to hers."

Two weeks later Elizabeth left her children with Arthur Loew, Jr., and flew to New York, saying she was en route to the French Riviera, where she had rented a villa for a month. Eddie was also in New York, taping his television show for Coca-Cola. He invited her to join him for the Labor Day weekend at Grossinger's, where he was dedicating a new indoor swimming pool. The Catskills resort was special to him as the place where he had launched his career in 1949. He also had married Debbie Reynolds there in 1955, when he was the number one singing star in the United States.

Elizabeth accepted his invitation. During the drive through the Upstate mountains they held hands in the back of the limousine and she put her head on his shoulder. After a carefree weekend in the company of his friend Danny Welks; his manager, Milton Blackstone; and resort owner Jennie Grossinger and her 1,500 guests, the couple returned to New York. There they closeted themselves in Elizabeth's hotel room before dining at Quo Vadis, drinking at the Harwyn Club, and dancing at the Blue Angel. They also attended a cocktail party hosted by Elizabeth's first husband, Nicky Hilton. In public they were always with another couple to avert suspicion about their liaison.

"At Quo Vadis, Dick Hanley and I were their 'beards,' " recalled Mike Todd's secretary, "and I still remember in the ladies' room saying to her, 'Please cool it with Eddie. You really don't need this right now. You really don't.' But Liz didn't listen. She wanted Eddie Fisher and that was that."

"Liz was the one who pursued Eddie," said his former publicist. "He didn't pursue her. When she called on him after Mike Todd's death and wanted sympathy, she gave more than he gave. Let's put it that way."

"She went after Eddie, all right," said Ketti Frings. "No question about it. She tried Mike Todd, Jr., first, but his wife said no and put a stop to it before it could develop. She got young Mike out of town fast before Elizabeth could move in on him."

Privately, Elizabeth confided to syndicated columnist Max Lerner that it was this trip to New York which had brought her together with Eddie. "They were in a New York hotel together," said Lerner, "and Elizabeth told me that they spent four days and nights mostly in bed together. She said that was how Eddie got her out of her grief."

Publicly, Elizabeth said, "I've felt happier and more like a human being for the past two weeks than I have since Mike died."

By the time Eddie returned home, ten days later than planned, pictures of him with Elizabeth had appeared in the newspapers with stories of their evenings together.

"I am deeply shocked by what I have read in the papers and there is nothing further I can say at this time," said Debbie Reynolds.

Pigtails flying and red-faced with anger, she confronted her husband the minute he walked into the house. "What's the matter with you, anyway?" she screamed.

The next day Eddie Fisher walked out of the house. He told reporters that he and his wife were separating.

Debbie appeared minutes later with diaper pins fastened to the corner of her blouse, carrying her baby's vinyl bottle bag. The wirephoto of her in pigtails standing in the doorway of her house flashed around the world, making her the object of international sympathy.

"I am still very much in love with Eddie," said Debbie with tears in her eyes. "I just hope this separation will iron out the difficulties so that we can get together and be happy again. . . . We were never happier than we have been in the last year. Don't blame Eddie for this, though. It's not his fault. He's a wonderful guy."

After reading those comments Elizabeth threw down the newspaper. "That little bitch!" she exclaimed. Knowing that Debbie had filed for divorce twice in the past, Elizabeth was incensed that she was now pretending otherwise, and she said as much to Hedda Hopper later.

"You can't break up a happy marriage," Elizabeth said. "Eddie's not in love with Debbie and never has been. Only a year ago they were about to get a divorce but stopped it when they found out she was going to have another baby."

"This will hurt you much more than it ever will Debbie Reynolds," warned the columnist. "People love her very much. . . ."

"And what am I supposed to do?" snapped Elizabeth. "Ask Eddie to go back to her and try? He can't. And if he did they'd destroy each other. I'm not taking anything away from Debbie Reynolds because she never really had it."

"And what do you suppose Mike Todd would say to all this?"

"Well," said Elizabeth, "Mike is dead and I'm alive. What do you expect me to do? Sleep alone?"

That interview knocked the national Quemoy-and-Matsu debate off the front pages. Even the resignation of presidential adviser Sherman Adams for accepting a vicuña coat became secondary news to the love triangle involving America's favorite singer, a popular pug-nosed actress, and the most beautiful widow in the world.

"Hollywood was caught with its make-believe down," chortled *Life* magazine.

"The storybook marriage of Eddie Fisher and Debbie Reynolds skidded on a series of curves yesterday—Liz Taylor's," reported the New York *Daily News*.

From that point on, all the principals communicated through reporters and newspaper stories. Debbie stayed at home with her two babies. Eddie moved in with his friend Joey Foreman. Elizabeth stayed with Kurt and Ketti Frings.

"I don't want this marriage to break up," Debbie told the press. "We have our two lovely children and a beautiful life ahead of us."

"The breakup is inevitable," retorted Eddie. "We've been having problems for a long time and it has nothing to do with Liz Taylor."

"It seems unbelievable that you can live happily with a man and not know that he doesn't love you," said Debbie. "But that —as God is my witness—is the truth."

"Bullshit," said Elizabeth.

"Oh, I hope they blast the daylights out of that Elizabeth Taylor," said Debbie Reynolds' mother. "Everybody knows exactly what she is!"

The Liz-Eddie-Debbie headlines continued for weeks, with most Americans cheering Debbie, booing Eddie, and scorning

Elizabeth. As the sweet and innocent victim, Debbie Reynolds watched her career soar, while Eddie Fisher, cast as the villain, saw his fan clubs turn against him, his record sales wane, and his television show canceled by NBC-TV. Comedians joked about the Eddie Fisher doll which sang "Oh, My Papa" off key when punched in the belly. "It's not a toy but a voodoo hex," they wisecracked. "You send the Eddie Fisher doll to your enemy on his honeymoon and watch his bride run off with the bellboy."

Publicly denounced as a "home wrecker," Elizabeth suddenly went from an object of sympathy to a target of contempt. "The facts seem to me to prove she has been aggressive in her romances, ruthless in her disregard for the feelings of those who have stood in her path, and indifferent to the wreckage she has left behind her," wrote Elsa Maxwell.

Capitalizing on the scandal, MGM released *Cat on a Hot Tin Roof*. It featured Elizabeth slinking across the screen in a silk slip and satin pumps in a persistent effort to seduce an unwilling husband. Aided by the free publicity, the movie became the studio's top money-maker for 1958 and the tenth-biggest hit in MGM history. It also earned Elizabeth her second Academy Award nomination, catapulted her into the top ten box-office stars, and won her the "Star of the Year" award from the Theater Owners of America.

But as Elizabeth's notoriety grew, the trade association had second thoughts and eventually voted to take back its award.

"The movie industry is at the mercy of public opinion," the Theater Owners announced, "and to award Miss Taylor the honor at a time like this is simply out of the question."

Later, NBC barred Elizabeth from the studio before Eddie's last television show. "Her appearance in the studio would seem to be flaunting things that are not too wholesome," said an executive. "This is something that the public does not approve."

CHAPTER 13

SAVAGED BY THE PRESS AND SCORNED BY HER FRIENDS, Elizabeth turned again to Rabbi Nussbaum for comfort. At a meeting with the Hebrew scholar, Elizabeth said that she wanted to convert to Judaism, the religion of Mike Todd and Eddie Fisher.

"I feel as if I have been a Jew all my life," she said.

The highly publicized and controversial conversions of Marilyn Monroe and Sammy Davis, Jr., initially made the Rabbi reluctant. He suggested that Elizabeth think more about her decision. But her mind was made up. She insisted on instruction in the Reform philosophy. For six months she studied the Bible, read numerous books, and discussed with the Rabbi the ancient traditions and modern problems of Jews throughout the world. When her instruction was completed, she pledged $100,000 in war bonds to Israel—a pledge that touched off an immediate ban of her films in the Moslem countries of the Middle East and Africa.

"I'm proud to be a Jew," she said. "Now Eddie and I have so much in common."

Delighted by her decision to embrace his religion, Eddie Fisher began calling her "my Yiddena," which to him meant "my little Jewish woman." She chose Elisheba Rachel as her Hebrew name and asked the Rabbi to read Eddie the story of Rachel from the Book of Genesis, illustrating how Jacob served seven years in bondage to win Rachel, won Leah instead, and then served another seven years in bondage because it was really Rachel he loved.

"I would have done that for you," claimed Eddie.

Elizabeth's Christian Scientist mother was hardly happy about her daughter's adoption of the Jewish faith. She attributed it to Elizabeth's love for her own daughter, Liza.

"Elizabeth now says she is Jewish, but she isn't really," said her mother. "She converted to Judaism after Mike Todd died so that his child—their child, Liza—would not be the only one in the family of the Judaic religion. She didn't want the little girl to feel that she was Jewish and no one else was Jewish. It was really for Liza because she didn't want Liza to feel alone."

Claiming that her conversion was based on much deeper feelings, Elizabeth said, "I felt terribly sorry for the suffering of the Jews during the war. I was attracted to their heritage. I guess I identified with them as underdogs."

She certainly knew what it was to be vilified. She and Eddie were so ostracized that they were forced to spend most of their time secluded in the Bel Air home she rented from Linda Christian. With their publicity-conscious agents advising them not to be seen together, they lived for months in isolation and employed security guards around the clock to protect them, and especially Elizabeth's children, from angry rock-throwers and religious zealots who wanted to preach to them on their front porch. The guards also were there to protect them from reporters and photographers.

Public condemnation seared Elizabeth. She could not understand why people turned against her. She called friends like Sidney Guilaroff in tears. Later she sought redress in the courts, suing at least six publications which she felt had printed libelous stories. Filing suit soon became a habit.

"She can't believe that someone else's husband is a luxury that even she will have to pay for," said writer Joe Hyams.

Years later Eddie Fisher confided: "She does not like to read bad things about herself. She reads all the gossip columnists and the fan magazines, and she gets very easily hurt by anything that might not cast her in the light of the sweet innocent child she played in *National Velvet*. I guess that she always thinks of herself as being the same sweet child. She has never gotten used to the fact that the movie public no longer thinks of her in that way."

Elizabeth refused to go out in public with Eddie until Debbie Reynolds filed for divorce. "We did not dare," she said. "Friends—at least, people I thought were friends—didn't seem to want to have anything to do with us."

In February—eleven months after Elizabeth became a widow and six months after Eddie left home—Debbie marched into a Los Angeles courtroom. Without mentioning Elizabeth by name, she told the judge that her husband had become interested in another woman. Inside five minutes she was granted a divorce that would be final in a year. She was also awarded custody of the two children and a million-dollar settlement. This included two houses in Hollywood and Palm Springs, plus all the furniture, stocks, securities, and an unprecedented alimony schedule of $10,000 a year for twenty years even if she were to remarry.

So acrimonious was the divorce that Debbie bitterly disavowed her former husband. Years later she said, "I had two children by him who could have been sired by anybody. So that's not a great deal of credit on his part. I raised them, supported them, and took care of them. He didn't help at all." *

Elizabeth privately ridiculed the girl-next-door as "Little Miss Homespun." Flashing her 29.7-carat diamond ring from Mike Todd, she mimicked Debbie, who had publicly disparaged the 7-carat diamond engagement ring she had received from Eddie in 1955. "Sometimes I hate to wear this," Debbie had told reporters. "It's so big and it makes all the girls who have little diamonds feel bad."

"When Eddie gave Liz a bracelet with fifty big diamonds as an

---

* When Eddie Fisher decided to write his autobiography, Debbie Reynolds heard that he might allege a lesbian relationship between her and Agnes Moorehead. She publicly denied such a relationship and announced that if he did make such an allegation she would sue him for millions. For the sake of his children, Eddie promised to write about Debbie only as "the perfect girl-next-door."

engagement present, guess what she said?'' recalled a friend. '' 'Sometimes I hate to wear this because it's so big and it makes all the girls who have little bitty diamonds feel bad.' She imitated Debbie's voice perfectly.''

Eddie indulged Elizabeth the same way that Mike Todd had—with spectacular jewelry, which she flaunted. For her twenty-seventh birthday he gave her an evening bag studded with twenty-seven diamonds, one for each year of her life. He also gave her a surprise party at the home of Ketti and Kurt Frings, inviting the only people in Hollywood still speaking to them: Janet Leigh and Tony Curtis, George Burns and Gracie Allen, Rock Hudson, Peter and Pat Lawford, Richard Brooks, Joe Pasternak, and Ronald and Nancy Reagan.

In the spring Eddie landed a six-week engagement at the Tropicana in Las Vegas. He decided to take up residence there so he could get a quick divorce and marry Elizabeth right away —a step that the California court said he could not take for a year without Debbie's approval. Debbie objected.

"I've already given him a divorce," she said. "I don't approve of divorce, especially the Nevada kind. It would be embarrassing to my children to one day find that their father had two wives at the same time."

"Oh, Jesus," wailed Elizabeth to a friend. "I'll kill that bitch."

Instead, she leased the Hidden Well Ranch in Paradise Valley for $500 a week for herself, her children, and Eddie, telling reporters she adored the singer and planned to marry him as soon as possible.

"Debbie was very hurt at first to find out that Eddie and I were in love," she said. "I think the hurt has now left and she will consent to Eddie getting a divorce here. What has she got to gain by opposing it?"

The next day Debbie Reynolds admitted that she had nothing to gain by opposing the divorce and grudgingly gave her consent.

"Liz is flipping," Eddie announced when he heard the news. "She's jumping all over the room."

That night Eddie walked onto the stage of the Tropicana flashing an apple-cheeked smile. "I opened here two years ago," he said, "and since then nothing much has happened."

The audience cheered, and Elizabeth beamed from her ringside seat as he sang all his songs to her, ending with "Another bride, another groom, another sunny honeymoon . . ."

After the show, Eddie received a rousing three-minute ovation. Elizabeth followed him to his dressing room, trailed by her parents, her two young sons, her agent, her secretary, and her hairdresser, and ran into his arms.

"Oh, darling," she said. "You were wonderful, just so wonderful!"

"No, you were wonderful," yelled a reporter, who said it was her devoted attention that made Eddie's opening such a colossal success.

"It has nothing to do with me," she said. "It's not as though Eddie had been a no-talent kid. He's a great talent. . . . He has a wonderful presence. I don't think our relationship has anything to do with the fact that he's a smash. I don't think I'm speaking as one who's prejudiced when I say Eddie is one of the *finest* performers today!"

Columnist Earl Wilson later said, "The one thing that impressed me about her relationship with Eddie was the actually wide-eyed looks of adoration she kept giving him."

Unquestionably Elizabeth was in love with Eddie Fisher. She assured friends that she was not marrying him for the wrong reasons. "When I began to grow fond of Eddie as a man, I wondered whether it was because I was seeing him as Mike," she said. "That was something I carefully searched my mind about. I knew you could not re-create someone in someone else. If that was what I was trying to do, it had to be disastrous. Mike isn't somebody I could ever forget—or ever want to. I will always love Mike, but that's something different and separate. Eddie does have a lot of Mike's qualities, but finally I was sure I was not trying to marry an image. I knew I was truly and deeply in love with Eddie. We have a marvelous relationship of tenderness, fun, and understanding."

The Las Vegas wedding was set for May 12 in Temple Beth Shalom, three hours after Eddie received his Nevada divorce. His best man was Mike Todd, Jr., and Elizabeth's matron of honor was her sister-in-law, Mara Taylor. The night before, the couple had given a champagne party for their wedding guests: Eddie's parents; Elizabeth's parents; MGM vice-president Benny Thau; Sidney Guilaroff; Ketti and Kurt Frings; Dr. Rex Kennamer; Dick Hanley; comic Joey Foreman; Elizabeth's press agent, Patricia Newcombe; Eddie's press agent, Gloria Luchenbill; Mr. and Mrs. Eddie Cantor; Eddie's manager, Milton Blackstone, and his lawyer, Martin Gang.

"Elizabeth, of course, was a half-hour late for the wedding, but she looked so gorgeous we all would have waited a week," recalled one guest.

Wearing a spectacular moss-green chiffon dress designed by Jean Louis with a dramatically draped hood, high neck, and long sleeves, Elizabeth swept into the temple on the arm of her father.

Wearing the traditional *yarmulke,* Eddie waited patiently for her beneath the *chuppah,* or canopy, of carnations and gardenias. There they repeated their vows in English and Hebrew; signed the *Kesubah,* or marriage contract; and kissed each other lovingly. Afterward the beaming bride turned to everyone and said, "I've never been happier in my life!"

Outside, throngs of tourists in shorts and sandals were held back by police so that the couple could proceed to an adjacent gymnasium where reporters and photographers were waiting. Spotting Vernon Scott from United Press International, Elizabeth snarled, "Why don't you go screw yourself, Vernon?"

"She was mad because I'd done a story on her and Eddie a few days before that was less than flattering," recalled Scott.

To the rest of the reporters the bride was gracious. She and her husband would honeymoon in Europe, she told them, before she began work in London on *Suddenly Last Summer,* her next movie.

"I'm so happy, so very happy," she said. "Eddie and I are going to be on our honeymoon for thirty or forty years. And as soon as my contracts run out I want to retire and devote my life to being a wife and mother."

A couple of reporters wanted to know why she always announced her retirement with each new husband. Elizabeth ignored the question.

The next day, columnist Robert Ruark published his opinion of the wedding. It was the result, he said, of an illicit love affair only five months after Mike Todd's death. "This monument to busting up other people's homes, this solid statue to the ignoring of the ordinary tenets of widowhood and girls' marriages—especially when great female friendships were involved—seemed a little gamey for a Temple," he wrote.

In the *New York Post,* Max Lerner defended the marriage: "I like the fact that . . . they are quite frank about their feelings for each other. This is a case where a joyous candor is far better than a hypocritical show of virtue. Where so many people have been desensitized in our world, I welcome this forthright celebration of the life of the senses."

Touched by his words, Elizabeth and Eddie told Milton Blackstone they wanted to meet the columnist. Lerner was ready to go to London to cover a meeting between President Eisenhower and Prime Minister Macmillan before leaving for a year in India.

"I called them at their hotel," recalled Lerner, "and spent a very spontaneous evening with them, talking and laughing. We all liked each other immediately. Elizabeth was her usual seductive self, and I fell in love. She was careful to tell me how stimulating Eddie had been in bed the night before. 'Three and a half times, Max, three and a half times,' she bragged. They were definitely reveling in their sensuality at the time."

Completely captivated by Elizabeth, the fifty-seven-year-old political columnist began a love affair with her which continued intermittently until 1961.

"It was a giddying experience," he said. "At one point we were so involved we even talked about getting married."

All the time swearing eternal love to Eddie Fisher, Elizabeth was secretly meeting Max Lerner in the pubs of London and in her bedroom at the Dorchester, where, he said, she confided that her new marriage was already shaky.

"I thought I could keep Mike's memory alive that way, but I have only his ghost," she told Lerner.

Yet at Shepperton Studios, where Elizabeth was filming *Suddenly Last Summer*, people remember her wrapped around Eddie and obviously very much in love.

"She's a highly sexed woman," recalled one man. "And she was spending a lot of time in bed with Eddie then. She'd come up for air once in a while, ask if someone was taking care of the kids, and then go back to sex with Eddie. Dick Hanley and John Lee were with her then and they were devoted to the children, so Liz didn't have to worry about them too much."

"No question that she was very much in love then," said Harold Salemson, the film's publicist. "She was crazy about Eddie, who had a lot of influence on her. I could get things done if I went through him. He'd go to Liz and then she'd do it. Otherwise she wouldn't.

"Once I had to tell him to tell her to stop using such foul language on the set. It was making a terrible impression on the British crew. She was always hollering, 'Hey, shmuck,' 'Hey, asshole,' and making everyone very uncomfortable. So I went to Eddie and asked him to get her to clean up her language, and it worked—for a while."

Filming *Suddenly Last Summer* was a nerve-racking experience for everyone involved. The dark gothic tale, adapted from Tennessee Williams' one-act play about homosexuality, cannibalism, and psychosurgery, seemed to counterpoint the disturbances of the people creating the movie.

"Everyone connected with the film was so unhappy," recalled Mercedes McCambridge. "The ambiance and the vibrations were terribly upsetting."

Producer Sam Spiegel had assembled a cast of monumental egos whose creative talents were severely challenged by their own personal demons at the time. Katharine Hepburn was suffering through Spencer Tracy's fatal illness. Montgomery Clift was in the throes of alcoholism and drug addiction. And Elizabeth Taylor was so enraged by the British press coverage of her marriage to Eddie Fisher that she demanded that the set be closed to reporters and photographers.

From the first day of shooting the set bristled with hostility. The director, Joseph Mankiewicz, became so anguished over his problems that he developed a skin disease on his hands and had to wear white gloves every day. He accused the publicists of promoting the producer above the director. He clashed bitterly with Katharine Hepburn for resisting his direction. He raged at Montgomery Clift for being so drunk and drugged that he could not remember his lines or his marks. He fought with Elizabeth for reviling him for his maltreatment of Clift.

The personal problems of the cast were intensified by the horror story enacted in front of the camera. Gore Vidal had written the screenplay, which concerns a brain surgeon, played by Montgomery Clift, who is summoned by an imperious Southern lady, played by Katharine Hepburn, to perform a prefrontal lobotomy on her beautiful but hysterical niece, played by Elizabeth. Mercedes McCambridge was cast in the role of Elizabeth's greedy, babbling mother.

The plot revolves around a homosexual man, Sebastian—never shown on screen—who uses his mother (Hepburn) as a decoy to attract men for his sexual pleasure. He discards her when her beauty fades, trading her in for his exquisite cousin (Elizabeth), whom he takes to Spain. There he buys her a revealing white bathing suit which supposedly turns transparent when wet. She wears the suit swimming, a provocative act that attracts a horde of urchins. As she watches in horror, they turn in fury on Sebastian, clawing and tearing at his body and then, in a frenzy of cannibalism, devouring him.

Traumatized by the sight of her cousin's dismemberment, the young woman arrives home babbling incoherently about Sebastian's grotesque death. Her aunt institutionalizes her and arranges to have her lobotomized to prevent her from ever recounting the macabre scene and thereby defiling the memory of her beloved son.

The film reaches its dramatic peak when the brain surgeon

engaged to perform the psychosurgery assembles the family in a desperate effort to help the young woman unblock her memory. The doctor's plan works, prompting a gushing forth of the unspeakable recollection in a nonstop monologue which some critics felt was the best acting of Elizabeth Taylor's career.

"If there were ever any doubts about the ability of Miss Taylor to express complex and devious emotions, to deliver a flexible and deep performance, this film ought to remove them," stated the *New York Herald Tribune*.

Not everyone was so admiring. Of *Suddenly Last Summer,* Tennessee Williams said, "It made me throw up." The playwright felt that Elizabeth was totally miscast. "It stretched credulity to believe that such a hip doll as our Liz wouldn't know she was being used for something evil," he said. "I think Liz would have dragged Sebastian home by his ears and so saved them from considerable embarrassment. . . ."

Bosley Crowther of *The New York Times* labeled the movie "sheer vocal melodramatics." He said that Elizabeth's "wallow of agony at the climax is sheer histrionic showing off."

Joe Mankiewicz defended his star, who was nominated for an Academy Award along with Katharine Hepburn. "It was the best performance Elizabeth Taylor ever gave," he said.

Elizabeth agreed. *"Suddenly Last Summer* was the most difficult, most complex picture I've ever worked on. It certainly was no musical. Katharine Hepburn, Monty Clift—in fact, everyone —had to concentrate to make it what it was. It is a startling theme, but even the idea of cannibalism is presented, I think, beautifully and artistically."

"Elizabeth seems to do especially well when the role revolves around sex," said Harold Salemson. "She is quite a professional movie actress, and I stress the word 'movie' because she knows how to play to the camera. She will blink on the same syllable every time. She will do each scene letter perfect, and she will do it exactly the same way each time for hours on end. Every one of her takes match. On the other hand, you can't get such a smooth performance out of Katharine Hepburn because her takes don't match. She's much too creative. She refuses to limit herself to doing the same thing over and over and over from different angles the way Liz will.

"During *Suddenly Last Summer,* Hepburn would say, 'Let's try one take high key, one low key, and one medium key and then see which is the best.' This drove Mankiewicz insane. At one point he threatened to close down the production, saying, 'We will resume shooting, Miss Hepburn, when the Directors Guild card which I ordered for you arrives from Hollywood.' Katharine stormed off the set that day." *

Worried about presenting such taboo subjects as cannibalism and homosexuality to the 1959 moviegoing public, the publicity department came up with an unusual advertising campaign. It featured a seductive picture of Elizabeth Taylor in an alluring low-cut white bathing suit with the copy line "Suddenly last summer Cathy knew she was being used for evil."

"Getting that publicity picture of Liz took everything I had," recalled Harold Salemson. "She did not want to do anything extra—ever. So we had to make a deal with her that we would find a beach on the Costa Brava with no tourists. That was the only way she would pose for the picture, and then we had to swear that we would never ask her to do another thing to publicize the film.

"We found the beach, got Liz there, and started taking the pictures. Since she was going in and out of the water, I was holding a big terry-cloth towel to dry her off. At one point I was kidding her, or at least trying to kid her. 'Oh, Elizabeth,' I said, 'tell me you're really doing this because you love getting dried off by me this way.' She turned on me and said, 'I get paid to do movies, not publicity.' Obviously, I had overstepped the boundary between star and serf."

Elizabeth Taylor was not just a star at that time. The $500,000

---

* The last day of shooting, Katharine Hepburn contemptuously spat in the director's face. Mankiewicz retaliated by calling her "the most experienced amateur actress in the world . . . whose performances . . . though remarkably effective . . . are fake!"

she earned for eight weeks' work in *Suddenly Last Summer* made her the highest-paid actress in the world. As one of the top ten box-office stars in America she commanded her own price. She informed producer Walter Wanger that for $1 million she would play Cleopatra for 20th Century–Fox, although she still owed MGM one more film before she was totally free to form her own production company and select her own scripts. In anticipation of that freedom, Eddie was already lining up for her such properties as Pearl Buck's *Imperial Woman* and *Anna Karenina*. Together they formed several corporations—Ramrod Records, Pisces Productions, MCL Films—to finance these independent projects which Eddie planned to produce.

Elizabeth wanted to retire, but she and Eddie had to work to maintain their extravagant life-style. "I really haven't any money," she told Truman Capote. "Eddie doesn't either. Debbie Reynolds—if you'll pardon the expression—got it all."

Still, there was always enough money for presents. During filming in London, Eddie flew Elizabeth to Paris to shop at the House of Dior. There he bought her ten dresses designed by Yves Saint Laurent. In return, she bought him a Jaguar and a beaver-lined raincoat. In addition to property in Jamaica which Elizabeth christened "Eddie's Eden," he bought her a thirteen-room white brick mansion in Purchase, New York, with five acres of land, tennis courts, and a swimming pool. He also bought her a $325,000 chalet in Gstaad, Switzerland, and she presented him with a dark green Rolls-Royce convertible. To celebrate their six-month wedding anniversary, he gave her a mink sweater and she gave him a pair of gold cuff links diamond-studded with X's. "Those are for all my kisses," she said. On the back of the cuff links she had engraved a more personal endearment: "I LOVE AND NEED YOU WITH MY LIFE FOR THE REST OF TIME."

Moved by his wife's expressions of love, Eddie tried hard to reciprocate. One of his most spectacular gifts was a first-anniversary present: a leather-bound library of all her movies.

"Eddie gave her a set of thirty books for every movie she had ever been in," recalled his publicist. "Each book contained a copy of the script, plus a selection of twelve photographs from the movie. They were bound in lavender leather, and the inside was imported lavender paisley paper. Each title was written in 14-karat gold on the cover. He had a lavender bookmark made with the inscription 'TO MY LIFE, MY WIFE, ELIZABETH—LOVE, EDDIE.'

"She nearly fainted with pleasure when she saw all those books. I think she realized what an extraordinary gesture it was to do all that for somebody. It took me months to assemble everything, and the price was astronomical, because each book was magnificently done."

"It is my good fortune to be married to a man who likes the real things of life as much as I do," Elizabeth said. "And that is why, despite heartaches and the tragedy I've known, I say I am a doubly blessed woman. I have known real love twice in my life. Some never know it once."

In memory of her first love, Elizabeth carried Mike Todd's photograph with her wherever she went—a habit that Eddie encouraged. "Why not?" he said. "We both loved him. He was a great influence on me and he was the greatest influence on Elizabeth. He actually taught her how to love. . . . Mike gave her many things, but the greatest gift he gave her was the gift to love."

Elizabeth defined love in terms of constant companionship. She needed that kind of attention and affection as a flower needs full sun. Before marrying Eddie, she made him swear that they would never be separated for more than one night. He promised to accompany her on film locations, and she in turn vowed to be with him during his nightclub engagements. That way they would work together, help each other, and never be apart.

Elizabeth's appearances in Las Vegas and New York ensured full houses for the run of Eddie Fisher's engagements. Wrapped in diamonds and displaying décolletage, she strolled through one nightclub after another to her seat, seemingly oblivious to the gawking patrons and the glare of exploding flashbulbs. Putting her cigarette into its long jeweled holder, she smoked, smiled, and sipped champagne while waiting for her singing husband to appear on stage.

At the end of every act, Eddie thanked all the people who had helped him with the show and introduced the celebrities in the audience. Finally he concluded, "Well, that's all. I guess I've mentioned everyone." Inevitably, the audience yelled, "What about Liz? What about Liz?"

Eddie reacted with mock surprise and then looked lovingly at his famous wife.

"I'm so proud and I feel so lucky that she's here tonight," he said. "I think you know how I feel. Ladies and gentlemen, I'd like to present—Mrs. Eddie Fisher!"

The audience cheered and whistled as Elizabeth stood up. She waved to the crowd and blew a kiss to Eddie, who burst into his finale, singing "That Face" directly to her: "Those eyes, those lips, that fabulous smile . . ."

In New York, Elizabeth staged an opening-night party honoring her husband for seventy-two people in the Waldorf-Astoria's Empire Room. Her guests included Gloria Vanderbilt; boxing champ Ingemar Johansson; Aly Khan and his French girlfriend, model Bettina; Arthur Loew, Jr.; and Eddie's father, Joe Fisher, a retired suitcase salesman from South Philadelphia. Elizabeth reserved six tables for the late show and ordered three massive tins of caviar for each table, plus $1,500 worth of assorted liquors.

Minutes before Eddie was to go on, Elizabeth walked into the Empire Room and saw what she called "a couple of *shleppers* from Brooklyn" sitting at one of her tables. She approached to say that the table was reserved, but the couple laughed at her. She told them to leave, but they refused.

"Goddamn it," she yelled, "get your asses out of here!"

"Listen, lady, we knew Eddie when he was just a waiter at Grossinger's, and our money is as good as yours."

Letting loose a string of invective, Elizabeth summoned a waiter, paid the couple's $500 check, and claimed the table for her embarrassed guests. Trying to smooth things over, Eddie's father quickly sat down and started a conversation with Aly Khan.

"Here ya go, Prince," he said. "Have some caviar. Me, I like herring."

"Oui, Monsieur Fisher père," replied Aly gravely. "When a herring is good it is very, very good, but when it is not good it is awful."

One guest later recalled: "Liz didn't get the joke and it's just as well, considering her foul humor that evening. Aly was mocking her with that childhood rhyme about the little girl with the curl in the middle of her forehead who was just like Liz. When she was good she was very, very good, but when she was bad she was horrid."

CHAPTER 14

ELIZABETH, KNEW SHE OWED MGM ONE MORE MOVIE, for which she would be paid $125,000. First, though, she wanted to accept her million-dollar role in *Cleopatra*. Since the studio had allowed her to do *Suddenly Last Summer* for Columbia Pictures, she assumed it would release her now to 20th Century–Fox.

"She was so greedy for that money she figured Metro would roll over and let her out of her contract," said Pandro Berman. "But I wasn't going to let her get away with that. I wanted her for the lead in *Butterfield 8*. I had bought the movie with her in mind, and she was perfect for the part."

Elizabeth knew that MGM was capitalizing on her notoriety by casting her as the call girl in John O'Hara's novel, and she refused to make the movie. "The leading lady is almost a prostitute," she said. "She's a sick nymphomaniac. The whole thing is so unpalatable I wouldn't do it for anything—under any conditions."

With this announcement she sent her agent, Kurt Frings, to Sol Siegel, head of MGM production, followed by a phalanx of lawyers, in hopes of extricating her from her contract. But Siegel remained firm. If she didn't do *Butterfield 8* for MGM, he said, the studio would suspend her and under terms of the contract legally prevent her from accepting work from another studio for two years.

Finally Elizabeth went to see Siegel herself, convinced that she could persuade him to let her do *Cleopatra* first. She offered to put the $1 million from 20th Century–Fox into escrow as a guarantee that she would return to MGM. The studio executive refused her offer. He knew that Metro would make millions on a movie starring Elizabeth Taylor. Her reputation as a woman who would stoop to any level to get the man she wanted, including an adulterous love affair with her dead husband's best friend, made her the most tantalizing property the studio had. Since MGM production was at an all-time low in 1960, with only twelve features emerging from Culver City, the studio could not afford to free her.

"Is this the way to end a seventeen-year relationship?" she asked Siegel.

"Fortunately—or unfortunately—Miss Taylor," the MGM executive replied, "sentiment went out of this business long ago."

That sent her storming out of his office. "It's a terribly mean thing they've done to me," she told reporters. "I refused the role for two reasons. First, it's the most pornographic script I've ever read, and secondly, I don't think the studio is treating me fairly."

Elizabeth's public denunciation enraged John O'Hara. Written in 1935, his novel had been sitting on the shelf at MGM for several years, and he was anxious to see production start.

"Her basic mistake was in giving the remarkable opinion that the heroine of my novel was 'practically a prostitute,' " O'Hara said. "Bear in mind she was eager to play Cleopatra, not Joan of Arc. Bear in mind too the fact that the then Mrs. Eddie Fisher had already been Mrs. Todd, Mrs. Hilton, and Mrs. Wilding, though not yet thirty years old, and had long since changed her public image from that of the little girl who loved that horse in *National Velvet*."

After a week of suspension Elizabeth finally gave in. She had no choice. She could not afford to be out of work for two years. But she never forgave the studio and retaliated by denouncing Metro-Goldwyn-Mayer every chance she got for subjecting her to eighteen years of "penal servitude." She took immediate revenge by threatening to stall production of *Butterfield 8*.

"Nothing you can say will make me like this movie and nothing you can do will make me want to play it," she told Pandro Berman. "If you think I've been trouble in the past, you just wait. You've seen nothing yet. I'll never come to the set on time. I'll be late every day. I'll cost you a fortune in delays and sicknesses, and you will regret the day you ever forced me into making this crummy film."

"You are a member of the Screen Actors Guild," the producer replied, "and you will be working with other SAC members—Laurence Harvey, Mildred Dunnock, Dina Merrill—and you won't have the guts to do those things to them. You would be too humiliated."

"Like hell!" screamed Elizabeth. "You just wait and see what I'll do to them—and to you too!"

"Just play the part and you'll get the Academy Award," Berman said.

The producer had decided on David Janssen for the role of the platonic piano player in the film. But Elizabeth wanted the role for Eddie. She told Benny Thau that Eddie had been offered an Australian tour and would have to turn it down to be with her.

"Benny came to me and said, 'You'll be lucky to use him,' " recalled Berman. " 'She won't make as much trouble if Eddie's there on the set with her.' So I had to do it. I hated doing it, but I had no choice. Fisher was a bum. He was a drug addict, and on top of that he was a lousy actor. But I was forced into using him."

At the time, Eddie was receiving regular injections from Dr. Max Jacobson, later revealed to be the notorious "Dr. Feelgood." Jacobson's celebrity patients, including President John F. Kennedy, Andy Williams, and Alan Jay Lerner, were given vitamin shots laced with methamphetamine, or "speed."*

---

* In 1974 Eddie Fisher revealed that he frequently visited President Kennedy in the White House, where they both discussed their drug habits. "I could not live without those shots," said Eddie. "I used to go down to Washington often and visit the President. It's no secret that he was on them too."

Elizabeth too began getting these "health shots" from the doctor. They overstimulated her, causing attacks of rapid heartbeat, nervous exhaustion, insomnia, fits of depression, and bouts of hysteria. To counteract the regular amphetamine injections, she began taking sleeping pills, which made her late for shooting. It was not unusual for her to keep the cast and crew waiting as long as three hours until she arrived on the set.

Accustomed to consulting several doctors at the same time, Elizabeth was treated by at least six different physicians during the shooting of *Butterfield 8,* with each doctor prescribing drugs for her. She supplemented these by frequently seeking stimulants from friends.

"She was always asking me to get her pills and bring them to her on location," said Ketti Frings, "but I wouldn't do it."

The MGM legal files show a series of medical memos concerning Elizabeth during the filming of *Butterfield 8,* including one dated February 29, 1960, when she complained of feeling feverish about 5 P.M. The nurse on the set recorded her temperature at 99.8 degrees—nearly normal for that time of day, but Elizabeth still demanded that a doctor be summoned to examine her. Throughout shooting she complained of various maladies including colds, flu, a respiratory infection, a sprained ankle, a severe case of diarrhea, migraine headaches, and emotional exhaustion.*

Shooting began in New York in January, with Elizabeth telling the press that *"Butterfield 8* stinks."

"I hate the girl I play," she said. "I don't like what she stands for—the men, the sleeping around."

She became so distressed over her role as a prostitute that she secretly hired writers to revise the script in an effort to appear less tawdry. She also decided that Eddie's role should be rewrit-

---

* A production memo from June 16, 1960, reads: "At approximately 9:15, Wednesday, June 15, Hank Moonjean (asst. director) called me to say that Dick Hanley just called him to say that Elizabeth Taylor would not be in tomorrow, that she had been crying for an hour and is emotionally upset from nervous exhaustion and just can't stop crying."

ten, so her writers secretly reworked his lines as well. Then she called the director, Daniel Mann, and producer Berman to her apartment and presented them with the revised script.

As Pandro Berman took a seat opposite her, Elizabeth looked at him curiously. "Say, aren't you the guy who gave me that horse in *National Velvet?*" Puffed with pride, Berman replied that he was indeed that man.

"Well, I want to tell you something, you stupid son-of-a-bitch," she said. "That goddamn horse has been breaking my ass for fifteen years with his fucking feed bill!"

Elizabeth then handed Berman a stack of pages. "Eddie doesn't like his part and so he rewrote it," she said, "and now we are both very happy with it."

Berman picked up the bundle of papers and with a flourish dropped them into the wastebasket next to his chair to show her what he thought of her revised script.

"I'm not going to touch this crap," he said.

Elizabeth lunged at him. "She flew across the room screaming like a banshee and with her long fingernails aimed for my eyes," Berman recalled. "Danny had to hold her off. He was willing to use the material—anything to make her happy and avoid her wrath—but I refused to tarnish the John Michael Hayes screenplay with crap from Eddie Fisher's cheesy television gag writers."

Lashing out, Elizabeth proceeded to punish everyone connected with the film. She was hours late to location, hours late to wardrobe, hours late to makeup. "She was constantly sick and purposely late," said the producer. "She made life miserable for the studio," said the assistant director. "Everyone suffered through the making of the film," said the costume designer.

Elizabeth could not have cared less. Her only concern was Walter Wanger's visit to New York to discuss details of her million-dollar *Cleopatra* contract. Over dinner at the Colony she informed him that she wanted Sidney Guilaroff as her hairstylist on the film. She insisted on two penthouse suites in the Dorchester Hotel, plus a Rolls-Royce Silver Cloud limousine to drive her to and from the studio. In addition to her salary—$1 million for sixty-four days of work—she demanded $3,000 a week for living expenses, plus $1,500 a week for Eddie, whose job would be getting her to work on time. She insisted on first-class round-trip transportation from Los Angeles to London for herself, her husband, her three children, and her agent. Then she said she wanted the studio to abandon CinemaScope and shoot the film in Todd A-O, from which she would derive royalties. Since shooting was scheduled to begin in less than two months, Wanger acceded to all her demands. He knew that she was the star who was to save 20th Century–Fox from financial ruin. Besides, he felt that she was the only actress in the world who could portray the Egyptian queen who was destroyed by love.

Still, Elizabeth refused to sign the contract. She knew that Spyros Skouras, president of 20th Century–Fox, considered it risky for his financially troubled studio to rely on her for the title role. He balked at paying her $1 million, preferring instead to use one of his contract stars like Joanne Woodward, Joan Collins, or Susan Hayward. Knowing this, Elizabeth wanted to torment him by delaying her signing until the last possible minute, thus reinforcing his fears. By July 28, Fox executives were so frantic that they sent Wanger back to New York with orders to "get her" to sign.

"At the Park Lane, Elizabeth was lovely in a negligée and no makeup," Wanger recalled. "In the living room of their suite she was demonstrably affectionate with Eddie. She promised to sign the contract later in the afternoon, but told me to tell Skouras she was 'still looking it over' to keep him on edge a little while longer."

After two years of historical research, studio technicians had re-created the ancient city of Alexandria on eight and a half acres of the Pinewood Studios in England. Over $600,000 worth of temples and palaces, ponds and pools stood gleaming in the rain, awaiting the arrival of Elizabeth Taylor as Cleopatra, Peter Finch as Julius Caesar, and Stephen Boyd as Mark Antony.

On the first day of shooting, Rouben Mamoulian, the director, received a phone call saying that Elizabeth was not reporting to work because of a sore throat. The next day she had a cold. The following day she had a 100-degree fever complicated by hysteria touched off by Eddie's decision to return to New York for a few days.

"I went to Elizabeth's suite to say goodbye to Eddie," recalled Wanger. "Elizabeth was in tears. She didn't want Eddie to leave. She kissed and hugged him. After he left, she ran to the telephone to have him paged in the lobby. She told him on the telephone to be careful and hurry back. She said she was planning to stay up all night until he called her."

Every morning more than one thousand extras reported to Pinewood Studios in a drizzling rain while the director continued shooting around Elizabeth, who remained in bed at the Dorchester with a fever. By the end of the month, apoplectic executives estimated the studio was losing $121,428 a day, with a total loss of well over $2 million. Spyros Skouras screamed at the producer who had insisted on signing Elizabeth in the first place.

"You've ruined us by having that girl in the picture. I wish to hell we'd done it with Joanne Woodward or Susan Hayward— we'd be making money now."

In her bed Elizabeth was reading the British newspapers, which claimed that the delays in filming were all her fault. She was enraged by these stories because she knew that sets were still being constructed and the script rewritten. In addition, there were two technicians' strikes the first day of shooting. Even with the extra time provided by her illness, the production remained disorganized. Despite a long list of troubles she had nothing to do with, Elizabeth was singled out for criticism. She also was blamed for inciting riots within the hairdressers' union by insisting on having Sidney Guilaroff do her hair. When the London *Daily Mail* reported that she was really hiding in her hotel because she was too fat to appear on the set, she called her lawyers and insisted that they file a $2-million libel lawsuit against the newspaper.

The next day, Elizabeth was carried out of the Dorchester on a stretcher and rushed by ambulance to the London Clinic. Doctors extracted an abscessed tooth. Despite antibiotics, Elizabeth still ran a fever. Days later she developed a severe cold and excruciating headaches, indicating possible meningitis. By November 18 she was still too sick to work. Production was closed down until she recovered. Her sickness had so far cost Lloyd's of London $2 million, and the insurance company demanded that she be replaced by Marilyn Monroe, Kim Novak, or Shirley MacLaine.

"No Liz, no Cleo," vowed Walter Wanger.

"We cannot abandon her just because she has been ill," said Spyros Skouras, who was now convinced that only Elizabeth Taylor as Cleopatra could rescue his studio from liquidation.

Shooting resumed seven weeks later, when Elizabeth showed up at Pinewood Studios to do a scene in which a naked Cleopatra, rolled in a rug, is presented to Julius Caesar. By this time, though, Peter Finch was inching toward a nervous breakdown and Stephen Boyd was almost stiff from the inactivity. The rest of the cast had done nothing for two months but watch the palm trees, imported from California, being fitted with fresh fronds that were flown in every day from Egypt. Scriptwriters seemed to come and go weekly, and when two additional writers were hired to revise the script for the fifth time in two months, the director quit and Elizabeth pleaded to be released.

Clutching his worry beads, Spyros Skouras tried to convince 20th Century–Fox stockholders that $7 million for twelve minutes of usable footage was a wise investment. To salvage the film, he then spent another $3 million to hire Joseph Mankiewicz as the new writer-director. He told Mankiewicz that he had only two months to rewrite their script, scout locations, and begin shooting. "Save the picture" and "Use Liz" were his orders.

Collecting $50,000 a week in salary, plus $3,000 for expenses, Elizabeth cheerfully went back to her bed in the Dorchester. There she and Eddie lived like royalty, surrounded by children and nurses, dogs and cats, maids, secretaries, retainers, and applicants for favor. Celebrities called daily from Hollywood, Switzerland, and Rome, and famous people visited regularly to pay homage to the most publicized couple in the world.

Truman Capote stopped by and was appalled by what he saw. "I'd visited that same penthouse often, as another friend had once lived there," he said. "Oliver Messel had tarted it up and it was rather pretty, or had been. During the Taylor residency, the rooms were so crowded with shedding cats and unhousebroken dogs and a general atmosphere of disorderly paraphernalia that one could not easily espy the Messel touch."

Three weeks later that fashionable penthouse suite looked like an intensive-care unit as Elizabeth lay close to death in a transparent oxygen tent. She had been suffering from the Asian flu, which steadily worsened. By the morning of March 4, she was gasping for breath and turning blue.

Grabbing a phone, Eddie Fisher told the hotel operator that his wife was suffocating and needed a doctor immediately. Within minutes, an anesthesiologist who was attending a party at the Dorchester bounded into the penthouse, to find Elizabeth unconscious.

"There had been a sudden collapse," he said, "and she didn't have more than fifteen minutes to live."

The doctor shook her heels to loosen the congestion and struck her on the chest, trying to revive her. Finally, in desperation, he took a thin plastic tube from his bag and thrust it down her throat into her windpipe. Attaching the tube to an oxygen tank, he pumped pure oxygen into her lungs until she regained consciousness. Then he told Eddie that the only chance his wife had to live was with an immediate tracheotomy. He explained that it was necessary to cut a hole in Elizabeth's throat and open her windpipe to ease the congestion that was choking her. The surgery, he said, would leave a scar, which could possibly be concealed later with plastic surgery.

Eddie quickly called Dr. Rex Kennamer in Hollywood and then gave permission to operate. He accompanied his wife to the London Clinic in an ambulance.

"I have no doubt that the decision to move her for the operation saved her life," said the London doctor.

Unconscious and with a temperature of 103 degrees, Elizabeth was wheeled into surgery, where an incision was made above her breastbone for the insertion of a plastic tube connected to a respirator. Suffering from acute staphylococcous pneumonia and weakened by anemia, she was now listed in critical condition. Because she was slipping into and out of consciousness, the Queen's physician was summoned to monitor her breathing.

"The prognosis is not good," Dick Hanley told reporters.

Newspaper, radio, and television newsmen flocked to the hospital, which issued health bulletins every fifteen minutes. The world was on alert that Elizabeth Taylor might die. Outside, the streets were jammed with sobbing fans holding rosary beads and prayer books. Flowers and gifts poured into the hospital as well as cables and telegrams, including a sympathetic wire from Debbie Reynolds and her new husband, Harry Karl. A telegram from Seattle, Washington, read: "SIX THOUSAND OF US ARE PRAYING FOR YOU AT THE BOEING PLANT."

Eddie Fisher, still recovering from an emergency appendectomy two weeks before, looked worn and haggard. Refusing to eat or sleep, he stayed at his wife's bedside praying for her recovery while she remained in a coma. Although Elizabeth was receiving blood transfusions and being fed intravenously through an incision in her ankle, she was not responding to the antibiotics. Finally she stopped breathing completely, and the doctors took Eddie aside to tell him that it looked hopeless. At that point the thirty-one-year-old singer broke down.

"I'm going to lose my girl," he sobbed over the transatlantic phone to his manager, Milton Blackstone. "Oh, God, I love her so much. If she dies, I die. Please, Milton, help me to help her live."

He begged Blackstone to find a certain serum in the United States to replace the impotent antibiotics Elizabeth was taking. Within hours Blackstone had located the drug—staphage lysate —which was available only from an American medical laboratory. He arranged with the hospital to fly the medicine to London, saving precious time by skipping Customs. The hospital stated that an ambulance would be waiting for him at the airport if Elizabeth was still alive.

For the next four days and nights Eddie never left Elizabeth's side. Occasionally she regained consciousness, once scribbling a note to ask, *"Am I still dying?"* At another point she wrote, *"I love you."* Then she became delirious and whispered, "I want my mother."

Elizabeth's physicians immediately summoned Sara Taylor, who quickly called a Christian Science practitioner and then headed for the hospital with her husband, Francis. She arrived carrying her Christian Science books close at hand in a zippered leather case. Going directly to Elizabeth's room, she spent the night at her daughter's bedside reading Mary Baker Eddy's *Science and Health with Key to the Scriptures.*

Hours later, as Elizabeth neared the point of no return, her will to live somehow pulled her back from the brink of death. By early morning she was breathing normally, though aided by an iron lung. The next day she was declared out of danger.

Sara Taylor always took credit for Elizabeth's salvation. It was her strong belief in the healing power of Christian Science, she said, that had saved her daughter's life. "That is true," she said in 1980, "but I don't think Elizabeth would like to have that printed."

Christian Scientists believe that a respiratory ailment often stems from an inharmonious relationship such as the one that had existed between Elizabeth and her mother since Elizabeth's divorce from Nicky Hilton. Once that mental conflict is healed, the physical disease disappears. The healing involves a distinct change in the thinking that has produced the problem, so that when Elizabeth called for her mother on her deathbed, she had resolved the mental conflict between them and opened the door for her physical recovery.

Elizabeth gave Christian Science part of the credit for her recovery. But she said the one person who really pulled her through was her husband. "I saw Eddie," she said. "He had been there every time I became conscious, encouraging me to fight for my life and telling me I was improving, even though I knew I wasn't. I felt an overwhelming sense of love for him."

Days after her ordeal, she sat up in bed, drank champagne, and told friends over and over again how it felt to stop breathing four times and almost die.

"It was like riding on a rough ocean," she said. "Then slipping over the edge of the horizon. With the roar of the ocean in my head, which I suppose was really the noise of my trying to breathe."

When Truman Capote visited her, Elizabeth playfully pulled out the small rubber plug covering the tracheotomy wound in her throat. "If I pull this out, my voice disappears," she said merrily, pulling the plug and sending her laughter into soundless oblivion.

Her experience touched off worldwide sympathy, and Elizabeth basked in the public's affection for the first time since Mike Todd's death. Accompanied by Eddie, her parents, and her Hollywood physician, Dr. Rex Kennamer, she flew home to California to recuperate for six months before resuming work on *Cleopatra* in Rome. So strong was the public sentiment for her that by the time she arrived in Los Angeles she was the odds-on favorite for the Academy Award.

"The Oscar should go to Elizabeth," said Deborah Kerr, also a nominee. "Not because of her grave illness but because her performance in *Butterfield 8* is superb. She deserves the prize as Best Actress. She has been in the running many times, and perhaps this will be the lucky time."

MGM launched a mammoth campaign, taking ads in all the trade papers to promote Elizabeth and the movie. Days before the presentations, all straw polls showed her to be the winner. Still, she remained publicly doubtful. Only her former husband Michael Wilding knew how confident she really was about winning, and this he found out inadvertently when he went to the airport to pick up his children, who were flying in to be with their mother.

"I remember when our son Chris was seven and I picked him up at the airport," Wilding recalled. "He sat in the back seat and began giving a little speech, holding a Coke bottle up in front of him. Then he pretended to cry. 'What are you up to?' I asked. Chris said, 'I'm Mommy collecting her Oscar and I have to look like I'm crying.' "

On the evening of April 17, when Yul Brynner announced her name as Best Actress of 1960, Elizabeth clapped both hands over her mouth and stared in astonishment. She turned to Eddie Fisher, kissed him, and with his help limped slowly to the stage, her ankle bandaged from the intravenous feeding in the hospital. The applause grew as she reached the podium. She stood trembling before the audience of 2,500 people who had finally opened their hearts to her. In a hushed, halting voice, she said, "I don't really know how to express my gratitude. All I can say is Thank you very much."

She looked as if she were crying.

CHAPTER *15*

"ELIZABETH WAS CONVALESCING FROM HER TRACHEOTOMY at the Beverly Hills Hotel when we resumed our affair," recalled Max Lerner. "I think she was a little tired of Eddie at this point, and I began seeing a lot of her. I was writing articles on Latin America at the time and working on them in one corner of her room while she entertained her friends in another corner. She always introduced me as 'my professor.' She was proud of my professional standing. She said I was her intellectual Mike Todd."

In 1961 the syndicated political columnist was Professor of American Civilization at Brandeis University, having returned from a year in India as a Ford Foundation Professor at the School of International Studies. With a B.A. from Yale University, an M.A. from Washington University, and a Ph.D. from the Robert Brookings Graduate School of Economics and Government, Max Lerner possessed the most impressive intellectual credentials of anyone Elizabeth Taylor had ever met.

"Her picture of us was of Sophia Loren and Carlo Ponti," Lerner recalled. "There was a general feeling in her group that I was her man. Her group then consisted of about ten people—actors and agents who were always around. People like Alain Delon and Kurt and Ketti Frings. There was a general feeling among them that Elizabeth and I were going to get married. We discussed it a lot. It was obvious to everyone that she wanted to be with me, and I, of course, was very much under her spell.

"I remember she was drinking too much in those days, and I took over—or rather, I was allowed to take over. 'You're not to drink so much,' I told her. 'Who says?' 'I say!' 'Well,' she said, 'I guess you're the boss.' "

This affair between a fifty-nine-year-old professor and the world's most beautiful movie star was complicated by the fact that both were married to other people. But this did not stop them from seeing each other not only privately but publicly.

"We were out so much together that we began getting gossip items," said Lerner. "The president of Brandeis University even called me into his office at one point. He said, 'I've been hearing about you and Elizabeth Taylor. Is it true?' I said that yes, of course, it's true. Then he asked me what I was going to do about it, and I said, 'Well, I might conceivably marry her. You aren't telling me to lay off, are you?' He didn't say another word—just shook his head."

Lerner recalled being caught up in the ecstasy of his romance and trying at one point to impress his lover, only to be aggressively quashed. "We were having lunch and I guess I was boasting a little bit. I said, 'When we get married we'll have fascinating dinner parties. I know so many heads of state and so many congressmen and senators. You'll meet them all, darling.' Elizabeth said, 'Fuck you! I see these people now without you. I attract them myself. I sure don't need you to attract them for me.'

"I realized then how competitive she was and how much she enjoyed the exercise of power, especially sexual power. A good deal of sexuality comes from concentration on self, and she certainly had that. She was quite narcissistic and derived great pleasure out of that; but there was something missing, so she had to show constantly that she could triumph and get whatever man she wanted. For instance, she constantly taunted me with Richard Brooks. She had a way of telling me about other men who wanted her. She was not reticent about telling men who loved her about the other men in her life. It was boasting for her. Everyone wanted her and she'd let you know they did."

Elizabeth's candid remarks about her sexual conquests did not shock Max Lerner. Instead, they flattered him and invigorated the relationship. "I was not nearly as secure and confident then as I am now," he said years later. "I was finding my way then. Elizabeth was very important in giving me the feeling that the world was mine. If a woman like this—the most beautiful and sought-after in the world—could fall in love with me, then anything was possible."

In return, Max Lerner gave Elizabeth the same thing Arthur Miller gave Marilyn Monroe—the feeling of being elevated by the love of an intellectual man whose professional accomplishments and scholarly credentials transcended the box office. It was the perfect complement of The Brain and The Body, a melding of the cerebral and the sexual. Both Lerner and Miller were older than their lovers, and neither was handsome by conventional standards. Yet both had the love of the most beautiful women of their era.

Having published eleven books, including *America as a Civilization,* Max Lerner was now asked by his lover to write a twelfth, to be titled *Elizabeth Taylor: Between Life and Death.* "I'll do the recalling," she told him, "and you do the heavy thinking."

"We had a legal agreement to do her autobiography which was worked out with Louis Nizer, who was her attorney and mine as well," he said. "We started working with a tape recorder a couple of mornings in bed, but as you might suspect we didn't really get much work done on the book there. Later Elizabeth talked to me a great deal about Monty Clift and the car accident he had coming from her home. She told me how she had cradled his bloody head in her lap in the ambulance. She felt very responsible for that accident and said that she felt that she had let Monty down. He had been very much in love with her. She talked a great deal about dying then, about Mike Todd's death and about her own brush with death in the hospital."

Work on the book was a good excuse for the two of them to spend legitimate time together, but Elizabeth still wanted to allay any suspicions Max Lerner's wife might have.

"If we are going to be seeing so much of each other, I guess I'll have to meet that old bitch of a wife of yours so she won't think anything is going on between us," she told Lerner.

"I said that Edna was not a bitch, but that perhaps it was a good idea for Elizabeth to come by the house to meet her. So she came to our New York town house for a visit and was on very good behavior. Edna was cordial too, but a bit frosty, as I recall. Afterwards, she told me that Elizabeth was going to be fat when she got older, but of course, I didn't believe it at the time."

In New York, Elizabeth and Lerner went to the Floyd Patterson–Ingemar Johansson heavyweight fight at Madison Square Garden.* They attended a party beforehand hosted by Roy Cohn, the political antithesis of the liberal columnist.

"Elizabeth was the center of all attention that evening," recalled Lerner, "and I loved it. I adored being there with her and seeing the envy in all the men's eyes. When Roy Cohn saw me he said, 'Get that lousy left-wing son-of-a-bitch out of here.' He didn't want me at this party because of my liberal politics, not because I was publicly having a love affair with Elizabeth Taylor.

"During the fight Elizabeth kept saying to me, 'Now, don't get me wrong about Ingemar. I'm not fucking him.' But I think she was. I remembered in London and Paris, when Elizabeth was making *Suddenly Last Summer,* how Eddie and I and Ingemar were always waiting hours for her to get dressed so we could go out to dinner.

"As we were leaving the Garden after the fight, a crowd of people recognized Elizabeth and started shouting. Some of their comments were insulting, and when she had heard them she

---

* The year before, Elizabeth went to Yankee Stadium with Eddie Fisher to watch Patterson fight her good friend Johansson, whom she had met at Grossinger's. Tania Grossinger remembers this scene at the fight: Elizabeth was wearing "a revealing low-cut blouse that left nothing to the imagination. Suddenly out of nowhere a gentleman walked over, picked a breast out of her top, held it up for all to see, and shouted: 'Ladies and gentlemen, I ask you—isn't this a beautiful sight?' All agreed it was that, and Elizabeth, completely nonplussed, majestically put it back where it belonged, and round six began."

raised her left fist at the crowd and gave them an international hand signal. The men, most of whom were drunk, turned ugly and started yelling. I couldn't believe it, but Elizabeth yelled right back at them, and finally cops had to be called to form a flying wedge to get us out of there. If it hadn't been for those cops, we would have been killed. I screamed at her afterwards, saying she could not tell men like that to fuck themselves. She said, 'Oh, fuck them all. I don't give a damn.' ''

Elizabeth flew back to California, planning to meet Lerner and his wife a few weeks later in Las Vegas when Eddie opened at the Desert Inn for a six-week engagement. "We were going to work on her autobiography through the summer, but none of it ever happened, because Elizabeth spent that night back in Hollywood with Ketti Frings drinking and talking, and the next day Ketti told Eddie everything.

"That's when Elizabeth called me in New York and said, 'Well, darling. The shit has hit the fan. Eddie knows all about us now and he wants to kill you. Will you please come out here right away and get me?'

"I would not fly out to California. I said no to Elizabeth because I did not want the relationship to be on this level. I tried to explain that to her, but it was difficult.

"Unfortunately, when Elizabeth called me, Edna answered the phone. I took the call in my den and shut the door for privacy, which only angered my wife. Afterwards Edna said, 'Well, what the hell did she want?' I said that it was none of her business, to which she said, 'When Elizabeth Taylor calls you at home, it sure as hell is my business!' My wife was very hurt by my affair with Elizabeth, and it caused a rupture in our marriage at the time.

"Later I got a call from a friend of mine who knew Elizabeth well. She had spent the afternoon with him talking about us, and he called to tell me not to marry her.

" 'Max,' he said, 'you must not marry her. She's a bad bet. She's tried suicide three times and drugs of every kind.'

"He warned me because he cared about me. Still, it was a

terrible decision, and I went through great agony about it. There was a crisis in my marriage over Elizabeth because I was very much in love with her. In the end, though, I realized I could not marry her because I figured that she would use me the way a beautiful woman uses an older man—as a front while she goes on fucking everything in sight. Elizabeth was quite adventurous sexually, and while I certainly could have loved her completely in that way, it might not have been enough for her.''

The romance ended abruptly and did not mellow into a friendship for many years. Lerner remained with his wife and Elizabeth returned to Eddie Fisher. The ''silly little affair,'' she told Eddie, meant nothing to her and certainly had nothing to do with her passion for him. Still, Elizabeth was frightened that Eddie might leave her. She reassured him of her love by reciting the inscription she had had engraved on his anniversary present two years before: ''I LOVE AND NEED YOU WITH MY LIFE FOR THE REST OF TIME.'' She told reporters she adored her husband. She kissed and hugged him in public. In her off-key voice she sang to the tune of ''Bloody Mary'': ''Eddie Fisher is the man I love . . . Eddie Fisher is the man I love . . . Eddie Fisher is the man I love. Now, ain't that too damn bad!''

To cement their marriage, she said she now wanted to have a baby with Eddie. Since her tubal ligation prevented her from conceiving, she suggested that they adopt a child. First they went to Michael Wilding and asked if Eddie could adopt his two sons by Elizabeth. Wilding said no. Then Eddie and Elizabeth talked to Kurt Frings about adopting a foreign baby, since U.S. adoption agencies frowned on placing children with entertainers who had no permanent home and lived out of various hotels. Frings knew it would be impossible for Elizabeth and Eddie to adopt in Italy because neither was Catholic. So he asked Maria Schell, another client, to inquire about adopting a German baby in Munich.

''It is my belief that Liz sees herself as a mother-goddess figure,'' said Walter Wanger. ''Part of her function, in her mind, is to bear a child by the man she loves. Since she has had three children by cesarean operation, it is dangerous for her to have another. So the adoption was terribly important to her and Eddie.''

Elizabeth had loved being pregnant with each of her children, but the role of mothering did not come easily to her.

"She likes babies, puppies, and kittens," said one friend, "and she doesn't always differentiate among them. They're all pets to her."

Disdainful of the cooking, cleaning, laundering, housekeeping, and grocery shopping required of most mothers, Elizabeth hired maids and nurses and cooks to do these chores for her. For years she had Dick Hanley, who took care of everything for her. Her work schedule and constant traveling, especially with Mike Todd, had left her little time to spend with her children. When she did see them, she had difficulty asserting her maternal prerogatives. Mike Todd once mentioned this problem in passing to a friend of his.

"Being a mother is a woman's most important job, and you can't tell her she's being a poor mother because then she gets hurt, real hurt," Todd had said. "Now, I can tell Liz about her acting. I can say, 'You were lousy.' And I can tell her, 'When a guy's talking, pretend you're interested—listen.' But I can't say, 'Don't compete with the nurse—you're the mother. Let the children know you're the mother.' I've got to keep quiet because Liz has to be the one to discover these things. And I can keep quiet because I know she's smart and I see her learning all the time."

When she married Eddie Fisher, Elizabeth began spending more time with her children. Michael Wilding, Jr., was eight years old at the time; Christopher Wilding was six; and Liza Todd was three. She took them to London during the filming of *Suddenly Last Summer* and planned to take them to Rome for *Cleopatra*. She also planned to adopt another child, preferably a baby girl.

In the summer of 1961 she had signed a $100,000 contract with *The Saturday Evening Post* to tell her life story. Since she had ripped up her book-collaboration agreement with Max Lerner and he had returned all her tape recordings, she now needed another writer. The magazine, anxious to publish the exclusive autobiography of the number one box-office star in America, sent several writers to her bungalow at the Beverly Hills Hotel. Elizabeth turned them all down. Weeks passed before she selected a writer she considered suitable.

"I'll be delighted to accept you," she told the young man. They agreed to begin work in Las Vegas during Eddie's engagement at the Desert Inn. "We'll go into the desert for a picnic and work on it that way," she said.

Looking forward to his assignment, the writer flew to Las Vegas a few days later and arrived at the Desert Inn just as Elizabeth and Eddie were going out.

"She looked right through me," he recalled. "I reminded her of our agreement and she said, 'Oh, didn't you get my telegram?' Apparently she had decided not to do the project and had sent me a wire long after my plane had left. So, of course, I hadn't received it. I called my editor and he called her attorneys, who immediately flew to Las Vegas to try to convince her to stick by her contract. Eddie was cooperating with us as we all tried to get Liz to settle down to do this book. I tried to persuade her by suggesting that we do one trial session in the morning.

" 'I can't do it then because Eddie and I like to fuck in the morning—all morning long,' she said. "Those were her exact words, and that certainly took care of any morning work. She dangled me for a week or so and then finally said no."

Elizabeth did not possess the discipline necessary for the serious and sustained work such a project required, and she was in no mood to try. After her illness she became even more self-indulgent. "After what I've been through, I'm entitled!" she told friends who worried about her excessive drinking. "When you've suffered as I have and nearly died, well. . . ."

She said she wanted to celebrate life to the fullest. Even so, she was preoccupied with death. Her strange and strong premonitions, she said, made her psychic. She claimed to have a mysterious sensitivity to nonphysical forces that went beyond sheer intuition. Most of her friends dismissed this as yet another example of her need for melodrama. But Eddie Fisher's mother remembered receiving a call months before from her son and daughter-in-law in London that indicated either an unnerving coincidence or possible psychic awareness on Elizabeth's part.

His mother told Eddie how worried she was about an illness in the family, and he said, "That's funny. Liz bounded in here an hour ago and said, 'What's Mama's number in Philadelphia, Eddie? I want to call her. I have a feeling something is wrong.' "

These feelings were messages to her, claimed Elizabeth, who swore that the angel of death knew her name. She said that the night Mike Todd left to fly to New York in his twin-engined plane she awoke from a terrible nightmare full of exploding fire. Hours later she learned that her husband had died in a fiery airplane crash.

Another subject of her psychic knowledge, she said, was Gary Cooper. All of Hollywood knew in 1961 that the actor had incurable cancer. On the night of May 12, Elizabeth had a strange dream about dolls and little children, she said, and woke up declaring that Gary Cooper would die the next day. Shortly after noon on May 13, the actor died quietly in his sleep.

Fixated on the general subject of death, she particularly relished her own memories of dying. She was convinced that she had actually died "at least four times" during her hospitalization in London. In a morbid form of intimacy, she often relived her encounters with death for her friends.

In 1961 she was the guest of honor at a fund-raising dinner for the Cedars of Lebanon and Mount Sinai hospitals in California. She was asked to appear as "a symbol of the miracle of modern medicine." This is how she detailed her rendezvous with death for the assembled guests: "Dying, as I remember it, is many things. . . . I have never known, nor do I think there can be, a greater loneliness. . . . And then it happened. . . . I coughed. I moved. I breathed. And I looked. That hanging lamp—the most beautiful light my world has ever known—began faintly to glow again."

In 1964 she wrote about the experience: "Four times after the initial time I stopped breathing. Once I started to go when I was awake. I tried to draw breath and nothing happened. I could feel the oxygen leaving my whole system. Instead of blood, it was like boiling water flowing through my whole body, and it was like tons on my chest and the terrible thing of pulling, sucking, and not being able to get any breath and finally getting dizzy."

Over and over she told this story of her death and her miraculous recovery. It was, she said, "like I was, I don't know, twenty-nine years old but had just come out of my own womb."

The perilous melodrama of dying and coming back to life became one of her most prized roles. The part ensured attention and awe from everyone besides bestowing a touch of immortality. She was no mere mortal anymore. Nor was she just a movie star. She was now extraordinary, and in a sense untouchable. Beating back death was a triumph that magnified her box-office appeal and guaranteed intense and profitable public interest in everything she did.

For this reason, 20th Century–Fox swallowed its first $5-million loss and sold 260 acres of its back lot to push on with the production of *Cleopatra*. Running headlong into financial ruin, the studio bowed to Elizabeth's stardom, indulging her every whim.

"What do you care how much *Cleopatra* costs!" she asked Spyros Skouras. "Fox pictures have all been lousy. At least this one will be great—though expensive."

With that, Elizabeth charged 20th Century–Fox a second $1 million to start production in Rome in September. She demanded the same terms as in her original contract, plus $25,000 and all expenses for Dr. Rex Kennamer to travel with her for six weeks. As always, she insisted on such personal prerogatives as not working for the first two days of her menstrual period.

Acceding to everything, the studio responded extravagantly. It bound her script in Moroccan leather and ordered her a chair custom-designed of California redwood. Fox also converted an entire building into her dressing room, christening it "Casa Taylor."

The production soon devoured $500,000 a week and made *Cleopatra* the most expensive motion picture ever made. The $40-million spectacle eventually became renowned not only for capsizing a movie studio but for launching filmdom's most famous scandal.

CHAPTER *16*

"WELL, I GUESS I'VE GOT TO DON MY BREASTPLATE ONCE MORE
to play opposite Miss Tits," Richard Burton announced when he
left for Rome to play Mark Antony in *Cleopatra*.

"I hope you realize that Elizabeth will get all the publicity on
that picture," said his press agent. "You must watch out for
yourself."

"Don't worry," replied Burton. "I can take care of myself."

The Welsh actor, frequently described as "Britain's Brando"
and "the poor man's Laurence Olivier," had won the 1961 Tony
for Best Actor on Broadway as King Arthur in *Camelot*. A few
months later, 20th Century–Fox paid $50,000 to buy him out of
that show and signed him for $250,000 for three months' work in
Cleopatra as one of Elizabeth Taylor's leading men.

It was the most money Burton had ever made to do a movie,
and he bragged about being paid more than Rex Harrison, who
was playing Julius Caesar. He also boasted that the studio was
providing him and his family with a lavish villa, a car, a driver,
and several servants.

"It's no good playing a small role in a big film like Olivier in
Spartacus," he said. "His dressing room was one-half Tony Curtis' size and he got one-half Tony Curtis' money. This is ridiculous. I always demand two Cadillacs and the biggest dressing
room. It impresses them. Of course, the girl is getting even
more."

196

The thirty-six-year-old actor was holding court in "Burton's Bar"—his Broadway dressing room—and regaling friends with Rabelaisian stories. Dismissing Elizabeth Taylor as a "fat little tart," he recalled the first time he had met her, at Stewart Granger's house in Hollywood, when she was pregnant and married to Michael Wilding.

"That was before the Busboy," he said, referring to Eddie Fisher.

Then, with remarkable mimicry, he imitated Elizabeth's voice and spewed forth obscenities which convulsed his audience.

"Be careful, Richie," laughed a friend. "She just might ensnare you yet."

"No, luv," said Burton. "She's dark . . . dark—I think she probably shaves."

Again everyone roared, knowing Richard's reputation with his leading ladies and his compulsion to romance them all. "I cannot act with a person unless I'm powerfully sexually interested in that person," he had said many times. "I can't bear to be on the same stage or screen with them otherwise. . . . It's absolutely hell to make love to someone professionally if she leaves you cold personally."

Although Burton had been married to his Welsh wife, Sybil, for more than twelve years, he blatantly carried on love affairs with such leading ladies as Jean Simmons, Claire Bloom, and Susan Strasberg. Romancing them, he told more stories than Scheherazade. He recited the poetry of Dylan Thomas in his chiffon-and-cut-glass Oxford accent. He spoke Shakespeare with ringing felicity.

Even now he was in the midst of yet another fling, with Pat Tunder, a beautiful twenty-two-year-old blond chorus girl who was to follow him to Rome.* Also accompanying him was Roddy

* Enjoying his reputation as a womanizer, Burton once said, "There was a song in *Camelot* which began with the chorus behind me singing, 'I wonder what the King is doing tonight?' More than once it came out as, 'I wonder who the King is screwing tonight?' The audience never appeared to notice."

McDowall, who had been bought out of *Camelot* at Elizabeth's request to play Octavian. He and his friend John Valva flew with Richard and Sybil to the Burton home in Switzerland and drove with them and their two young daughters to Rome. There they all lived in one villa on the Appian Way.

By September 25, 1961, worldwide attention was focused on the production of *Cleopatra,* which had already suffered $7 million worth of setbacks and the near-death of its star. An entirely new cast had been assembled, plus a new director, a new costume designer, a new cinematographer, and sixty new sets. Every week there was a new estimate on the final projected cost, which escalated from $8 million to $10 million to $14 million to $20 million. Naturally, the first day of shooting on this epic motion picture was considered an international news event. The arrival of Elizabeth Taylor, Richard Burton, and Rex Harrison at the Cinecittà Studios in Rome brought forth a full complement of reporters, including hordes of boisterous paparazzi.

Rex Harrison and Richard Burton were already in costume and waiting with the director when Elizabeth swept onto the sound stage, trailed by her husband, her secretary, her hairdresser, her chauffeur, her wardrobe lady, and her three children. The crew all but bowed to her as she entered. Mankiewicz left his two male stars to rush to her side and give her a kiss.

"How are you feeling, darling?" he inquired solicitously.

Burton was still talking with Rex Harrison when he cast a sidelong glance at his leading lady, who was spilling out of her costume. As all the other actors moved to their places on the set, he walked over to Elizabeth and whispered in her ear.

"You're much too fat, luv," he murmured caressingly, "but you do have a pretty little face."

Elizabeth laughed her broad whinny, walked quickly to her chair, and plopped down on Eddie Fisher's lap. She was awed by Burton's reputation as a Shakespearean actor whose performances at the Old Vic were highly acclaimed. Although none of his movies had ever made money, he was regarded as a gigantic talent with the potential of becoming the greatest English-speaking actor in the world. Roddy McDowall and Joe Mankiewicz had told her how "brilliant" he was, and in that sense she was properly intimidated. She was not as impressed with his reputation as a womanizer. That, she said, she intended to steer clear of.

"I stayed with Elizabeth in Rome for a couple of weeks after shooting started," recalled a friend, "and I remember her telling me then that she was going to be the one leading lady that Richard Burton would never get. She was determined."

Elizabeth saw *Cleopatra* as the greatest woman's role ever written and believed that it was going to be the most important movie ever produced. Under the direction of Joe Mankiewicz she felt she would give her finest performance and probably win her second Academy Award. She considered the director a genius. He shrewdly deferred to her as if she were the most talented actress with whom he had ever worked.*

"Usually Liz is a bit off-and-on about parts she has to play," Mankiewicz said, "but not now. She has a new maturity after her operation and sees this film as a challenge."

Cleopatra, he said, was not a vamp. "She was a highly complicated, intelligent woman who was carried to great heights in her ambition. Elizabeth Taylor has an understanding of this."

"To me," said Elizabeth, "Cleopatra was more like a tigress than a sex kitten, even at nineteen, when she first met Caesar and had been queen for only two years. She was even more mature in her passions and political feelings by the time she met Antony."

Elizabeth had never read Shakespeare's *Julius Caesar* or *Antony and Cleopatra*. Nor had she read George Bernard Shaw's

---

* Christopher Mankiewicz, working as a second assistant director on *Cleopatra*, was amazed at the deference his strong-willed father showed Elizabeth. "I waited for the day he'd get ticked off and really tell her off, what with a hundred people just sitting around waiting for her, while such huge sums were being spent. . . . I have never seen such directionless behavior on his part toward other people, and if ever there was a picture that needed a director to shape it up, it was this one."

Caesar and Cleopatra. Her impressions of the Egyptian queen were formed from a quick reading of *The Life and Times of Cleopatra* by C. M. Frazero and frequent dinner discussions with Mankiewicz. Still, she identified with Cleopatra. Mike Todd, she explained, had been to her what Julius Caesar had been to Cleopatra. After Caesar's death, Cleopatra was drawn to Mark Antony the same way Elizabeth said she had been drawn to Eddie Fisher.

Mankiewicz was forced to start production without a completed script. The director took regular amphetamine shots so he could work twenty-one-hour days, including all-night writing sessions. With no time to cut the script or rewrite, he shot everything he wrote, costing the production millions of dollars in wasted time. He ordered sets built at exorbitant overtime costs, only to see them go unused for months. He was plagued by friction between the Italian and American crews, by strikes, by the emotional upheavals of his stars, by rampaging elephants, and by unrelenting corporate harassment from studio executives responding to outraged stockholders. By the end of the first month he was gnawing his knuckles and wearing white gloves, the result of an outbreak of the nervous skin disease that had plagued him throughout *Suddenly Last Summer*.

"He was semi-mad at that point," recalled an associate. "Reality and Joe had parted company, and though it was hard to talk to a thoroughly exhausted man at the end of the day, he had a manic sort of extra dimension from lack of sleep."

Every day brought wires from 20th Century–Fox complaining about the film's mounting costs. Studio emissaries visited every week trying to cut back on those expenses.

In the beginning Elizabeth entertained some of the visiting moguls with small dinner parties at the Villa Papa, the fourteen-room pink marble mansion with a swimming pool, a tennis court, and eight acres of pine trees that she and Eddie shared with their three children, ten dogs, four cats, two secretaries, three maids, and two butlers.

"It's the first real home that Eddie and I have ever had," she said.

In her role as mistress of the manor, Elizabeth insisted that the beds be changed every day with the finest linen. "Each set of linen had four matching pillows," recalled her butler, Emmanuele Feo. "Liz's passion for clean sheets accounted for much of the high laundry bill. Despite the fact that we had one woman washing, our laundry bill in ten days once came to over a hundred and sixty dollars."

"She also insisted on first-class food and service," said Feo, who estimated her food bill at $150 a day and her liquor bill at $450 a week. "She insisted on a formal service, too. The table —even in the bedroom—had to be laid perfectly with four glasses on the right hand of every plate. One glass was for white wine, one for red, one in case champagne was served, and the fourth glass for water. Almost every night Liz came into the dining room a few minutes before dinner to look at the table."

The Italian butlers were baffled by Elizabeth's insistence on color-coordinating everything—flowers, cigarette holders, matches, candles, napkins, tablecloths—to match the dress she wore for her formal dinner parties. This attention to detail seemed to contrast sharply with her instructions during the meal.

"I remember one dinner where Eddie sat smoking Romeo y Julieta cigars and Elizabeth gave orders to the Italian waiter, who did not understand a word of English. She smiled sweetly at him and said, 'Please pass the motherfucking roast beef.' Hearing her speak, the waiter rushed around with his silver platters and bowls, saying, 'Yes, madame. Yes, madame!' Those were the only two English words the poor fellow knew. Then Liz smiled at him again and said, 'Okay, asshole, you may pass the motherfucking peas now.' 'Yes, madame. Yes, madame!' Liz really thought she was quite amusing and Joe Mankiewicz fell about laughing, telling her how clever and funny she was," said a man.

The first night Richard and Sybil Burton came to the Villa Papa for dinner, the Welshman went directly to the bookcase in the living room to look at the thirty lavender leather scrapbooks of Elizabeth's movies that Eddie had given her for their first anniversary. Eddie told him about the present as Burton paged through the books, obviously quite impressed.

"Richard said this has got to be the most beautiful gesture ever made," recalled one guest. "He said it was the most overwhelmingly generous thing anyone could think of doing for somebody else. That compliment coming from the erudite Richard Burton was quite an accolade for Eddie."

Later in the evening the Welsh actor, sloshed with champagne, began spouting Shakespeare in stentorian tones. Eddie and Elizabeth sat entranced listening to his deep, rich voice while others at the table, accustomed to these inebriated performances, yawned. Finally, one guest, fed up with the slobbering monologue, yelled at Burton, "For God's sake, sit down, will you, Richard? You're making an ass out of yourself."

The guest then turned to the 20th Century–Fox executive next to him and said, "These damn actors! If you don't give them their exit lines, they don't know how to leave a room."

At these parties Eddie, who drank only Coca-Cola, tried to make sure that Elizabeth did not drink too much liquor. He also counted her cigarettes and watched her diet, but mostly he worried about her drinking. He told Emmanuele Feo to cut down on her wine, leaving her glass empty after the fifth refill.

"I understand, sir, but it is rather difficult if Madame asks me. . . ."

"Pretend you don't understand," said Eddie.

His efforts to take care of his wife were sabotaged whenever they went out and Elizabeth sat next to Burton, a marathon drinker, who surreptitiously refilled her glass while distracting her husband so he would not notice. When Eddie insisted on leaving early, Elizabeth begged to stay later, and Burton again began talking to him while quickly refilling his wife's glass.

"I thought," said Elizabeth later, " 'I absolutely adore this man.' "

"This was just part of Richard's seduction technique," observed a friend who was there.

Despite his acne-pitted face, Burton was devastatingly irresistible to women. Physically virile, with astonishingly broad shoulders, he still had enough of the motherless child about him to appear vulnerable.

"He has that marvelous quality of making a woman feel as if she's the only one in the world worth talking to, and it's bliss, it really is," said Lee Remick.

"I was madly in love with him for at least four days," said Tammy Grimes. "He makes women feel beautiful."

Actor Fredric March said Burton had "a terrific way with women." Said March: "I don't think he has missed more than half a dozen."

"He's a born male coquette," agreed producer Frank Ross.

Burton acknowledged his vaunted sex appeal while charmingly disparaging it. "Really, luv," he said, "I'm more frog than prince."

Still, he felt compelled to seduce other women, especially in the presence of his wife. Some of his sexual overtures were quite blatant. One night he made a pass at a pretty blond houseguest of the Fishers' in full view of Sybil, who so adored him that she tolerated the humiliation. Only once did she ever take exception. That was at a New Year's Eve party in Hollywood when Richard swept Jean Simmons into his arms at the stroke of midnight and kissed her passionately. Sybil, who had bravely tried to ignore the affair for months, marched onto the dance floor and walloped her husband across the face before storming out. Usually, though, she looked the other way, as she did the night Richard entertained Elizabeth with amusing anecdotes after a champagne dinner at the Villa Papa.

"Liz was laughing with Richard Burton when suddenly Eddie started playing the piano and singing," recalled the butler. "Liz shouted, 'Shut up, we can't talk.' Eddie was furious. He slammed the piano top down and stalked out of the living room into the small salon. A minute later, the conversation was blasted by a record player—playing Eddie's songs at full strength. Eddie put it on in the next room. Liz put her fingers in her ears. She was furious."

Unlike Eddie, Sybil ignored this particular incident, knowing that her husband was merely flexing phallic muscle as he did with all his leading ladies. Granted, this leading lady was a world-class beauty whose international fame surpassed even that of the Pope, the Queen of England, and the President of the United States, but Sybil was not too worried. She had lived through her husband's affairs before and understood how desperately he needed these sexual conquests to prove himself. Besides, she had the security of knowing that once the dalliance was over, Richard always came back home.

With prematurely gray hair, Sybil appeared years older than her rakish mate, to whom she was almost maternal in her role as the supportive, all-sacrificing wife. "You do become an absolute nursemaid," she admitted, "because your husband has to face the public every day. You worry about his sleep and his health, the way you do with a child."

Richard had insisted that Sybil give up her acting career shortly after their marriage. Although he admitted that she had been upstaging him, she happily obliged, knowing there was room for only one ego in the family. She devoted herself entirely to her husband's career, reading his scripts, reviewing his contracts, and picking his clothes. She even postponed having children for ten years in order to get him launched.

In 1952, Burton left the London stage for the international exposure and gigantic sums of money offered by Hollywood. Several critics felt that he had sacrificed his art to his ambition when he signed a movie contract with 20th Century–Fox. "This is a man who sold out," said his agent, Harvey Orkin. "He's trying to get recognition on a trick. He could have been the greatest actor on this planet." But Sybil understood her husband's driving need to make money. It was the only way he could blot out all his years of humiliating poverty as a child.

Born Richard Jenkins, the twelfth of thirteen children, he had lived in a shanty with no toilet facilities and no running water. He never knew his mother, who died giving birth to her last child. His father, an alcoholic coal miner, was too poor to pay for the funeral.

"The ten pounds we borrowed to pay for my mother's funeral haunted us for years," Richard recalled. "There was a tremendous celebration when our family finally paid off that debt. We were terribly poor. There were years when we lived on free soup doled out by charitable organizations.''

Since his father could not afford to raise his last two children, Richard was sent to live with his oldest sister, Cissie, and her husband. In high school he was befriended by Philip Burton, a benevolent schoolmaster who taught him to speak English, to lose his rough Welsh accent, and to develop a deep, far-ranging voice. The teacher trained him in drama and literature. He also taught him manners and how to use a fork.

Afterward, Richard had no desire to return to his natural father* or to his home in Pontrhydyfen. Instead, he asked his teacher to adopt him legally. Immediately he changed his Welsh name to Burton, knowing it would bring him more success in the West End theater district of London and in Britain's class-stratified society. Although Wales belongs to the British Crown, the English have always despised the Welsh and considered them poor and uncivilized. Their wet, gloomy peninsula seemed to produce nothing but coal-smeared miners whose lives were shortened by tuberculosis and malnutrition, giving them the highest mortality rate in all of Britain.

''We Welsh are absolutely different from the English,'' explained Sybil Burton. ''We haven't that immune quality. . . . We all want to be loved. It's a minority thing, really.''

''It's difficult for somebody who comes from a majority to know quite what it's like to be in a minority, to be a Jew or a Welshman or an Irishman,'' said Burton. ''After what I am and what I've come from, where can I go but to the top? It seems to me that coming from the very depths of the working class, if I'm going anywhere I must go as high as I possibly can.''

Burton liked to give reporters the impression that he was an Oxford graduate. Actually, his formal schooling ended with high

---

* ''He never knew which son I was,'' said Richard of his natural father. ''He was fifty when I was born. . . . He sometimes frightened me.'' For the rest of his life he considered Philip Burton his true father, so that when he was informed in 1957 that his father had died, he said, ''Which one?'' When told, he did not return to Wales for the funeral.

school in Wales, but he did on occasion attend lectures at Oxford University while based for six months in a Royal Air Force camp near the Oxford campus—a privilege that the university granted the airmen.

"The idea of a Welsh miner's son going to Oxford University was ridiculous beyond the realm of possibility," he told *Time* magazine.

Dropping octosyllabic words in great profusion made this pose quite convincing. He spoke fluently in four languages and dazzled people with his knowledge of literature and his ability to recite pages of poetry from memory.

Although he hated Hollywood, he longed to be a star. He craved the adulation and the applause, but rationalized his motives. "You simply have to do movies to keep your reputation— and your earning power—at a peak," he said.

Accumulating money obsessed this man who never forgot that his family had subsisted on 5 shillings ($1.25) a week during the Depression. He saved everything he earned in the beginning, and when he married Sybil he allowed her to work for a short time so they could live on her salary and bank his. "As soon as we could, we bought a house in London and made it into four apartments we could rent," she said. "Richard's a marvelous businessman and always wanted security."

Sybil was the perfect wife for a man who loathed spending money and rarely carried cash. She said she felt it was "wicked" to spend large sums on clothes. As for jewelry, she said, "I hate the lot on me." The only luxury she seemed to enjoy was the silver mink coat her husband finally gave her for Christmas one year to match her silver hair. The gesture lost its luster when she later learned that Richard had given Susan Strasberg a white mink scarf and muff that same Christmas.

Richard eventually realized that he would never be rich if he continued to live and pay taxes in England. In 1957 he moved to Switzerland, causing a national furor. "I am moving because of the blasted income tax," he said. "I am not trying to entice people in my business to Switzerland, but what I would like to make people understand is this: if enough top-ranking actors and writers left Britain, it would make the Chancellor of the Exchequer more alive to the vicious, punitive tax situation."

By the age of thirty-seven he was independently wealthy, with immense property holdings plus part ownership in a Swiss bank. He was stunningly successful as King Arthur in *Camelot,* but his fame seemed limited to the Broadway stage. Still nursing monumental ambitions, he began telling reporters that his next movie would be *The Taming of the Shrew* with Marilyn Monroe. Sybil realized that there was no such plan and that the claim was merely Richard's way of associating his name in print with the reigning sex goddess of the twentieth century. By the time they went to Rome in 1961, she also knew that a recognized celebrity such as Elizabeth Taylor would never be ignored by her husband, who was aching for the same kind of acclamation himself. Still, Sybil wasn't worried.

Before *Cleopatra,* Burton had dismissed Elizabeth as "MGM's Little Miss Mammary." Despite her Academy Award, he judged her acting ability as "quite pathetic, really; on a par with her education, I'd say." Roddy McDowall, who knew that Burton had never seen one of Elizabeth's movies, defended his childhood friend. He said that Elizabeth was an amazingly good actress.

"Good at getting sick and getting married," Burton said.

"You just wait until you see her come through the camera," Roddy said.

After seeing the first rushes, Burton began to change his mind. He was impressed by Elizabeth's ability to captivate the camera and come through the lens in another dimension. "She surprises the devil out of you," he said. "If you don't know her, and you watch her rehearse, you say, 'Oh, dear. Here comes nothing.' She goes through rehearsals sort of like a sleepwalker. 'Is this the way I should walk? Is that the way you want me to talk?' But when that camera starts whirring, she turns it on, the magic, and you can't believe your eyes."

The admiration was mutual, for Elizabeth was just as fascinated by this man, who spoke so articulately about the theater, as he was by her screen artistry. His moods were as mercurial as her own. One minute he was refined; the next he was savage. She also sensed the violent rages and melancholic depressions lurking beneath his charming surface. "He is a devious snakepit of ramifications," she said. "If a prefrontal lobotomy was performed on his skull, out would fly snakes, frogs, worms, tadpoles, and bats!"

In this one man seemed to be all the men she had ever loved. As rich as Nicky Hilton, Richard Burton possessed Michael Wilding's quicksilver humor and Mike Todd's energy and command. He was as physical as Ingemar Johansson, as intellectual as Max Lerner, as mellifluous as Frank Sinatra and Eddie Fisher. "I get an orgasm just listening to that voice of his," she confided on the *Cleopatra* set.

Eddie too liked Richard and enjoyed the evenings he and Elizabeth spent with the Burtons. He agreed with Elizabeth that Burton treated his wife miserably but was just as awed as she was by his acting ability. Eddie made a point of accompanying Elizabeth to the set one day to watch Burton do a complicated scene in which he had to kiss a dancing girl and place her on top of an elephant. Afterward, the three of them retired to Elizabeth's dressing room, where they discussed the next scene, in which Cleopatra was going to be massaged by her handmaidens. Eddie had suggested that Elizabeth do the scene nude, and she had agreed. The set was to be closed, with only Eddie and the necessary members of the crew present. No visitors were allowed, although Burton threatened to sneak in dressed as a handmaiden.*

"They say that this movie will cost over twenty million dollars, but it will still make a fortune," Richard said later. "For Liz is absolutely marvelous. They did a breathtaking shot of her the

---

* Elizabeth also allowed her close friend Roddy McDowall on the set to photograph her nude and seminude in a transparently sheer nightgown for *Playboy* magazine, which published the pictures in its January 1963 issue.

other day lying absolutely nude on a daybed. That ought to be good for around twenty million dollars on its own. I must say that Liz fascinates me. What is it about her, I wonder, that makes her so good? Off the screen she's just a nice, charming girl. But on the screen, she is absolutely compelling. She looks at you with those eyes and your blood churns.''

Despite Richard's public enthusiasm for his leading lady, Sybil remained unconcerned about their relationship. Eddie joked that he was jealous of the lines that Mankiewicz was writing for Burton to say to Cleopatra, but Eddie never felt that his marriage was threatened. Elizabeth was as affectionate as ever, and together they had just adopted a baby girl from Germany whom they named after Maria Schell, the actress who located the child for them.

Elizabeth had desperately wanted a baby to make her marriage to Eddie complete. She did not flinch when informed that this child had been born with a crippling hip deformity and needed a series of expensive operations if she was ever to walk. Unable to finance the necessary surgery, the child's working-class parents had put her up for adoption, and Elizabeth felt blessed to have found her.

"She was nine months old, covered with abscesses, suffering from malnutrition, had a crippled hip that was going to cripple her for life—and I just loved her," she said.

Despite friends' warnings about adopting such a child, Elizabeth insisted on taking the baby, saying, "I want her all the more because she is ill. Maybe I can do something to help."

To celebrate this joyous event, Sybil and Richard Burton hosted a New Year's Eve party with Elizabeth and Eddie as the guests of honor. It was weeks before either Sybil or Eddie realized what was happening. Only the director, who worked with Elizabeth and Richard every day, knew they were no longer just reading the lines of Antony and Cleopatra. By January 22, 1962, when they went before the cameras to play their first scene together, everyone on the set realized they were actually living their parts.

"There comes a time during a movie when the actors become the characters they play," said Walter Wanger. "This merger of real personality into the personality of the role has to take place if a performance is to be truly effective. That happened today. . . . The cameras turned and the current was literally turned on. It was quiet, and you could almost feel the electricity between Liz and Burton."

Within a few weeks the rest of the world felt the first shocks of that combustion as the romance became front-page news. LIZ AND EDDIE TO SPLIT headlined newspapers as reporters flocked to Rome from all over the Continent. They stood outside the Cinecittà Studios like beggars waiting for bread. The paparazzi swarmed around Elizabeth and followed her everywhere; they even hid in trees and hung from buildings in their desperation for her photograph.

"I've had affairs before," Burton said, "but how did I know the woman was so fucking famous? She knocks Khrushchev off the bloody front page."

In New York, Montgomery Clift was flabbergasted by the publicity. "It's lunatic," he exclaimed. "Bessie Mae is now the most famous woman in the world!" He told close friends that he suspected Richard Burton of promoting the romance simply to promote himself. "Richard wants to be famous at any cost," he said.*

Fame indeed had suddenly struck Burton. Photographers clamored for his picture, reporters begged for interviews, fans hounded him for autographs. No longer just an actor, he was now an international movie star known throughout the world. Overnight his market price doubled, assuring him $500,000 for his next film. "Maybe I should give Elizabeth Taylor ten percent," he joked.

---

* Montgomery Clift was not at all impressed by Richard Burton. Photographer Blaine Waller, a close friend of Clift's, remembers him saying that Burton was a self-indulgent actor. "Monty said that when Richard spoke he had the feeling that he was listening to himself and getting off on his own voice, which just disgusted him. Monty did not consider that acting."

"He was casual and unconcerned in his debonair British way, admitting frankly that he was enjoying all the publicity," Sheilah Graham reported, adding that Burton had sworn to her he'd never get a divorce. "I shall never leave Sybil. She loves and understands me, and thinks I'm a genius."

Reveling in his new notoriety, Burton bragged to a friend about his conquest of the most famous woman in the world. "Now Liz will be on the set every fucking day I'm on," he said. And he was right. For the next ten days Elizabeth was there to watch him work, although she had no scenes herself. While the lights were being set between takes, they went to his dressing room to make love, emerging later smiling and laughing. On the eleventh day, Roddy McDowall appeared at Cinecittà to tell Richard that Sybil was packing to leave for New York. Burton paled and immediately took Elizabeth aside. As much as he loved her, he told her, the romance was over. He could not further jeopardize his marriage and risk losing his wife and two children. Elizabeth became hysterical.

"Mank and W.W. try to calm her down, but she's coconuts," said one of the film's publicists. "She wants to junk everything. Imagine, a guy turning her down!"

Worried about Elizabeth's emotional stability, Wanger later drove to the Villa Papa to talk to her. The producer was panicked. The entire production of *Cleopatra* hung on the fate of its star. If Elizabeth did not complete the film, 20th Century–Fox faced sure bankruptcy. The studio also would be ruined if a scandal erupted and killed her at the box office.

By the time Wanger arrived, Elizabeth was sedated and in bed wearing a pale gray Christian Dior nightgown. "She was upset about her life and future," he recalled. "She said, 'I feel dreadful. Sybil is such a wonderful woman.' She said she hated all the trouble. . . . Mike Todd was the great love of her life. . . . She really loves Eddie, and now she is confused."

The producer comforted her, telling her that everyone loved her and would do whatever she wanted. Finally Elizabeth said she wanted to sleep and be alone, so Wanger went downstairs into the salon to talk with Dick Hanley. Later he went back to look in on Elizabeth, who was now heavily sedated and nodding. She mumbled that she had taken an overdose of sleeping pills. Someone in the house immediately called an ambulance and Elizabeth was rushed to Salvator Mundi Hospital to have her stomach pumped.

Eddie, who had been in Switzerland looking over their new house, called his wife later and learned that Elizabeth was in the hospital. He did not know about her emotional crisis over Richard Burton earlier in the day. He was told only that his wife wanted him to come and get her. However, when he arrived he was kept waiting seven hours because the doctors did not want to disturb her rest.

The studio claimed that Elizabeth was suffering from "nervous exhaustion." Walter Wanger said it was "food poisoning due to bad beans." Her doctor, Richard Pennington, said that "low blood pressure" had caused her collapse. Her friends knew better.

Elizabeth's suicide attempt so frightened Richard Burton, who was in Paris at the time, that he immediately tried to spike rumors by denying that the romance had ever occurred. Upon his return to Rome he talked privately with Walter Wanger, telling him that he had no intention of divorcing his wife. "I'm a selfish man," he said. "I don't want anything to interfere with my acting career. I'm happy with Sybil, who I know will help me in my career. . . . And I won't do anything to harm Liz, who is a wonderful person."

After taking Elizabeth home from the hospital, Eddie tried to repair his damaged marriage by going to Bulgari, one of Elizabeth's favorite jewelers, and selecting a $250,000 emerald necklace for her.

"One thing I learned with Elizabeth was the value of gifts," he said later. "Just a little fifty-thousand-dollar diamond would make everything wonderful for up to four days."

Elizabeth reassured her husband of her love by writing him letters which she left on his pillow every night. "The lady expresses herself very well," recalled Eddie's secretary. "I saw one of Liz's letters with my own eyes in which she said that despite what was going on between her and Burton, Eddie was still her love, her wondrous love, her forever love. She wrote that there were all kinds of different loves, and she said her love for Eddie, or 'Sunny Boy,' as she called him, was very special. She was leaving him those letters every night when things were disintegrating quite rapidly.''

It was the sentiment in those letters which kept Eddie by her side. For her thirtieth birthday, a few days later, he bought her an antique mirror and a large diamond ring. He knew how traumatized she was by this birthday. ''I came into her dressing room and found her gazing into the mirror,'' he said. ''I couldn't believe that look. Here was the world's most beautiful woman scared to death of turning thirty. It was sad.''

Wanting to make her feel better about herself, Eddie planned an elegant party in the Borgia Room of the Hostaria del' Orso, the most famous night spot in Rome, and invited eighteen people for dinner and dancing, including Joe Mankiewicz, Roddy Mc-Dowall, Hume Cronyn, and Cesare Danile from the *Cleopatra* cast. Richard Burton was not invited.

Eddie's wooing of his wife amused Burton, but the actor was rankled by Eddie's possessiveness of her time, especially when the singer helped Elizabeth study her part. Describing him as ''this fellow always standing around like a waiter,'' Burton made Eddie the butt of every joke. One man recalled: ''Rich especially liked the one about Eddie getting out of bed in the middle of the night to go to the bathroom and saying to Liz, 'Save my place, okay?' ''

Soon the boyish singer paled in comparison with the sophisticated actor. Eddie did not read books and he could not quote poetry. Elizabeth complained that he gave in too easily and never seemed to have an opinion of his own and would rather sleep than argue. Richard, on the other hand, gave her the howling, roaring, tempestuous brawls she craved. He also gave her stimulating conversation and all-night revelry. Still, as enchanted as she was with him, she clung to Eddie for comfort and security.

"I believe that Elizabeth is in a very difficult situation with very deep feelings toward two men," said Wanger at the time.

Eddie had no idea of the passion between his wife and her leading man until he visited the set one day—unannounced. "It wouldn't have mattered if I had sent them an engraved announcement telling them the time I was coming," he recalled. "They couldn't keep their eyes, not to mention their hands, off each other."

The crowning blow came when Burton announced to Eddie, "I think you should know that I'm in love with your girl."

"She's not my girl," Eddie said. "She's my wife."

"Well, then, *Dummkopf,* I'm in love with your wife."

Elizabeth sat beaming with joy and looking adoringly at Burton. Eddie left the next day for New York, still denying the breakup of his marriage. He told reporters that there was nothing to the rumors of an affair between his wife and Burton. To prove it, he offered to get Elizabeth on the phone to deny the rumors herself. But Elizabeth refused to cooperate.

"Eddie," she said, "I can't do that because there is some truth to the story. I just can't do that."

The next day's headline: LIZ TURNS DOWN EDDIE'S OCEAN PHONE CALL LOVE PLEA.

CHAPTER 17

WITH EDDIE FISHER IN NEW YORK and Sybil Burton in London, Elizabeth and Richard luxuriated in their love affair on and off the set. Arm in arm, they dined and danced on the Via Veneto. They picnicked at Tor Vaianica. They sunbathed on the island of Ischia. They made love at Porto San Stefano. Every step of the way they were pursued by paparazzi and journalists. This was the biggest story—short of the death of a Pope—to come out of Rome in years. "Le Scandale," as Burton now called it, dominated headlines around the world. In the spring of 1962, nuclear testing, disarmament, and the Berlin crisis were secondary news to what was happening between Elizabeth Taylor and Richard Burton in the Eternal City. As a result, *Cleopatra* became the most publicized motion picture ever produced.

Finally, the Holy See could no longer tolerate the illicit romance taking place almost within its sacred borders. Vatican Radio censured the "caprices of adult children" and "this insult to the nobility of the hearth." *Il Tempo* castigated Elizabeth as "an intemperate vamp who destroys families and devours husbands." The Vatican City weekly, *L'Osservatore della Domenica,* accused her of "erotic vagrancy," condemned her as a mother, and berated the German agency that had permitted the adoption of Maria.

"Don't these institutions think before handing children to somebody?" it asked. "Don't they request moral references?

Was it not better to entrust this girl to an honest bricklayer and to a modest housewife rather than to you, my dear lady, and to your fourth ex-husband? The housewife and the bricklayer would have worked harder and would have seriously made sacrifices for their child. You, instead, have other things to do.''

Le Scandale whipped up a furor in the United States as well. From television host Ed Sullivan: ''You can only trust that youngsters will not be persuaded that the sanctity of marriage has been invalidated by the appalling example of Mrs. Taylor-Fisher and married man Burton.'' From the New York *Daily News:* ''When persons such as these make spectacles of themselves with their mockeries of love and of the sanctity of marriage, is it any wonder that the U.S. image abroad is a trifle tarnished just now?''

In the House of Representatives, Congresswoman Iris Blitch (D.-Ga.) claimed that Elizabeth Taylor had ''lowered the prestige of American women abroad and damaged good will in foreign countries.'' She demanded that the Attorney General revoke the passports of the lovers, making them ineligible to reenter the country on the grounds of undesirability. Representative Michael Feighan (D.-Ohio) asked the State Department to confiscate Burton's visa because his behavior was ''detrimental to America's morals.''

Eddie Fisher exploited the scandal by launching a full schedule of nightclub appearances. Asked why he opened each act singing ''Arrivederci Roma,'' the baby-faced singer said: ''What did you expect me to sing—'Take Me Out to the Ball Game'?'' Later Eddie appeared at the Winter Garden in New York with Juliet Prowse, who slinked onstage singing ''I'm Cleo, the Nympho of the Nile.'' Bumping and grinding, she purred: ''She uses her pelvis Just like Elvis. . . . There was not a man she couldn't get —That was Cleo's problem on and off the set.''

Elizabeth complained bitterly to the AP's Jim Bacon when she heard about the act. ''Eddie wants to make me look like a nymphomaniac,'' she said.

Bacon put his arm around her and said, ''Elizabeth, I've never met a nymphomaniac I didn't like.''

But Elizabeth didn't laugh. Instead, she summoned her lawyer to Rome and announced plans to divorce Eddie, who in turn agreed to file in Nevada. Sybil Burton, meanwhile, maintained that her marriage to Richard "is fine, just fine, thank you very much." To prove it, she stormed back to Rome to reclaim her husband. Richard was with Elizabeth in the pink stucco bungalow they secretly rented in Porto San Stefano. When he received a call saying that his wife was on the way, he prepared to leave. Elizabeth insisted that he stay. He told her that he had to return to his wife. Elizabeth screamed and threatened to kill herself if he left her. "Go ahead," yelled a very drunk and distraught Richard Burton.

Hours later, Elizabeth again was sped by ambulance to Salvator Mundi Hospital in Rome to have her stomach pumped. Her face was so bruised from the efforts to revive her that she could not return to work for days. Suddenly sober, Burton told his wife to return to London until he finished the picture. To appease Sybil, he made a public announcement that there would be no divorce. Somewhat mollified, she left Rome. Elizabeth returned to work and to appease her, Richard went to Bulgari and bought a $150,000 emerald brooch.

Filming on *Cleopatra* was now so far behind schedule and so far above budget that studio executives threatened to cut off production. They insisted that Elizabeth, who was earning $50,000 a week in overtime, had to complete her scenes by June. Joe Mankiewicz was told to wrap the film two weeks later. Corporate wrangling reached such a pitch that 20th Century–Fox's stockholders fired Spyros Skouras as president. His successor fired Walter Wanger, the producer of *Cleopatra,* and Joe Mankiewicz, the director. Finally, the studio retaliated against its stars and sued Elizabeth and Richard for $50 million, claiming that their personal conduct had destroyed the film.

After 215 days of shooting, Elizabeth completed her last scene in June. But she refused to allow the studio to make a public announcement, for fear that Sybil would fly back to Rome. She stayed with the company to be with Burton on the set, and as the last day of filming approached, people began making bets on what would happen. Most assumed that Richard would return to his wife, as he had always done in the past. Some were so convinced of a disastrous ending to this love affair that they ordered an ambulance to be on hand when Elizabeth got the news. "I was there and I saw the ambulance waiting outside," recalled film critic Hollis Alpert.

Although she was hopelessly in love with Burton, Elizabeth knew that he was consumed with guilt about his family, especially his younger daughter, Jessica, who was born mentally retarded. She sent him a letter breaking off the affair. She loved him too much, she wrote, to destroy his life.

"Nobody could look anybody else in the eye, and the children were being badly affected," said Burton.

With the affair over, Elizabeth felt lonely and distraught and began calling Eddie regularly in the United States. She had sent a bunch of lavender roses to his dressing room for each of his nightclub openings. Now she pleaded with him not to go through with his plans for a Las Vegas divorce.

"No," Eddie said. "I'm going to file. . . . I don't want to go through it all again. It's over." To an associate standing next to him he whispered, "I'm going to show her I'm a man."

But Elizabeth persisted, and—as Eddie admitted years later —they secretly agreed to reconcile. "She even had an air ticket to fly back from Rome," he said. "But it was Richard Burton who stopped a reconciliation."

Burton was at home with his wife and children in Switzerland when he heard that Elizabeth was going to fly to New York. He called her at her chalet in Gstaad and invited her to lunch, saying that he was worried about her. She saw him again and decided not to reconcile with Eddie. Instead, she would make herself available to her lover whenever he wanted her.

"Maybe I could have made him want me more if I'd acted unattainable, made him jealous," she said. "But it would have been dishonest, because I loved him so much. By making myself so readily available, I lowered my stature in everyone's eyes but mine—and, as it turned out, but Richard's."

To be with Burton, Elizabeth agreed to co-star with him in *The V.I.P.s* for $1 million. She left her children in Switzerland and moved with Richard to London, where they maintained the charade of separate suites at the Dorchester Hotel. Wracked with guilt and drinking around the clock, Burton began going back and forth from his hotel with Elizabeth to his home with Sybil and his children. "If it was possible for a man to have two wives, I believe that would have been Richard's solution," said his brother Graham.

Loving both women, he found his dilemma real and "quite awful," he told a friend. "I love Sybil but in a different way," he said. "My love for Elizabeth is more complete, more . . . more necessary, I suppose. I wasn't terribly conscious of it and I didn't rationalize it, but I would say my love for Sybil was much more the love of a man for his daughter. I felt very protective towards her. She was very giggly and bright and sweet and innocent and selfless."

He admitted that his love for Elizabeth was basically lust, which he felt was not enough reason to divorce his wife. "You mustn't use sex alone as a lever, as a kind of moral, intellectual, psychic crutch to get away from your wife," he told critic Ken Tynan. "You can't say to her, 'I'm terribly sorry but I can't sleep in the same bed with you anymore because I simply have to run off with this infinitely more fascinating girl.' There is no such thing as a more fascinating girl. They're all the same, because our appetites are all the same."

Burton said his appetite for Elizabeth was insatiable. "The woman who brings out the best in a man—who is good in bed—is very rare," he said. "In my entire life I have known only three. The qualities they possessed were a responding passion and a responding love."

Wanting to be Mrs. Richard Burton more than anything else, Elizabeth held tightly to her lover. She never left his side and tried desperately to ingratiate herself with the few friends still speaking to him. She bought him a $257,000 Van Gogh landscape to hang over the fireplace in his hotel suite. She ordered for him a custom-made library of five hundred leather-bound books for $10,000. She accompanied him on his rounds of pubs and bars and drank with him through the night. She indulged his black, melancholy moods, which she called his "Welsh hours," and doted on him as Sybil once had done, cutting his hair, selecting his clothes, reviewing his movie scripts. She also consecrated herself to his career.

"Before I met her I was making any kind of film in sight just to get rich," he said. "Then Elizabeth made me see just what rubbish I had been doing. She made me do the film *Becket* when I didn't want to—and it was a turning point in my career. She also made me do *Hamlet*."

Elizabeth vowed to give up her own acting career, if necessary, to be with Burton. She accompanied him to the set of *Becket* every day, took long wine-drenched lunches with him and his co-star, Peter O'Toole, and steered him back to the Dorchester every night.

"The drinking that was going on during that time was something to behold," recalled Mike Mindlin, the publicist for *Becket*. "I remember Elizabeth and Richard so drunk one day we couldn't do an interview for the Ed Sullivan show. Ed had wanted to get Richard and Peter on his program, and they both agreed to do it; so Sullivan flew to London for the sole purpose of doing that segment, but Burton suddenly decided that he wanted to be paid. At the very last minute he had his agent call me to say that unless he was paid his television fee, he was not on call.

"I was frantic. I drove to the Dorchester and waited for Richard and Elizabeth to arrive so I could talk to them. They walked in around five-thirty P.M. and the three of us sat down in the lobby for a drink. It was the height of the tourist season, and there were hundreds of people standing there staring at us.

"Richard begins drinking and Elizabeth is drinking, and they keep drinking and drinking and drinking. Finally Richard agrees to do the Sullivan show. Then he begins quoting Dylan Thomas and reciting poetry. Suddenly—without a second's warning—he throws up. He literally vomits all over himself, all over the sofa, all over the coffee table, as hundreds of tourists gape in horror. Elizabeth immediately jumped up and went over to him, putting her hand on his forehead. 'Oh, my dear,' she says loudly. 'I think you have a fever. You haven't kicked the flu yet.'

"Well, Richard is so humiliated that he can't move. He doesn't utter a word. Vomit is all over the place, and the waiters are now scurrying around to clean it up because the smell is so awful. At that very moment Otto Preminger walked through the revolving door. He doesn't know what has just happened but he sees the crush of people. Then he spots the Burtons and walks over to say hello. Just as he gets to the table and starts to say something, Burton, who is humiliated to be found this way, yells at him, 'Will you fuck off? Just fuck off?' Without saying a word, Otto turned on his heel and ran.

"Thinking I have the Ed Sullivan interview sewed up, I walked Elizabeth and Richard to the elevator and said I would talk to them later. The next day the director, Peter Glenville, called me. 'You better get here before lunch so you can keep an eye on Burton,' he said. 'Richard and Peter will go to lunch together and they'll get so drunk you'll be very sorry.' So I made up some story, saying that Richard had to be in the studio at noon for the interview. Ed Sullivan was there, and we waited hours and hours. By three P.M. there was still no sign of Burton. Three-thirty passed, no Burton. Four o'clock came and went and no Richard. Finally, around five, Elizabeth called. 'We are here,' she said. 'We're in Richard's dressing room.'

"I walked in and found the two of them absolutely insensate. Richard was so drunk that he was putting his tights on over his trousers, and Elizabeth, thinking it was the funniest thing she'd ever seen, was howling with laughter. Poor Ed Sullivan was so ill at ease he didn't know what to do. But he started the interview anyway. Turning to Richard with a nice, polite warm-up question, he said, 'This is the first time that you and Peter O'Toole have ever worked together, isn't it?'

"Richard responded: 'Yesh, and it will prolly fucking be the lashed.' Peter, who was completely sober at the time, was so thrown by the remark that he didn't know how to handle it. We continued filming for about fifteen more minutes, but it was hopeless. The segment couldn't possibly be used, and there was no way of splicing it so that you wouldn't know Burton was drunk.''

Except for the times Richard slipped away from the Dorchester to be with his family, he and Elizabeth were inseparable. Still, he could not bring himself to ask his wife for a divorce, and Sybil, although humiliated by his public love affair, would not bring up the subject because she desperately wanted to keep the marriage together.

"I would never allow the father of my children to become the fifth husband of Elizabeth Taylor,'' she said. "I have him bound hand and foot like so much Lend-Lease. I'm not going to cut the leash, and when I get him back I'll be two million dollars richer.''

That statement was partially true. Without ever discussing divorce, Richard did mention a separation when he traveled to North America, first to film *The Night of the Iguana* in Mexico, and then to play Hamlet in Toronto and New York. Ordinarily Sybil would have accompanied him, but under the circumstances, he said, it was best if she and the children did not disrupt their lives. To assure them total financial security, he instructed his lawyer, Aaron Frosch, to draw up papers stipulating that he deposit $1 million into Sybil's Swiss bank account and pay her $500,000 a year for the next ten years. Nothing was said about divorce. So, still believing in an eventual reconciliation, Sybil moved with her two daughters to New York while Richard remained in the Dorchester chained in taffeta.

"I love Liz,'' he said, "but marriage is out. Liz and I aren't made for marriage. She has not had much luck in her love life. Apart from Mike Todd and myself, of course, she hasn't known any real men.'' Proceeding to characterize each of Elizabeth's husbands, he labeled Nicky Hilton "a complete mistake,'' Wilding "handicapped by enormous difference in ages,'' Todd "perfect but dead,'' and Eddie Fisher "deplorable, absolutely deplorable.''

Cleopatra was released in June of 1963. Elizabeth, who had believed that this movie would bring her a second Academy Award, was lacerated by the critics.

"Overweight, overbosomed, overpaid, and undertalented, she set the acting profession back a decade," said television critic David Susskind.

"When she plays Cleopatra as a political animal," said *Time* magazine, "she screeches like a ward heeler's wife at a block party."

"Miss Taylor is monotony in a slit skirt," said the *New Statesman,* "a pre-Christian Elizabeth Arden with sequinned eyelids and occasions constantly too large for her."

"She is an entirely physical creature, no depth of emotion apparent in her kohl-laden eyes, no modulation in her voice that too often rises to fishwife levels," wrote Judith Crist in the *New York Herald Tribune.* "Out of royal regalia, in negligee or au naturel, she gives the impression that she is really carrying on in one of Miami Beach's more exotic resorts."

"Miss Taylor is a plump, young American matron in a number of Egyptian costumes and make-ups," said *The New Republic.* "She needs to do no more than walk around the throne room to turn Alexandria into Beverly Hills."

"Cleopatra, in the person of Elizabeth Taylor," said the *New York Post,* "falls flat, disastrously so."

"Despite her great beauty," said *Cue* magazine, "Miss Taylor simply does not possess the emotional range—in voice control or movement—to match consistently the professional perfection of Rex Harrison, superb as Caesar . . . or Richard Burton as the tempestuous, passionate and utterly tragic Antony."

Devastated by the critics, Elizabeth became hysterical, locked herself in her hotel suite, and refused to get out of bed for days. "When Elizabeth read the reviews of *Cleopatra,* she had an attack of the vapors, and retired to her bed at the Dorchester for an indefinite period," recalled Hal Wallis, producer of *Becket.* "Her phone calls from bed to set were many, and interfered with Richard's work. He told me one morning, 'If you've got a picture for Elizabeth, I think you can get her today for twenty-five thousand dollars.' "

Later, Burton announced: "I want to marry Elizabeth and I will marry her. No ifs. No buts. She wants to marry me. I want to marry her." Later he added, "Of course, you may be quite certain that I shall be in the center of the stage. Elizabeth will be in the wings—knitting."

During the filming of *Becket,* Elizabeth made her television debut. CBS-TV's *Elizabeth Taylor in London* gave viewers a glimpse of famous British locales, and Elizabeth in a Dior wardrobe reciting snatches of Winston Churchill and Elizabeth Barrett Browning. Paid $500,000 to conduct this tour, she was the highest-salaried television performer ever to do a single one-hour show. Still, the critics were unimpressed.

Observed *Variety:* "What might have been a diverting and entertaining travelog unfortunately turned out to be something else altogether, for to be quite blunt about it, Miss Taylor, pompous and so very, very cultured, got in the way of the cameras— and for nearly two-thirds of the program. As designed by the producers, it was as though Miss Taylor were in competition with London. It's too bad that Miss Taylor won out."

In the fall Elizabeth sent her sons, eleven-year-old Michael and nine-year-old Christopher, to Los Angeles to live with their father and start school. Her adopted child, Maria, remained in England with her nurse for further hip surgery while six-year-old Liza accompanied Elizabeth and Richard to Puerto Vallarta, Mexico. There Burton began work on *The Night of the Iguana* with Ava Gardner, Deborah Kerr, and Sue Lyon.

The film company seemed as intrigued by Le Scandale as the rest of the world. The director's secretary kept a diary on location, recording that Elizabeth had arrived with forty bikini bathing suits from Paris. There were other observations as well.

Sept. 26: At one point Burton said to Taylor, "May I take some snapshots of Sue Lyon and the others?" She an-

swered, "Of course. Why do you ask me?" And he said,
"Because I'm afraid of you."
Sept. 27: Elizabeth is wearing a fancy bikini outfit and I
noticed that she seems to have a wonderful time picking at
her navel with a fingernail.
Oct. 4: Elizabeth, as always, was there watching. Today
she wore big black flowers on her head. They were made of
human hair from Paris; beaded thongs made of turquoise
on gold and a Mexican-made green and white shift over a
bikini bathing suit. She has huge rolls of fat around her
stomach.
Oct. 24: Elizabeth arrived on the set wearing a loose top
and bikini bottom of sheer white batiste trimmed with red
embroidery. She had no bra on and you literally could see
the complete upper structure. Imposing. She was also
wearing a magnificent gold ring loaded with pearls and
what looked like either pink diamonds or rubies. She said
the King of Indonesia gave it to her. Richard said, "She's
seducing me again."

Le Scandale was still raging in the world's newspapers when
Sybil conceded defeat in December. Richard's refusal to visit her
and the children in New York before traveling to Mexico was the
final blow. She announced that she was filing for divorce on the
grounds of abandonment and cruel and inhuman treatment.

Elizabeth said it was the best Christmas present she ever got.
Immediately she called Irene Sharaff to design her wedding
dress. Then she called her lawyers to get her free from Eddie
Fisher. However, Eddie refused to sign the divorce papers, saying that the financial settlement she wanted was unfair. In addition to all the jewelry he had given her, Elizabeth insisted on
keeping the dark green Rolls-Royce she had given him for his
birthday and Chalet Ariel, the $350,000 house he had bought for
her in Gstaad, plus all the profits from MCL Films, the corporation they had formed for *Cleopatra*. Eddie was allowed to keep
only the undeveloped property they had purchased in Jamaica.

Elizabeth told the press that Eddie was demanding $1 million
for a divorce. Eddie said she was hallucinating. "The nature of

the dispute is not my request for money," he said. "It is the determination of our mutual property."

Finally Elizabeth instructed her lawyer to release some of the money from MCL Films to Eddie, but only on condition that he sign an affidavit swearing never to do anything in the future to embarrass or exploit her. She was still enraged by his nightclub act which featured "Cleo, the Nympho of the Nile," and she was determined that he would never hold her up to such public ridicule again. Despite her appearance of flouting convention, Eddie knew how much she cared about public opinion.

"She's very conscious of her public image," he said later. "When we were in public she'd smile at me, the photographers, everyone. But as soon as the door closed in our room, she'd explode."

Eddie signed the affidavit promising not to exploit Elizabeth,* and she filed for a divorce in Mexico on the ground of abandonment—but only after she and Burton met with Eddie in New York to ask him to relinquish Maria.

"There was some question that Maria would have to go back to Germany, to the people she came from, because of a broken home," Fisher said a few days later. "So, very reluctantly, I agreed that Burton and Elizabeth could have Maria. And if she is happy with them, I will not object if he adopts her. But I will never allow anyone to adopt Liza. I regard Liza as a trust from Mike. And if anything should go wrong for Elizabeth and Burton, I would be there to pick up the pieces for her."

"That *shmuck*, that fucking *shmuck!*" screamed Elizabeth when told what Eddie had said. She was so incensed at him for holding up their divorce and fighting her on the settlement that she never spoke to him again. Worse, she told everyone that marrying him had been the biggest mistake of her life. She denied

---

* Years later Eddie was prohibited from publishing his autobiography because of this legal agreement in his divorce settlement with Elizabeth. "I had written the book for him and went to New York in July of 1968 to read Eddie the manuscript," recalled Ketti Frings, "but we couldn't publish it because of the agreement with Elizabeth."

ever loving him. She swore that the only reason she had married him was that he had been Mike Todd's best friend and she had wanted to keep Mike's memory alive forever. She said that Eddie had been nothing more to her than a substitute—a very weak substitute—for the ghost of her dead husband. Later she embroidered that story, telling friends that Mike Todd had had strong premonitions about his death and had said that if anything ever happened to him, she was to marry Eddie and let him take care of her. Claiming to have been in a state of shock after his death, she said she "went through with the marriage to Eddie only because Mike wanted me to."

Disavowing Eddie as the adopted father of Maria, Elizabeth lied and said that she had adopted the child by herself. Despite court records and newspaper accounts to the contrary, she also denied that Eddie had ever adopted Liza Todd.

Completely disregarding her four years with Eddie Fisher, Elizabeth said she had been spiritually and emotionally dead until she met Richard Burton during *Cleopatra* and started to live again. "He was like Prince Charming kissing the sleeping princess," she said.

"Elizabeth would like to blacken me out of her life as if I never existed—which is why I will always be on her conscience," Eddie said years later. At the time, he was too humiliated to contest her petition for divorce in Mexico; so it was granted on March 6, 1964, in Puerto Vallarta, on the ground of abandonment. Elizabeth was with Richard Burton in Toronto, where he was starring in *Hamlet*.

"We will be married properly, by a rabbi, in our own dignified good time," she said. But nine days later the couple sneaked off in a chartered plane to get married secretly in Montreal. "I remember that day so well," recalled Ronald DeMann, Elizabeth's hairdresser. "Richard was drinking himself silly on the plane at ten o'clock in the morning and Liz begged me to get him to eat something. 'He's got to have some food in him,' she said. 'I don't know why he's so nervous. We've been sleeping together for two years.'"

Hours later the thirty-eight-year-old groom, drunk but standing, waited in the eighth-floor bridal suite of the Ritz-Carlton for his thirty-two-year-old bride. The Presbyterian Welshman and his converted Jewish fiancée were to be married by a Unitarian minister, the only clergyman they could find who did not object to the four divorces that preceded this marriage. For her fifth wedding in fourteen years Elizabeth wore a low-cut bright yellow chiffon gown with the $150,000 emerald brooch Richard had given her during their *Cleopatra* days. For her birthday he had given her an emerald-and-diamond necklace, and now for a wedding present he gave her matching emerald-and-diamond earrings.

True to the tradition of her past weddings, Elizabeth was more than forty-five minutes late, causing Burton to bellow, "Isn't that fat little tart here yet? I swear to you she'll be late for the Last bloody Judgment!"

Finally she floated into the room, wearing $600 worth of Italian hairpieces which DeMann had entwined with Roman hyacinths that trailed down her back. She was unattended and unescorted. Her parents were there, but not her children. Bob Wilson, Burton's black valet and dresser, served as best man.

The service took ten minutes, after which the groom announced, "Elizabeth Burton and I are very, very happy."

"Oh, God, yes," gasped Elizabeth. "I'm so happy you can't believe it. This marriage will last forever."

"I have been so nervous about this and having to play *Hamlet* eight times a week that I've lost twelve pounds," Burton said. "Now I just feel terribly relieved."

At the next performance of *Hamlet,* the star took several curtain calls and then stepped forward. "I would just like to quote from the play—act three, scene one," he said. " 'We will have no more marriages.' " The audience and the cast roared their approval. The cast prepared a special celebration for the newlyweds, and Burton started the festivities by taking Elizabeth's lipstick and scrawling a heart on a mirror with the message "'E loves 'er."

"They were madly in love then and couldn't take their hands off each other," recalled Robert Milli, the actor who played Horatio. "She was captivated by his poetic brilliance, and he was—to the extreme—inordinately proud that he, Richard Burton, the twelfth of thirteen children born to a barmaid and a Welsh coal miner, had married the most beautiful and most famous woman in the world. He loved her for all she brought him, and he kept saying over and over, 'I'm married to the most beautiful woman in the world.' He couldn't get over it.

"He bragged like a little boy about how much money he paid for Elizabeth's emerald earrings and necklace. He would show them to you and then tell you how much they cost. 'Over a million dollars I paid for them,' he'd say. It was tacky but very endearing. Money meant quite a lot to him. In fact, he told me his life's ambition was to be the highest-paid actor in the world. He loved the idea of being so mercenary and scandalizing the old knights who were holding the mantle ready for him as the greatest Shakespearean actor of his generation."

In Toronto the Millis gave a party for the *Hamlet* company but did not invite Richard and Elizabeth, assuming they would not come. Midway through the evening there was a bang on the door. Mary Jane Milli opened it to find the newlyweds begging to come in and be included.

"We heard you were having a party and we wanted to know why we weren't invited," Richard said.

"May we please come in and join you?" asked Elizabeth.

After a few hours of drinking, the Burtons invited their hosts to their suite in the King Edward Hotel, where a framed photograph of Mike Todd peered down at them from the mantel in the bedroom and the 29.7-carat diamond engagement ring he had given Elizabeth sparkled on top of the commode. "I still remember that incredibly expensive diamond, which was the size of a locomotive light, just sitting there on top of the toilet where it could easily have been flushed away," recalled Mary Jane Milli.

The party continued until four in the morning, with Richard

getting convivially drunk and telling stories about President John F. Kennedy, who had invited him to the White House after seeing *Camelot*. He played directly to Robert Milli's pretty wife, trying to woo her. He kept smiling and saying, "Give us a kiss, luv. C'mon. Give us a kiss."

Elizabeth, not at all amused, was standing in the corner cracking hard-boiled eggs in hopes of sobering him up while he was trying to seduce another woman. Finally she walked over to Mary Jane Milli.

"I think you are very attractive, and Richard obviously does too," she said, "so I'm just going to have to ask you to get the hell out of here."

"Liz didn't like me at first because of Richard's flirting, which was just laughable to me, and I tried to tell her so," recalled Mary Jane Milli. "I know what it's like to have a handsome husband whom women are attracted to. It's hell. But I realized then how insecure she was about Richard. She was tremendously possessive of him and told me later how she always worried about him playing around with other women. She wanted to make sure that he wouldn't ever leave her and walk off with someone else."

Trying hard to please, Elizabeth made efforts to ingratiate herself with the director, Sir John Gielgud, and the rest of the *Hamlet* company. She took great pains to be nice. On opening night she had two bottles of vintage wine delivered to everyone's dressing room with a handwritten note wishing each one good luck. She insisted on Richard's picking up the tab whenever the company dined out. When one of the actresses popped her zipper, Elizabeth whipped off her $150,000 emerald brooch and used it as a safety pin.

"She was there every night to see Richard," recalled Robert Milli. "She would sit in the wings wearing form-fitting pants and lavender suede pirate boots. With a bottle of champagne in one hand and a copy of *Hamlet* in the other, she'd watch the performance."

By the time the company left Toronto for two weeks in Boston the production was still uneven, and Richard's performance was unpolished in parts and extremely inconsistent. Realizing this, he asked for extra rehearsals. He also drank continuously.

Sensing his anxiety, Elizabeth was desperate to help him. Also, she wanted to remove the last remnants of guilt she knew he was feeling about Sybil and the children. So she telephoned Philip Burton, the foster father who had turned against Richard and sided with his wife during Le Scandale.

"Richard needs you," she told him. "Please come."

After restoring this very important relationship, Elizabeth called Emlyn Williams, the Welsh actor who had begged Richard not to leave Sybil to marry "a third-rate chorus girl."

"I was appearing in *The Deputy* when Elizabeth telephoned," recalled Williams. "She was sweet and very nervous, and it was very touching that Richard wanted to see us the night before he opened. You can't keep up a nonfriendship indefinitely, and anyway, Sybil was doing very well and it was all working out wonderfully."

After reuniting Richard with his father and his best friend, Elizabeth called his family in Wales and invited each one to come to New York to see *Hamlet* at her expense, now that it was on Broadway. She arranged first-class flights, deluxe accommodations at the Regency Hotel, and the best theater seats. When she called his oldest sister, Cissie, the woman who had taken Richard in when his mother died, Elizabeth told her to bring nothing but an empty suitcase. Then she sent Dick Hanley and John Lee shopping to buy Cissie a complete new wardrobe, including a gold lamé dress for the opera.* Elizabeth made a great effort to win over this careworn woman who had been so horrified by the great scandal surrounding her brother.

"Cissie is on the staid side," explained her sister Hilda. "She doesn't believe in divorce, and she always liked Sybil."

---

* Elizabeth began sending trunks of her discarded clothes to Burton's sisters in Wales, and the women of Pontrhydyfen wore her large-printed silks, sequined caftans, and thick velvet gowns to their local bake-offs and picnics.

When Cissie James and her husband, Elvid, arrived in New York, Elizabeth escorted them to the theater. She appeared in a short black dress, a full-length white mink cape, an emerald ring, the emerald-and-diamond earrings Richard had given her, and a magnificent strand of pearls.

"Those are beautiful pearls you're wearing," said her sister-in-law.

"Yes," said Elizabeth. "I just bought them today, and they only cost seventy-five thousand dollars."

Sometimes Elizabeth spent all day getting her hair done and selecting the perfect dress, the right fur, and the best jewelry to wear that evening. Throughout the seventeen-week run of *Hamlet* she never appeared at the theater twice in the same outfit. Like an old-time movie queen, she dressed for her fans, the thousands—literally thousands—of people who gathered every night on the corner of Broadway and Forty-sixth Street to catch a glimpse of her arriving at the Lunt-Fontanne Theater in her chauffeured Rolls-Royce to pick up her husband. As she and Richard emerged, policemen mounted on horseback had to use their clubs to hold back the surging mob.

Burton reveled in the mass adulation. "It's just a phenomenon," he told Truman Capote. "Every night Elizabeth comes to pick me up after the show, and there are always these . . . these . . . these . . ."

"Sex maniacs," said his wife.

"These enthusiastic crowds," he corrected her, "waiting . . . waiting. . . ."

"To see a pair of sinful freaks," snapped Elizabeth. "For God's sake, Richard, don't you realize the only reason all this is happening is because they think we're sinners and freaks?"

Richard was unconcerned about the motivation. He cared only that these squealing hordes showed up every night. Their presence validated his stardom.

"Frank Sinatra was with us the other night and he couldn't get over it," bragged Burton. "He said he'd never seen anything like it. He was really impressed."

And so were the other celebrities who paid $100 to listen to the celebrated lovers recite poetry. To raise money for the American Musical and Dramatic Academy, an acting school run by Philip Burton, Richard and Elizabeth agreed to do a poetry reading in June, and Elizabeth spent six weeks rehearsing beforehand.*

"She knew that many in the audience would come for the ghoulish joy of watching a high-wire artist working without a safety net," said Philip Burton.

When Elizabeth walked onto the stage that evening with purple flowers dripping from her high-piled hair, she was applauded before she even began reciting.

"Now she'll make a mess of it," muttered Burton.

She started slowly and fumbled a bit. Looking up at her husband, she made a face. "I'll begin again," she said. "I got it screwed up."

Watching apprehensively in the audience were Lauren Bacall, Dina Merrill, Hume Cronyn, Beatrice Lillie, Lee Remick, Montgomery Clift, Kitty Carlisle Hart, Alan Jay Lerner, Carol Channing, Patricia Kennedy Lawford, Jean Kennedy Smith, Anita Loos, Walter Wanger, Myrna Loy, and Adolph Green.

After Richard recited "To His Coy Mistress" by Andrew Marvell, Elizabeth read "The Ruined Maid" by Thomas Hardy with a Cockney accent. Then, with conviction and perfect inflection, she recited "Three Bushes" by William Butler Yeats.

"If she doesn't get worse soon, they'll all be leaving," whispered Bea Lillie.

The audience stayed until the very end and gave Elizabeth a

---

* Until meeting Richard Burton, Elizabeth knew nothing about poetry and was humiliated every time he asked her to recite something. "I don't know any poetry," she protested. "Oh, come on, luv, you must know something," he insisted. Finally she recited the only poem she had ever learned:
"What'll you have?" the waiter said,
As he stood there picking his nose.
"Hard-boiled eggs, you son of a bitch!
You can't put your fingers in those!"

standing ovation. "I've never had an ovation like that before," said her husband. "I didn't think she'd be this good."

"I've never had an ovation, period," interrupted Elizabeth, adding heartily, "I like it."

Burton later recalled the evening: "Oh, the smell of wealth, all those minks and perfumes, that awful strong silence in the audience that night—I thought, 'The knives are out.' But," he said, pointing to his wife, "this awful sort of raucous intellectual Ethel Merman won them over."

Afterward, outside in the street, the crowds were as impressive as ever. Burton told a reporter that it was a mystery to him why they were always there, every night. "At first I thought the somewhat illicit quality of our relationship before we were married was bringing them. We assumed that once we were married, it would stop."

"Nonsense," said Elizabeth. "You're the one they're coming to see. You're the Frank Sinatra of Shakespeare."

"The what?"

"I said the Frank Sinatra of Shakespeare."

"Oh, come now, get ahold of yourself, luv."

New York's high society paid homage to the Burtons for seventeen weeks in 1964 as Richard in his most spectacular stage triumph broke all records as Hamlet. The play drew standing-room-only crowds at every performance and grossed over $6 million, of which the star received 15 percent. Having survived worldwide censure for their immoral conduct, Elizabeth Taylor and Richard Burton now emerged from Le Scandale with new-found fame and wealth and professional stature.

"I learned in New York," said Elizabeth later, "that there is no deodorant like success."

CHAPTER 18

THE ROLE OF MOTHER WAS HARDER than any movie part Elizabeth Taylor ever played. She loved her children, but her love for Richard Burton was more consuming. The demands of their marriage and their film work sapped her emotional energies.

"Elizabeth was so well-meaning," said Paul Neshamkin, the tutor hired in 1964. "She really wanted to be a good mother, but she and Richard were so involved with themselves that first year. They spent all their time with each other and had nothing left over for the children."

After *Hamlet,* when the Burtons were scheduled to film *The Sandpiper* in California and Paris, Elizabeth felt that her children needed her attention more than ever. Michael and Christopher Wilding were having to adjust to their mother's third husband since their father, and they had been shifted into and out of so many classrooms around the world that they were behind in their schoolwork. Seven-year-old Liza, who had never finished the first grade, still could not read, and four-year-old Maria could speak no English and was not being educated at all. Yet rather than enroll them in boarding schools while she and Richard were abroad, Elizabeth decided to take the children with her, and hired a tutor to travel with them from New York to Mexico to California to France to Switzerland and finally to England and Ireland, where Richard Burton would film *The Spy Who Came In from the Cold* in 1965.

"I tried to tell her that I thought it was a bad idea to drag the

236 • ELIZABETH TAYLOR

kids around the world like that," said the tutor. "I told her that they needed to be with other children their own age, but Elizabeth insisted. She had fantastic dreams about spending time with them."

With good intentions, Elizabeth had ordered reading primers the year before so that Liza could be tutored during the filming of *The Night of the Iguana*. The primers soon took a back seat to bar-hopping with Burton. A member of the film company remembered how Elizabeth tried to drag Richard away from one of his marathon drinking bouts by reminding him that they had promised Liza to be home by three o'clock that afternoon and they were already two hours late. "He just looked at her and ordered what must have been his twenty-second tequila," the woman said.

John Huston's secretary recalled Liza as being a very beautiful child, but extremely precious and completely undisciplined. "Out on the beach, Liza said to another little girl, 'Did you see *Around the World in 80 Days?*' The kid said no. Liza said, 'My first daddy made that. My second daddy made a movie too, and Richard makes movies, and my only mommy makes movies.' "

The secretary recalled a time when Elizabeth took Liza to the set to watch Burton work. During a break the youngster jumped into his lap, kissed him, and called him "Daddy." "Don't ever call me Daddy again," Burton told her. "I am not your daddy. Your daddy was Michael Todd and he was a very wonderful man, and don't you forget it."

During Thanksgiving vacation Michael and Christopher arrived to visit their mother. The secretary recalled seeing them on Thanksgiving day. "At six P.M. they were sitting in the bar watching their mother and Burton swilling tequila with beer chasers," she said.

"In all fairness, Richard knows he drinks too much and tries every now and then to cut down," said newspaperman Jim Bacon, who was with them at the time. "But Elizabeth never lets up. And she could be a barracuda at times. She can outdrink any man I have ever known, including Burton."

He recalled one evening when everyone but Burton was drinking. "Richard, take a drink," Elizabeth told him. "You are so goddamn dull when you're not drinking."

She had hit him where he was most vulnerable. His worst fear, he once admitted, was being sober and "boring the piss out of everyone." "Without alcohol, when I'm stone-cold sober, I feel I belong in a university town somewhere teaching literature and drama to grubby little boys," he had said. So when Elizabeth ordered him to take a drink that evening, he dutifully did so.

"That was the night I saw him drink twenty-three street shots of tequila with a few bottles of Carta Blanca beer as chasers," said Bacon. "It's a wonder it didn't kill him."

"Both of them were drinkers, I can tell you," said the tutor. "I drank with them every night until about four in the morning. I used to spend all day with the kids and then I would spend the evening entertaining the Burtons. . . . We'd start drinking and talking and reciting poetry and, of course, debating Jews versus Protestants."

Recognizing their shortcomings as parents, the Burtons later told the tutor to let them know when their behavior was not in the best interests of the children. "Both Richard and Elizabeth told me to order them around if they screwed up," he said. "Well —they screwed up royally. They never saw those kids for weeks. They did have a heavy shooting schedule, but when we were in Paris staying at the Lancaster Hotel they were living one floor away from the children and would go weeks without seeing them.

"Unfortunately, when they did see them, it was as if it was a royal visit. The children were invited up to talk to Elizabeth and Richard for an hour or so, and their governess, Bea, prettied them and slicked them and sent them upstairs to be received. They did not even see the apartment their parents were living in for at least a month after we arrived.*

"Another thing," recalled the tutor. "The children's posses-

---

* During that time the Burtons, their children, and their entourage occupied twenty-one rooms at the Hotel Lancaster, which with room service cost $10,000 a week.

sions were constantly being given away. It was not Elizabeth's fault, but there was no continuity to the kids' lives. They never had the same toys or went to bed in the same place. Although we traveled with a hundred and fifty-six pieces of luggage, there just never seemed to be enough suitcases to carry their toys, so they were always left behind and new ones were bought at each new destination. It upset me terribly.''

There was little the twenty-two-year-old tutor could do to force the Burtons to be better parents to their children. "I don't want to dump on them," he said, "because I liked them a lot. It's just that their definition of family was weak." At one point Maria's nurse was so outraged by their disregard for the children that she admonished them to see more of their kids. The Burtons fired her the next day.

"Understandably, the kids were difficult to handle," said the tutor. "They felt completely regimented, and they were. If I wasn't there with them all the time, the governess was, and she was terrible—really awful. She must have been seventy-eight years old and quite crotchety, but she was, in effect, their mother at the time. She was the one who was always there. She told them what to do, and if they didn't do it, she beat them. This was particularly disturbing to Michael. He was forced to take a bath at a certain time and to wear what the governess wanted him to wear and to do what she wanted him to do. Naturally, he was rebellious. All the kids were. They acted as a team and were very destructive. I liked them a lot, but they sure knew how to act like spoiled brats. Richard, especially, felt that the problem was lack of discipline. He said that one of the biggest drawbacks to American education was that it was too lax.

"Richard was all for getting the children into a British boarding school, but they were not prepared for it at the time. So he and Elizabeth wanted me to be stern and formal and run a structured classroom with desks from nine to three each day. I was teaching first grade for Liza, fourth grade for Christopher, and fifth grade for Michael. There was no thought given to educating Maria at that time. She had had her final hip operation in Paris that year and was not yet treated as part of the family by the rest of the entourage.* The kids themselves had not adjusted to her.

"On the first day I started teaching, there was a formal introduction to school by Richard and Elizabeth. They arrived at nine in the morning. They had already told the kids, who had a bad attitude toward employees, that I was a friend of theirs, an equal, and was *not* to be treated as an employee by them. They made that clear from the beginning. So on the first day Richard said to the kids, 'It is all right for you to call him Paul, although we would have preferred you to call him Mr. Neshamkin.'

"Then he turned to me and said, 'Now we want to give you something, Mr. Neshamkin.' With that they handed me a wooden paddle which had written on it: *'Dear Paul, If the children act up you are to use this paddle with our blessing. Richard and Elizabeth.'* I told them that I could not discipline the kids that way. I wanted to get through to them as a friend, and it took me one-third of the year to do that. I'm afraid in the end the kids took advantage of it."

The children did not seem to miss Eddie Fisher, who had spent so much time with them in the past. "They liked him as a friend," said Elizabeth, "but when Eddie left, they didn't even ask where he had gone."

"I'm afraid the kids just laughed at Fisher," said Paul Neshamkin. "They used to put on Eddie's record of 'Oh Mein Papa,' which had been left at the chalet in Gstaad, and they would mug to it and crack themselves up laughing. They loved Richard, all right, but saw him so infrequently that they didn't always call him by the right name. I remember after one of the Burtons' visits with the children Richard said to me, 'The kids kept calling

---

* In 1964 and 1965 the Burtons' entourage included Dick Hanley, Elizabeth's executive factotum; his assistant, John Lee; Gaston Sanz, the chauffeur; the tutor, Paul; the governess, Bea; and Maria's nurse. Later Richard's dresser, Bob Wilson, and his makeup man, Ron Berkeley, were added, along with Claudie, one of Elizabeth's hairdressers, and Gianni Bozzachi, her personal photographer, who also substituted on occasion as a bodyguard.

me Paul. Tell me, do they ever call you Richard?' I had to tell him no, they didn't.''

During that time in Paris, the Burtons were publicly confronted in the lobby of the Lancaster Hotel by German journalists who had Maria's natural parents in tow, demanding money from Elizabeth for their daughter. "It was really very, very sad," recalled the tutor. "I think at that point it was the final buy-off. Richard and Elizabeth had to pay those people to get rid of them, and Elizabeth was shattered by the experience—truly shattered. I'd never seen her that way before. She did not think those people deserved their child. They had not kept her because she was malformed, and now they were merely out for the money—trying to exploit her.''

After Aaron Frosch worked out the legalities, Elizabeth paid Maria's parents, and Burton legally adopted the little girl, giving her his name.

By this time Elizabeth Taylor was a very wealthy woman. She still owned 40 percent of all rights to *Around the World in 80 Days,* and her earnings from *Cleopatra* totaled nearly $7.5 million. Because of the lawsuit 20th Century–Fox had lodged against her, she had gone without a movie offer for two years until MGM signed her for *The Sandpiper.* Metro agreed to pay her $1 million plus 10 percent of the gross* and $4,000 a week in living expenses.

Her other demands for *The Sandpiper* included a five-day week beginning no earlier than 10 A.M. and ending no later than 6 P.M. She refused to work Saturdays, Sundays, or evenings.† Again, she refused to work during the first two days of her period. She insisted that she start work with Richard Burton and not be held after he finished. She specified her hairdresser, her makeup man,

---

* *The Sandpiper* grossed $14 million worldwide, giving Elizabeth $1.4 million in addition to her $1-million fee.

† On Yom Kippur, Elizabeth approached Mike Mindlin, the film's publicist, and said, "I'm Jewish and I want the day off. If you won't work, I won't either." Mindlin laughed. "You're Jewish until we have our first pogrom." They did not take the day off.

and her costume designer. She also demanded approval of the director. Her billing was to be first, followed by Richard's, and both billings had to be above the title and 100 percent the size of the title. Both Burtons demanded that no one else get billing of more than 70 percent the size of the title, and no one else was allowed billing above the title unless they gave their permission. Elizabeth was billed as Elizabeth Taylor, but signed her contracts Elizabeth Taylor Burton and insisted that the daily call sheet carry her as Mrs. Richard Burton. Both Burtons demanded the day off on March 1, St. David's Day, so that Elizabeth could accompany Richard while he drank himself senseless to celebrate the patron saint of Wales. In addition to their fees, both demanded to be paid extra money for still photographs, and for advertising if their names were used.

The legal fees for negotiating the Burtons' contracts for this film alone totaled $30,000, which MGM also paid—$15,000 to Weissberger & Frosch and $15,000 to Gang, Tyre, Rudin & Brown.

With so much money coming in, Elizabeth incorporated herself under Interplanet Productions, while Burton incorporated under Atlantic Programmes Limited. These were just two of several corporations they formed over the years to shield their money. Since British subjects living outside England could enjoy a far better tax break than Americans living abroad, Elizabeth decided to renounce her American citizenship and become totally British. This would require her to abjure allegiance and loyalty to the United States. She insisted on doing this in private instead of in a public declaration as called for by the State Department.

"As I recall, the U.S. stood to lose something like two million dollars in taxes," said Paul Neshamkin, "but Elizabeth refused to renounce her American citizenship in public because of the scandal it would cause."

Refusing to appear in person at the American Embassy, Elizabeth signed her expatriation papers in her hotel room in Paris. She claimed that she was becoming a subject of the Crown for no other reason than Richard Burton. "It's not true that I love

America less, but I love my husband more," she said. "It is true that I am trying to give up my American citizenship and become completely British. I want to become British more than anything else. I like the British best of all."

For the next few years Elizabeth earned $1 million for every movie she starred in, plus 10 percent of the gross and $4,000 a week for expenses. Burton's fee ranged from $500,000 to $750,000 per movie, plus $2,000 a week for expenses. They made eleven movies together—nine as husband and wife—and with outside investments, they accumulated over $50 million, much of which was banked in Switzerland, their legal residence, and not subjected to U.S. income tax.

Richard made no secret of his overriding ambition to be a rich man. "I care about money," he told a friend. "I've never had any, and now I do, and I want—well, I don't know what you consider rich, but that's what I want to be."

"That's all he ever talked about," recalled Paul Neshamkin. "He told me that the only thing he was concerned about was getting as rich as Elizabeth. He said he had to make as much as she made per picture. He argued that the only thing he cared about was money. I'd say, 'What about your art?' And he'd yell, 'Fuck the art. I want to be rich, rich, rich.' "

During *The Sandpiper,* the first movie the Burtons made after their marriage, Richard argued with Vincente Minnelli over one of his directions. "It's absurd," he said, "but for the money we will dance."

After the film was released, movie critic Judith Crist made this comment on that dance: "Miss Taylor and Mr. Burton were paid $1,750,000 for performing in *The Sandpiper.* If I were you, I wouldn't settle for less for watching them."

The Burtons shrugged off the criticism. "Every once in a while you have to make a potboiler," Richard said. "We never thought it would be an artistic masterpiece," said Elizabeth.

After grabbing an enormous hunk of diamonds from the producer as her reward for being the star, Elizabeth and the entourage followed Richard to Dublin, where he began *The Spy Who*

Came In from the Cold. She had made the same promise to him that she had made to Mike Todd and Eddie Fisher—never to leave his side. In the case of Richard Burton, a man whom director Martin Ritt described as "the greatest phallic symbol in the world," there was even more reason for this dogged companionship, and her fifth husband admitted as much.

"In making movies, when actors play lovers in a film—even when each one is well married in real life—strange chemical things happen," Burton said. "I don't try to explain it—but believe me, they do. And your marriage is just not the same afterwards—no matter how good it may be—and why should it? I don't want this happening to us. Elizabeth's a good girl. The least flirtatious in the world. She's loyal and good. I want us to stay together. So she keeps me company when I work and I keep her company when she works. There it is."

In this particular movie, Richard's leading lady was Claire Bloom, who Elizabeth knew was once the great love of his life. Although thirteen years had passed since their affair, Elizabeth still felt possessive and jealous. "When I see a woman he knew before me, something happens to me inside," she admitted. "But I know intellectually that it's emotional and stupid and my problem." Still, she never let Richard out of her sight and was none too cordial to his leading lady.

"They were both rather aloof to me," recalled Claire Bloom. "In fact, in all the months' shooting in Ireland I was never asked to dinner by the Burtons."

Undismayed by the slight, the actress expressed no renewed interest in her former lover. "He hadn't changed at all," she said. "He was still drinking, he was still boasting, he was still late, he was still reciting the same poems and telling the same stories as when he was twenty-three. . . . He was interesting years ago, but now I found him rather boring."

Julie Andrews, his leading lady in *Camelot,* agreed. "He can entertain you nonstop for three weeks with his conversation, but in the fourth week he starts to repeat himself."

By 1965 Burton had finally broken into the list of the top ten box-office stars in America, joining Doris Day, Jack Lemmon, Rock Hudson, John Wayne, Cary Grant, Elvis Presley, Shirley MacLaine, Ann-Margaret, and Paul Newman. Elizabeth followed him as number eleven—a position he never let her forget. With the public still feeding on Le Scandale, the combination of both of them was unfailingly bankable at the box office.

"When I saw the lines around the block for *Night of the Iguana,* which was just Burton, I thought to myself, 'Imagine the lines around every block in every city in the world if Elizabeth Taylor and Richard Burton were to star together," recalled producer Ernest Lehman, concluding that they would be perfect for *Who's Afraid of Virginia Woolf?*

After scripting Edward Albee's lacerating play, Lehman sent the property to Elizabeh to read. He wanted her to play the part of Martha, the profane, jeering wife of a spineless college professor, George. "I saw a lot of Martha in her," admitted the producer, who had never forgotten the picture of Elizabeth Taylor howling at Mike Todd in the London airport. However, no one else agreed with Lehman at the time. In fact, his desire to cast Hollywood's reigning beauty as a fat, foul-mouthed slut was derided by everyone in the industry.

After reading the script, Elizabeth decided that the role of Martha was her Hamlet. She ached to play the part. She was even more determined after Richard told her she couldn't do it. "I don't think you're old enough to be Martha," he said. "And I'm sure you haven't the passion or power. But you'd better play it to stop anyone else from doing it and causing a sensation."

Elizabeth's agent had difficulty keeping from the producer and Warner Brothers just how much she wanted for the part. She demanded $1.1 million (the extra $100,000 in lieu of her customary fee for living expenses) and 10 percent of the gross, plus approval of the director, her co-star, and the cameraman, hairdresser, and costume designer. "She laughed uproariously when we caved in and gave her everything," said an executive, "because she would have done the part for free."

The story focused on the brutal interplay between a middle-aged couple and a younger faculty couple one drunken night in a New England college town. The language was raw and obscene, and the sexual scenes graphic. Yet it was through such searing coarseness that these four people revealed their awful truths. The producer cast George Segal as the ambitious biology professor saddled with a whiny little wife played by Sandy Dennis, a celebrated Broadway actress making her motion-picture debut. Casting the part of George, the mediocre college professor married to Martha, the castrating daughter of the college president, proved to be more difficult. Aware of their masculine screen images, Jack Lemmon and Glenn Ford turned down the role and Robert Redford refused even to discuss it. "I would not play that part for all the money in the world," he told the producer.

"What about Fatso here? Old What's-his-name?" said Elizabeth, jabbing Burton in the ribs.

"He's too strong to play George," said the producer.

"Well, luv, if you don't get who you want, I'll be there in the bull pen," Burton said.

Realizing that Richard's presence on the picture would be a steadying influence on Elizabeth, the producer wrote to Jack Warner suggesting that he be cast in the role. Warner agreed and paid him a flat fee of $750,000. Elizabeth gave her husband nothing, keeping her full percentage and her top billing.

"There was never any question about who the star was on the film," said a member of the company. "Elizabeth not only got all the money and a piece of the action, she also got the biggest and best dressing room. When Richard saw that it was better than his, he had a huge, ostentatious star painted on the door. Also, I remember that Elizabeth had eight hundred dollars' worth of champagne waiting in her dressing room, while Richard only got a twenty-two-dollar bottle of Scotch. George Segal and Sandy Dennis got something like a two-ninety-five bottle of Liebfraumilch."

After securing the part, Burton began to fret about playing

George. "I'm worried about doing the American accent," he said. "I don't know—the man is so weak, so overrun by that woman."

"Well, honey," said Elizabeth. "You were kind of *nebbish-shlemiel* in *The Sandpiper* too."

The producer flew to Paris to confer with the Burtons about the next step—the selection of a director.

"What about Fred Zinnemann?" he said.

"Terrific," said Elizabeth.

"I don't want Zimmerman," said Burton.

"It's Zinnemann, asshole. Not Zimmerman," said Elizabeth, slugging him.

"I don't care. I don't want him!"

Hours later the producer broached the subject of cinematographer, suggesting Haskell Wexler.

"God, no!" yelled Burton, who was painfully sensitive about his pockmarks. "He would make my face look like the craters of the moon."

Finally the Burtons selected their friend Mike Nichols as director—another unorthodox choice, since the thirty-four-year-old comedian, though successful as a director on Broadway, had never directed a movie. "But he was a good choice, because he was the only one who could handle them without getting swamped by their personalities and eaten alive," said the producer. "The Burtons were quite intimidating, and we needed a genius like Mike Nichols to combat them. He was the rage at the time, and having his name on the picture gave it more prestige and kept it from becoming a Richard-and-Elizabeth production. That was important because our reputations were on the line with this project."

After three intense weeks of rehearsal, shooting began in Hollywood. Elizabeth, who had gained twenty-five pounds to play Martha, was so skittish that she insisted on closing the set to everyone not·connected with the film. There was also a "No press" policy, and reporters were barred by armed guards.

On the first day of shooting the director received a call from

Jacqueline Kennedy wishing him good luck with the movie.
"Mike was dating Gloria Steinem at the time, but he seemed to
be very much in love with Jackie," said an executive. "In fact,
we later lost an entire day of shooting—twenty-four hours—just
so Mike could fly to New York to have lunch with Jackie."

As a director, Mike Nichols was painstakingly slow and demanding, especially of Elizabeth, who frequently exploded in
bursts of frustrated rage. "To direct an actress and to have to tell
her to do it again and again is to say that what she did wasn't
good enough," explained the producer. "Mike was especially
tough on her because he wanted the picture to be good and she
needed the most help. We were all under a lot of pressure, but
Elizabeth was really out on a limb. Everyone said she'd make a
fool of herself."

Even after Elizabeth ate herself up to 155 pounds, Nichols still
had to make her look like a forty-five-year-old woman. She tried
eight different makeups until she got the blowsy, disheveled look
he wanted.

"Everyone on the set stopped cold when she stepped in front
of the camera," said Irene Sharaff, the costume designer. "You
could almost feel a current between Liz and the lens. There was
a sizzle. She came through in another dimension."

Even Burton was awed. "God, how that lady comes through
the box!" he exclaimed. "Margaret Leighton is a much better
actress than Elizabeth, but nothing comes through the box with
her."

Ordinarily, Richard assumed a superior position to his wife
and tried to play down his adoration by describing her to reporters as nothing more than a short, fat peasant girl. "All this stuff
about Elizabeth being the most beautiful woman in the world is
absolute nonsense," he said. "She's pretty enough, and her eyes
are nice, but she has an insipid double chin, big feet, stumpy
legs, a potbelly, and she's as pouty-breasted as a pigeon."

"Those ungallant remarks he makes about Elizabeth are usually kidding," explained a friend, "or he is trying to play it cool."

Despite his comments about Elizabeth's looks, he never withheld his respect for her ability in front of the camera. "She has this something which makes her the biggest star in the world," he said. "The only star in cinema."

He was fascinated by his wife's stillness in front of the camera and her ability to minimize her actions. He studied her closely during the filming of *Virginia Woolf* and tried to follow suit by paring down his own exaggerated movements. "It was immensely challenging, but it was such agony," he said. "Playing everything down, down, holding myself in all the time. The tiniest gesture, the slightest word was crucial in characterizing. . . . I had to watch myself constantly. I really felt like a very tensed-up labyrinth."

While Burton concentrated on his film technique, Elizabeth spent hours troweling on makeup. "She suggested that the mascara should run in a certain way," the director said. "She suggested the black smudges under her eyes and said that's the way it looked when makeup is put on carelessly. She suggested a particular blouse to wear because she knew it would ride up and make her look middle-aged. She did it all without vanity, and I must say with great gusto that I was and am deeply impressed.

"She had painful things to do. She had to spit in Richard's face, take after take after take. He didn't mind, but she finally became very upset. On a piece like this something bad has to come out of everyone, but I'd say it came out of Elizabeth only once. It was anger."

While Elizabeth transformed herself into a hard, lewd, castrating wife, Richard slipped into character as the passive, repressed, henpecked husband. "I'm convinced that somewhere within this man is someone who wants to be lacerated," said the producer. "I remember when I first saw him in costume as George, I was bowled over. 'By God, Richard, you are George. You really are,' I said. And he replied, 'Of course I am, Ernie. Didn't you know that? I am George. George is me.' "

The shooting, scheduled for two months in 1965, dragged on from July to December. Elizabeth caused some of the production delay when she got a black eye from her nephew's popgun toy and could not work for several days. "We should have figured on something like that with her," said an executive. "Elizabeth's always been high risk on a film." The picture went way over budget, and nerves became extremely frayed as the corrosive material of *Virginia Woolf* affected everyone. Richard sniped at Mike Nichols behind his back, complaining that he was too slow, and Jack Warner agreed but did not want to criticize him for fear of upsetting Elizabeth. George Segal became temperamental. Sandy Dennis, pregnant at the time, lost her baby. The Burtons grew depressed and turned on each other as the savage script eroded their real-life marriage.

"We all got possessed by the picture," Mike Nichols said later. "The Burtons told me they talked about nothing else when they got home."

After battling each other in character during the day, Richard and Elizabeth could not shrug off Edward Albee's bitter story at night. People around them remember drunken evenings after work when he would call her "monkey nipples" and, still in her Martha suit, she would scream at him, "For Chrissakes, shut your fucking mouth! I'm not finished talking yet."

In the movie, Martha pummels George around the chest and lashes out at his eyes. He reacts by trying to choke her and then attempts to crack open her head on the side of a station wagon. Some of this violence toward each other on screen spilled over into their marriage, but most of it was already there.

"Elizabeth loves to fight," said the producer. "She was always ready. She was constantly hitting and punching Burton."

Elizabeth admitted as much, saying that on occasion Richard struck back, clouting her about the ear.

Though brutal on occasion, the Burtons also demonstrated real thoughtfulness at times. During the shooting someone threw a party for George Segal, whose wife was virtually ignored until Richard and Elizabeth rescued her. "The wife of an actor gets less attention than the waiter with the martini tray, and Segal's wife wound up standing around with nobody to talk to until the

Burtons realized what was up," recalled a guest. "I don't think they left Marian Segal's side for the rest of the night."

Drained by their work, Richard and Elizabeth did little socializing. An exception came in November, when they went to a party in honor of Princess Margaret and Lord Snowdon at Le Bistro in Los Angeles. Richard proceeded to get extremely drunk. Now accustomed to imperial treatment himself, he was infuriated to find that he and his wife were seated near the kitchen instead of at the head table. Later, when Judy Garland got up to entertain, she caught her shoe on her mike cord and had to be helped by her publicist. In a voice for all to hear, Richard said, "She's drunk again." Shortly afterward, he and Elizabeth walked out.

"I thought they would never leave!" exclaimed Joanne Woodward later, vowing never to speak to them again.

Richard recovered the next day and sent his apologies to the Princess for their abrupt departure. He explained that he and Elizabeth had had an early call on the set the next morning. Clearly, though, the pressure of playing George and Martha was getting to them. They never shook the parts they played in that movie, and Elizabeth especially went into and out of her harridan role when she was angry or drunk, bellowing profanities and hurling invective at her husband. They seemed to exchange sex roles, with Elizabeth calling him Harriet or Agatha and Richard referring to her as Sam or Fred. Many years later, explaining their divorce to a friend, she said, "I just got damn sick and tired of playing *Virginia Woolf*."

By the time the film was wrapped in January, everyone needed to celebrate. The Burtons hired an orchestra and had a huge party at their rented Bel Air mansion. They presented Mike Nichols with a pair of gold David Webb cuff links with two jade wolf heads. He gave them a silver-framed photograph of themselves between takes on the set. The picture showed Elizabeth fat and completely bedraggled as Martha, and Richard wearing baggy dungarees and his wife's wig—backward. Ernest Lehman received a rare book—a 1633 first edition of Francis Bacon. Elizabeth also gave the producer an autographed copy of her own book titled *Elizabeth Taylor.** Earlier she had received a pair of diamond-and-ruby earrings from Mike Nichols and had sent word to Jack Warner that she wanted an $80,000 diamond-and-ruby brooch to wear with them.

"I'm paying her a million one hundred thousand, plus ten percent of the gross," snarled Warner. "Let her buy her own brooch."

As a result, the executive producer did not receive a set of gold cuff links or a rare book from his star. He was not even presented with an autographed copy of *Elizabeth Taylor* by Elizabeth Taylor.

---

* Elizabeth was paid $250,000 to write her autobiography, which was 177 pages of edited tape recordings discussing her various husbands, sicknesses, and surgeries. There were also fifty-six photographs by Roddy McDowall. Published in 1964 by Harper & Row, the book bore the dedication: "To the Lady from Pismo Beach," which was Elizabeth's designation for the anonymous public matron "who reads that made-up stuff (about me) and believes it, wants to believe it, and is going to believe it regardless. . . ." Critics reviewed the book as "thin," "superficial," and "prattling."

CHAPTER 19

THE GRAND GESTURE WAS NOT FOREIGN TO ELIZABETH, who was renowned for her generosity. Some friends felt that she had reached her zenith with the adoption of Maria. Others wished she had not been quite so public about her goodness at the time. However, no one questioned the love and loyalty she showed to Montgomery Clift in the last two years of his life.

When Elizabeth saw Monty in New York in the spring of 1964, she was appalled. Sickly and malnourished, he weighed barely one hundred pounds. He had cataracts in both eyes, and his once-handsome face was ravaged by his addiction to drugs and alcohol. Worst of all was the fact that he had not worked in four years. Elizabeth was convinced that it was the professional inactivity that was killing him as much as his own self-destruction.

"If he doesn't work soon, he'll die," she told a friend.

As the top movie star in the world, she had her choice not only of scripts but of co-stars as well. She decided to save her friend by making a picture with him.

They always had wanted to do a comedy together, so they discussed *The Owl and the Pussycat* and read the parts out loud. But the producer balked, saying Monty was too big an insurance risk.

Later Elizabeth was approached to play the nymphomaniac lead in *Reflections in a Golden Eye,* a Southern gothic by Carson McCullers. She called Monty about the role of the latent-homosexual Army officer. She felt that his vocal hesitations and pecu- liar mannerisms were perfect for the part. He read the script and agreed to do it. Elizabeth persuaded John Huston to direct the film and then announced to the press that she and Monty were going to co-star for the first time since *Suddenly Last Summer* in 1959. But Ray Stark, the producer, again informed her that Monty was uninsurable.

Knowing how desperately her friend needed to work again, Elizabeth refused to drop the project. Instead, she offered to put up her $1-million fee as insurance for him.

"Miss Taylor was determined to have Monty in *Reflections* and to make another picture with an actor she admired greatly and loved as a friend," said his agent, Robbie Lantz. "Her im- mense devotion to him was not only responsible for the accep- tance of Clift by John Huston, but she also overcame certain insurance problems."

Elizabeth informed Warner Brothers and Seven Arts that if they wanted the film with her in it, they had better take Monty as well. They had no other choice. Still, Monty worried that they might renege.

"We've got 'em by the balls, baby," Elizabeth assured him every time he called, frightened that the deal might be off.

"I can't get a job," he confided to a friend, "but Elizabeth Taylor is the greatest friend. She keeps trying to help. Everybody else has deserted me."

Warner Brothers and Seven Arts kept postponing production on the film, because nobody believed that Montgomery Clift could act anymore and Elizabeth was preoccupied with the roles she had accepted in order to work with her husband. She flew to England to appear on stage with Richard Burton in *Doctor Faus- tus* at Oxford University and then to Rome to make *The Taming of the Shrew* with him. Monty kept calling her to get a firm starting date. Finally they were both informed that shooting on *Reflections* would begin in September 1966. But tragically, after two years of waiting, Montgomery Clift died of a heart attack in his bed on July 22, 1966, at the age of forty-five.

His naked body was found by his houseman, who immediately phoned close friends to spare them the shock of reading the news in the morning papers. Roddy McDowall called John Springer, the Burtons' publicist. He relayed the news to Richard, who said he would tell Elizabeth privately. The next day she told the press, "I am so shocked I can barely accept it. I loved him. He was my dearest friend. He was my brother."

From Europe, Elizabeth called Monty's houseman and spent a long time with him on the phone discussing the details of Monty's last day. Then she called Dr. Rex Kennamer, the Beverly Hills physician she had met the night of Monty's careening car accident in 1956 when she cradled the actor's bloody head in her arms. She relived details of that accident with Dr. Kennamer. She recalled how much Monty had loved her and how changed he had been the last time she had seen him from the Adonis she had known during *A Place in the Sun*. She talked about his death, telling the doctor she had known it was coming. She repeated what Roddy McDowall had said about Monty's friends' being unable to do anything for him except hold his hand to the grave.

The Burtons did not attend Monty's funeral in New York, but sent two huge bouquets of white chrysanthemums, which were placed near the closed coffin. Their card read: "REST, PERTURBED SPIRIT—ELIZABETH AND RICHARD."

Days later, Elizabeth announced that she was establishing a heart-disease research foundation in Monty's memory and endowing it with her $1-million fee from *Reflections in a Golden Eye*, the money she had pledged as insurance on her friend. The Montgomery Clift Foundation was to be administered by the American Heart Association. However, when the Heart Association later inquired about Elizabeth's reported philanthropy, her spokesman replied, "The contributions that she will make will be anonymous." After her public announcement, the Heart Association never received any money from Elizabeth Taylor in memory of her "dearest friend."

"As far as I know, it was only an idea, although announced in the press," said Montgomery Clift's biographer Patricia Bosworth. "[The foundation] never came to pass."

"This is where her vaunted generosity gets a little embarrassing," said a friend.

Elizabeth's publicized acts of charity did not always materialize, especially when actual cash donations were involved. "She's more inclined to make a personal appearance in behalf of a good cause or contribute her talent through the receipts of one of her movies to a fund-raiser than to give hard currency," said a friend, pointing to her numerous appearances in behalf of Israel. "But I'm afraid there's not much anonymous giving on Elizabeth's part. Although she says otherwise, she definitely wants credit for her generosity. It helps soften her public image."

Both Burtons boasted about their donations and frequently claimed that they contributed more than $1 million to charity every year. After Robert Kennedy's assassination in 1968, Elizabeth spent $50,000 for a full-page ad in *The New York Times* advocating gun control. Burton later bragged about his wife's philanthropy, saying that Elizabeth was single-handedly supporting the Biafran relief effort. She insisted that this generosity was not motivated in any way by tax deductions. "Donations give me such a warm glow in my private parts," she said, "so why worry about deductions?"

A great deal of their giving was directed toward British charities in the hope that Queen Elizabeth might close her eyes to their refusal to pay British taxes and bestow knighthood upon Richard. Despite the Burtons' contributions to Oxford University and their social courtship of Princess Margaret, Wales's most celebrated son never received more than the honorary title of Commander of the British Empire.

Through their lawyers and accountants the Burtons established trust funds for themselves and their children. They lavished upon their families first-class trips around the world to attend their movie premieres. Each of Richard's sisters and all their daughters wore Elizabeth's hand-me-down gowns to those events. Richard also presented his brothers and sisters with either houses or cars, plus annual checks.

"He was always talking about giving money away," said a member of the Burton entourage, "but I think he did more talking than giving. I still remember how astonished he was when Sybil gave up a fortune in alimony in 1965 to marry Jordan Christopher, a rock-and-roll musician twelve years younger than she was. Richard just couldn't believe it. Afterwards, he bought Elizabeth a house in England with the money that the remarriage had saved him. Elizabeth called it 'Sybil's Folly.'

"Both of them were generous, but Dick Hanley used to say that the closer you were to Elizabeth, the less you got. If you were totally unknown to her—someone she'd just bumped into —you'd probably get a mink coat or a really expensive piece of jewelry."

Mrs. Harvey Orkin, the wife of Richard's agent, recalled meeting Elizabeth for the first time and being offered a fur coat. "She said she had been given a beautiful mink with a hood but she had so many furs that she didn't need another one, and since I didn't have one she urged me to take it, and I wish I had. Then she offered to have Alexandre of Paris, her hairdresser, do my hair."

Rather than giving to organized charities, Elizabeth directed her generosity toward friends who needed medical treatment. When the wife of Richard's dresser, Mrs. Bob Wilson, became critically ill in Rome, Elizabeth insisted on the finest care available and arranged for her to be hospitalized in Harkness Pavilion at Columbia Presbyterian Hospital, where she paid for everything. She also purchased ten first-class seats on a commercial jetliner so that Mrs. Wilson could be flown from Italy to New York in as much comfort as possible.

"The quickest access to the Burton hearts is through misfortune," said the director Peter Glenville. "On the film *Becket* I had an assistant who was visited one day on the set by his wife and child. The boy had been a cripple since birth, and the doctors had pronounced the damage incurable. When Elizabeth, who as usual was on the set watching Richard's performance, noticed the child moving in the background, she asked why the youngster was limping. Quietly and secretly, she made a date with the mother and child in London for the next day. She took them straight to Oxford. One of England's finest surgeons subsequently performed an operation of great delicacy on the boy's leg, completely curing him. Elizabeth took care of everything and told no one. I found this out much later from the assistant.''

Yet this same woman who raised thousands of dollars for Israel, bestowed mink coats on mere acquaintances, and financed the costly surgery of friends also expected priceless gifts to prove her worth.

"She was always trying to get Ernie Lehman to buy her expensive presents," recalled an assistant on *Who's Afraid of Virginia Woolf?* "She'd show off the hunk of diamonds that Marty Ransohoff bought her during *The Sandpiper* and say, 'Oh, Ernie. Look what Marty gave me. Isn't he terrific?' She was enraged when Jack Warner refused to buy her the eighty-thousand-dollar brooch she wanted.''

By the time *Who's Afraid of Virginia Woolf?* was released in June of 1966, the film, at $7.5 million, was the most expensive black-and-white movie ever made. It was also the most shocking in terms of explicit language, violating nearly every section of the industry's thirty-six-year-old conduct guide. Hoping to avoid condemnation from the Catholic Church's rating board, Jack Warner told exhibitors that no one under eighteen could be admitted unless accompanied by an adult. He was astounded when the Catholics did not ask for one cut in the film. When they let stand the torrents of blasphemy as an example of tragic realism, Hollywood was catapulted into a new era.

"It means that we are finally accepting the same contemporary change in our films that we accept in our lives," said one executive.

Having beat the censors, the controversial film became a leading contender for the Academy Award. Elizabeth was hailed for "the finest performance of her career," and Mike Nichols was credited with getting the performance out of her. But it was Richard's riveting portrayal of the henpecked husband which was applauded as "a work that actors dedicated to their profession can use for a textbook.''

"What Elizabeth lacks is Burton's heroic calm," said *The Vil-*

lage Voice, "particularly in the all-too-rare quiet moments when she is supposed to be listening and reacting, moments that are the supreme test of acting. It is at those moments that a sullen coarseness invades her dulled features, and Burton simply soars by contrast, with inscrutable ironies flickering across his beautifully ravaged face. Without Burton the film would have been an intolerably cold experience."

Elizabeth and Richard were both nominated for Academy Awards, along with Mike Nichols, Sandy Dennis, Richard Sylbert for art direction, George James Hopkins for set decoration, Haskell Wexler for cinematography, and Irene Sharaff for costume design.

Excitement mounted for the Burtons as Elizabeth received the top acting award from the National Board of Review and Richard claimed the prize of the British Film Academy. Both received the Silver Masks of Italy as the year's Best Foreign Film Actors. Their final triumph would be to win the Academy Awards for Best Actress and Best Actor; but Richard knew that he didn't have a chance when Paul Scofield won the New York Film Critics' award for *A Man for All Seasons*.

"Burton really had tremendous competition from Scofield, whereas Liz was hardly threatened at all by Vanessa Redgrave [*Morgan*], Lynn Redgrave [*Georgy Girl*], Anouk Aimée [*A Man and a Woman*], and Ida Kaminska [*The Shop on Main Street*]," said a member of the Burton entourage.

"It was a foregone conclusion that Elizabeth would get the Oscar," recalled Ernest Lehman, "but not Richard. He gave the best performance of the year, probably of the decade, but he had too much opposition from Paul Scofield, who was favored."

By the time of the Awards ceremony in April 1967, the Burtons were in the south of France finishing *The Comedians,* their seventh film together and the only one in which Richard got top billing. Elizabeth, who had promised Jack Warner that she would attend the Oscar awards, was preparing to fly to Los Angeles when her husband said he did not want her to leave. She insisted on going, saying she had given her word.

"I've gone to those Award dinners four times," she said. "Won it once—for not dying. The only time I didn't go was when I was nominated for *Raintree County* and the dinner was just two weeks after Mike was killed. They didn't expect me to go. But most of the time you're supposed to, if you possibly can, whether you've got a chance of winning or not. It's for the industry."

Knowing how much she wanted to go, the Burton entourage encouraged her to make the trip. "There's no guarantee she'll win," said her irritated husband. "She could fly all that way and lose."

The next day Elizabeth told the entourage she had changed her mind about attending because Richard had awakened with a terrifying nightmare. "I was up all night," she said. "He dreamt the plane I was flying back to California in crashed—and he saw me dead. We've almost never been separated, and now he doesn't want me to go. He's my husband and I'm not going. . . . He gets into a terrible state when I'm away, especially when he gets tanked up. He just needs me. . . ."

She cabled Jack Warner her change in plans and within hours received a wire begging her to reconsider. "DO NOT BURN THE BRIDGES YOU HAVE BUILT," he pleaded.

"Piss on him," muttered Richard, who composed another telegram for Elizabeth, expressing profound regrets but explaining that she had promised to appear only if her husband would be free to accompany her. Since he was still shooting *The Comedians,* she said, she could not leave.

"The idea of Elizabeth being away from him for a few days was too much for Richard," explained John Springer. "Elizabeth said to me that the Academy Award was the most important thing in the world to her, next to her marriage—but she decided not to come."

"What she really wanted most, I think, was to have him win it and bring it back for him," said Dick Hanley.

Others felt that Richard could not bear the public humiliation of losing the Oscar himself and then watching his wife win, especially in front of 150 million television viewers. Unable to leave him, Elizabeth stayed in the South of France, where she received her congratulatory call. Only four actresses had ever won the Oscar twice, and Elizabeth was delighted to take her place alongside Luise Rainer, Olivia de Havilland, Vivien Leigh, and Ingrid Bergman. She expressed her delight when called, but then screamed profanities into the phone when told that Burton had lost to Paul Scofield, Mike Nichols to Fred Zinnemann, and *Virginia Woolf* to *A Man for All Seasons*.

In California, as Anne Bancroft walked to the stage to accept Elizabeth's Academy Award, Bob Hope quipped: "It must be nice to have enough talent just to send for one."

"Everybody was talking about it backstage," recalled Walter Matthau. "When the winners aren't present, it denigrates the whole thing, it cheapens it, it lessens the value, the drama, the excitement."

"Yes, everyone was disappointed that Elizabeth didn't show up," said Bob Hope, "but then again, leaving Richard alone on the French Riviera is like leaving Jackie Gleason locked in a delicatessen."

The prestige of winning that second Oscar did little to burnish Elizabeth's career. Professionally, she never again reached the heights of her performance in *Virginia Woolf,* and neither did Burton. After their flamboyant romp in *The Taming of the Shrew,* they filmed *Doctor Faustus* and were criticized by *The New York Times* for "an awfulness that bends the mind." Richard was accused of having "exchanged the gift of art for money," and Elizabeth was blistered for her melodramatic walk-on. "When she welcomes Burton to an eternity of damnation, her eyeballs and teeth are dripping pink in what seems to be a hellish combination of conjunctivitis and trench mouth," said *Time* magazine. "Mercifully mute throughout, she merely moves in and out of camera range, breasting the waves of candle smoke, dry-ice vapor and vulgarity that swirl through the sets."

For twenty years Elizabeth had been typecast as the most beautiful woman in the world, playing pretty-rich-girl roles for Metro-Goldwyn-Mayer. After *Virginia Woolf* she developed a new persona. With a raunchy laugh and *double-entendre* lines she became the cinema's quintessential shrew, cursing and castrating her way across the screen in a series of unsuccessful movies. "It was a rough stretch for Elizabeth Taylor with or without Richard Burton," said *Variety*. "The year that counted her *The Comedians, Reflections in a Golden Eye,* and *Boom!* had to subject this $1 million-a-year film star to some discount as box office insurance." She toppled from the list of the Top Ten Box Office Stars in 1968 and then tried to slash her way back in *Secret Ceremony,* a bizarre film that prompted Rex Reed to observe: "The disintegration of Elizabeth Taylor has been a very sad thing to stand by helplessly and watch, but something ghastly has happened over the course of her last four or five films. She has become a hideous parody of herself—a fat, sloppy, yelling, screeching banshee. . . ."

At first Elizabeth did not seem to comprehend her dwindling box-office appeal. She got an initial clue the day Hal Wallis came to lunch with the Burtons and talked to Richard about playing Henry VIII in *Anne of the Thousand Days*. She listened attentively as Wallis discussed the picture. Then, taking a deep breath, she said, "Hal, I've been thinking about it for weeks. I have to play Anne Boleyn!"

"My fork stopped halfway to my mouth," recalled the producer. "Anne Boleyn? Elizabeth was plump and middle-aged. Anne was a slip of a girl."

Burton turned to his wife and patted her hand. "Sorry, luv," he said. "You're too long in the tooth."

At the age of thirty-six, Elizabeth had to watch the extraordinary role go to an unknown young actress by the name of Geneviève Bujold, whose youthful beauty captivated her husband.

"Oh, God, was that a terrible time!" recalled a member of the entourage. "Elizabeth nearly berserked over that girl, especially when Richard nicknamed her 'Gin' and started telling reporters how terrific she was. The nickname was Elizabeth's proof of a love affair, because she knew that Richard nicknamed all his lovers. He called Tammy Grimes 'Shining'; Susan Strasberg was 'Baby Angel'; and during *Cleopatra* Elizabeth herself was 'Ocean.' So when Miss Bujold became 'Gin,' and Elizabeth was demoted to 'Tubby,' there was real hell to pay.''

Threatened and insecure, Elizabeth telephoned the set constantly, checking up on Richard. She sent her chauffeur out to find him whenever she suspected that he was with the young actress. Burton did not deny the rumors of a romantic involvement with his co-star. Instead, he indicated that his attraction to other women had nothing to do with his marriage.

''I might have some middle-aged catastrophe and fall in love with some pretty little blonde for five minutes,'' he said, ''but Elizabeth would be prepared for that, I think.''

Totally unprepared, his wife screamed at him, slugged him, and publicly threatened him every time he started toward his costar. ''Watch it, Buster, or you'll be singing soprano soon,'' she warned. The day Richard was scheduled to film the final scene of the picture, Elizabeth insisted on being present and swept onto the set with her entourage.

''I was afraid her presence, her jealousy, might affect Geneviève's performance,'' said the producer. But the twenty-seven-year-old actress was so enraged by Elizabeth's arrival that she flung herself into the scene, saying, ''I'm going to give that bitch an acting lesson she'll never forget.''

So spectacular was Geneviève Bujold's performance that she was nominated for the Academy Award and won Hollywood's Golden Globe as the best dramatic actress of the year. When she accepted the award, she again sent Elizabeth into spasms of rage. ''I owe my performance all to Richard Burton,'' she said. ''He was generous, kind, helpful, and witty. And generosity was the one great quality.''

''That one cost the bugger a boatload,'' laughed a friend. ''I think Richie had to apologize by giving Liz another whopping diamond or something.''

It is true that Burton's extramarital dalliances frequently cost him hundreds of thousands of dollars in gems, but he also enjoyed giving well-publicized jewels to his wife. "It made me feel good," he said. "A feeling of power—real power."

"He gave me fabulous gifts and all the world knew about them," Elizabeth said later. "But he also gave me other gifts for no apparent reason and asked me not to tell the press about them. And while he was giving me these gifts he looked at me in a certain way, as if he had to beg my pardon for some things he didn't tell me."

Burton made his spectacular purchase of the 33.19-carat Krupp diamond in 1968, the same year that Elizabeth began slipping at the box office. Taken alone the two incidents seemed unrelated, but when they are viewed in sequence there is a poignancy to the professional decline of the world's highest-paid movie star and the purchase of a $305,000 diamond for her. Such sensational jewelry commands attention for a woman and guarantees her a compelling spotlight.

The Krupp diamond was followed by the $37,000 La Peregrina pearl, to be worn on a $100,000 Oriental pearl, diamond, and ruby necklace; a 40-carat sapphire brooch surrounded by diamonds costing $65,000; rubies and diamonds worth $60,000; a heart-shaped diamond valued at $100,000; a rare pink 25-carat diamond in a 16.5-carat diamond setting; and—the crown of her collection—the 69.42-carat Cartier-Burton diamond that cost over $1,050,000.*

It was this diamond—one of the most expensive gems ever sold at auction—that Elizabeth craved. When she heard about it, she called Ward Landrigan, the head of Parke Bernet's jewelry department, demanding to know if it was the "finest stone available." Assured that it was, she cried: "I want it! I really want it! I'd even be willing to pay a million for it."

The Burtons' lawyer, Aaron Frosch, made arrangements to place their bid at the New York auction and fully expected to win

---

* The jewels that Richard bought were owned by Atlantic Programmes, one of several corporations formed by the Burtons, as a tax shelter. In fact, all their investments—gems, properties, and paintings —were officially listed as company assets.

the prize for his client, only to be outbid by Robert Kenmore of Cartier. When Frosch phoned the news to Elizabeth she burst into tears, prompting Burton to grab the phone and bark, "Get that frigging stone at all costs."

This sent Frosch into frantic negotiations with Kenmore, resulting in the end in the Burtons' paying more than $1 million for Elizabeth's 69.42-carat diamond. She also spent another $100,-000 for a diamond necklace on which to display the phenomenal gem—and insisted that a man fly from New York to Gstaad to measure her neck so that the famous diamond would cover her tracheotomy scar. As part of the sale she had to agree to let Cartier show the gem in its window. This display attracted thousands of people and prompted editorial outrage from *The New York Times:*

> The peasants have been lining up outside Cartier's this week to gawk at a diamond as big as the Ritz that costs well over a million dollars. It is destined to hang around the neck of Mrs. Richard Burton. As somebody said, it would have been nice to wear in the tumbril on the way to the guillotine.
> Actually, the inch-long, inch-thick Cartier diamond is a smart buy because it goes with everything. It won't clash with the smaller Krupp diamond already given by Mr. Burton as a modest gift to his wife. It won't seem out of place on the yacht parked in the Bahamas or the Mediterranean where Beautiful People spend much time, not to mention money, impressing each other.
> In this Age of Vulgarity marked by such minor matters as war and poverty, it gets harder every day to scale the heights of true vulgarity. But given some loose millions, it can be done—and worse, admired.

"I know I'm vulgar," said Elizabeth, "but would you have me any other way?"

Then she gleefully piled diamond rings on both hands, diamond bracelets on each arm, a diamond belt around her waist, diamond earrings on her ears, a diamond tiara on her head, and the dangling Cartier-Burton diamond on her décolletage. "Them that has 'em wears 'em," she said. No one knew better the value of costumes, sets, and scenery than Elizabeth—and sparkling under the weight of all her gems she felt more secure, more beautiful, more famous.

Seeing her so bejeweled, one reporter said she looked like the Wife of Bath after colliding with a Brink's truck. *Look* magazine called her "a fading movie queen who has much and wants more." Sheilah Graham wrote that she "looked like a woman who has made it rich and was wearing all her possessions on her ample back."

"She's full of crap," snorted Elizabeth.

That sentiment was properly toned down when she met Princess Margaret at a wedding and flashed her blinding 33.19-carat Krupp diamond.

"That's the most vulgar thing I've ever seen," said the Princess.

"Want to try it on?" asked Elizabeth.

"Oh, yes, please," said the Princess, putting the big zonking diamond on her finger and holding it up to the light to admire it.

"See, there," purred Elizabeth, "it's not so vulgar now, is it?"

Other friends were just as flabbergasted when they saw the mammoth jewel, which came from the estate of Vera Krupp, former wife of the convicted Nazi munitions magnate. "It can't be real," said one man. "It just can't."

"You bet your sweet ass it's real," said Elizabeth. "It's the Krupp diamond, and I think it's fitting and charming that a nice little Jewish girl like me has ended up with the Baron's rock."

"Richard benefited as much as Elizabeth from those jewels," said a friend. "With the Krupp diamond he got the pleasure of finally topping Mike Todd's 29.7-carat engagement ring. Elizabeth's mania about acquiring jewels was matched by his obsession with buying and publicizing them. Those behemoth gems allowed Richard to look like one of the richest men in the world, and that was more important to him than anything. In fact, he claimed that he outspent Aristotle Onassis. Both he and Elizabeth needed to impress the world with their wealth; but Richard, especially, needed to flaunt it."

By 1967 Burton was telling reporters that he and his wife were paid $1,250,000 each to star in a film, a bold increase from their usual $1-million fee. "We broke the sound barriers," he said. "The price of food is going up." "And diamonds, too," she said.

Later he announced that he had spent $192,000 for their yacht, the *Kalizma,* named after their three daughters Kate, Liza, and Maria*—adding that it had cost another $240,000 to refurbish. "The reason, you see, is Elizabeth and her extravagance. She spends a thousand dollars a minute," he said. Then he announced that he also had paid $1 million for a ten-passenger twin-jet with a kitchen, lounge, bar, and movie screen, which Elizabeth had named *The Elizabeth.* "I bought it so we could fly to Nice for lunch," he said.

Ostentatious and monarchical, the Burtons lived like potentates, buying and spending and reveling in their money. He announced paying $200,000 for two seats on the board of Harlech Television, and she reminded him of their $50,000 investment in a Paris boutique. He talked fervently about the $215,000 mink coat he had had designed for her from forty-two Kojah pelts, and she burbled on about the $120,000 Monet landscape she had bought for him.

"They say we generate more business activity than one of the small African nations," said Burton.

"And why not?" said his wife. "We get such pleasure out of spending money."

Still, Elizabeth claimed that she tried to budget herself, spending "only a hundred thousand dollars" on clothes every year. She added hastily, "That's not including jewelry, of course."

"Elizabeth wears a dress only once—just once," said Evan Richards, the owner of Tiziani of Rome, which designed most of her wardrobe. "This pink dress is to be thrown away; five or six hundred dollars' worth of ermine are on this cape." Not liking the fourteen little pearl buttons that he had put on the cape, Elizabeth summoned him from Rome to Paris and insisted that

---

* Richard did not mention his younger daughter, Jessica. Born mentally retarded, she never spoke and lived for years in a home for the mentally handicapped in Pennsylvania.

he remove them, cover them with pink velvet, and sew them back on.

"Sometimes I might feel that all the hand sewing, the little refinements, aren't worth it, but Elizabeth would be the first to notice if they were missing," said the designer. "She once asked me if the lining of a dress was real silk."

Such "little refinements" were important to a woman who once had more than three hundred diamonds sewn on the bodice of her evening dress just so she would not have "cheap rhinestone shine" under klieg lights. Another time she took her Pekingese dog to a Hollywood hairdresser and commissioned a wig so she could look exactly like her favorite puppy.

She thought nothing of spending $960 every six months to replace the Super Peerless Wilton carpet on the yacht *Kalizma* which the dogs had soiled.

"Les chiens pissaient partout!" screamed the French mate hired to clean up after her pets. ("The dogs were pissing everywhere!")

Elizabeth Taylor and her incontinent animals became well known to the finest hotels in Europe. At the Plaza Athénée in Paris a concierge said, "When she leaves, the carpets have to be taken up after her dogs have used them."

Her puppies were so important to her that in 1968 she and Richard chartered a yacht in London and moored it in the Thames to house the animals, which were under British quarantine and not allowed into the country.

"Yes, luv, we did spend twenty-one thousand six hundred dollars a month to keep the dogs on board," said Burton, "but what else could we do? Elizabeth wouldn't be separated from her pets!"

With money no object, she indulged every whim in deluxe style whether it was ordering a dozen $250 Dior nightgowns or a $150 bottle of Lafite-Rothschild for lunch. Food was a primary passion that could be satisfied only with the very best cuisine. Depending on her mood, that might mean flying chili from Chasen's in Los Angeles to Paris or London or Rome.

Aghast and unbelieving, reporters stretched for superlatives to describe the hedonistic Burtons and their excessive life-style, but Elizabeth enjoyed the extravagant image and helped cultivate it on occasion. In describing one of her houses, she said, "It's such a cozy, sweet place with bits and pieces around—bits and pieces of Renoir—and, you know, things that make it homey."

She took great pride in her art collection, which included "bits and pieces" of Picasso, Utrillo, Degas, Rouault, Monet, Pissarro, Renoir, Mary Cassatt, Modigliani, Vlaminck, Van Gogh, Frans Hals, and Andy Warhol. But after spending hundreds of thousands of dollars to buy these precious art works, she was not above economizing when it came to insuring them.

"I remember when the premiums started skyrocketing," recalled the children's tutor. "Rather than pay the insurance, Elizabeth started storing the paintings in the chalet in Gstaad. One day when the Burtons were in Paris and the kids and I were in Switzerland, we saw two armored trucks drive up. I had to sign for the contents, and I couldn't believe it: there I was with about a million and a half dollars' worth of art. Dick Hanley just told me to stick them all in the garage."

Traveling was a monumental undertaking for the Burtons that required the assistance of several retainers. They were accorded privileged entry into all foreign countries and waved through Customs after airline officials greeted their planes, then ushered them out of the first-class section, into VIP lounges for champagne, and on to waiting limousines. Hotel concierges and bellmen snapped to attention when the heralded couple arrived with their 156 suitcases, four children, one governess, three male secretaries in mink battle jackets, one hairdresser, one nurse, four dogs, a turtle, and two Siamese cats with diamond-studded collars. Rex Harrison once watched aghast as they swept into the lobby of the Lancaster Hotel. "Why do you suppose the Burtons have to be so filthily ostentatious?" he muttered.

"I remember when they visited Sicily for the Taormina Film Festival," recalled Fred Hift, a former film publicist. "They sent two advance men ahead of them to check out the hotel and make sure everything was suitable. The fact that the Burtons were actually going to be at The Principia had everyone in the hotel in a dither. Maids scrubbed and scoured around the clock to prepare for their arrival.

"When the advance men arrived, they stormed around inspecting everything in the eight-room apartment suite reserved for the two gods. Then they summoned the proprietor and all the employees to the lobby, where they started screaming at them, saying, 'We are disgusted with the way you have prepared for this visit. Don't you understand that Elizabeth Taylor is coming to this hotel and that she must have nothing but the very best?' "

Living like monarchs, the Burtons were isolated from the real world. Few friends could break through the barrier of bodyguards, lawyers, secretaries, servants, chauffeurs, and press agents that protected them. Rarely did they fraternize with their co-stars. With the exception of a few of Richard's Welsh drinking pals like Stanley Baker, Hugh Griffith, John Morgan, and Emlyn Williams, they socialized only in the exclusive moneyed circles of Baron and Baroness Guy de Rothschild, Princess Elizabeth of Yugoslavia, and Princess Grace and Prince Rainier of Monaco.

Like royalty, they were always accorded their special privileges. Producers reconstructed sets in Paris and Rome just so they would not be separated from each other. Both insisted on filming in foreign countries to avoid heavy taxation, so hundreds of dollars were spent to accommodate them. On location they were indulged with sumptuous dressing rooms for themselves and their entourage, fresh flowers, food, liquor, and long lunches, which frequently cost thousands of dollars in delayed production time.

Hal Wallis recalled lunching with them on the set of *The Taming of the Shrew* and eating off porcelain plates, drinking from the finest Venetian crystal, and being served the best food from the most expensive restaurant in Italy.

"Lunch dragged on and on," he said. "Hundreds of extras waited while the stars languished at the table in full costume. . . . Perspiring assistant directors appeared at fifteen-minute intervals to inform the players that they were required for the scene. The group laughed and ate and drank and paid no attention to them. I was embarrassed at their self-indulgence and lack of discipline.''

As indolent as the Burtons appeared, both felt the insecurity of trying to hold on to their international fame. Elizabeth claimed that she could give it up with fewer regrets than Richard, and told him so. "She wonders if I could get along without being famous," he said. "I mean living that sort of life. . . . I think I would be bloody angry if I were not treated absolutely first class. The best table and all that. It would take a little reorganizing of my mind, I suppose.''

Driven to hold on to his phenomenal status, Burton felt a sense of urgency to make as much money as possible as fast as possible. Consequently, he refused to stop working, but Elizabeth finally did quit. After filming *The Only Game in Town,* another cinematic bust, she retired for two years because there were no more million-dollar offers coming her way.

CHAPTER 20

THE CATACLYSMIC FIGHTS BETWEEN THE BURTONS shook the walls and sent the animals and the entourage scurrying for cover. When Richard's volcanic temper erupted, Elizabeth's piercing shrieks threatened to shatter the windows. Then came the physical blows. "I used to belt him a lot, and he hated it," she confided. "Finally he belted me one back, and my eardrum did not function correctly for some time."

These violent brawls were usually triggered by her lateness or his taunting her about being a pseudo Jew. "Elizabeth doesn't have a drop of Jewish blood in her," said Burton. "I've told her so. Makes her furious. I tell her, 'You're not Jewish at all.' She turns white with rage."

The worst fights started over his drinking or his other women. One occurred when he forgot her name and introduced her as someone else. "I have the most appalling memory for names," he said afterward. "When I said, 'This is my wife, er, Phyllis,' that meant she didn't speak to me for four weeks because she wanted to know who Phyllis was."

Ordinarily it was Burton who didn't speak, storming off to his own bedroom and locking the door so Elizabeth could not enter. He had always insisted on separate bedrooms for this reason. In Puerto Vallarta he had a bridge built between their two properties so that he could get away from his wife. Yet she refused to be left alone and would stand outside his door for hours, pounding and screaming and swearing until he let her in.

After their fights, they made up with demonstrative affection followed by public embraces and exhibitionistic statements to the press, each participant proclaiming undying love for the other.

"Terrible fights we have," Elizabeth told United Press International. "Sometimes they're in public and we hear whispers of 'That marriage won't last long.' But we know better. Once we're cuddled up in bed it will all be forgotten."

Richard enjoyed telling reporters that his wife had once called him to say, "It's absolutely extraordinary when you are away. I wandered round the bedroom last night and found a pair of your socks the dogs had been chewing, and I mooned over them."

"I was very flattered," Burton reported. "I told everyone that Elizabeth goes to bed with my socks when she is on her own."

"The truth is we live out for the benefit of the mob the sort of idiocies they've come to expect," he told the *Daily Mirror*. "We will often pitch a battle purely for the exercise. I will accuse her of being ugly. She will accuse me of being a talentless son-of-a bitch, and this sort of frightens people. . . . I love arguing with Elizabeth, except when she is in the nude. What I am saying is that it is quite impossible to take an argument seriously with Elizabeth naked, flailing around in front of you. . . . She throws her figure around so vigorously she positively bruises herself."

Some of the friction between them stemmed from Richard's need to assert himself. When Elizabeth finished her role in *The Comedians,* she sent the director, Peter Glenville, to Richard's dressing room to tell him to join her and the cast for a drink.

"Mabel thinks because she's through with the film, the film's over," Burton responded. "But I'm not through with the film. I'm going to see these people for two more weeks. Why should I go to a goodbye party? You tell Mabel Burton that!"

Minutes later Elizabeth strode into the room. "It's my last day, luv," she said. "I have to go."

"All right, luv. You go. Without me."

"But it's just common courtesy for you to come!"

"Be courteous on your own time, Mabel!"

Sensing that he had lost the Academy Award for *Who's Afraid of Virginia Woolf?*, Richard was in no frame of mind to humor his wife, who he knew was going to win.

"Yes, there is a tiny bit of rivalry there," admitted their friend John Gielgud. "I would suspect that he knows what a marvelously good film actress she is, and I think she rather longs to act on the stage. And he certainly, I feel, longs to act on the stage to show that he acts better than she does."*

Losing that Oscar always nagged Burton. He was bitterly aware of his wife's two Academy Awards and wanted desperately to win one of his own. "I want the Oscar," he admitted. "I've won all kinds of little Oscars but not the big one."

Richard also envied Elizabeth's higher salaries. "All I know is that if Liz asks for a million dollars for a film, then I demand a million plus ten," he insisted. "I've always believed that a husband should have a larger pay packet than his wife."

Sometimes they teased each other about who would get top billing, although in the end it always went to Elizabeth. During *The Taming of the Shrew* Richard accidentally got top billing in one of the original ads and gleefully posted it with a note to his wife: *"Dear Snapshot: I couldn't help it. Honest. They just insisted that the money should come first. Your ever-loving leading man, Richard (First Billing) Burton."*

Elizabeth laughed and then had a gag ad reproduced with huge letters proclaiming: "ELIZABETH TAYLOR, ACADEMY AWARD WINNING ACTRESS, IN *THE TAMING OF THE SHREW* . . . and introducing richard burton."

Elizabeth liked to point out to people that she had been signed before her husband for *Virginia Woolf*. He countered that she had only a walk-on in *Doctor Faustus*. Later the lighthearted

* The competition between the Burtons was obvious to everyone who ever worked with them. British actress Margaret Rutherford, who co-starred with them in *The V.I.P.s*, recalled: "It's no secret that they both can act beautifully. But at times it became a 'who-is-the-better?' contest. Elizabeth would play a scene to the very hilt and make it the zenith of perfection. Richard would come along and try to top it with his own brand of dynamism. They would then ask someone to select the winner."

bantering turned into nasty one-upmanship. During the filming of *Hammersmith Is Out*, Richard made an effort to entertain Beau Bridges' little boy by turning to his one-eyed Pekingese, E'en So, and causing the animal to roll over three times with commands in Welsh. The child was enchanted with the puppy's performance and laughed and clapped his hands. "I could make it do that too," Elizabeth shouted across the set, "if I could speak Welsh."

Later, during a scene between Elizabeth and Bridges, Richard made a move in the wrong direction. "For God's sake, Richard," she screamed. "Not that way. You're throwing shadows on Beau and me." Burton took the lashing, according to one bystander, "with the docility of a tranquilized lion." He simply continued drinking.

In the beginning of the marriage, Elizabeth kept up with Richard drink for drink. The drinking then was fun, sociable, entertaining; and the voluble Burton entertained and educated his wife. She was his best audience. "He is the ocean," she said. "He is the sunset. . . . He is such a vast person."

Occasionally, though, when the drinking got out of hand, she tried to pull Richard away from the bar before he sank into one of his black depressions. She never succeeded if there were other people with full glasses who wanted to listen to his articulate Welsh monologue. She dreaded those "death moods," as she called them, knowing that if Richard gulped down more than two quarts of vodka, he might turn from a charming raconteur into a churlish nuisance. It had happened so many times before. At a formal dinner party in London he drank all evening and then sprang on the guest of honor. "You bore me!" he snarled.

"We've got to get Richard out," Elizabeth told the hostess. "He's been ghastly. Did you hear what he said?"

Before they could wheel Burton out the door, he drunkenly lambasted the hostess for inviting them in the first place. "You're a cunt," he said. "I hate all this fucking privilege—all these people going round saying you sit here and so on."

The next day Elizabeth sent flowers and insisted that Richard go and apologize in person for his behavior.

"Okay, Tubby, I guess I overdid it again, didn't I?" he said contritely.

"I'll say you did, Boozy."

Elizabeth usually coped well with her husband's alcoholic binges. "I think you'd better take a nap, old shoot," she would often say. "You're drunk again. I mean—the hair of the dog was the whole hound this time." Burton would growl good-naturedly and stumble off to bed. But in public she had greater difficulty with him. One night in Beverly Hills he became so sodden that he turned on her and in front of everyone referred to her as "Elizabeth the Fat."

"I've had enough of this and I've had enough of this drunk!" she screamed. "I'm leaving."

She streaked for the Burtons' rented limousine and raced to the Beverly Hills Hotel. Richard stumbled to their suite minutes later, but Elizabeth would not let him in.

"You're not coming in here!" she shouted. "I don't want to sleep with a drunk. Go up to the desk. They'll give you a room."

"The hell with you!" roared Burton, nearly breaking down the door. "I'm sleeping in this bungalow tonight."

Elizabeth left and had the chauffeur drive her to the home of Edith Goetz. Arriving at three in the morning, she said, "He's drunk and I'm fed up. Let him sleep alone."

The next day she headed for the Polo Lounge in the Beverly Hills Hotel and found Richard drinking with a friend. She marched to his table and smashed a hand in his face, nearly knocking him off the chair.

Later she accused her husband of being an alcoholic. He said he wasn't. She bet him that he could not go without a drink for three months.

"Of course I can," he said.

"All right. Start—now."

Richard accepted the dare. He went on the wagon, and Elizabeth automatically cut down on her own drinking. She refused, though, to completely give up her doubles of Jack Daniel's.

"Why should I?" she said. "Drinking has never been a problem with me. No one has ever had to roll me home from a pub. Why should I quit because he has? I think it's admirable that he has been so good about it, but every time I order a drink he gives me the fish eye. First thing I know I'll be sneaking them like Ray Milland in *Lost Weekend*."

Burton was convinced that Elizabeth's drinking was as much a problem as his own, but she claimed that she simply had tried to keep up with him, to stay in the mood. However, when he stopped she continued, and so did their fights.

Performing without liquor was difficult for Richard. He told Lucille Ball that he was extremely nervous during the Burtons' television appearance on *I Love Lucy*. "This is the first time I've worked without a drink since I was sixteen years old," he said.

Socializing was even harder, especially with Elizabeth drinking. Richard would glare at his wife morosely throughout the evening and then grab her hard by the arm. "Come on, luv. You had better leave before I have to carry you home."

Elizabeth became incensed and their fights escalated. "He was so priggish it was absurd," she said. "If I had so much as a single bourbon before dinner he'd say, 'My God, the smell of whiskey on your breath is disgusting.' "

While sober, Richard smoked four packs of cigarettes a day. His nerves bristled and his hands shook. He seemed to have less patience than usual, especially with his wife's many ailments. He despised sickness of any kind, shook with fright at the sight of a hypodermic needle, and never quite accepted Elizabeth's illnesses as real.

"I remember when we were in Paris shooting *The Sandpiper* and Liz was not feeling well," said Mike Mindlin, recalling a time when Richard was still drinking. "She was in her dressing room, and when I walked in she had a fever and was whimpering in real pain. I ran into Richard's dressing room and said, 'Elizabeth is really sick.'

" 'Fuck it,' he said.

" 'Richard, it's your wife and she's really ill. You'd better go in there and help her.'

" 'How dare she interrupt me in the middle of a story!'

"When he finally finished telling the story I got him to leave, but he refused to help Liz to the car and he ignored her on the way to the hotel. He did not express one little bit of sympathy or concern. So I called a doctor to meet us at the hotel, but Richard insisted on waiting for him in the lobby so he could continue drinking. He was so unkind to her."

The mainstay of Elizabeth's conversations was her physical ailments. She tended to repeat her melodramatic medical history over and over: "When my eye was almost gouged out . . . when I choked on my phlegm . . . when I almost died four times . . . when they nearly amputated my leg . . . when my back was fused . . ."

"I think that kind of stuff was a lot easier for Richard to tolerate when he was boxed," said a friend. "He absolutely detested any kind of physical frailty. So imagine what it was like for him sober."

Knowing his aversion to illness, Elizabeth always claimed that she hadn't been sick a single day since falling in love with him. But she actually continued to catch colds, get the flu, and go into and out of hospitals for back traction and surgery, including two operations for hemorrhoids and another, a hysterectomy, which emotionally traumatized her.

"I would give up everything I have," she said. "I would even live in a shack—if I could just give Richard a baby." No longer able to conceive, Elizabeth began making public announcements about her plan to adopt another child. First she said she wanted a Jewish child; then an African child; then a Vietnamese child. Burton was not so sanguine about his wife's plans. "To adopt a child requires more thought and more preparation than the probable accident of conception," he said. "We have the money to indulge ourselves with pets, but we can take no risk at all with a child that is going to bear our name."

The general subject of children was not a good one to broach with Burton at the time, as he was having considerable difficulties with fifteen-year-old Michael Wilding, Jr. "Let's face it," he said. "Our son is a hippie. His hair lies on his shoulders and we can't keep him in school. I tell Elizabeth that we should do either one of two things—ignore him or kick the living daylights out of him. It bothers Elizabeth too, but she goes around sermonizing, 'He has the right to wear his hair any length he wants; it's his right as an individual.' We argue all the time about it, and amazingly, the only one who sides with me is Mike Wilding, Michael's father. He approves of my taking stern measures."

Bouncing around the world, the Burtons continued to leave the care and discipline of their children to others. Young Michael ambled into and out of various boarding schools until he finally was asked to leave Millfield, the most expensive preparatory school in England. The Burtons sent him to live with Elizabeth's brother, Howard, in Hawaii, and there he met Beth Clutter. In 1970, to cap a romance that had included a trip to the Middle East, Michael and Beth decided to marry. Michael was seventeen. Beth was nineteen.

Burton was furious upon hearing this news. Michael had no high school diploma, no job, and no professional training. But Elizabeth was delighted and said that a wife might settle him down. She insisted that the young couple be married at Caxton Hall in London, where she had married Michael's father in 1952.

"I think that was the event that caused Richard to fall off the wagon," said a friend. "He must have needed a few stiff ones to stand up as best man for a boy who wore a maroon velvet caftan and had hair as long as a girl."

In front of hundreds of photographers, Elizabeth walked by her son's side wearing a white ensemble. The bride, also wearing white, was almost ignored at her own wedding: HERE COMES THE MOTHER OF THE GROOM! proclaimed the next day's headline. Elizabeth arranged a champagne reception for the couple in the Dorchester and treated them to the hotel's honeymoon suite. Later she gave them a Jaguar, plus a hefty check "to get started on," while Richard presented them with a $70,000 house in London.

Weeks later Beth Wilding announced her pregnancy. "I

wanted the baby," she said, "but Michael didn't know if he did. He didn't know what he wanted. I didn't know what to do. . . . I turned to Elizabeth and she spoke to me like a mother. She told me how happy she was that I was pregnant. She made me feel as though she were right there, holding my hand. She reassured me that everything would turn out well and to go ahead and have the child. She said she would always be there to help me whenever I needed her."

For the next nine months Elizabeth showered her daughter-in-law with gifts, including a stunning diamond ring. "She enjoyed giving me things, and she was very generous. She would have some designer send over part of a collection of clothes, and she would choose outfits for herself and for me, or occasionally she let me choose. She bought me some beautiful things, many of them frilly chiffon-type gowns."

Beth Wilding gave birth to her daughter, Leyla, while the Burtons were vacationing on their yacht in Monte Carlo. They immediately flew to London to be with her. Elizabeth arrived at the airport wearing huge gold hoop earrings, a pair of white lace hot pants, a low-cut white lace top, and white boots with white lace eyelet decorations sewn up to the knee.

"I'm so excited," she told reporters. "I can't get over it—this is the baby Richard and I could never have."

"It's true," said Burton. "We've been thinking about adopting another child for some time now."

"Hey, Liz," yelled a reporter. "How's it feel to be a granny?"

"You know, everybody assumes that this whole thing would upset me. That's silly. If you want to be honest, I feared turning thirty more than I fear being called Grandma."

The next day's newspapers proclaimed the thirty-nine-year-old beauty the world's most glamorous grandmother. But Elizabeth secretly considered herself more of a surrogate mother.*

---

* Richard felt the same way about the child that Sybil gave birth to after marrying Jordan Christopher. "It's an awful male thing," he said, "and I know female lib will hate me for it, but in some extraordinary way I consider the child mine."

"When Leyla was born, Elizabeth was so happy," recalled her daughter-in-law. "She would buy the baby Christian Dior clothes, and she even had fun taking baths with her. She paid a lot of attention to Leyla then."

To keep the baby close to her, Elizabeth insisted that Michael Wilding, Jr., be hired as a photographer's assistant on her film *Zee & Co.* But he did not like getting up early in the morning to work, and quit. Still, Elizabeth kept supporting him and his new family. But she refused to subsidize the street people he began bringing home. Michael decided to vacate the $70,000 house, leave London, and head for the rugged hills of western Wales to start a commune.

"I really don't want any part of my mother's life," he announced. "It seems just as fantastic to me as it must appear to everyone else. I just don't dig all those diamonds and things. I suppose I've always rebelled against it."

Elizabeth pleaded with him to change his mind, but he refused to listen. He packed his wife and baby, three mattresses, a color television set, and $40,000 worth of electronic equipment, including speakers, drum, and guitars, and left for Pnterwyd, a barren village in the Welsh mountains.

Richard Burton did not think kindly of his stepson's abandoning his life in London for a meager existence in Wales. "I made it up and the boy's trying to make it down," he said. "I try not to interfere, but I still get goddamned mad. When I think what it took to climb out!"

Beth Wilding's life at the commune included cooking and cleaning for six other people, plus taking care of her baby. After several weeks, she left Michael and went with Leyla to live with the Burtons in the Dorchester. "I had a bedroom that I think was Liza's or Maria's room," she said. "At one point Elizabeth got me a job in Italy as an assistant to a photographer, and she took Leyla to Switzerland with her for a while."

Beth Wilding lost her job with the photographer and felt even more insecure. Rejected by her young husband, she was overwhelmed by the grandiose life-style of the Burtons and the possessiveness of her famous mother-in-law toward her baby daughter. Feeling frightened and alone, she returned home to Portland, Oregon, and began divorce proceedings. At this point, Elizabeth withdrew all her financial support and demanded that Beth bring the baby to her for regular visits and family reunions.

"Because I was trying to start a new life for myself here in Oregon, I didn't want to go—and turned her down," she said. "Then Elizabeth cursed me and shouted, 'Beth, nobody tells me whether I can see my own grandchild!' But when she realized I meant what I said—that I would not change my mind—she blurted, 'I'll never help you again.'

"Elizabeth is very possessive and she's used to having her own way," said her former daughter-in-law. "It seems that if she wants something, she wants it now. Leyla was like a new toy, a new amusement to her. She didn't want to let go. I don't think she's often told that she can't have her way. When I said, 'No, you can't have her, I'm going to keep her, Leyla is the only thing I've got,' it upset Elizabeth. She wanted Leyla to be where she could say, 'Well, I want her this week.' But I wanted Leyla with me."

Poor as she was, Beth Wilding did not want her daughter to be brought up as her father had been. "It wouldn't be good for her to have all the material things she wanted and so little real family life," she said. "Elizabeth was away so much that instead of a parent it was always a nanny, a secretary, or a chauffeur doing things for Michael. He dropped out of school at fifteen and lived on what Elizabeth gave him. . . ."

Placing her other children in boarding schools, Elizabeth spent the next two years living as Richard's camp follower. She accompanied him on locations for *Sujetska* and *The Assassination of Trotsky,* moving with their vast entourage from hotel suite to hotel suite. In January of 1972 the Burtons headed for the presidential suite of the Inter-Continental Hotel in Budapest, Hungary, where Richard began work on *Bluebeard* with eight beautiful women, including Raquel Welch, Virna Lisi, Nathalie

Delon, and Joey Heatherton. Elizabeth accompanied her husband to the set every day. In her spare time she planned three separate parties to celebrate her fortieth birthday.

"Nothing like them had been seen in Budapest since Emperor Franz Josef's last Hungarian wingding before World War I," said *Bluebeard* director Edward Dmytryk. "And it created more stir than the revolution of 1956."

The proletarian atmosphere of Communist Hungary was hardly suitable to Elizabeth's taste, so she telephoned Larry Barcher, the designer who had decorated Vicki Teal's Paris boutique. "I flipped when she called me in Paris," he said. "I was broke at the time, and although she never paid me for my work, she did give me a lovely piece of jewelry afterwards—a twenty-five-hundred-dollar medallion from Van Cleef and Arpels. All my tickets were taken care of, and cars met me, and I immediately became part of the family. I brought three thousand gold balloons from Paris and had access to everything at the film studio, including flowers."

Elizabeth telegraphed two hundred invitations around the world, saying:

WE WOULD LOVE YOU TO COME TO BUDAPEST AS OUR GUEST FOR THE WEEKEND OF 26 AND 27 FEBRUARY TO HELP ME CELEBRATE MY BIG 40 BIRTHDAY STOP THE HOTEL IS VERY HILTON BUT THERE ARE SOME FUN PLACES TO GO STOP DRESS SLACKS FOR SATURDAY NIGHT IN SOME DARK CELLAR AND SOMETHING GAY AND PRETTY FOR SUNDAY NIGHT STOP DARK GLASSES FOR HANGOVERS IN BETWEEN STOP LOTS OF LOVE ELIZABETH & RICHARD STOP P.S. COULD YOU RSVP AS SOON AS POSSIBLE TO INTERCONTINENTAL HOTEL BUDAPEST SO I KNOW HOW MANY ROOMS TO BOOK.

"After all the telegrams were sent, Richard wanted another one to go out saying 'NO GIFTS,' " recalled the designer. "He felt it was not nice of Elizabeth to have a party for herself and ask for gifts. 'But I invited [the jeweler] Gianni Bulgari,' she wailed. Actually, the only additional telegrams she sent were to Richard's beautiful co-stars. She came to me with the guest list and said, 'Oh, Larry. It's getting so crowded. I think I will just have to disinvite the broads.' She sent them each a telegram 'disinviting' them, but a few, like Raquel Welch, showed up anyway.''

Elizabeth instructed the designer to redecorate some of the hotel suites for the more important guests, such as Princess Grace. She even arranged for him to visit various homes throughout Budapest to borrow the antiques and paintings he would need.

"We can't move out of our suite because it would take weeks to get my things out of there, so make a royal one for Grace," said Elizabeth. "Make it pretty enough for a Princess, Larry, but remember that she's just like us."

People like Ringo Starr, Michael Caine, David Niven, Susannah York, Joseph Losey, Alexandre the hairdresser, Victor Spinetti, Stephen Spender, and seven ambassadors arrived in Budapest for the celebration. To appease the reporters and photographers, Richard Burton held a press conference and announced his birthday gift: a $50,000 heart-shaped diamond inscribed with a promise of everlasting love.

"I would have liked to buy the Taj Mahal for Elizabeth," he said, "but it would have cost too much to transport it."

Richard posed for photographers with the jewel on his forehead. For the rest of the press conference, the precious stone hung around the neck of a seven-year-old Hungarian boy who had walked into the room.

Such a capitalistic exhibition in socialist Budapest caused resentment in the Hungarian news media and aroused some of the Burtons' young friends. Michael Wilding, Jr., refused to attend his mother's birthday party, and Emlyn Williams' son criticized Elizabeth for her opulent self-indulgence. "You mean to say the Hungarian Revolution means nothing to you?" he said, describing her as "a beautiful doughnut covered in diamonds and paint." Elizabeth burst into tears, and Burton immediately announced that whatever he and his wife spent on her birthday party would be matched by a contribution to the United Nations Children's

Fund. "Elizabeth and I do this sort of thing to square our own consciences," he said.*

Richard, who was still abstaining from alcohol, managed to get through the birthday celebration sipping only soda water. But soon after the occasion, he received news that his brother Ivor had died. Months before, when the two brothers were in Switzerland together, Ivor had broken his neck in a fall. He had spent the remainder of his life completely paralyzed.

"Richard regarded this brother as a father figure," said Edward Dmytryk, "and he was deeply affected. He took a few days off to attend the funeral in Wales. When he returned, he had left the wagon behind somewhere in the Welsh countryside."

Drinking now to blot out bleakness and rage, Richard rarely drew a sober breath.

To repay the Burtons for their birthday-party invitation, the British Ambassador and Mrs. Derek Dodson honored them with a dinner party on their eighth wedding anniversary, inviting the Swiss Ambassador and his wife; Edward and Jean Dmytryk; Joey Heatherton; and a U.S. Embassy attaché and his wife. All remember that Richard's drinking ruined the evening for everyone, turning the party into a shocking replay of *Who's Afraid of Virginia Woolf?*

"It was so awful," recalled the attaché's wife. "It felt like a week, not just a night. Richard got roaring drunk and made an ass out of himself by insulting everyone, including Elizabeth. They fought each other back and forth. . . . Oh, it was terrible!"

Richard arrived at the Ambassador's residence and demanded a drink from the butler. He was served an aperitif from a silver tray. "I don't want any of that crap," he said. "I want a drink. Where's the liquor?"

Elizabeth grabbed the arm of the embassy attaché. "Please help me," she said. "I don't know what to do."

---

* On July 8, 1972, Richard Burton presented a check for $45,000 to Peter Ustinov, a roving ambassador for UNICEF, saying, "All I had to do with it was to make the stake by giving a party in Budapest and saying that whatever I paid for the party she [Elizabeth] would have to give to UNICEF."

Richard passed the cocktail hour drinking and reciting the poetry of Dylan Thomas for the Dodsons' teen-age daughter. Everyone was enthralled listening to his melodious voice fill the room, but when he sat down to dinner he ignored the specially prepared quail and continued drinking. He put his hand on the thigh of the attaché's wife, sitting next to him, and in a loud stage whisper said, "Aren't you thrilled to be meeting me, luv?"

"Not drunk," she replied.

"You know, you would be quite spectacular in the movies."

"Really?"

"I'd say it again if I wouldn't choke on it," he hissed.

"He kept saying how much he hated being an actor and how demeaning it was," recalled his dinner partner. "He almost seemed to hate himself."

Without warning, Richard turned to the embassy attaché and said, "You don't look like an American diplomat. You look like a Greek ambassador."

The attaché bridled but, feeling protective of Elizabeth, sitting next to him, he said nothing. The Swiss Ambassador's wife tittered nervously and, by doing so, became the next victim.

"You remind me quite distinctly of a hungry vulture," Burton said to her. "You Swiss are a bad lot."

"Richard!" cried Elizabeth.

"If you can't find anything nice to say about anyone at this table, I'm afraid the evening will be quite dreary for you," said the hostess.

"Quite so," said Burton, who then belched loudly and left.

Humiliated by her husband's drunken performance, Elizabeth apologized to everyone and tried to make amends by remaining at the party and chatting brightly. "She put on a grand front," said one guest. "She talked to all of us and was quite open about herself. I remember she asked me about raising children, saying, 'How do you do it?' She said her son had just gone into a commune and she didn't know what to do. She talked a lot about antiques and Lalique crystal, of which she apparently has quite a collection. Later she told us that she was the first person in her family to ever get divorced and how humiliating it was for her, but she said she just couldn't stay married to Nicky Hilton because he beat her up so much."

The next day the British Ambassador and his wife received a huge bouquet of flowers and an apologetic phone call from Burton, who invited them and their daughter to the set to watch him work. Mercifully, the invitation was not extended for the next night—because the Dodsons would have been subjected to more of the same. Richard, who was supposed to be shooting late on the streets of Budapest, arrived on the set drunk, took Nathalie Delon by the arm, shoved her into his Rolls, and drove off.

"That was the beginning of a long nightmare," recalled the director. "Burton was often drunk when he arrived at the studio in the morning and always drunk when he left in the afternoon. . . . But the leading ladies—Miss Lisi excepted—were still falling in love with him, and when Elizabeth left Budapest he was reciprocating their affections."

Informed by her entourage of what was going on, Elizabeth stopped accompanying Richard to the set every day and appeared only when he was scheduled to do his love scenes. "If anyone had reason to be jealous, it was me over that *Bluebeard* film," she said later. "There was somebody who put too much passion into certain scenes. And moreover, she was naked. I smacked her face for her pains—and Richard! Well, I don't know how many plates I broke over his head. . . . What I couldn't stomach was that he seemed to like the excessive show of passion put on by that actress."

Elizabeth was on the set the day Richard was to play a love scene with Joey Heatherton, who later admitted how unnerved she had been by Mrs. Burton's presence. "I was supposed to be kissing him and looking into his eyes when I was kissing him," she said. "Elizabeth was so close to the camera I was looking into her eyes instead of his! She was very nice and smiled at me, but it was a nervous time."

It was a loathsome time for Elizabeth, who could no longer control her husband's drinking or keep him exclusively to herself. Desperate and depressed, she stayed in the Inter-Continental Hotel, practically imprisoned by her entourage, while Burton continued courting his co-stars. Finally, in defiance, Elizabeth struck back by going out with the only man who could possibly make him jealous. She called Aristotle Onassis in Rome and arranged to meet him for dinner at the Hostaria Dell' Orso. The evening was ruined when police created an uproar by evicting twenty-seven paparazzi who stormed the restaurant to photograph Jacqueline Kennedy's husband and Richard Burton's wife dining with friends but without their spouses.

Elizabeth returned to the Grand Hotel alone, phoned her entourage in Budapest, and then at five in the morning called Richard. "Get that woman out of my bed!" she screamed.

Hours later on the set, when Burton told Edward Dmytryk about the phone call, he marveled at his wife's clairvoyance. "How did she know?" he asked. "How did she ever know?"

"You don't really know you're surrounded by agents?" asked the director in disbelief. "Why, you can't pick your nose without Liz finding out. You must know that."

Days later the Burtons' publicist announced that his famous but fading clients would be starring in a made-for-television movie created specially for them and appropriately titled *Divorce: His/Divorce: Hers*. This was their eleventh film together since *Cleopatra*—and their last. After it was shown in February of 1973, even they knew that their screen magic was gone.

"A matched pair of thudding disasters," said *Time*.

"A boring, tedious study of the crumbling marriage of two shallow people," said the *Hollywood Reporter*.

"Holds all the joy of standing by at an autopsy," said *Variety*.

Professionally, the Burtons had bottomed out, while personally, their life became even more strife-torn, anguished, and bleak. The dismal dismantling of their celebrated marriage followed a few months later.

CHAPTER 21

"BEFORE ELIZABETH, I HAD NO IDEA WHAT TOTAL LOVE WAS," said Richard Burton in June of 1973. "The only trouble is that when a woman like Elizabeth loves you she is not happy until she owns your soul. And me, I demand absolute loyalty. I demand obedience. I must have my own way. Our natures do not inspire domestic tranquillity."

Filled with rage toward her husband, Elizabeth flew to California by herself so that she would not inadvertently set off the detonator and blow their marriage to bits. In Beverly Hills she had dinner with old friends—Peter Lawford; Laurence Harvey and his wife, Paulene; Dr. Rex Kennamer; Roddy McDowall; George Barrie. They ate chili con carne, drank Stolichnaya vodka, and viewed *Night Watch*, the film that Elizabeth and Harvey had recently completed. Never during the evening did she mask her desperate unhappiness.

"Women have always surrendered to Richard Burton without condition, without so much as a bloody whimper," she said at one point. "Not me. He has no rights over me, none at all."

Yet when Burton called—days later—to say that he did not want to join her as planned, she immediately flew back East to stay with him in Quogue, Long Island, at the home of their attorney, Aaron Frosch. Fortified by a day's drinking, Richard met her at the airport in a chauffeured limousine. But by the time they reached their attorney's cottage he had told her to leave, to get as far away from him as she possibly could. In tears, Elizabeth obeyed, instructing the chauffeur to drive her to the Regency Hotel in New York. There she called her publicist and on July 4, 1973, made her own declaration of independence.

"I am convinced it would be a good and constructive idea if Richard and I are separated for a while," read her proclamation. "Maybe we loved each other too much—I never believed such a thing was possible. But we have been in each other's pockets constantly, never being apart but for matters of life and death, and I believe it has caused a temporary breakdown of communication. I believe with all my heart that the separation will ultimately bring us back to where we should be—and that's together. I think in a few days' time I shall return to California, because my mother is there, and I have old and true friends there too. Friends are there to help each other, aren't they? Isn't that what it's all supposed to be about? If anybody reads anything lascivious into that last statement, all I can say is it must be in the mind of the reader, not in mine or my friends' or my husband's. Wish us well during this difficult time. Pray for us."

Never before had a movie star issued such a public monograph of her personal distress; but then, Elizabeth Taylor knew that she was not simply any movie star. At forty-one, she was a legend whose beauty and notoriety had commanded worldwide attention for thirty years. She was such an international phenomenon that her pronouncement grabbed headlines across the world, sharing front pages with Nixon and Watergate. After delivering her statement, she flew to California on a private plane while reporters and photographers raced to Long Island to interview Richard Burton.

Sitting with a glass in one hand and a bottle of vodka in front of him, he held court for the press and seemed amused by his wife's melodramatic exodus.

"It was jolly well bound to happen," he said. "You know, when two very volatile people keep hacking constantly at each other with fierce oratory and then, occasionally, engage in a go of it with physical force . . . well, it's like I said: it's bound to happen. You can't keep clapping a couple of sticks together without expecting them to blow up.

"Perhaps my indifference to Elizabeth's personal problems triggered off this situation," he said. "I have only twenty-four hours a day. I read and write and film. Elizabeth is constantly seeking problems of one kind or another. She worries about her figure, about her family, about the color of her teeth. She expects that I drop everything to devote myself to these problems. I cannot. . . .

"Maybe it was something else. I don't know. Women are strange creatures. She is a splendid child, and I am very fond of the lady. But who knows what goes on in the feminine secret mind? I haven't spoken to her since her extraordinary statement. The frightful thing is I'm amused by all this. I find the situation wildly fascinating."

When one reporter asked him about the possibility of divorce, Burton no longer sounded so amused. "There is no question of our love and devotion to each other," he said. "I don't even consider Elizabeth and I are separated. . . . It is just that our private and professional interests are keeping us apart. I even have Elizabeth's passport in my possession. Does that look as if she has left me?"

The rest of the world wondered as well, but no one believed that the separation was permanent.

"They have been driven apart by the pressure of being the Burtons," said Peter Ustinov. "I think there will be a reconciliation."

"I can see that burly Welshman going down on his knees to beg her forgiveness with a sly glint in his eye," said Laurence Harvey. "Elizabeth, after listening to him and forgiving him, will go down on her knees in ecstasy—and they'll fall back into each other's arms."

"I was with the Burtons six weeks ago in Rome," said the director Franco Zeffirelli. "I could see then that Elizabeth was struggling to cope with Richard's increasing aggressiveness and his intolerance for the way she bossed him around. She's been used to bossing him right from the start of their relationship. I feel that Elizabeth has artificially created a disaster to test whether their feelings are still as strong as ever. She's trying to shock Richard into realizing how much he loves and needs her."

Terrified by the alcoholism now dominating his life, Burton finally consulted a New York internist and began a detoxification program to dry out. He was trying desperately to get in shape to film *The Voyage* with Sophia Loren in Rome. He called his co-star in Italy and asked if he might stay with her and her husband, Carlo Ponti, at their villa in Marino.

"He explained that he did not want to stay in a hotel, which I could understand because he would constantly be surrounded by paparazzi and find no peace," recalled Sophia Loren. "I told Richard we would be delighted to have him come and stay in the guesthouse."

Announcing that he had been on the wagon for two weeks, Burton left Rome on July 13 with a doctor, a nurse, a secretary, and two bodyguards. The next day his lawyer announced that all the difficulties between the Burtons had been resolved. He admitted that the reason for the separation had been Richard's drinking. "This has now ceased; he has not been drinking, and his intention is not to drink," the lawyer said. "Why, even the other night when we celebrated my forty-ninth birthday, he toasted me with a diet soda."

Reassured of her husband's sobriety, Elizabeth immediately made plans to meet him in Rome, where she was to film *The Driver's Seat*. She offered a betting tip to friends in California: "Get some money on us being together again, and make yourselves a bundle."

On July 20 Richard was waiting in a Rolls-Royce at Rome's Fiumicino airport when his wife stepped off the plane wearing blue jeans, an orange T-shirt, and her 69.42-carat diamond ring. Security guards escorted her through a maze of reporters and screaming photographers to Burton's limousine. Richard kissed her cheek gently, then nuzzled her neck and finally buried his head hard in her shoulder. The crowds applauded and Elizabeth wept as the chauffeur headed for the Ponti villa.

"They're very happy to be together again," announced their publicist. "They will have absolute privacy. There will be no phone calls, and they will make it clear that the separation was not serious but just one of those things."

Nine days later the reconciliation faltered. Elizabeth again left in tears, and both Burtons placed separate transatlantic phone calls to their lawyers to begin divorce proceedings. This time the publicist had a sadder message. "It is not much more than the story of two very intense people in a world of crisis," he said.

"I don't approve of divorce as a blank thing," declared Richard Burton, "but if two people are absolutely sick of each other or the sight of one another bores them, then they should get divorced or separated as soon as possible. That is certain. Otherwise life becomes intolerable—sort of waking morning after morning and having to have breakfast with the same miserable face."

This rejection was devastating to Elizabeth. While Richard remained secluded with Carlo Ponti and Sophia Loren, she moved into a seven-room suite in the Grand Hotel and tried to pull herself together to begin shooting. Hours passed before she was in any condition to show up on the set.

"Elizabeth arrived at five o'clock in the afternoon, after we'd waited all day for her," recalled the director. "With tears in her eyes she addressed fifty extras who'd been waiting to do a scene with her. She told them, 'Please forgive me, for I have had a very difficult day. I am not usually late.' Everyone knew what she was talking about, and they gave her a standing ovation. Then Elizabeth proceeded to work. She worked for three hours and proved herself the perfect actress, totally and completely dedicated to her work."

Earlier in the day she had called the producer and, choking back sobs, said, "It takes one day to die and another day to begin living again. I have had one sad day in my life and that was when Mike Todd, my husband, was killed. I never thought I would have another. I was wrong. Today is the second sad day in my life. I am desolate.''

Emotionally unstrung, Elizabeth needed to ventilate her anguish. She grabbed Andy Warhol, who had a cameo role in the film, sat him down at a glass table, and talked for hours without stopping.

"The whole time Liz was talking she was pulling leaves off a bush next to the table," recalled Bob Colacello, executive editor of *Interview*, Warhol's monthly tabloid. "One by one she plucked every leaf off that tree and then stacked them all in the middle of the glass table. It was such bizarre behavior. She kept telling Andy how much Richard Burton meant to her and how important it was to her to be married to him and how destroyed she was by the breakup. When she started getting really agitated, Andy looked nervous, so I went over to him, but Liz screamed at me, 'Get out of here! Just get the hell out of here!' So I backed off. Poor thing. She was truly devastated. I never saw her that way again. It was touch-and-go emotionally all day. She'd cry at a moment's notice."

Sick with her misery, Elizabeth remained in bed in her baroque suite, where, between bouts of hysteria, she talked openly to friends. "I don't want to be that much in love ever again," she said. "I don't want to give as much of myself. It hurts. I didn't reserve anything. I gave everything away . . . my soul, my being, everything. . . . And it got bruised and hurt. Like a snail, I guess, I'm retreating. . . . I know I can't retreat. That's why it's bad at the moment, because I'm retreating. In the beginning it was horrible. I wouldn't go out. I just sort of holed up in the hotel until I realized I was sick and it wasn't helping me to get over my personal agony."

A few days later, when Elizabeth forced herself to go out for lunch, she saw a friend from Puerto Vallarta and begged him to get Richard on the phone so she could hear his voice. Fighting tears, she pleaded, "Oh, please, please call him. He won't take calls from me, but from you he would. Please call him. Please." The friend refused to get involved, and Elizabeth, hysterical, had to be taken to her hotel. Watching her leave, Andy Warhol said, "Gee, she has everything—magic, money, beauty, intelligence. Why can't she be happy?" *

Aware of Elizabeth's tormented emotional state at the time was Henry Wynberg, the forty-year-old used-car salesman she had met through Peter Lawford weeks before in California. He immediately flew to Rome, registered at the Grand Hotel, and phoned to see how she was. She invited him to her suite for drinks. From that point on they were inseparable.

"Poor Elizabeth," he said. "She needs much comfort at this stage, and I am able to give it. She really needs me."

Unable to be alone any longer, Elizabeth began a very public love affair with the attractive Dutchman, clinging to him for comfort and security. They were photographed holding hands, dining, dancing, and kissing. "Let's just say that our friendship is a very friendly one," he told reporters.

"I'm in good Dutch hands," said Elizabeth as she continued working on *The Driver's Seat* with Henry accompanying her to and from the set every day. Afterward, they flew to Holland for his father's sixty-fifth birthday. In Amsterdam Elizabeth helped raise $184,000 at a benefit for the widows and orphans of Israelis killed in the Middle East war. Accompanied by Henry, who is half-Jewish, she bought a diamond collar for $2,400 and sold the pearl necklace she was wearing for $800. "The reason I am doing this Elizabeth Taylor stunt for war victims is that we have to care for those who are bereaved," she said. "I am clearly pro-Israeli, but even more pro-humanity." From the Netherlands she and Henry flew to London to visit Laurence Harvey, who was in the final stage of terminal cancer.

"I tried to show a cheerful interest in their arrival," recalled Paulene Harvey, "but . . ."

The actor's wife was apprehensive about Elizabeth's unex-

* After filming his walk-on part, Andy Warhol returned to New York. Days later he took Jacqueline Onassis and Lee Radziwill to the Brooklyn Museum to see a show of Egyptian art. "Jackie wanted to know all about Elizabeth Taylor," he said. "She kept asking, 'What is Elizabeth Taylor really like?'"

pected visit, as she knew how morbid and depressing her recent telephone calls had been. "Elizabeth's bedside manner remained brooding and dramatic," she said. "She went on and on about life and death. 'It seems to be her favorite subject after diamonds,' Larry growled to me after one of her calls. . . . 'I'm not well enough to talk to her anymore,' he said. I saw that his cheeks were wet. 'Next time she calls, tell her I'm not in.' "

Laurence Harvey found Elizabeth's self-absorption boastful and boring. "She is such a terrible downer," he told his wife, Paulene. "She has no humor in her. And I really have no desire to hear all about her damned distempers and nostrums and endless surgical adventures. Do you know she's had thirty-two operations in thirty years?"

"I think that's rather grand, don't you?" replied his wife.

"It's showing off," said Harvey.

Now here she was, uninvited and unannounced, demanding a drink and one last look at her beloved friend.

"Elizabeth drinks Jack Daniel's on the rocks," said Henry Wynberg. Paulene Harvey poured Elizabeth a bourbon, then urged her not to disturb her husband.

"I just want to *look* at him," Elizabeth said.

"He has trouble sleeping; please don't disturb him."

"I just want to *look* at him," Elizabeth said again.

When Mrs. Harvey left the room for a moment, Elizabeth slipped into the dying man's bedroom, climbed into his bed, and lay down beside him. She put her arms around his neck, sobbed, and told him she wanted to go with him. Although heavily sedated, Laurence Harvey was wide awake and weeping. Months before, he had been able to fight her off, saying, "We certainly live dramatically, you and I, Fat Ass. . . . The likes of you and me would be done for without a little torment in our life." But now, weighing barely 110 pounds, the actor had no strength left with which to resist her overwhelming commiserations. Three weeks later he died. Elizabeth, undergoing tests for abdominal pains at the University of California Medical Center, emerged from her suite to talk to reporters.

"He was one of the people I really loved in this world," she said. "He was part of the sun. For everyone who loved him the sun is a bit dimmer."

Elizabeth and Peter Lawford arranged an Episcopal memorial service in California for their friend—a gesture which puzzled everyone who knew that Laurence Harvey was a Lithuanian Jew. John Ireland delivered the eulogy as Elizabeth stood in the back of the church in a low-cut black velvet gown. She wept openly as she passed out small nosegays of violets.

"I still can't believe that I'll never see him again," she said. "I just can't believe it."

By this time Elizabeth had survived the deaths of Mike Todd, her third husband, in 1957; her best friend, Montgomery Clift, in 1966; her father, Francis Taylor, in 1968; her first husband, Nicky Hilton, in 1969; her beloved assistant Dick Hanley, in 1970;* Richard's brother Ivor, in 1972; and now her close friend Laurence Harvey in 1973. Feeling bereft, she returned to her room at the medical center, and after Henry Wynberg left, she called Richard Burton in Italy. She told him she did not want to live and die alone.

"Please," she begged. "Can I come back home?"

Burton, who had passed six miserable months indulging in what he called "cathartic infidelities," was pleased to hear her voice. "I had told her to go. 'Get out,' I said. 'Get out.' And to my astonishment she went. Time went by. Six months of torture, agony. And then the telephone rings. And there is this strange woman, very strong, very odd, very perverse, very curious, who says, 'Can I come back home?' or something like that. And I said, 'Oh, sure.' "

However much he wanted his wife back, he was still smarting over her public love affair with a used-car salesman nine years

---

* The death of Dick Hanley affected Elizabeth more than the death of her own father, for Hanley had been taking care of her and every aspect of her life since her marriage to Mike Todd. At the time of his death in California she paid for a lavish funeral and a wake that was held at the Beverly Hills Hotel. Her flowers, prominently displayed, carried a card saying, *"I will love you always—Elizabeth."*

his junior. He also refused to sit through another one of her elective surgeries. "I'll be happy to have my wife back," he told reporters. "I love her very much. But I can't desert the film I'm making here to be with her. And I'm not going to do any chasing."

The next day Elizabeth was operated on for a bleeding cyst, which Richard was relieved to hear was not malignant. "Thank God, it wasn't cancer," he told Sophia Loren. The following weekend he flew over the North Pole from Italy to California and walked into Elizabeth's hospital room. "Hello, Lumpy," he said. "How are you feeling?"

"Hi, Pockface," she smiled.

Burton then ordered Henry Wynberg out and told the nurses to bring in another bed so he could spend the night alongside his wife. The next day he pushed her out of the medical center in a wheelchair and headed for the airport to fly her to Naples for the holidays.

"Richard and I are back together again," said Elizabeth, "and it will be the happiest Christmas of my life."

"It took a little salesmanship, but I won her back and I know it will be for good this time," he said. "Both of us are very happy. The happiest we have ever been."

"I believe in Santa Claus again," said Elizabeth.

In London, the effigies of Richard Burton and Elizabeth Taylor which had been separated at Madame Tussaud's wax museum in July were put back together. "But not quite so close," admitted an official.

On the NBC-TV nightly news John Chancellor announced: "Elizabeth Taylor and Richard Burton are reconciling permanently—(pause)—as opposed to temporarily."

For Christmas Richard gave his wife a 38-carat cognac diamond and a painting of two naked lovers embracing. "Neither the painting nor Richard will ever leave me," Elizabeth said.

"Until Elisabetta came back, Richard was a man who was ready to die, a man killing himself," confided Vittorio De Sica, who was directing *The Voyage*. "He drank; he came onto the set shaking, in a daze. It broke my heart to see him, because he has pride and you knew he didn't want it to be that way. Then Elisabetta came and he was a changed man. Even if he betrays her, even if he goes with another woman, he has one and only one great love of his life—Elisabetta.''

The betrayals now cut both ways. Although Burton denied it, Elizabeth accused him of having had, as she phrased it, "a go with Sophia." She was aware of their weekend together on the *Kalizma*. She also knew that in one of their scenes Madame Ponti, as she snidely referred to Sophia, had cried real tears when she had to say, "I can't marry you or go away with you." To complicate matters, Richard was in the process of writing a warm tribute to his co-star for *Ladies' Home Journal*, something he had done in the past only for Elizabeth.

For public consumption, Burton wrote that Sophia was "as beautiful as erotic dreams. Cold as gold sometimes. Warm as fresh toast other times. . . . Adore her. She me. Platonically, of course."

Privately, though, he indicated otherwise.

"I was working on the film with him at the time," recalled Larry Barcher, "and I remember him moaning, 'What to do about these two women. Oh, what to do!' He tried to intimate to all of us that he was having a go with both of them."

Understandably, the relationship between Elizabeth Taylor and Sophia Loren was strained. They were cordial to each other, but just barely. Although both were renowned international beauties, they had nothing else in common except perhaps their phenomenal jewelry collections, although some rivalry was evident there as well. Sophia had once discussed Elizabeth's 69.42-carat diamond with *Photoplay* magazine. "The stone had been offered to Carlo before the Burtons bought it," she said. "He appraised it and decided that it was not worth the price. And I assure you, Carlo knows the value of jewelry."

Elizabeth refused to be insulted by the remark. She later told friends that she thought Sophia was "too piss-elegant for words." She said Sophia spent hours applying her makeup and never got her hair wet when swimming. Elizabeth's secretary, Raymond Vignale, pointed out that she had been clad in blue jeans, a T-shirt, and assorted gold chains when first introduced to the Italian movie queen. "That is the way she dressed to meet Sophia," he said. "Madame Ponti wore a Dior suit, matching handbag and shoes."

During her six months with Henry Wynberg, Elizabeth had affected a much more casual life-style. She not only wore blue jeans and T-shirts but, according to Larry Barcher, had also learned how to smoke grass. "Elizabeth had discovered marijuana, but she did not have any with her and she wanted some," he said. "We then called a well-known movie star to get some, but he said his was not good enough quality. He said if I would go to Milan, he would make a connection for us and I could take it back to Venice for Elizabeth. So I took a cab from Venice to Milan to get the stuff, but I was too late and arrived back empty-handed."

After filming in Italy, the Burtons flew to Puerto Vallarta and celebrated Elizabeth's forty-second birthday. Then she and the private nurse attending her since her surgery accompanied Richard to Oroville, California, where he began work with Lee Marvin in *The Klansman*. But by the time they arrived, Richard's new passion for his wife had again been overtaken by alcohol. He drank continuously and recklessly—including tumblers of vodka martinis before breakfast—and careened through the day with bloodshot eyes and trembling hands. Elizabeth was drinking as well, starting each day with a bottle of champagne, but by the time she got high he was insensate. As a result, they quarreled violently.

"A woman will try and dominate a man," she explained. "She will try and get away with it. But really, inside herself, she wants to be dominated. . . . She wants the man to take her. And she wants to lean on him—not have him lean on her. If he does lean on her, everything goes slightly off key, like a bad chord. She hopes it will pass, that the guy will come through. When it doesn't, she begins to needle him. If nothing happens, she goes on needling—until he stops listening. At that moment, she becomes bitter and he goes deaf. Finally, there is no more dialogue, they have no rapport.''

And that's the way it was in this gaudy marriage. The forty-eight-year-old husband, debauched and out of control, publicly humiliated his wife by presenting a ruby-and-diamond ring to an eighteen-year-old waitress amid rumors of their romantic involvement. "A sweet, lovely child," he said. "Reminds me of my oldest daughter, Kate." When he ordered the director to give the young woman a role in *The Klansman,* Elizabeth departed in rage. The real threat to her marriage, she finally realized, was not younger women but her husband's overwhelming love for his own pain.

"Richard was a terribly sick man," recalled the director, Terence Young. "When I saw how bad it was, I told everybody that we'd just better wind up the shooting. He was making a great effort, having to force his whole body just to get the words out. . . . I got a doctor down here and the man said, 'This man is dying. He'll be dead in three weeks.' ''

Immediately, Richard was taken by ambulance to St. John's Hospital in Santa Monica with a temperature of 104 degrees. Suffering from diseased kidneys, influenza, and tracheobronchitis, he was given emergency blood transfusions and placed in detoxification. Weeks later he emerged, heavily tranquilized. He walked by leaning on two bodyguards. His face, once described as "deliciously ravaged," was pale and haggard, and the white in his hair made him look pathetically old and feeble. He insisted that he did not have cirrhosis of the liver, but agreed that he should never drink again.

"I nearly killed myself," he said. "I can't go through the headaches, the shakes, and the terrible feeling of a hangover again. No more—ever. . . . I'm not an alcoholic, but I'm the kind of drinker who can't have one martini before lunch. Instead, I'll have thirty-two martinis and then I'll have seven bottles of wine during lunch and when the waiter brings the Rémy Martin I say, 'Just leave the bottle.' But that's all over now. Never again.''

That promise, made so many times before, no longer mattered to Elizabeth. Having instructed her attorney to file for divorce in Switzerland on the ground of irreconcilable differences, she was already back in the arms of her used-car salesman. Weeks later, on June 26, 1974, she left him for a few hours to walk into a wood-frame courthouse in the ski resort town of Saanen, near Gstaad, to divorce her fifth husband. He had sent a medical certificate from New York saying that illness prevented him from attending in person, much as Nicky Hilton had done twenty-six years before. Now, at the age of forty-two, Elizabeth, many times married and facing her fourth divorce, was more in control of her emotions than the first time she appeared in a domestic-relations court. Still, she had to use sunglasses to hide her tears.

"Is it true that to live with your husband was intolerable?" asked the judge.

"Yes," she said. "Life with Richard became intolerable."

"Why has the reconciliation period failed?"

"There were too many differences," she said. "I have tried . . . everything."

The judge was satisfied, and minutes later the divorce was granted.

CHAPTER 22

FRESHLY DIVORCED, ELIZABETH FLEW TO LOS ANGELES to go house-hunting with Henry Wynberg. One place they liked, in the Hollywood Hills, had Greek statues in the living room, an outdoor pool with fountains, and a patio filled with tropical flowers. Elizabeth, ever superstitious, suggested that they make love in the bedroom "to check out the vibes." The house was perfect, she concluded, except for the bedroom, which was too dark and depressing. She insisted that it be papered with silver metallic wallpaper so she and Henry could watch distorted images of themselves in bed. She also insisted that they sleep together in a double bed so she could have constant touching and reassurance.

"And then, because she need someone around to do all the other things for her, she call me," said Rudy Uribe, an urbane Latin who functioned as her majordomo. Since Dick Hanley's death, Elizabeth's entourage had been scaled down to Raymond Vignale, her French secretary from Gstaad, and Arthur Bruckel, her Beverly Hills hairdresser; but never having been without a keeper before, she needed someone there to run the house.

"Elizabeth, she say, 'Oh, Rudy, you must come live with me and do all the things I need,' and so I go. I moved in with her and Henry, and I cooked and cleaned and drove her everywhere in her Rolls-Royce and I prepared everything in the house for all her parties. Elizabeth say to me, 'Now, Rudy, you open the door for all my friends but if I don't want to see someone, you say that I'm in the bedroom sick and cannot be disturbed.' So I say okay and I only let in who Elizabeth wants to see."

Her regular visitors included Peter Lawford; Altovise and Sammy Davis, Jr.; Roddy McDowall; Dr. Rex Kennamer; Desi Arnaz, Jr.; Liza Minnelli; Olivia Hussey; and Max Lerner, who now was teaching at Pomona College. Lerner had not seen Elizabeth in thirteen years—since the end of their love affair in 1961—until he renewed contact that summer in Southern California. They visited regularly and spoke almost every day by phone. "We weren't in love then," he said. "Just very good friends."

The other visitors—the ones Elizabeth never knew about—were the young women whom Henry Wynberg entertained at nude swimming parties when she was away.

"I remember going to the house once—the one that Elizabeth was paying rent on and sharing with Henry—and finding three different girls there at the same time," said one man. "Two of the girls were waiting in an adjoining room for Henry to finish with the third."

"Henry would drive Elizabeth's Rolls-Royce around and pick up girls when she was away," said Don Crider, one of her hairdresser friends. "But we loved her so much we would never tell her about it."

The forty-year-old man Elizabeth had selected for her lover was attentive in her presence, but friends often heard him complain about the constant reassurance that she required. "Henry said that if he didn't tell Elizabeth five times a day that he loved her, she'd pout," said one business partner.

"With her friends Elizabeth needs to love and she needs to be constantly assured that she is loved," explained Max Lerner. Having always needed reassurance of her beauty and her importance, Elizabeth needed it more than ever after her divorce from Richard Burton. She wisely surrounded herself with people like Rudy Uribe and Don Crider who gave unstintingly of their time and attention.

"A lot of time Elizabeth say, 'Come to my bedroom and come in bed with me to watch TV Westerns,' " said Rudy. "I always stay with her watching the television so she would have company."

"We were always in bed with her," said Don Crider.

The constant attention from her claque took some of the pressure off Henry Wynberg, who could not sustain the emotional intensity that Elizabeth required. Still, she loved him enough in the beginning to unburden herself completely, telling him about her past sex life. She withheld nothing. In intimate detail she discussed all of her marriages, all of her divorces, and each of her affairs, including a brief fling with Frank Sinatra when she was young. Then, as she had done with every other man in her life except Mike Todd, she asked Henry to marry her. But unlike the others, this one turned her down.

Already divorced once, with a young son, Henry had no desire to marry again. His idea of a commitment was to live with Elizabeth. At her insistence, he bought matching gold friendship rings, which they wore for a time on their left hands. But marriage, he maintained, was out of the question. In fact, he claimed that when Elizabeth proposed to him he went to the bathroom and wrote a marriage certificate on a piece of toilet paper and pasted it on the mirror. "Most pieces of paper," he told her, "end up in the toilet bowl anyway."

Elizabeth pasted a toilet-paper comment of her own on the bathroom mirror. It asked him to legalize their relationship in front of a judge. "I've had enough troubles with judges," Henry replied. "I can make up my own certificate."

Some of Wynberg's troubles with judges stemmed from his arraignment in a California municipal court on four counts of grand theft involving the sale of used cars on which the odometers had been rolled back. He pleaded no contest. The judge later reduced the grand-theft charges to misdemeanors, fined Wynberg $1,000, and placed him on three years' probation. This highly publicized case was later followed by prosecution against him for "fondling" teen-age girls, plying them with liquor and drugs in his Beverly Hills home, and then taking photographs of a "sexual nature." *

Some of Elizabeth's friends voiced reservations about her involvement with this man. Many felt that he was an opportunist interested only in courting rich and famous women like Dewi Sukarno, Tina Turner, and the ex-wives of Dean Martin and Clint Eastwood. Yet no one could deny how radiantly happy Elizabeth looked when she was with him.

"The secret of Henry Wynberg was that he took care of everything," said Max Lerner. "Elizabeth told me, 'I love him, Max. I know that no one else likes him, but I don't care. He's good to me and he takes care of me. He fucks me beautifully, and I know he's not a big mind like you are, but he takes care of me, and that is what I need.' "

Across the ocean, Richard Burton agreed. "What she really needs," he said, "is me for entertainment and a nice little fellow to run errands for her—a sort of ménage à trois." Refusing to take Elizabeth's "nice little fellow" seriously, Burton professed not to know Henry Wynberg's name. He referred to him as "that Wiseberg chap" or "What's-his-name Winborger." Usually he dismissed him with "that awful used-car salesman." When told of Henry's reputed sexual endowments, Burton replied, "I'm sure that like the used cars he sells, it will fall off just at the psychological moment."

In Elizabeth's choice of a man eight years younger than Richard Burton and in perfect physical condition, there were strong overtones of revenge calculated to infuriate the Welsh actor, who struggled to appear unruffled. "He may be an interim bloke for all I know," Richard told reporters. "Elizabeth and I talk on the phone quite a lot. It's funny, but she never refers to him in any way."

The contempt was mutual. Wynberg, who genuinely believed

---

* Wynberg pleaded no contest to one of the counts against him. He was ordered to serve ninety days in the Los Angeles County jail and was later placed on probation. The other counts against him were dismissed.

he was now the love of Elizabeth's life, viewed Burton as a failure who had drowned his genius in alcohol. At the time, Henry Wynberg could afford to be confident. He knew he had Elizabeth's attention and affection. She cared about him and genuinely wanted to help him succeed. Together they formed a cosmetics company to market Elizabeth Taylor perfume. Henry negotiated a contract for Elizabeth to go into the diamond business. He profited from both arrangements. Later Elizabeth insisted that he accompany her to Leningrad and be hired as the still photographer on *The Blue Bird,* the first Soviet-American coproduction in film history. Recognizing the value of her presence, Henry frequently asked her to go with him on business trips. She never refused him. Even while suffering one of her frequent back spasms, she got out of bed to fly with him to San Clemente because a Japanese friend of his was going to interview Julie Nixon Eisenhower and wanted Elizabeth Taylor along for the ride.

"Given her condition, it was either foolish or heroic, perhaps a little of both," said Max Lerner. "But if she felt it important to give Wynberg that kind of support, he was also strong enough to exact it."

For a while Max Lerner might have been viewed as either foolish or heroic for having written a magazine article entitled "Elizabeth Taylor: Survivor." Although the piece was extremely loving, Elizabeth nearly tore him to shreds after reading it.

"She called me in a rage," he said years later. "I had written that she was a legend but that Marilyn Monroe was a myth— perhaps *the* American myth of a love goddess—and Elizabeth really let me have it for that. 'You goddamned son-of-a-bitch!' she screamed. 'You have a nerve saying that Marilyn was a myth and I'm just a lousy legend. . . . I'm much more beautiful than Marilyn Monroe ever was and I'm certainly a much better actress. What the hell do I have to do to be a myth? Die young and at my own hand?' "*

---

* Word of Marilyn Monroe's death at the age of thirty-six had reached Elizabeth in Europe on August 6, 1962. At the time she said she did not believe that it was· a suicide. She felt that Marilyn had accidentally

In his article Lerner theorized that Elizabeth lived her life swinging from strong men to weak men. He said the pattern had started with her first husband, Nicky Hilton, who, although young, had certain qualities of strength. He was replaced by the sweet but weak Michael Wilding, who was superseded by the bombastic strength of Mike Todd. Then came dear Eddie Fisher, who was vanquished by Richard Burton. Now, maintained Lerner, Elizabeth was in her weak-man phase with Henry Wynberg.

"Oh, bullshit!" she screamed. "You know, people are very wrong about Henry. They think of him as weak. He isn't. In some ways Richard was weaker than they thought, and Henry is strong."

The days with Henry Wynberg were spent beside the pool, sunning and eating and drinking. Nights of pleasure were sometimes heightened by the use of amyl nitrate, an antiangina drug which some people claim increases the impact of orgasm.

"Elizabeth had tremendous sexual fulfillment with Henry," said one of his business partners, "and a great deal of fun and games. I remember when they sent me off to buy one of those life-size rubber sex dolls with hair and all the anatomical parts— the kind you blow up and inflate. Liz wanted to put it in the guest bedroom so that the doctor visiting them would have something to play with at night. So I went to a sex shop in Santa Monica and bought a real cheap doll with a wide-open mouth, which I took back to the house. We blew it up, named it Marianne, and Henry photographed the ghastly thing in Elizabeth's bed. Later she put it in the doctor's bed, turned the lights down low, and told him that he was going to get full hospitality while staying with them. 'We provide all the services here you could ever want,' she joked. That night the guy walked into his room and nearly fainted when he found Marianne. Henry and Elizabeth were standing outside the door giggling. Later they said they took the doll to their bedroom and played with her themselves."

---

overdosed on sleeping pills. Elizabeth confided that it was something she herself could easily have done, since she was so accident-prone. She told Marilyn Monroe's publicist, "I was stunned. I thought it would have been me."

In California, Elizabeth began seeing more of her mother, Sara, who was living in Palm Desert. She visited old friends from MGM like Sidney Guilaroff and Helen Rose, and she entertained at dinner parties for people like George Cukor, Rock Hudson, Myrna Loy, and Marlon Brando.

"I remember once when Elizabeth call Chasen's to cook the dinner and I'm serving it in the kitchen," recalled Rudy Uribe. "All of a sudden I hear this voice. . . . So I run into the dining room and there is Elizabeth screeching and swearing and screaming. Suddenly she has become Martha from *Virginia Woolf*. She do that all the time and I tell her she scare me, but she such a great actress she no can help it. Even when she get out of bed in the morning she playact and pretend she is someone else. One morning she was Margaret Rutherford, and she talk just like her, too."

For an actress who lived the parts she played and played the parts she lived, the dividing line between fantasy and reality was not always clear, but Elizabeth seemed most comfortable when playacting. "She try to help Olivia Hussey all the time," recalled Rudy Uribe. "Elizabeth give Olivia lessons at the house and show her how to walk and talk and be best in front of a camera. Elizabeth knows everything about lights and movies and production."

Late one afternoon, as Uribe prepared a small dinner party for Marlon Brando, the actor called to ask what time he should arrive. "I tell him to come over now because Elizabeth and Henry are on their way home, but he won't listen to me. He say, 'You call me when Elizabeth gets there.' I tell him, 'But Mr. Brando, she's on her way right now.' Then Marlon Brando, he start laughing and he say, 'No, man. You don't understand. That woman has no conception of time. I remember once I invited her to dinner and she never showed up. She called me three days later from Rio and said she was on her way. So I'm not leaving here until I know she's there in the house.' "

Getting Elizabeth ready on time for her appointments was Rudy Uribe's biggest problem. "One time a lady come to the house to talk to Elizabeth about *The Blue Bird,* the movie she was going to do in Russia with George Cukor, the famous director. Elizabeth told me to give the lady a drink, so I do that. The lady waited sixty minutes for Elizabeth. I felt bad so I went to the bedroom and told Elizabeth, who was fixing herself, to hurry. Elizabeth said, 'Well, tell her to wait. If she wants me, she'll wait. Don't worry.' And it's true, too," he said adoringly. "Everyone, they will always wait for Elizabeth.

"The only thing that ever really made me nervous was the diamond—the big one. I cleaned it a lot for her and I always put it in its box. But one day Elizabeth screamed she cannot find the diamond. She said, 'Oh, I think I flushed it down the commode last night when I got drunk.' We called a plumber and then we looked in all the tropical fish tanks, because Elizabeth was always feeding her fish with that ring on, but the ring never showed up. So she finally told me to tell Raymond to call the bank and contact Aaron Frosch. We don't say Elizabeth was drunk and flushed it down the toilet. We just say that she can't find it. Then one day my friend Don Crider found the ring by the pool and he put it on his little finger and started to make Elizabeth a drink. At first she didn't see the ring, but then she saw it sparkle and started screaming, she was so happy. I told her she must be more careful because the worry over that jewel was making me an old man."

As sweet, easy, and sensual as the days with Henry Wynberg were, Richard Burton still cast his long shadow over Elizabeth's life, especially in October of 1974, when his engagement was announced to Princess Elizabeth of Yugoslavia. Days later Elizabeth suffered a crippling back spasm and was laid up in traction in her silver-papered bedroom. Her friends flocked to her side, worried about the twenty-pound weight pulling at her spine. No one doubted her pain, but all assumed that it was connected with the thirty-eight-year-old princess. Yet Elizabeth became indignant if anyone suggested a psychosomatic connection between her back pain and the new love in Richard Burton's life.

"I have a disintegrating vertebra!" she cried. "You can check the X rays. Just ask my doctor!"

When Max Lerner called later in the day, Elizabeth said, "Have you heard the news? Richard is marrying a princess."

"That's no news—he already had one," said Lerner gallantly. "Tell me about her. Do you like her?"

"She was one of my dearest friends," hissed Elizabeth.

"How long do you give the marriage—if they get married?"

"Oh, I hope forever."

"How will she feel when he starts wandering? Will she give a damn?"

"She'll give a damn," said Elizabeth. "She'll give a damn."

Gritting her teeth, she called her former husband in London to wish him and the second Elizabeth happiness, but she hung up feeling dejected. Burton told reporters, "She's fine. We're old friends."

Days later Elizabeth's spirits revived when she read an article that ridiculed the betrothal. "Listen to this," she crowed to a friend on the phone. " 'After being deposed by a queen, Burton is lucky to find a princess who would be bloody foolish enough to marry him.' "

The princess, who was separated but not divorced from her second husband, told reporters that Burton, a friend since 1968, had been proposing to her for three weeks—the first time at a centenary exhibition in London honoring Sir Winston Churchill. "He kept on and on and on, and I said yes. It was as simple as that."

Phone calls between Elizabeth and Richard became more frequent that fall. With the approach of Christmas, her mood toward him had softened enough for her to suggest that their adopted child, Maria, spend the holidays with him and his princess in Switzerland. She gave her brother, Howard, and his family the use of her chalet in Gstaad while she remained with her mother and Henry Wynberg in Los Angeles. She was joined there by Christopher Wilding and Liza Todd.

"I still remember the Christmas holidays," recalled Rudy Uribe. "For my birthday four days before, Elizabeth gave me a

beautiful French sweater. Raymond did all her shopping for her
and so he picked it out, but the card she wrote herself and it was
beautiful. Elizabeth said, 'I hope you are very happy and I hope
you spend every birthday with me. Love, Elizabeth.'

"But what I never forget is the Christmas present she gave me
and Liza Minnelli and Arthur Bruckel and Olivia Hussey and
Roddy McDowall and Raymond Vignale. It was a ring with gold
circles and a diamond initial. Richard had given her one, and
Elizabeth liked the design so much that she sent Raymond to Van
Cleef and Arpels in Beverly Hills to have it duplicated for all of
us."

During the weeks before Christmas, Elizabeth made a huge rag
doll for Liza from bits of lace and velvet and silver lamé brought
to her by Edith Head. Lovingly she sewed on long black yarn
curls and lavender sequins for the eyes. "It was such a beautiful
doll, and Liza was so excited because Elizabeth never did such
a thing before," recalled Rudy. "She put it on top of the piano
on Christmas day, and I told her that when I wrote my book I
would tell this story so everyone would know what a wonderful
mother she is; but Elizabeth say, 'No, I prefer to be a bitch in
the eyes of people and not a very good mother.' Then she scream
at me: 'What book?' and I tell her I was only kidding." *

Having accepted the lead in *The Blue Bird*, Maurice Maeterlinck's childhood fantasy, Elizabeth began dieting to get into
shape before leaving for Leningrad. During this time she stayed
in touch with Richard Burton and secretly hoped for a reconciliation.

After inviting several friends to Dean Martin's house for a

---

* Elizabeth started worrying about kiss-and-tell memoirs by former
employees, lovers, and friends when she heard that Eddie Fisher, after
declaring bankruptcy, had decided to write his autobiography. At that
point she instructed her attorney to send letters to various people telling
them not to talk without her permission. In 1980 when John Lee, a
former employee, decided to write about the years that he and Dick
Hanley had spent with Elizabeth, he received a letter from Aaron Frosch
saying that Elizabeth was the only person allowed to write about her
life. "Anyone else who does a book on her life will be sued for dam-
ages," he warned.

screening of *The Driver's Seat*—a strange, morbid psychological study of a woman going mad—Elizabeth pulled Lerner aside to talk to him about her secret desire.

"Come in here, Max," she said, motioning him into another room. "I don't want Henry to hear this. Let me tell you about Richard. He's still with that terrible princess, but I know he doesn't give a damn about her. I feel that we are destined for each other. I really do."

Lerner listened sympathetically as Elizabeth told him that she loved Burton more romantically and passionately than she had ever loved even Mike Todd and that she could not get him out of her system. "She really wanted to go back to him and reconcile and remarry," he said later. "My slogan at the time was to follow the organism, and so I told her that she should do what she really wanted to do. 'If it works, great,' I said. 'If not, it will come full circle and you'll know.' "

"I'm so glad you said that, because no one else supports me," she said.

A few nights later, Elizabeth and Henry were entertaining Henry's mother at their house when Elizabeth got up to leave in the middle of the party. "She was not feeling well," recalled Rudy Uribe. "Her teeth were paining her. She wanted to go to her bungalow at the Beverly Hills Hotel, where she had some pills. She told me to get Henry to drive her, but he wouldn't do it. He didn't want to leave the party. So I offered to take her, but she said she was going to spend the night there and be relaxed. Then she said, 'This is the moment I have finally decided to leave Henry, to not be serious with him, to not think of the future with him anymore. He's going to be sorry, because I'm going to go back to Richard. But first I need to make this film in Russia. I'll use him for that, but afterwards I'm leaving him and then I'll marry Richard.' " *

* So determined was Elizabeth to reconcile with her former husband that she refused to change anything in her will, including the clause stipulating that when she died she was to be buried alongside Richard Burton and placed next to his parents in the Jerusalem Chapel graveyard in Wales.

Elizabeth threw a farewell party in January of 1975 to celebrate her departure for Russia. "Hollywood's elite were present," recalled writer Gwen Davis. "Elizabeth entered her own party nearly an hour late. She was wearing brilliant green flowing chiffon, and her hair was strung with what seemed to be beads of light."

"Oh, it was all so beautiful!" exclaimed Rudy Uribe. "Elizabeth spent so much money on the decorations to have everything in lavender. There was five thousand dollars' worth of flowers—purple orchids in the dining room and violet orchids for the centerpiece and five-foot-tall lavender orchids all around the pool and lilac orchids in the living room. The tablecloths were lavender and the matches were purple and the napkins were violet. Everything went together in all different shades of lavender and pastel purple. All around the pool were white candles that sparkled like Elizabeth's diamonds. She had Japanese food and Japanese people to serve it. She also had special police there because of all the jewels. Henry Fonda and Edith Head and all the big stars were there."

Days later Elizabeth left California with Henry Wynberg; 2,800 pounds of luggage; her male secretary, Raymond; a maid; her hairdresser, Arthur Bruckel; two Shih Tzu dogs; and one Siamese cat. They headed first for her chalet in Gstaad. En route they got the news that Princess Elizabeth of Yugoslavia had found Richard Burton romping around Nice with Jeanne Bell, a young black woman who had been a *Playboy* centerfold model. The princess immediately broke their engagement and returned to London. "I didn't realize it takes more than a woman to make a man sober," she told friends. "I thought I could do it and failed."

Burton publicly claimed the engagement was still on, swearing that he had not had a drink since June of 1974—"except for an occasional glass of wine." Feeling remorseful, he chased back to London, begging his former fiancée to see him. She finally consented to a meeting but kept him waiting in the lounge of the Dorchester for two hours, during which time he drank so much that he required assistance in reaching her suite. There she told him, "I love you and I will do anything for you. I will be a friend, a mother, a wife, or a nurse. But darling, you are killing yourself by drinking so much."

Burton took the pledge once again and returned to Nice; but while the will was strong, the flesh was weak. He soon was back in the arms of the *Playboy* model, and his engagement to Princess Elizabeth was off.

Before leaving for Russia, Elizabeth called Max Lerner. "I don't know the intimate details," she said, "but I do believe their romance is over."

Days later Elizabeth woke up in Leningrad with a 104-degree temperature and a severe case of amebic dysentery. "They sent over some Russian doctors that looked like butchers to me in white hats, masks, and aprons," she recalled. "I was a little delirious anyway. I thought they were going to take me off to the slaughterhouse."

For the next six months Elizabeth battled the flu, colds, and Tsar's Tummy, losing eighteen pounds in the process and looking thinner and more beautiful than she had in years. "I've lost a ton of weight," she said, "but what a hell of a way to diet."

Nearly everyone on the film got sick. Ava Gardner refused to drink the water. Cicely Tyson was so nauseated that she ordered people around her not to smoke. Jane Fonda broke out in a rash. James Coco, who had spent thousands of dollars reducing for his role, gained twenty pounds because all he could eat was bread and butter. The illnesses caused one delay after another. Elizabeth was one of the few who did not threaten to quit. "I stand to lose two million dollars, so I'm not about to do that for anybody," she declared.

By this time the perquisites of her prima donna days were over. There was no $1 million fee—only a percentage of the picture if it succeeded. There was no $3,000 a week in expense money. In fact, she spent $8,000 of her own money on costumes for which she was never reimbursed. There was no mobile dressing room and no star on her dressing-room door. Instead, she shared a bathroom with Ava Gardner.

"It was not the most comfortable picture to make for someone accustomed to first cabin," said the producer, Paul Maslansky. "I was brought in to replace Ed Lewis when the picture had been suspended and the crew was in confusion. We salvaged the project only because Elizabeth was willing to come back from London and start work again. She was terrific."

From Russia, Elizabeth made secret phone calls to Burton, who was drying out in Switzerland and living with Jeanne Bell, his centerfold friend. Elizabeth always made sure that Henry Wynberg was not around when she placed her calls, and Richard never called her back for fear Wynberg might answer the phone.

"Elizabeth is phenomenal in the way she lives for now—in the present," said Paul Maslansky. "She never even alluded to Burton in front of Henry, but everyone in her entourage knew that Richard was the love of her life, and consequently they were deeply resentful of Henry. . . . But I think they were unnecessarily harsh, because Henry was quite useful to Elizabeth at the time. He helped soothe a lot of her hurtings."

Richard, meanwhile, was trying to meet her demand to give up drinking so that they could be reconciled. "We arranged it all in advance by phone," he said later. "Then Liz called and said she would be finished shooting two weeks early. And our plan went into action."

On August 10, 1975, Elizabeth tossed a party in Leningrad to celebrate completion of *The Blue Bird*—a film that months later failed dismally at the box office. That evening, in true movie-queen fashion, she gave every member of the crew a framed autographed picture of herself. Capping her evening was a telegram from Richard asking her to meet him in Switzerland to discuss business. Four days later she and Henry Wynberg flew to Geneva.

"I believe Henry had no idea of what was going to take place," recalled Peter Lawford. "It was a bombshell for him—and for me."

It was also a surprise for the Burtons' children, especially their fourteen-year-old adopted daughter, Maria, who was the first person to be informed of the planned reconciliation.

"For how long?" she asked.

"Forever," promised Richard.

The next day Elizabeth walked into her Swiss lawyer's office to meet her former husband. That night they met at a friend's villa for dinner. He arrived without his *Playboy* playmate, and she came without her used-car salesman.

"There they were—the master and his lady—standing together in the middle of the room," recalled one guest. "Mr. Burton looked at her and smiled, and she just fell into his arms, the tears streaming down her face. It was a moment so incredibly moving. All the months of pain and bitterness had disappeared in just a few hours."

He toasted her with orange juice, and she sipped a glass of milk. Caught up in their own melodrama, they both wept a bit. The next morning Jeanne Bell moved out of Richard's villa, Henry Wynberg flew to London, and the Burtons' publicist announced to the world that his famous clients were once again reunited.

CHAPTER 23

IT TOOK ELIZABETH APPROXIMATELY SIX WEEKS to persuade Richard Burton to remarry her. Rationally, he knew it was the worst thing he could possibly do to either of them, but emotionally he could not resist.

"I can't remember the exact words that said we would remarry," she said. "I think I brought it up and he shied away—sweetly. Then I dropped it. The next time it came up was in Johannesburg and he asked me. I asked for an old-fashioned proposal and he actually did it—with no doubt more than a little mirth. He got down on his knees! He said, 'Will you marry me?' I fell about with laughter and said, 'Sure, honey bunny.' I don't think he really meant it. . . ."

Approaching his fiftieth birthday and still not free of alcoholism, Richard felt depressed and gloomy. He mourned his passage from vital youth to shaky middle age. He tried to explain to Elizabeth that he was a very different man from the man she had married many years before. But she would not accept that fact. "I'm a hopeless romantic and want to be romantically swept away," she said. She wanted the passion and ecstasy of their early love, begging for a dramatic remarriage in Africa, the Dark Continent. "That's where I would like us to be married again," she said. "In the bush, amongst our kind."

Richard, aware of how volatile their relationship was, sug-

318 • ELIZABETH TAYLOR

gested that they merely live together. But Elizabeth pushed and pleaded for marriage. In a note that she publicized, she said: *"Fear and doubt. Will marriage spoil our confident love, make us overconfident and smug and taking for granted all the lovely awareness again. . . . I love you, Richard, and I leave it up to you. Please answer."*

Burton's response: *"As always, the answer is yes, if that's what you want. . . . I could elaborate endlessly on why we should marry and why we shouldn't. But it is just, as you say, a piece of paper. Papers can be torn up. True promises cannot. Any road, I love you."*

Back and forth they went with their love notes—his resisting and hers insisting. Finally he agreed to marry her on an African riverbank. On October 10, 1975, the day of the wedding, he took his first drink in weeks and had drunk himself sodden by eight o'clock in the morning. Elizabeth put him to bed for a few hours before waking him to accompany her in a Land-Rover to Kasane, Botswana, to be married by the District Commissioner and then to the river to repeat their vows amidst hippopotamuses, hadedah birds, and vervet monkeys. "Even they seem to be smiling," she said. "Everybody is happy now that Richard and I are back together."

"Sturm has remarried Drang and all is right with the world," reported *The Boston Globe*.

Then came another public exchange of letters, with Elizabeth writing first, saying that there would never be any more marriages or divorces for either of them. "We are stuck like chicken feathers to tar—for lovely always," she wrote.

Richard responded by saying that there was nothing more he could ever want in a woman. "Without you, I was a ghost."

Days later he was felled by malaria, and Elizabeth insisted that a pharmacist be helicoptered to the bush to take care of him. The pharmacist, a beautiful young South African woman named Chen Sam, remained with the Burtons after Richard's illness and worked for Elizabeth as her secretary, traveling companion, and publicist. The three of them emerged in time to fly to London in

November to celebrate Richard's fiftieth birthday, an occasion he suffered through, sipping only mineral water.

"It was terrible to see someone like that standing there needing a drink and not able to have it," recalled one guest. "He seemed so quiet—and so ill."

"He didn't look well at all," said British writer David Wigg. "He looked like a man who wasn't really there."

Richard Burton knew that he had made a dreadful mistake in remarrying Elizabeth. Already they were fighting bitterly, and she was back in a London hospital complaining of neck and back pains and insisting that he stay by her side.

"I didn't think then that their second marriage would last ten minutes," recalled Brian Haynes, their personal bodyguard. "But I could also see that they seemed to need each other. The Burtons had a real love-hate relationship. When he was there she seemed to hate him. When he was away, she couldn't bear to be without him. They were often at each other's throats, and there was plenty of hard-core swearing on both sides."

When Richard refused to stay in the hospital, Elizabeth began having dark imaginings and insisted that Haynes come to her room. "Elizabeth was convinced there was a man in her room and would rest easy only after I had made a thorough search, including under the bed," the bodyguard said. "She frequently slept nude or topless, so that when I came racing in I would get a close-up of those famous boobs. . . . She never worried about how much or how little she was wearing on these occasions. One night when, as was so painfully often the case, she seemed lonely, she held up a very short, very sexy, and very transparent nightie and asked me what I thought of it. She added, 'I've just paid a hundred and fifty pounds for this.' I replied, 'I think they must have seen you coming, Miss Taylor.' "

The ex-detective had great respect for Richard Burton, whom he described as one of the boys. "In my book, he had to put up with a hell of a lot from Elizabeth, who was overdemanding," Haynes said. "He seemed to be trying to lead a normal business life, and it wasn't easy for him—or for others—when she was in full flight. Take the case of the Great Dubbing Drama.

"Elizabeth was supposed to go to Soho to dub some scenes in the film, *The Blue Bird,* that she had been making in Russia. For two weeks, while the whole film crew waited, she put the matter off. Finally Richard started shouting at her that unless she got her backside out of the hospital and back to work they would be sued. So at last she turned up at the dubbing studios."

On Christmas Eve, Elizabeth was due to leave Wellington Hospital in St. John's Wood and fly with Richard to Gstaad for the holidays. Brian Haynes was there to help her and watched as she walked around the wards cheerfully telling everyone good-bye. "Then she was told that reporters were waiting for her outside," he recalled. "Suddenly, she seemed to decide that everything was too much, and she had to be taken out in a wheel-chair to her waiting car."

When Burton wheeled his wife through the press throng, he kept a cigarette in his mouth and refused to give photographers the kissing picture they were waiting for. He knew that his marriage was over and he no longer wanted to pretend otherwise. He confided to friends that after sobering up, he could not believe what he had done.

"I don't know," he said. "Don't ask me. It's like a huge dream. I remember thinking: What am I doing here? Odd place to be married, in the bush, by an African gentleman. It was very curious. An extraordinary adventure doomed from the start, of course."

By the time the Burtons reached Gstaad for Christmas, Richard wanted to put as much distance as possible between himself and his clinging wife, who was almost frantic in her desperation to hold on to him. To get away from her, he went skiing with Emlyn Williams' son Brook. On the ski lift he saw a gorgeous blonde by the name of Suzy Hunt. He said later that despite his preference for short, dark-haired women with large bosoms, he couldn't help staring at this lithe twenty-seven-year-old who was five feet ten inches tall.

M·G·M presents

Cat on a Hot Tin Roof

Every sultry moment of Tennessee Williams' Pulitzer Prize Winning Play is now on the screen!

This is Maggie the Cat...

STARRING

ELIZABETH TAYLOR
PAUL NEWMAN
BURL IVES

JACK CARSON · JUDITH ANDERSON

Though Mike Todd's death left her in anguish, Elizabeth managed to complete the filming of Cat on a Hot Tin Roof.

Drawn together in the aftermath of Todd's death, Elizabeth Taylor and Eddie Fisher decided to marry. Here they apply for their marriage license in Las Vegas in 1959.

Eddie and Liz with Michael and Christopher Wilding and Liza Todd.

To dispel rumors of their feuding, Katharine Hepburn and Elizabeth Taylor stage a mock battle on the set of Suddenly Last Summer. *Sam Spiegel and Joe Mankiewicz carry on their own fracas in the background.*

[ABOVE] *Liz in the revealing white swimsuit she wore in* Suddenly Last Summer. *Author Tennessee Williams thought she was totally miscast.*

N° 10

Liz and Eddie in a between-scenes embrace at Shepperton Studios, London.

Eddie Fisher and Elizabeth in a scene from Butterfield 8. *"I hate the girl I play," she said.*

Elizabeth signs her one-million-dollar contract for Cleopatra.

Richard Burton and Mr. and Mrs. Eddie Fisher on the set of
Cleopatra *in Rome.*

Elizabeth being rushed to the London hospital where a trache-
otomy had to be performed to save her life.

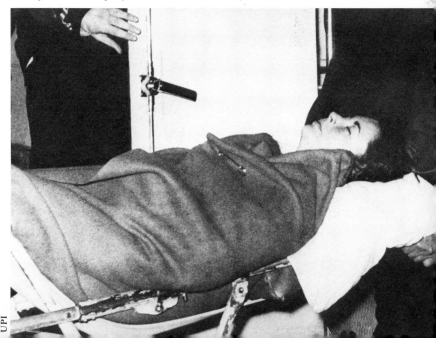

Elizabeth was awarded her first Academy Award for the call-girl role she hated in Butterfield 8.

Liz and Richard Burton share a quiet moment between takes of Cleopatra.

The most famous movie Cleopatra of all.

The photo that flashed around the world and launched le scandale.

To be with Burton, Liz agreed to co-star with him in The V.I.P.'s *for one million dollars.*

A stormy scene from **Who's Afraid of Virginia Woolf?**, *1966. The Burtons' on-screen battling was eroding their real-life marriage.*

[OPPOSITE] *The Presbyterian Welshman and the converted-to-Judaism movie star were married by a Unitarian minister in Montreal on March 15, 1964.*

Princess Grace of Monaco joins the Burtons on Elizabeth's fortieth birthday in Budapest, 1972.

Elizabeth, in disguise, with her lover, used-car salesman Henry Wynberg. "I'm in good Dutch hands," she said. Burton, for his part, was engaging in "cathartic infidelities."

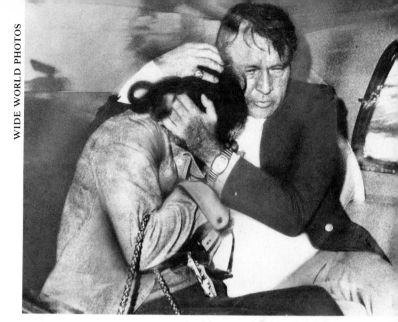

The Burtons.

Elizabeth marries Richard Burton for the second time on an African riverbank. "Sturm has remarried Drang and all is right with the world," reported the Boston Globe.

*Marrying a second time seemed to change nothing. The Burtons contin-
ued battling and Elizabeth's various ailments continued to plague her.
They were soon divorced—again.*

Elizabeth and former Iranian ambassador Ardeshir Zahedi in Washington, D.C., in June of 1976.

Elizabeth with Halston and Henry Kissinger at a fundraising gala for the American Ballet Theater in Washington. Estimated worth of her jewels: one million dollars.

Elizabeth was not amused by cartoonist Garry Trudeau's needling.

DOONESBURY   by Garry Trudeau

LACEY! DEAREST! I'VE BEEN LOOKING ALL OVER FOR YOU!

WE JUST ARRIVED, GAIL. SORRY WE'RE SO LATE!

DON'T BE SILLY! I WAS JUST AFRAID YOU WEREN'T COMING..

WELL, AS YOU KNOW, DEAR, I'M NOT WILD ABOUT FILM PEOPLE. BUT LIZ TAYLOR, WELL ..

THRILLING, ISN'T IT? WAIT UNTIL YOU SEE HER! SHE'S..

WE KNOW. "A TAD OVERWEIGHT, BUT WITH VIOLET EYES TO DIE FOR."

WHY, DICK! I THOUGHT YOU JUST GOT HERE!

WE DID. THAT'S FROM ONE OF THEIR BUMPER STICKERS.

The Warners at their annual Republican fund-raiser in Middleburg, Virginia. "Mr. Warner's rapid political rise is widely credited to the enormous publicity attracted by his famous wife," said The Wall Street Journal.

John Warner and Elizabeth on the evening of his election to the U.S. Senate. Warner waves a newspaper clipping of his horoscope which predicted he would gain popularity and "be a winner."

Elizabeth and John Warner talk to Marion Barry, mayor of Washington, D.C. "All our lives we have wanted to look like Elizabeth Taylor, and now—God help us—we do," moaned a middle-aged woman.

GAY DE LORT/WOMEN'S WEAR DAILY

Kim Novak, Rock Hudson and Elizabeth Taylor in The Mirror Crack'd.

UPI

Senator and Mrs. John Warner visit 92-year-old former Governor Alf Landon in Topeka, Kansas, in 1979.

Finally slim after weeks at a Florida spa, Elizabeth Taylor is congratulated by President and Mrs. Ronald Reagan following her triumphant opening night in The Little Foxes *in Washington, D.C.*

UP

"I turned around and there was this beautiful creature nine feet tall," he said. "Absolutely startling. She could stop a stampede. I kept wondering when she was going to appear again. I couldn't wait. 'Get James Hunt's wife up to the house,' I kept saying. Brook knew her a little, and my luck was in. She started coming up to the house—two, three, then four times a week."

The former fashion model was separated from James "The Shunt" Hunt, who was known throughout England as "the golden boy of British car racing" after winning the Dutch Grand Prix.

"Instinctively, Elizabeth recognized that Susan was something special," said Burton. "From the very beginning, she sensed a worthy adversary. I can't imagine how women know these things, but I assure you, they do. Elizabeth is by nature a jealous woman, and like a good many women, she believes that where there is no jealousy there is no love. She didn't very much mind about the other women who popped up now and again when we were separated and divorced and all that. She didn't think they were any real competition. But now the chips were down."

Shortly after Christmas, Richard was to leave for New York to begin rehearsals for *Equus,* the Broadway play by Peter Shaffer. This would be Burton's first stage appearance since *Hamlet* in 1964. He was terrified, he admitted, but determined to revive his career. "This has been a shabby period professionally for me," he said at the time. "Elizabeth couldn't believe I was going to tackle a play. She said, 'You have the guts of a blind burglar—you know they'll be gunning for you.' "

For strength and support he asked Suzy Hunt to accompany him and made no pretense of hiding the fact from his wife. Elizabeth turned on the young woman and snarled, "You'll last only six months with Richard."

"Perhaps," replied the green-eyed blonde, "but those six months will be very worthwhile."

Richard left London that evening for a few days in Geneva, and Elizabeth went to The Cave, a disco restaurant in the basement of the Olden Hotel, with Chen Sam and two young men.

She was dancing with one of the young men when Peter Darmanin, a thirty-seven-year-old advertising executive from Malta, walked in with a group of friends.

"The place was packed," he recalled, "but the minute I walked in I saw her and she saw me. The music stopped as I was in the doorway, and she came up to me and said, 'How nice to see you.' I kissed her hand and then sat down with my group. I told the owner, Heidi Donizetti, that I wanted to ask Elizabeth to dance, but Heidi said no one does that because Elizabeth won't dance with just anyone."

Confident that the forty-three-year-old movie queen would indeed dance with him, Peter Darmanin signaled to her, and she responded. "We started dancing and we never stopped for an hour," he said. "She kept saying, 'Don't leave me. Please. Whatever you do. Don't leave me.' Afterwards, she told me: 'Go ask Chen Sam to dance and then give her your number, and I'll call tomorrow.' I did exactly that.

"The next morning at ten o'clock Chen called me and said, 'Liz wants to talk to you.' She got on the phone and told me to go out on my patio and look for the chalet with the chaise on it. That would be hers. I did. I told her to come by for breakfast, and she did. We made love that first morning."

Darmanin recalled that Elizabeth was in a highly agitated state that morning, picking up the phone several times to call Richard. "She was trying to give back that diamond, and she was crying and screaming constantly at Richard. She was like a volcano. Erupting constantly."

Burton had bought his wife the diamond, a rare pink gem of 25 carats costing over $1 million, a few days after their jungle wedding ceremony. Elizabeth created international headlines at the time by announcing that she had planned to trade in the $1-million stone to build a hospital in Botswana. "I was deeply moved by Richard's gesture of giving me the ring," she said. "I know it was meant out of a happily returned love; but I really would rather the money be spent in a more worthwhile way. After long discussion we both decided that we would like to build a hospital-clinic in Kasane, Botswana, on the border of the Chobe Game Reserve. They need one badly and I certainly don't need another ring."*

Since their disastrous remarriage the pink diamond had become another wedge between the Burtons. Gavin de Becker, one of their security guards, said that he was sent back to the jeweler to return the stone. By that time, Richard was en route to New York with Suzy Hunt and Elizabeth had moved Peter Darmanin into her chalet in Gstaad.

"Our affair lasted seven weeks," he said, "but it was like seven months—no, seven years—because we were with each other every moment. That is the only way you can be with Elizabeth. She needs that kind of loving. She is passionate in bed, and I must admit that I did not sleep much during those seven weeks. I didn't want to waste any time. We'd stay in bed until two in the afternoon and not get dressed until dinner.

"We were together constantly. Even when the hairdresser came to do her hair she would call me on the intercom and say, 'Please come here, Peter. I want you to be with me. I need you near me.' So I'd go into the room and sit with her and look in the mirror with her at the most beautiful face God ever created.

"She was always screaming and yelling and hitting and socking me. An example is the time in bed I noticed a big bruise on her hip and asked how she got it. She said she had walked into a door—which I believed because she is so accident-prone. Later when we were in the middle of a huge fight she started toward me but smashed into a doorjamb. Sarcastically, I said, 'Oh, is that to prove that you really did bruise yourself walking into a door?' She got so mad that she took her arm and smacked me

---

* This grand gesture full of impulsive goodwill never fulfilled the promise of its dramatic publicity. Instead, Elizabeth changed her mind about funding a hospital in Botswana, and her legal representatives had to so inform the Ministry of Health in Gabarone. Later she was asked for assistance in expanding the existing health center at a cost of $347,-000, but she refused. Instead, she offered the government about $50,000 to build two health clinics. By 1979 she had contributed $25,000 toward the project.

right in the face, cutting my eye with her diamond ring. She loved fighting, so we had huge fights. Another time she crammed a burning cigarette into my hand, and that left a scar.

"She was also very possessive," he added lovingly. "I remember when a friend of mine from London called to say that she had had an armed robbery in her home. I was quite stunned and told Elizabeth about it when I hung up. 'Oh, what the hell,' she said. 'I had an armed robbery once.' She had to have a more dangerous story than my friend, and she couldn't be topped by anyone else. Her story had to be better and more dramatic than my friend's, and she also didn't want me to waste any time comforting my friend when I could be loving her.

"One night I wanted to go to the Eagles Nest with my friends. Elizabeth didn't want to go, but she didn't want me to go either. I said I was leaving anyway and got dressed. Just as I was ready to walk out the door she started crying hysterically about her Shih Tzu dog. 'Oh, Peter,' she screamed. 'I think Sally's dead. I can't find her anyplace. I think she has been crushed by the snowmobile.' Well, I ran around like crazy looking for that silly dog, and it finally occurred to me to just look in her normal place —the closet—and there she was, fast asleep. Then I realized that Liz was stalling and trying to keep me there with her."

During their seven weeks together Elizabeth poured out her heart to her young lover, telling him secret after secret as she had done with every other man in her life. "She told me all about Monty Clift and how deeply he loved her," Darmanin recalled. "She told me everything about that car accident and how she held Monty's head in her arms afterwards. She talked about how she wanted Monty to star in *Reflections in a Golden Eye* with her but no one would put up the money so she put it up herself and told the producer never to tell him. She also told me about how much she and Monty loved Frank Sinatra and how she once had had an affair with Sinatra when she was a young girl.

"Mike Todd is still big in her life, and she always talks about him as a little boy and how he was so poor that he would run into a restaurant, rush up to a table and reach for the bread, and then run out. How he used to have to take all the free sugar and ketchup just so he'd have something to eat. She talked about Richard that way, too. How poor he was as a child, how he did not speak any English, and how he learned and then saved himself from being a Welsh coal miner.

"Richard was terrible to her. He slept with many women. . . . She hated it. It made her terribly insecure. But she told me she would always love Richard. She could not stop loving him."

Burton phoned his wife in February and asked her to meet him in New York, where he was starting preview performances in *Equus*. "I did not see the necessity or the need to announce the separation," he said later. "Why announce something that is there and has been a fact for some time? But it is difficult to work these things out through the post when I am in New York and she in Switzerland, or through a lawyer traveling to see her. So she came here and we decided to break up."

Before leaving Gstaad, Elizabeth asked Peter Darmanin to accompany her to her bedroom, where she opened a treasure chest full of gold charms. "She picked up one that had *'Elizabeth Taylor Elizabeth Taylor'* written all over it about fifty times, but she said, 'No, this is too conspicuous.' Then she found a gold charm which she said had been given to her in Pisa. It was engraved in Italian with *'Obesanzo di Te,'* which means 'I need you.' She gave that to me," he said, "and I've worn it ever since."

Before leaving Switzerland the next day, Elizabeth made a promise that she did not keep: to meet Peter Darmanin in March. "I was in such pain after she cut me off," he said. "At first I didn't realize what was happening. I didn't know it was over. We had said we were going to meet after she came back from New York. She knew the thing with Richard was over and she said she wanted to see me again. I said I would never see her if she ever went back to that awful Wynberg guy. When she didn't come back in March, I spent hundreds of dollars calling her and waiting for her to call me, but she never did. She wouldn't talk to me and Chen Sam wouldn't put any of my calls through."

"I loved her then and I still love her," Darmanin said four

years later. "All she'd ever have to do would be to call me and I'd come to her no matter where she was."

Elizabeth was experiencing her own pain at the time, having been told in New York by Richard Burton that he wanted an immediate divorce to marry Susan Hunt. "Why the hell did you have me come all this way to tell me that?" she screamed as she moved out of his suite at the Lombardy Hotel. She then called Broadway producer Alexander Cohen to cancel a birthday party he had planned in her honor. By the time Cohen was telling invited guests that "You must realize this is a difficult time for her," Elizabeth was aboard a plane for California and headed for the comforting arms of Henry Wynberg.

"Richard Burton might as well have hit her in the face with a two-by-four," Wynberg said. Elizabeth's Hollywood friends immediately called Henry to arrange birthday dinners for her, but he turned them all down. "She doesn't want to see anybody," he said. "She sends love to all her friends, but she's not up to a party. She's too wounded."

Rather than celebrate a forty-fourth birthday in the wake of her husband's public rejection, Elizabeth remained secluded behind the palm fronds of the Beverly Hills Hotel. She then moved with Henry Wynberg to a rented house in the Trousdale section of Los Angeles. Intensifying her pain were newspaper stories and photographs of Richard squiring Suzy Hunt to the same little bistros where he had once taken her. When he walked into these restaurants with the British model at his side, diners stood up and applauded. In *Equus*, he had just achieved what *New York Times* critic Walter Kerr described as the best work of his life. After years of squandering himself on unimportant films, an enervating marriage, and self-destructive drinking bouts, Richard was now surpassing everyone's expectations. The Plymouth Theater was sold out every night, and he was once again the toast of Broadway. Much of the credit, he said, went to his twenty-seven-year-old lover, who he said had rescued him and resurrected his career.

"All I know is Susan saved my life," he said. "I met her just when I was putting my hand up for help for the last time. And she's rejuvenated me with her enthusiasm and interest. Now I enjoy things I never did before.''

Bitterly, Elizabeth read the interviews in which her husband said that he had given up alcohol in order to live for his new love and that he would try to stay sober for Susan as he had never done for Elizabeth. "I loved my silly image as the besotted Welsh genius, dying in his own vomit in the gutter,'' he said. "I think I must have been going through the male menopause; but I'm a changed man now.''

Asked about Elizabeth, Richard smiled indulgently. "I'm very fond of the old girl. I don't mean it in the sense it sounds. It's just that I was never really the man who bestrode the narrow world like a colossus, and she was never a real-life Cleopatra.'' Then he added: "I worry about Elizabeth. Financially she has no problems. But emotionally. . . . I worry that some idiot will get hold of her. She is surprisingly vulnerable. But you can't learn them, as they say, so there is no point in trying.''

Crying constantly and drinking heavily, Elizabeth refused to sign the separation papers that had been drawn up by the Burtons' attorney, Aaron Frosch. It would be months before she could admit that her sixth marriage was over and there was no hope for a reconciliation. In the meantime, her friends recognized that her only salvation was work. "She will be back on the screen within a few weeks,'' said her agent, Robert Lantz, as he negotiated a film contract for her in *A Little Night Music*. "Elizabeth is one of the greatest movie actresses in the world and should be working. It is unhealthy for a star of her talent not to work.''

On the arm of Henry Wynberg, Elizabeth finally emerged from her self-imposed exile to accept a dinner invitation with Secretary of State Henry Kissinger and his wife, Nancy, whom she had met at the King David Hotel in 1975 when she and Richard visited Israel. The Kissingers were vacationing for two weeks in Palm Springs with Ann and Kirk Douglas and wanted to see Elizabeth and wish her well. The Secretary of State, who had enjoyed meeting Richard Burton, was just as charming toward his stand-in, although he felt the used-car salesman did not measure up to the Welsh actor. A few weeks later Kissinger called Elizabeth, knowing how miserable she was, and invited her to Washington to attend the April fund-raising gala for American Ballet Theater at the Kennedy Center, and the party afterward at the Iranian Embassy which was to be hosted by the dazzling bachelor Ambassador, Ardeshir Zahedi.

Elizabeth immediately accepted, hung up the phone, and turned to the designer Halston, who just happened to be fitting her for a bright red halter dress to wear to the Academy Awards. She told him that she now needed something to wear to Washington. "What I really need, darling, is a yellow dress for my yellow diamonds. I've already got a blue for the sapphires, red for the rubies, and green for the emeralds." *

Halston agreed to accompany Elizabeth to Washington. Liza Minnelli then told him that she too wanted to go. So together the threesome, plus Arthur Bruckel, Elizabeth's hairdresser, descended on the nation's capital. The city that John F. Kennedy once described as a sleepy little Southern town woke up to gawk at Elizabeth Taylor.

"She swept into Washington like Cleopatra into Rome," gasped one newspaper, giving extravagant details of Elizabeth's diamond-and-emerald necklace, her matching diamond-and-emerald drop earrings, her glittering ring, her sparkling bracelet, and the eye-popping brooch on her cleavage. "Estimated value: $1 million," claimed *The Washington Post*.

At the Iranian Embassy, Elizabeth was photographed dancing

---

* Elizabeth had met the designer after calling him in New York. "Is this really Elizabeth Taylor—the real Elizabeth Taylor?" he asked. "Yeah," she said. "Is this really Halston—the real Halston?" They both laughed, and Elizabeth asked him to fly to California to create a dress for her. Although Halston doesn't usually make such trips for clients, he did for Elizabeth. He also promised her a 40-percent discount on everything. Days later he called Pat Ast and said, "You'll never believe this but I'm calling you from Elizabeth Taylor's house!" "Sure I believe it, Halston," said the singer. "This is Hollywood!"

a frantic hustle with Senator Edward Brooke (R.-Mass.). She nuzzled the Iranian Ambassador on the dance floor as they moved slowly to the music with both arms around each other. Polly Bergen watched from a divan in the Embassy's Persian room and said, "It looks like Liz is still carrying the torch for Burton."

Actually, Elizabeth was captivated by the dashing Ambassador. The next morning she sent Ardeshir Zahedi an orchid plant standing five feet tall and covered with forty blossoms. Accompanying this $500 gift was a note thanking him for the dinner dance. Elizabeth had already returned to Henry Wynberg by the time the Ambassador called and asked her to come back to Washington to be his guest at the Embassy. She accepted and asked him to escort her to the Washington premiere of *The Blue Bird*. He accepted and asked her to fly to Teheran on Iran Air's new nonstop service from New York. She accepted, and three weeks later, after he sent a chartered jet to bring her to Washington, they began their love affair.*

In Ardeshir Zahedi, Elizabeth found a sophisticated forty-eight-year-old man accustomed to wealth and opulence. Since his divorce in 1964 from the Shah's eldest daughter, the Ambassador had enjoyed a luxurious life-style as one of America's most sought-after bachelors. Representing the Peacock Throne in Washington gave him access to hundreds of thousands of dollars for entertaining. Only the ambassador of oil-rich Iran could curry favor by showering important journalists, politicians, and socialites with tins of caviar, magnums of champagne, and Persian rugs. Invitations to his embassy parties were coveted as a mark of social acceptance in Washington. Always there were music and feasts. Sometimes there were belly dancers, hashish, and pornographic movies. These attractions unfailingly drew the rich, the powerful, and the famous.

---

* A friend who visited Elizabeth at the time brought her a book on Iran "so she'd know where it was" and two peacock feathers. "She put the feathers in the bedroom where Henry could see them," recalled the friend. "That's her sense of humor."

Photographs of the Ambassador kissing the movie star began appearing hours after Elizabeth's arrival. For the next two weeks the couple were inseparable, clutching hands tightly in public and causing high-society gossip around the world.

"My husband and I went with them to a charity benefit one night and Liz was all over Ardeshir," recalled a Washington socialite. "She was quite in love with him. As he drove, she sat next to him twirling the hair on his neck and leaning over to kiss him every time he stopped the car. My husband accidentally dropped a gin and tonic on her dress, and he and Ardeshir began mopping it up with a lot of lewd comments that she just loved. 'Maybe I better lick it up, what do you think, Ardeshir?' 'No, no,' he said. 'I'll do it, but first I think I better take this dress off.' Later we all went back to the Embassy and Liz and Ardeshir lay down on the couch together and almost made love right there in front of everyone."

"When I fall in love I fall in love," Elizabeth told the woman, who later added: "And when she wants something she moves fast. . . . I found out later that she wanted to marry Ardeshir but the Shah had forbidden it. He informed Ardeshir that he could not remarry during the Shah's lifetime, and he certainly couldn't marry a commoner converted to Judaism and make her the step-mother of the Shah's grandchildren. The Shah was so incensed about all the publicity surrounding Ardeshir's affair with Liz that he commanded him to stay in Washington rather than accompany all of us to Iran on the New York-Teheran inaugural flight. So he flew to New York to see everyone off, but then returned the same day. After that trip Liz wouldn't leave the Embassy. At first Ardeshir didn't know how to get her out, but he finally managed, and they remained friends."*

---

* The Ambassador continued to publicly deny the love affair with Elizabeth while privately explaining to her the difficulties he faced in remarriage. After her trip to Iran she finally moved out of the Embassy, tipping all the maids $100 apiece and thanking them for their kindnesses to her. What followed was not an easy period for Elizabeth, who frequently appeared disoriented and distracted. One young man who met her asked where she was going next. "She looked at me straight in the

Elizabeth insisted on traveling to Iran with her hairdresser and a doctor friend named Lou Scarrone. The Ambassador sent a cousin, Firooz Zahedi, to accompany them and see that they were comfortable.

An early *faux pas* was avoided when Zahedi learned that a film starring Richard Burton was scheduled to be shown on the flight. He notified airline officials, who hastily came up with a French crime comedy. But the gracious diplomat could do nothing about the press that was swarming the airport in New York and ignoring Connie Stevens and Cloris Leachman to talk to Elizabeth.

As the Ambassador stood at her side, one reporter asked her if she planned to divorce Richard Burton to marry Zahedi. "You don't read the newspapers, do you?" said Elizabeth. "My husband is getting the divorce, and don't worry your pretty little mustache about it!"

Upon her arrival in Teheran eleven hours later she was again greeted by the press. Her first questioner inquired whether she was still seeing Richard Burton. "That's a very silly question to ask," she flared. "We are getting a divorce, you know!"

Aware of Elizabeth's past preference for being addressed by her husband's name, a second journalist made the mistake of calling her Mrs. Burton. "Please don't ever call me that again," she snapped. "My name is not Burton but Taylor."

The first reporter meekly asked Elizabeth if she was making any movies. "I couldn't be making any films right now or I wouldn't be here in this country, would I?"

Still, the urge for playacting was always there. A few days later Elizabeth and her hairdresser spent an entire afternoon dressing each other up in fantasy costumes and posing in front of a camera. "We didn't have anything else to do, so Liz and I

---

eye with her teeth clenched and said, 'I'm going to the moon.' It was so weirded-out you can't imagine."

Paul Neshamkin, the former tutor to the Burtons' children, also saw Elizabeth during this time. "I was at the Iranian Ambassador's residence in Manhattan and she crashed a party there," he said. "It was the first time I had seen her since 1965. I went up and talked to her and she just stared at me. She was completely out of it."

bought a bunch of junk—scarves and native dress and stuff like that,'' recalled Arthur Bruckel. ''She penciled in a beard around my mustache and wrapped my head in a turban. Then she wrapped me up in hundreds of silk scarves and I wrapped her up. We spent the whole afternoon posing on a couch for Firooz, who took a bunch of exotic photographs and later sold a couple to Andy Warhol's *Interview*.''

Firooz insisted that Elizabeth dress properly during the trip, and on more than one occasion he was heard telling her to go back and change her clothes into something more suitable. When she appeared in a tight T-shirt and wrinkled slacks wearing a scarf wrapped around her head, he refused to escort her through the streets of Teheran. ''You look like a slob,'' he said. ''You are a movie star and you must dress like a movie star. That's why you're here. You insult the Iranians looking that way. So go back and change and try to make yourself look like Elizabeth Taylor.''

By the time Elizabeth returned to the United States, Richard Burton was sneaking off to Haiti to get a quickie divorce so he could marry his blond traveling companion, who went along to get her own divorce from James Hunt. She received hers, but Richard returned empty-handed. He had come without a necessary document—his wife's notarized statement agreeing to the divorce.

That night the news was reported on network television—a further humiliation for Elizabeth, who looked to some like an overweight aging beauty desperately holding on to a husband who was determined to marry a much younger woman.

''Richard never asked for my signature,'' Elizabeth insisted. ''In fact, he never communicated his plans to me, and I was unaware of them until I heard them on a television news program. I would have done nothing to stand in the way of the happiness of Richard Burton and Susan Hunt.''

The next night Elizabeth attended a party in New York at jewelry designer Elsa Peretti's apartment in honor of Valentino, the Italian couturier. She swept into the room in a flowing caftan from Iran, headed directly for a young man named Kevin Farley, and stayed with him all evening. "We went on the balcony at Elsa's apartment and started throwing strawberries at all the ladies with the bouffant hairdos because Liz said she wanted to hit them in their little bird's nests," he recalled. "When we were out there she mentioned Richard Burton and called him a silly fool. She said, 'All he had to do was ask me to sign a piece of paper.' Then she started talking about when she had lived in New York. She said, 'We had a terrace then. That was with Eddie Fisher. Oh, God. This is so damn depressing I can't think about it.'"

Hours later the party moved to an all-black discotheque, where Elizabeth drank and danced and refused to be depressed.

CHAPTER 24

By THE TIME ELIZABETH RETURNED TO CALIFORNIA in the summer of 1976, her romance with Henry Wynberg was crumbling. Still, she did not expect to be thrown out of the house for which she was paying the rent; but after an acrid argument, that is exactly what happened. Wynberg not only told her to get out, but called a cab and directed the driver to take her to the Beverly Hills Hotel. Then he pulled all her clothes out of the drawers and closets and heaped them in the middle of the living room. He called a second cab, heaved everything inside it, and sent it after the first one. Henry remained in the house for several months afterward and enjoyed the use of Elizabeth's green Rolls-Royce until a letter from attorney Aaron Frosch asked him to return it.

Peripatetic and restless, Elizabeth began flying back and forth between California and the East Coast. On one New York stop she swept into a Democratic fund-raiser to endorse Jimmy Carter for President. "I have nothing against President Ford," she announced. "He seems like a sweet man. But Carter is very intelligent, quick-minded, and has a whole new image." Wearing a gold peanut, Elizabeth kissed the presidential candidate and gave him instant glamour. The next day she flew to Washington to have lunch with Vice President Nelson Rockefeller. Days later she flew back to New York to attend a fund-raiser for Democratic Congresswoman Bella Abzug, to whom she contributed $1,000.

On July 8 she was back in Washington for a dinner at the

British Embassy that Queen Elizabeth was giving for the President of the United States to celebrate the American Bicentennial. Without a husband or lover, Elizabeth decided to rely on her Hollywood hairdresser as an escort for the evening. Ambassador Ramsbotham explained that this simply would not be appropriate for such a formal affair. He offered to provide her a more acceptable date and contacted John W. Warner, the forty-nine-year-old former Secretary of the Navy* who had recently completed his duties as head of the American Revolution Bicentennial Administration. "Stick to her like a leech," said the Ambassador. "She can be quite willful. Keep a tight hold on her, because I don't want anyone to detract from the Queen or the President."

That evening Warner appeared at the Madison Hotel to pick up his blind date. When he rang Elizabeth's room, she quickly sent Chen Sam down to the lobby to see what he looked like.

"Hey, he's not bad-looking," reported the secretary. "He's pretty dishy."

"And so I went down," Elizabeth recalled. "He had his back to me and all I saw was that marvelous silver hair. I gathered this was my escort, since he was the only one in white tie in the lobby. He turned around. 'Ah, Miss Taylor.' And I thought, *Wow!*"

Rugged and handsome,† John Warner was an impressive sight in his white tie and tails. He had not concealed from friends how thrilled he was to be escorting the most famous movie star in the world. Since his 1973 divorce from Catherine Mellon, the daughter of multimillionaire philanthropist Paul Mellon, Warner had seemed interested in dating only rich and famous women like television personality Barbara Walters, to whom he had pro-

---

* President Nixon had appointed John Warner Secretary of the Navy in April 1972. After Nixon resigned, President Ford sought his advice about unloading an undesirable White House aide by appointing him to the position, but was worried about endangering the nation's naval posture. Nixon reassured him, saying, "It's a job anyone can do. Why, we even had John Warner in that job. . . ."

† When asked how he stayed so fit, Warner said he rode horses and played squash—and, he added bluntly, "I am a very active bachelor."

posed, and Page Lee Hufty, a blond Standard Oil heiress once linked with Senator Edward Kennedy.

"From a bachelor's perspective, if I want to have a date, I think how a woman would relate to the situation," he told the *New York Post*. "Page Lee relates to all of them. I look down my list of ten girls or so and I say, 'Now, let's see, which one can ski or go canoeing or ride or play tennis or go to an embassy dinner and talk about international affairs? If you had to say what was the best thing about Page Lee, it's that checkoff list."

While Elizabeth Taylor could not ski, play tennis, or canoe without capsizing, she certainly was someone to take to an embassy dinner. Following the Ambassador's instructions, John Warner remained at her side all Saturday evening and basked in her limelight. Afterward, he took her to a private club in Georgetown, where they drank and danced until five in the morning, when he took her back to the Madison Hotel. Hours later he picked her up again to drive to Atoka, the 2,700-acre farm in Middleburg, Virginia, that his former father-in-law had given to him as part of his divorce settlement from Catherine Mellon.*

"I'm just an old country farmer," Warner said as he drove up to his magnificent estate set amidst the richly manicured fields of Middleburg, an hour's drive from his home in Washington. A

---

* Born poor, John Warner was thirty years old when he married twenty-one-year-old Catherine Mellon in 1957. After their wedding he bragged to a friend that his income from the Mellon family trust was $9,000 a day. When his wife insisted on a divorce fifteen years later, he did not contest the action, and his father-in-law very gratefully gave him the $750,000 house they had built in Georgetown, the 2,700-acre farm in Middleburg, and a lifetime income from investments estimated at $9 million. Warner also received custody of their three children during the school year and provided for them from his divorce-settlement moneys. Understandably, he always appreciated his father-in-law for making him a multimillionaire. "At every stage Paul Mellon remained the perfect father-in-law," he said. "He gave me an absolutely free hand with respect to taking care of the children, using the financial resources made available by himself. And he was *very* generous to me. Through his generosity I am now able, and will be throughout my life, to pursue a career of public service."

long, winding stone-and-tar road bordered by blossoming fruit trees led to a twenty-room fieldstone house that was built in 1816.

Warner enjoyed showing his wine cellar and a Portuguese-tiled kitchen that he had designed, complete with a commercial six-burner stove. He pointed to some of his six hundred head of Herefords and said, "When cattle prices are up, I jingle." He showed Elizabeth all his horses, the cattle barns, the indoor swimming pool, tennis courts, spring and smoke houses, vegetable and flower gardens, several ponds, and his five-hundred-acre wildlife preserve.

"When she saw the farm I won her heart," he said later.

That first Sunday they spent the night at the farm. On Monday John Warner, a workaholic who had not taken a day off in eighteen months, called in sick to his office. Tuesday he canceled all his appointments. He finally stumbled back to work on Wednesday.

He invited Elizabeth to lunch with him later in the week in Washington. Looking forward to showing her off, he was embarrassed when she appeared at the Bicentennial office wearing a flowing black silk pajama outfit with a low-cut neckline. Commenting later to one of his assistants, Warner said, "That getup was a bit much, wasn't it?" For a man who had closets full of expensive pin-striped suits and wore tweeds cut in London, Elizabeth's choice of noontime attire was jarring. Still, her outrageous taste in clothes did not prevent him from proposing marriage a few days later at the farm.

"It just happened," he said.

"We both decided at the same time without really saying anything," she said. "We had taken a picnic and gone in a Jeep to watch the sunset high on a hill. There was a rainstorm all around us, and we sat there surrounded by thunder and lightning. It was like being in the center of a saucer. The storm circled around us, and finally the skies opened in a torrential downpour. We just lay back in the grass, hugged each other, soaked by the rain but in love. It was a magic moment."

"Instead of complaining and screaming that she wanted to go

home," he said, "Liz wanted to sit on the hill and watch the lightning. I thought she was special after that."

For years John Warner had wanted to run for the office of United States Senator from Virginia. In 1978 a vacancy was opening with the retirement of Senator William Scott, who once held a press conference to deny a magazine's claim that he was the dumbest man in Congress. Warner desperately wanted Scott's seat, and for someone with his political ambitions the choice of a wife was very important. He later admitted that he had not ignored the political impact of Elizabeth's six marriages and five divorces. As he told Barbara Walters: "Well, I have to say it certainly crossed my mind a little bit. But I feel that in my own association with Elizabeth—and she's been extremely frank with me about the entire period of her life—the early part, which is so highly criticized, gives way to the fact that she worked hard for over sixteen years to make her marriage work with Richard.* And I think both of them felt that it just couldn't go on any longer and it came apart. That is the period that I look at. If she had suddenly had, say, six or seven consecutive marriages of just two or three years apiece, right up to the point, I suppose it would have frightened me away a bit."

Warner told other reporters that, in addition to Elizabeth's previous marriages and divorces, her politics was also an important consideration. "Hell," he said, "if she had Jane Fonda's ideas I wouldn't bother with her for two seconds." Obviously he did not know that Elizabeth admired Miss Fonda and had even given her $3,000 to be used for Black Panthers who were in jail without legal representation.

An extremely conservative Republican, John Warner had worked for Richard Nixon for President in 1960; Elizabeth Taylor said that she had voted for John F. Kennedy that same year.

---

* John Warner was obviously confused about Elizabeth's marital history. She married Richard Burton in March 1964 and divorced him in June 1974. She then remarried him in October 1975 and was divorced from him in July 1976, a total of ten years and nine months of marriage to the man.

In 1968, Warner was director of National Citizens for Nixon and Agnew, contributed $100,000 of Mellon money to the campaign, and supported the war in Vietnam;* Elizabeth supported Senator Robert F. Kennedy's antiwar campaign effort. In 1972, Warner as Secretary of the Navy campaigned strenuously for President Nixon's reelection; Elizabeth, a British subject no longer able to vote in the United States, was outraged to hear that Sammy Davis, Jr., whom she described as "one of my best Jewish friends," had endorsed Nixon, a man she said she detested. In 1976, Warner, aspiring to the GOP Senate nomination from Virginia, campaigned throughout the state for Gerald Ford for President; Elizabeth supported Jimmy Carter.

Obviously there were more political differences than similarities between them, including party affiliation.

"I'm not a Republican," Elizabeth told a reporter.

"Oh, my God, you are too a Republican," insisted John Warner.

"I'll become a Republican when you come out for the Equal Rights Amendment," she said. At that point, Warner ran out of the room as if he were going to be sick. Elizabeth, realizing what she had said, tried to smooth things over. "Of course I consider myself a Republican," she said. "I was only teasing him. If you print what I said, I'll get my tit caught in a wringer."

---

* "I was very cautious because my first marriage broke up over politics," said John Warner. "We disagreed on Vietnam. I was in the Administration and thought we had to finish something we had started. My wife was almost a student radical. The marriage couldn't survive those pressures. I wanted to take it slowly with Elizabeth. I had to be convinced she not only accepted but enjoyed politics."

Catherine Mellon agreed with her former husband that their bitter disagreements over the Vietnam War had damaged their marriage. "I'd have these arguments with John. I'd say, 'But I'm right.' And then it would turn into something else. . . . Then John and I got into the horse business and that became one more thing we argued about. It seemed a little too much like what people would expect. I'd say, 'If you're going to run for the Senate, don't expect me to give those teas.' And he'd say, 'All you have to do is sit there while I'm on television and look pretty.' "

John Warner claimed that political leaders had warned him about marrying Elizabeth: "A number of the so-called pols talked to me when they heard I was falling in love with Elizabeth. They said, 'You can forget about a political career.' So if forced to make the choice, I was going to take Elizabeth. I was going to forget about a political career."

He said that these "so-called pols" told him that Elizabeth would destroy him politically "because of her numerous marriages, principally. And because religious heritage is very important in Virginia. It's a Southern Baptist, Methodist, and Episcopalian state." *

Some people dispute John Warner, saying that with that noble statement he was trying to cut a profile in courage. These people insist that Warner knew marriage to Elizabeth Taylor would instantly confer on him the first basic in politics: name recognition. "Not many people knew who he was outside of being Paul Mellon's former son-in-law," said one Virginia politician. "With Elizabeth Taylor beside him, people would remember his name, and they would also turn out in droves to suffer through whatever he had to say just so long as they could see her."

Former Virginia Governor Linwood Holton agreed. "Elizabeth Taylor's past won't make much difference now in John's political plans," he said. "She will attract attention for him and she won't hurt his campaign. The only thing John will have to do is overcome a possible, but incorrect, image as a playboy, and he will have to get rid of that marcel look in his hair."

Warner told Elizabeth of his ambitions and explained the kind of life she would lead as a politician's wife—campaigning constantly, shaking hands, smiling, kissing bald heads—anything to win the nomination at the GOP convention in June of 1978. To

---

* Elizabeth agreed with his assessment. "They'll never elect a man who's married to a woman who's been divorced five times. And Jewish!" she told Andy Warhol.

that end he insisted on presenting himself as a simple country
farmer. She would be the farmer's wife.*

"I can assure you I am an old-fashioned, traditional individual
and that's the kind of life we are going to lead," he told reporters.
"Elizabeth understands that and she understands that very well.
I took her to the farm several times and said this is the way it is
going to be."

Desperate to be securely married, Elizabeth promised to accommodate herself to his life. "If John wants to campaign as a
candidate, I'll be with him all the way side by side," she said.
"I love Washington and Virginia. I am not intimidated by politics. I think it's fascinating."

"All those days of big jewelry and that stuff are over," he
warned. "It's not my bag."

Elizabeth reassured him that her behemoth jewels meant nothing to her compared with the peace and serenity she felt being
with him down on the farm. "This reminds me of my childhood
home in England," she told him. She spoke lyrically about his
"cows silhouetted against the moon." She said, "I feel at home
here. It's a long time since I felt that way. I feel that at last I've
come to rest."

They decided they would spend six months after their wedding
"testing the waters," as John Warner said, to see if the people of
Virginia responded favorably to them as a political team. If they
did, he would announce his candidacy for the U.S. Senate. If
not, he would announce it anyway.

They agreed to premarital contracts securing their individual
assets for their children and not sharing in each other's estates.
"I have no desire to inherit from her, nor does she from me," he
said. However, Elizabeth, with her romantic notions of death,
insisted on having it written into their wills that their graves be
side by side. Unable to live without a husband, she was not going
to die without one. "I have indeed found my roots and they are

---

* "If John Warner is just a farmer then Mrs. Warner is the best known
Virginia farmer's wife since Pocahontas," exclaimed the *Richmond
Times-Dispatch.*

firmly planted," she said. "We've even chosen our burial site. I think that's sweet. We're going to be buried next to each other." Sharing a grave with her loved one represented the ultimate rendezvous to Elizabeth, who added, "When I love somebody I love them one hundred percent. I like to feel cozy, the idea of the family being together, growing up together, growing old together —and dying together."

She left in August for Austria to begin work on *A Little Night Music*. John planned to join her in Vienna in October, when they would announce their betrothal. "I am sort of a traditionalist," he said, "and so we are definitely going the engagement route." He began designing a red, white, and blue engagement ring for her with one small ruby, one small diamond, and one small sapphire, to commemorate their meeting during the Bicentennial year.

On August 21, Elizabeth was driving through the Vienna Woods on her way to a restaurant when three carloads of photographers started following her. "Their attitude was so hostile I turned my back on them," she recalled. "What is so unfair is that I wasn't aware of why they were following me until I got back and saw the papers reporting the Burton wedding and realized what had happened."

After Richard's ill-fated attempt to secure a quick divorce in Haiti, Elizabeth had agreed to give him whatever he wanted, and their divorce had been granted at the end of July.* "After that he got married and didn't let me know," she said. "I heard of it through the media, and I called him and Suzy and congratulated them, because I really wish them happiness."

---

* Private papers indicate that financially Elizabeth and Richard remained intertwined for many years through their various corporations —Safety Programs, Oxford Productions, and Taybur Productions. Through their legal representatives they haggled over their investments in Harlech Television and the Nassau Corporation, which they had formed for U.S.-inheritance-tax purposes. In 1979, Richard tried to completely disentangle himself from Elizabeth, saying he wanted to sell his percentage of the Vicky Tiel boutique and keep his apartment in Tenerife, in the Canary Islands. He insisted that Elizabeth pay him the $202,000 she owed him or he would sue her to recover the money.

Accompanied by eleven guests, Richard Burton and Suzy Hunt flew to Arlington, Virginia, where there was no waiting period for marriage and the necessary blood tests could be performed the same day as the ceremony. "Mr. Burton wanted it quiet and confidential and went to great detail to make sure it was kept quiet," recalled the county clerk.

After the five-minute ceremony, the fifty-year-old actor kissed his twenty-eight-year-old bride and said, "Stuck again!" Everyone laughed, and the couple headed for the airport to return to New York and the Lombardy Hotel.

"Marriage was the right thing for us to do," Richard told reporters. "I plan on it lasting forever."

"I am totally, one hundred percent in love with him," said the new Mrs. Burton. "Richard is the only man in the world who stops me dead in my tracks. I've made the promise that I'll be with him all the time—and do all the things a good wife should."

When asked what Elizabeth Taylor thought of his latest marriage, Burton smiled. "She's too much of a lady to say anything," he said. "Still, I don't think she feels particularly warm toward Susan."

In Vienna, Elizabeth dismissed her marriages to Richard Burton with one word: *"Kaput!"*

"I suppose when they reach a certain age some men are afraid to grow up," she said. "It seems the older men get, the younger their new wife is—so maybe I was just getting too old for him. . . . Of course, I am very fond of Richard—you can't have loved somebody for fifteen years and just completely throw them out of your life. But you can get over the agony of love."

Elizabeth's survival technique sprang from her ability to live in the present and look forward to the future, refusing to be dominated by the past. She did not believe in a life after death, only a life on earth which she insisted on living to the fullest. "I think one should do what one has to do now," she said. "While you are here. Not wait or hope and count on something else after one is dead. I think that attitude is wishful thinking."

344 • ELIZABETH TAYLOR

When Mike Todd died Elizabeth had been totally grief-stricken, but had quickly gravitated to Eddie Fisher for a new life. Criticized for the unseemliness of her affair with the singer so soon after her husband's death, she had shouted down her critics: "What do you expect me to do? Sleep alone?" After her marriage to Eddie had run its course, she had immediately moved toward Richard Burton. He had become the love of her life and the passion of her days. Yet when he no longer cared about her in the same way, she had forced herself to move on, determined to grab happiness. "Richard is a bridegroom with a bride," she said now. "I have John. . . . I have a whole new world ahead of me."

That day Elizabeth called John Warner, who flew to Vienna earlier than planned. He stayed with her at the Hotel Imperial and rode to the set daily in her seven-passenger Cadillac, the largest of its kind in Austria. "She introduced him to everyone and sounded just like a little girl," recalled Florence Klotz, the film's costume designer. "I thought John was very nice—though rather square and very stuffy—but Elizabeth was crazy about him. 'He's marvelous,' she said. 'I love him.' I was working on her wedding costume at the time and a traveling suit for her trousseau, but it was all a secret then because they hadn't announced their engagement or a date for the wedding."

John Warner was not intimidated in his first appearance on a movie set. When Elizabeth appeared before the cameras in an extremely low-cut dress, he called her back and suggested gruffly that she expose less bosom. She agreed, and alterations were made immediately in her costume.

"He's a take-charge guy, accustomed to giving orders and reminiscent of Mike Todd," one crew member reported. Warner agreed with the assessment, saying, "Yeah, I did. There's no question."

Not everyone around Elizabeth was impressed by his high-handed manner. "John still thinks he's the Secretary of the Navy," sniffed her hairdresser, Arthur Bruckel. "He tried to tell me to do something and I had to set him straight. I told him that

I worked for Elizabeth Taylor and that was a twenty-four-hour job. Then I suggested that he get his own secretary to run his errands.''

The engagement was announced on October 10 as Elizabeth and John sat in her hotel suite. Surrounding them were John's eighteen-year-old daughter, Mary; Elizabeth's twenty-three-year-old son, Michael Wilding, now divorced from Beth; Michael's common-law wife, Jo; and their baby daughter, Naomi. Liza Todd, nineteen, was also there, with Norma Heyman, a close friend of Elizabeth's from London.

"My engagement ring is not two hundred and ten carats," she told the press. "John designed it, and it means a lot more to me than any ring I've ever had. . . . It's really very simple, unostentatious. It's very lovely."

Playing the part of Désirée in *A Little Night Music,* Elizabeth said she identified with the aging actress who decides to retire from the stage and get married. "There is one line in the film that sounds very much like a cry from my own heart," she said. "Désirée is speaking to her daughter and she says, 'How would you feel about having a home of our very own and my acting only when I felt like it?' That's how I've felt for many years. I've always wanted to have a real home of my own and to act only when I felt like it."

Naturally, the engagement news of Elizabeth Taylor Hilton Wilding Todd Fisher Burton Burton made headlines, one of which read: HERE SHE GOES AGAIN, NUMBER 7 FOR LIZ. John Warner drew a few dubious looks in Washington when he piously announced that he was marrying Elizabeth "because my children need a mother." Neighbors quickly pointed out that his three teen-age children already had a mother, who had bought a home next door to Warner's house in Georgetown so that the children could come and go freely between both parents and not feel so estranged.

With few exceptions, most friends wished the couple well. "Liz is a woman who needs to be loved because she's a very sensitive, lovable person herself," said the diplomat Ardeshir

Zahedi. "She will be a great asset to John. . . . I am very happy for both of them, because both are friends of mine."

"I think their marriage will last," said Barbara Walters. "He is a genuinely nice man, devoted to his children. They each have something to give the other. He will be very good to her. He is not a man who is with one woman and looks for another. And— he doesn't drink."

The public reaction to the engagement was that John Warner had made yet another brilliant mate selection. "He's like Jackie Onassis in that sense," said one woman. "He always marries well." * The private reaction among those who knew Elizabeth was profound relief that she had found somebody to cushion the psychic blows she had suffered from Richard Burton.

"This bloke Warner might be dull as dishwater, but he'll look good on paper to Richard," commented one friend.†

"She had no place else to go but to this man," said another.

"The lady needed a home," said her secretary, Chen Sam.

After filming was completed in Austria, Elizabeth flew to Virginia. There she accompanied her fiancé as he campaigned for President Ford's reelection—while she very quietly continued to support Jimmy Carter. They made their debut as a political couple at Virginia Military Institute in Lexington, where John delivered the Founders Day speech and Elizabeth listened. He insisted that their appearance was strictly apolitical, saying, "I think it would be wrong for any individual to accept an invitation here and then use his presence on these really hallowed and venerable grounds to foster any political interest."

---

* Washington and Lee classmates of John Warner remember him sitting down at a desk, spreading out the folders of the freshman class, and looking up the girls from Sweetbriar, Hollins, Mary Baldwin, Randolph-Macon, and other nearby schools. "Nothing wrong with that," said one man. "We all checked out the girls in those folders. But John added a new twist to it by having the Social Register next to him and checking out the girls' family background as well."

† Richard Burton had already given his opinion of politicians. "Politics is a cheap profession, like acting. It's so cheap, nobody knows why it's important, or why it's not important."

In the middle of his speech he introduced Elizabeth by saying, "And my fiancée is here to salute the corps of cadets." Without a moment's hesitation she stood up and saluted rows and rows of young men, prompting them to break their stiff military stance and toss their hats into the air. At that instant John Warner knew for sure that he had the best partner an ambitious politician could ever have.

He soon was amusing audiences across Virginia with one anecdote that he would repeat five or six times a day. "I feel just like Ben Franklin," he would say. "He was born in Boston. Moved to Philadelphia. Met a lady on the street. She laughed at him. They got engaged. And then he discovered electricity. Ladies and gentlemen," he would conclude, turning to Elizabeth, "allow me to share some electricity with you."

The couple had planned to be married on Thanksgiving Day, but Elizabeth, having fallen off a horse the week before, spent the holiday in the hospital. By the time she was mobile her mother, Sara, and all her children had dispersed. She had already told them she was going to be married outdoors at sunset on top of the hill where John Warner had first proposed. "That was Elizabeth's desire," he said. The next day they would go to the Episcopal church in Middleburg as husband and wife, take Communion side by side, and then fly to Israel to dedicate a Bicentennial forest; go to England, where Elizabeth said she wanted "to show John off to everyone"; and then fly to her chalet in Gstaad for Christmas with their children.

The wedding took place on Saturday, December 4, 1976, at about 5 P.M. For twenty-four hours beforehand, Elizabeth and John, although living in the same house, deliberately did not see each other. "I'm a great believer in the solid, honest traditions," he said. "It sounds old-fashioned, but that's what we wanted." After fox-hunting all afternoon, he walked with his son to Engagement Hill, as Elizabeth had christened it, and stood with a small group of relatives, friends, and farmhands to wait for the bride. The Reverend Neale Morgan of Emmanuel Episcopal Church in Middleburg looked strangely out of place in that bucolic setting when he appeared wearing his white lace vestments. Another minister had refused to perform the ceremony, but the Reverend Mr. Morgan agreed to marry the couple despite all Elizabeth's divorces. He would read the Twenty-third Psalm, which John had requested, and a passage from the Book of Ruth for Elizabeth. "It was very simple," he said later. "No music— nothing but the lowing of the beasts."

Shortly before sunset, the bride appeared in gray suede boots, a lavender-gray cashmere dress, and a matching coat trimmed with huge flounces of silver fox fur. She wore an elaborate lavender turban and carried a bouquet of brush heather. Inside her gray kid glove she was carrying a gold wedding band for her husband which she had melted down from an ornament she had given to her father shortly before he died.

John walked toward her and then startled everyone by loudly summoning his herds of cattle with shouts of "Hoo-ee! Hoo-ee! Hoo-ee!" The curious cows meandered over to the grassy hill as Elizabeth grabbed his arm and squeezed tightly, promising to love, honor, and obey until parted by death. John then placed on her finger the modest gold wedding band that his father had given his mother fifty years before. He kissed her tenderly and then exulted with a wild yell: "We did it! We finally did it!"

"I have never been so happy," said Elizabeth with tears in her eyes. "I'm really so very much in love with John. I don't think I have ever really felt this good and lucky about being in love before. John is such a wonderful man."

For a wedding present the farmer gave his wife a blue corn silo on which he drew a heart saying "JOHN LOVES ELIZABETH." The farmer's wife gave her husband two cows and one bull.

CHAPTER 25

FOR YEARS ELIZABETH TAYLOR PERSONALLY APPROVED every photograph taken of her, except for paparazzi snaps. With scissors she slashed contact sheets of pictures she did not want used and returned them in shreds to photographers.* She never signed autographs. Her rare interviews were to people who she knew would be adoring. These were her prerogatives as a movie queen, and she exercised them without apology. Now, as a politician's wife, she would be subjected to slobbering fans, probing reporters, and inquiring photographers. On the campaign trail she would be expected to sign their autograph books, answer their questions, and smile for their cameras—while remaining sweet, self-effacing, and uncontroversial.

For a woman who smoked and drank, cursed freely, and talked frankly about her private life, the role of political wife was going to be a difficult part to play. Elizabeth promised her husband that she would cut down on the diamonds and décolletage. She said she would also try to restrain herself in other ways, but she made no guarantees. "As a person in my own right, I have always expressed my feelings, and I can't change that," she said. "It may be a problem, but that's the way it is."

---

* "Most actresses are repulsed by a still picture taken of them in action, because that's when the flaws show up. Liz has two chins. Monroe had three. Bette Davis is one of the few who's been able to accept her face. She's willing to take a chance," said photographer Larry Schiller.

The Warners' blitz of Virginia "to test the waters" began in January of 1977 with an appearance at the Hearts of Gold Ball in Richmond, which they reached by Greyhound bus. "Why not?" asked Elizabeth. "I'd never ridden on one before."

In February they flew to Cambridge, Massachusetts, where Elizabeth accepted the Hasty Pudding Institute's "Woman of the Year" award at the annual theatrical performance staged by members of the Harvard organization. Then to Marion, Virginia, where she was crowned with a hairnet and dubbed an honorary cafeteria maid of Emory and Henry College. She gave a drama seminar, stipulating no cameras, microphones, or tape recorders. She told the students: "You can ask me about *National Velvet* or anything else in my career but nothing personal."

In March, Elizabeth presided over a tea urn at a Salvation Army Auxiliary luncheon in Norfolk, presented a trophy to the winner of the Blue Ridge Ladies' Horse Race in Berryville, raised $17,500 for John Dalton's gubernatorial campaign by making one personal appearance in Alexandria, and kissed a bald-headed judge at a bar-association luncheon in Richmond. At each event she drew a record crowd, prompting a political reporter to observe: "Nobody ever thought that a movie star could do this. We didn't realize that it was not just a movie star but *the* movie star!"

In April, Elizabeth cut the ribbon at the grand opening of the Ice Cream Parlor in The Plains (pop. 374), handed out diplomas to graduating seniors of Handley High School, and crowned the queen of the Shenandoah Valley Apple Blossom Festival in Winchester.* When she and John Warner rode as the grand marshals in the Charlottesville Dogwood Parade, one woman shouted to her, "I'll swap my husband for yours!" Elizabeth shouted back, "No, you won't. I like him!" Later she popped two blood vessels

---

* For weeks on end Elizabeth was handed plaques and trophies and crowns to present to people for their notable achievements. At one function she handed over the award saying, "I think it is absolutely superb what you have done. . . . Of course, I'm not quite sure what that is, but congratulations anyway."

in her hand while shaking six hundred hands at a GOP reception in Hampton.

In May, Elizabeth attended the World 600 stock-car race at Charlotte, North Carolina. She did not repeat the mistake she had made months before at Virginia's Martinsville Speedway. "It's so exciting to be here," she had told twenty thousand beer-drinking stock-car fans in Martinsville. "I haven't been this thrilled since the Grand Prix at Monte Carlo."

In June she served as chairman of a Wolf Trap gala in Vienna, Virginia, that starred several of her friends—Halston, Liza Minnelli, Sammy Davis, Jr., and Henry Fonda. Stunned by her disoriented performance, *The Washington Post* reported that she appeared "dazed" and "totally out of it" when she tried to introduce the stars. "Not only did she ramble and repeat herself, but she seemed to be having the most terrible time remembering the names of her chums onstage," the newspaper said. The most embarrassing moment came when Elizabeth forgot to introduce Kay Shouse, the elderly and esteemed Wolf Trap founder. As she raced back on stage to do so, the automatically controlled curtain fell on top of her.

In July, at the fourth annual Virginia Scottish Games in Alexandria, Elizabeth reported that "my Scottish ancestry goes back to Queen Mary of Scotland—on the wrong side of the sheets, I might add." At a GOP fund-raiser staged by the State Nationalities Council, she told the crowd, "If you talk about ethnics, you've got the right chick up here."

In August, she was crippled by a flare-up of bursitis. She was pushed in a wheelchair to the forty-second annual Fiddlers' Convention in Galax and then spent two weeks in a hospital.

In September, she and John Warner held a "simple country supper" for three thousand paying guests at Atoka, raising over $45,000 for the Republican campaign of John Dalton. That same month she was honorary chairman of the Eye Ball in Washington, D.C., and willed her violet eyes to the International Eye Foundation.

In October, the Warners were cochairmen of the Washington

International Horse Show. Days later they flew to New York, where Elizabeth was honorary chairman of the Anglo-American Contemporary Dance Foundation and John Warner got to sit next to Princess Margaret. When he spotted a friend on the dance floor, he pulled Elizabeth over. "I want you to meet the little woman," Warner told the man. Turning to his wife, he said, "Al here is one of my oldest and dearest friends." Not without a sense of humor, Al said, "That makes how many of us now?" "About seven hundred," said an unsmiling Elizabeth.

In November, the Warners hosted a fund-raiser in Washington for a Republican congressman. There Elizabeth emotionally announced that for the first time in her life she was able to get close to people. "Before, I was always isolated and guarded against personal contacts," she said. "I have never been happier than in the seventeen thousand miles I have traveled with John." Days later she appeared at a Republican rally in the town of Amherst. "It's just lovely to be here," she said. "You all make me feel like I fit into Virginia like fried chicken." On the eve of John Dalton's election as governor, she rose from her sickbed to fly to Richmond. "I broke my hand, I broke my hip, and I busted my ear and my ass for Dalton," she said. "I'll be damned if I'm going to miss the victory party."

In December, she starred on CBS-TV's *All-Star Tribute to Elizabeth Taylor*—a Variety Clubs International extravaganza from which the proceeds went toward a $100,000 hospital wing for underprivileged and handicapped children in her name. Surrounded by celebrities like Paul Newman, Joanne Woodward, Janet Leigh, Margaret O'Brien, June Allyson, and Carroll O'Connor, Elizabeth said, "Only in America could a little farmer's wife from Virginia be here with all these big movie stars."

By the end of 1977, Elizabeth had broken all the rules for being a good political wife. She sipped bourbon as she shook hands in receiving lines. She screamed at photographers trying to shoot her from uncomplimentary angles. She refused to give in-depth interviews unless reporters submitted their copy for clearance.

She resorted to earthy idioms to express herself. At a GOP fund-raiser in Manassas, she said, "Everyone here has to mentally get their fingers out and go root for the Republicans." She yelled at her husband in public, used profane language, and even insulted potential voters. One man told her he would win $50 from his fellow factory workers if she would kiss him on the cheek, and she snapped, "Buddy, you just lost your bet."

She interrupted her husband as he, trying to sound statesman-like, read to a reporter Lord Chesterfield's definition of a politician. "What I've always heard about Lord Chesterfield was that he had this marvelous personal aroma," Elizabeth said. "In fact, his aroma was so wonderful that women competed to get his discarded shirts, which they rolled up and put in with their lingerie."

John Warner was speechless. The reporter, nonplussed, said, "You really have had a lingering interest in politics."

"No," said Elizabeth. "Just in underwear."

No other political wife would have risked being seen at Studio 54, the controversial New York discotheque, with Halston and Andy Warhol, a duo that might strike some conservatives as decadent. But Elizabeth didn't mind. She allowed Halston to toss one of his infamous birthday celebrations for her there without telling her husband about another party the designer had given for Bianca Jagger, at which a naked black boy had led a naked black girl around the dance floor on a white pony. Since John would be with her that evening, she cautioned Halston to make her party a little less pagan than Bianca's. He obliged by having thirty clothed Rockettes kick their way into the disco to present her with a five-hundred-pound chocolate cake shaped like her body.

"She blew out the candles and cut off her right tit and gave it to Halston," Andy Warhol recalled. "The TV cameras zoomed in as Halston ate it. Then they waltzed. John Warner ran away."

Most political wives would never have risked open disagreement with their husbands on any subject, but Elizabeth frequently chided hers for not supporting the Equal Rights

Amendment. "I've been working since I was ten," she said. "I have supported my family, a couple of husbands; I feel absolutely equal. I already feel I have equal rights. I feel women who are less fortunate than I have been may need this help. . . . I am for it."

When Warner expressed doubt that a woman could contribute to foreign policy or defense strategy, Elizabeth snapped at him: "There's no reason why a woman can't know as much about defense as a man—no reason at all. It's all in the training." He sensed a public dispute brewing and tried to quiet her, but she immediately started sparring.

"You don't own me like your cattle," she said.

"Oh, yes, I do," he countered. "I'm a Virginia farmer to the hilt—you're my property."

None of this wrangling seemed to make any difference in Virginia. Wherever Elizabeth went she generated excitement among admirers that bordered on hysteria. Autograph seekers even included blue-haired members of the Daughters of the American Revolution. Each outing stimulated more interest and curiosity and reams of publicity. No other unannounced candidate's wife in Virginia history had ever drawn the national press the way Elizabeth did, producing features in *The New York Times, The Wall Street Journal,* The Associated Press, United Press International, *Ladies' Home Journal, McCall's, Good Housekeeping, Esquire,* and a Barbara Walters television special. The raucous movie star so captivated the state's Bible Belt constituency that UPI's Helen Thomas quipped, "The Virginians have taken her to their bosoms—and that's a switch."

"Liz has brought the role of political wife out of obscurity and into the forefront," bragged her husband. She also brought him out of obscurity and into the forefront as a serious political contender. "Mr. Warner's rapid political rise is widely credited to the enormous publicity attracted by his famous wife," said *The Wall Street Journal.* "For not only in Virginia but also in the high society of neighboring Washington, D.C., Elizabeth Taylor is a smash hit. . . ."

"I'm delighted with the crowds," she said, "and I'm flattered. So much the better if it helps John."

"It doesn't bother me that Elizabeth gets so much attention," he said. "I'm glad she can bring happiness into the hearts of so many."

Many women who thronged to her appearances went away feeling better, once they saw for themselves that the woman heralded as the most beautiful in the world was so hefty she could no longer camouflage herself in tunics, caftans, and capes. Crowds poured into church bazaars and country fairs to see if they could still see any trace of the nymph from *National Velvet* or the voluptuary from *Butterfield 8* who had driven her spiked heel into Laurence Harvey's foot. Instead, they found a 175-pound matron.

"All our lives we have wanted to look like Elizabeth Taylor, and now—God help us—we do," moaned a middle-aged woman.

One result—not just in Virginia—was a spate of Elizabeth Taylor fat jokes.

"Every time Liz Taylor goes into McDonald's, the numbers on the sign outside start changing," quipped Joan Rivers. "When she looks up and sees five billion, she thinks it's her weight."

"Liz has more chins than the Hong Kong phone book."

"Got to watch the weight, girls," said Debbie Reynolds in her Las Vegas act. "I've been trying. Know what works for me? On my refrigerator door I've pasted a picture of Liz Taylor."

"Liz has a new bumper sticker," a comedienne told the *Tonight* show. "It says HONK IF YOU HAVE GROCERIES."

"At forty-five, Elizabeth Taylor reminds one of the trademark for Mike Todd's *Around the World in 80 Days:* the hot-air balloon," said *Esquire* magazine in an article titled "National Velveeta."

Even the movie critics took swipes at Elizabeth, with some expressing the hope that *A Little Night Music* would be her last film. "Her appearance is something of a shock," said *New West* magazine. "Couldn't she have been persuaded to spend a few weeks on liquid protein?"

"What brought us all dangerously close to rolling in the aisles was the forlorn attempt to squeeze Elizabeth's quart-sized goodies into a pint-sized ensemble," said the *Daily Mirror*. "Torturously nipped in here, flowing out there and heaving out of you-know-where, it only required heavy dark blue eyeshadow to complete the impression of a superannuated Madam."

"Liz Taylor as actress Désirée Armfeldt, all calories, cleavage and camp, is pitifully miscast," claimed *Cue* magazine. "The one good laugh comes when her lover sings 'If she'd only been faded, if she'd only been fat.' "

Elizabeth tried to make light of her extra poundage and the jokes at her expense. "It's happy fat," she maintained. "I eat because I'm so happy."

"She can take it off," added her husband, who nicknamed her "Chicken Fat" and called her "my little heifer."

"I have lived every second of my forty-five years," she said. "I have never lied about my age. I am proud of my age. It is nothing to hide. I am happy. I am content. I don't want to starve myself because my looks don't matter that much to me. John is interested in having a happy human being, not a model-type beauty."

"I can say she is prettier inside than she is outside," interjected Warner.

"Why, thank you, John," she said.

Later Elizabeth became enraged at the public reaction to her weight gain. "The media's preoccupation with my weight really bugs the hell out of me," she said. "I am not a monument that pigeons can doo-doo on. I am a living human being, and if I want to eat fried chicken six times a day and can still function, that's up to me!"

Shocked and incredulous, many assumed that Elizabeth was eating herself into oblivion because of heartbreak over Richard Burton. Few really believed her when she said she was in love with John Warner, a nice but dull attorney who wore a black sleep mask to bed and a Navy flight suit around the house with

SECRETARY OF THE NAVY stitched above the breast pocket.* She was continually bombarded with questions about the Welsh actor, a ghost that haunted her in every backwater of Virginia.

"What do you really think of your husband?" asked one woman.

"He's very dishy," replied Elizabeth.

"Like Richard Burton?"

"I haven't noticed," she said, with tears in her eyes. "John's the most honest man I've ever met, and one of the kindest."

Despite her protestations, some people remained unconvinced. Others questioned her intelligence. "What kind of good sense could that woman have to give up Richard Burton twice?" asked one matron.

One reporter asked if she felt the same way about John Warner that she had about Richard Burton. Elizabeth replied: "Richard acted as if he was on stage most of the time. It was hard for me to get a word in edgeways. . . . I felt a bit in his shadow, and that's not a constructive way to live. Whatever John and I do, we share completely together. We are a partnership."

She told everyone who inquired that she had never been happier than she was as the wife of a country squire. "John and I have the most gorgeous thing going between us," she said. "I don't think of him as husband number seven. He's number one all the way. And," she added, "he's the very best lover I've ever had.

"The difference in this marriage is the extra effort we both put in. It is not a fifty–fifty proposition but a fifty-one–fifty-one," she said. "John is his own man, secure in his shoes, confident but not smug. He is not threatened by my image—whatever it might be on any given day."

Warner agreed, assuring reporters that he was not at all worried about being compared with Richard Burton. "There's no way to compare us," he insisted. "I have no opinion on him. I

---

* "I always wear the flight suit to write speeches," said John Warner. "It doesn't grab your balls, and it's so seedy a woman won't touch you. You can work!"

am perfectly neutral. I have never met him, and I do not care to meet him." Yet they did meet during the Christmas holidays in Switzerland, when their children came together for a reunion. Afterward Warner said, "We had a nice talk and I found him a fascinating individual."

Finally, in a public announcement designed to dispel sentimentality, Elizabeth declared that she was selling the 69.42-carat Cartier-Burton diamond that her former husband had bought for her in 1969 for more than $1 million.*

After unofficially campaigning through Virginia for a year, John Warner officially announced his candidacy for the Senate on January 6, 1978, joining a field of seven Democrats and four Republicans. He launched a hard-hitting campaign that saw his famous wife throwing rubber footballs through hanging toilet seats at county fairs and teetering into small towns on her four-inch heels to stick JOHN WARNER FOR SENATE buttons on passersby. "I just want to help my husband," she said. "I'm just doing what any wife would do."

In addition to stumping through the countryside of Virginia, the Warners crashed the Washington social circuit and participated in every charitable event that came their way, volunteering themselves, their house, and their hospitality for a host of organizations. Among them was the Corcoran Gallery of Art, which held a fund-raiser and auctioned off a dinner party for six to be hosted by Elizabeth and John Warner at their Georgetown home. The prize went for $500 to three couples who later admitted they might have paid $5,000 for the experience.

"It was the most thrilling night of my life," said one of the men.

"I won't forget that performance as long as I live," said his wife.

After receiving a call from Chen Sam, who told them what to wear, requested they arrive promptly at 7 P.M. for cocktails, and

---

* The diamond was on the market for over a year before a buyer could be found, and then Elizabeth had to accept far less than her $4.5-million asking price.

instructed them to bring no cameras, the sextet decided to send a spectacular bouquet of lilacs to their hostess beforehand.

"We spent seventy-five dollars for the flowers and then looked around the house all night trying to find them," recalled one woman. "Finally we asked about them, and Elizabeth was so embarrassed that she didn't know where they were."

The hostess answered the door wearing a red Halston caftan which matched the red walls of her living room. "Just call me Elizabeth," she told her guests. She sported an eye-popping necklace of what a guest said were egg-sized canary diamonds and amethysts as big as her fist. Her matching earrings were so heavy that one fell off when she moved her head, causing her to yell, "Don't move! Don't move! Don't step on it!"

"We began with drinks, although we didn't need to," recalled one woman. "All of us had had a few beforehand because we were so nervous. Elizabeth had been drinking too, and by the time we arrived she seemed very relaxed. The waiters kept bringing her glasses of Jack Daniel's without her ever having to ask for another drink. She was wearing a back brace that night and carrying a cane. I remember she had to be helped out of the sofa to go in to dinner. 'I'm crippled with arthritis,' she said."

John Warner kept going back and forth to the kitchen to check on the caterer while the three couples sat in the living room entranced by Elizabeth's accounts of her various surgeries. Then one woman asked about her relationship with Montgomery Clift. Elizabeth's mood immediately changed. "I was extremely close to him," she said haltingly. "I was with him the night of his terrible accident when he was so badly hurt. I rode with him in the ambulance holding his bloody head. We were so close—so very, very close—and . . ."

Seeing that she was on the verge of tears, one of the men smoothly changed the subject. "Without knowing it, we had hit on a very touchy subject," he said later. "She got very agitated at the mere mention of Clift's name and very, very maudlin."

At this point John Warner walked back into the room, and the men, all prosperous and professionally successful, asked him about his political campaign. "John was so condescending when we inquired about how it was going in Virginia that instead of answering the question, he pointed to a glass-topped coffee table filled with a collection of cigarette lighters and said, 'Take a look at these, will you? Khrushchev gave that one to me. And here's a PT-109 lighter that John F. Kennedy gave to me.' "

"He was haughty and patronizing and obviously bored with us," said one of the group. "His attitude said, 'Who are these peons and why are they bothering us?' But 'Just Call Me Elizabeth' was wonderful, full of warmth and humor. She made us feel comfortable. One reason I loved her was when we sat down for dinner she ate like a horse and took second helpings. John kept getting up from the table and running into the kitchen or off to his wine cellar, which he seemed to be very proud of."

Every time he left the room, Elizabeth began chatting about another of her husbands. She spoke warmly of Michael Wilding and Richard Burton, whom she referred to as simply "Burton." She said she had never considered herself an actress until after Mike Todd died. "Before that I didn't know what I was doing on the screen," she said. "I was just being myself. But then Mike died and I was left with a little girl and two little boys to raise. I had to work, and I was already in the middle of *Cat on a Hot Tin Roof*. I had to finish the movie, and that's when I learned to act, which is doing something that doesn't come naturally. I was so grief-stricken that I didn't want to go to work, but I did. I got out of my agony by being Maggie the Cat."

"Wasn't that your Oscar in the living room?"

"Yeah," said Elizabeth, "but that's the one for *Butterfield 8*. The other one is for *Virginia Woolf,* and that's at the farm."

"Wow, I remember *Butterfield 8,*" said the man. "I loved you in that film, but I forget who starred with you."

His wife piped up: "I remember. It was Eddie Fisher!"

Dead silence engulfed the room for a few seconds. Elizabeth pushed her chair away from the table, bounced to her feet, and started screaming: "Get out! Get out of here! Leave my house this instant! I will not have that name mentioned in my presence. I will not tolerate it!"

Dumbfounded, the woman wanted to bury herself in the parsleyed potatoes. "Oh, God, I'm so sorry," she stammered. "I—well, I—I'm just so sorry . . ." Quickly her husband tried to rescue the evening by asking Elizabeth about her children, and complimenting her on her pretty dress and the dinner—anything to distract her. Everyone else fussed around and patted her and finally simmered her down.

"That sobered us up real quick," said one guest. "And for the first time all night I was genuinely glad to see John Warner walk back into the room."

After dessert and coffee, the candidate abruptly announced that the $500 dinner was over. "I'm sorry," he said, "but tomorrow at six-thirty in the morning we have to start campaigning in southern Virginia, so I'm going to take the little woman off to bed now."

"Weuh hayuv ta go daown Saouth tamarra and eyut peanut sandwiches," said Elizabeth in her worst Southern accent.

"John didn't like her making fun of mingling with the local folk like that, but she said, 'Oh, I can say whatever I want,' " recalled one guest. "She was being a bad little girl to his Big Daddy. Then I remembered that I had made some disparaging comment about Southerners' being slow and poky, so I apologized to John as we were leaving. He was so smarmy about it I couldn't respond. He patted my hand and in one of those *March of Time* voices he said, 'You were fine, dear, just fine. I don't take what you said personally and I want you to know that. You have a perfect right to express yourself and I want you to feel free to express yourself and not feel that I would ever hold it against you.' "

The three couples left the Warners that evening wishing that Elizabeth Taylor were running for office instead of her husband. "I can't imagine what she sees in him," said one man. "He almost makes Eddie Fisher look good, doesn't he?" said his wife.

In the months that followed, John Warner began looking better to Virginia Republicans, grateful for the $500,000 that he and his famous wife had raised for the party. The farmer and the movie star attracted more people than the circus as they barnstormed small towns and rural counties, campaigning for various GOP candidates. Still, John Warner needed to persuade 1,541 conservative delegates to the convention in June that he was a better candidate than the former governor, Linwood Holton; State Senator Nathan Miller; or Richard D. Obenshain, the former GOP national cochairman and the man most conservative party regulars supported. To that end John Warner campaigned relentlessly for six months. He spent $561,000, twice as much money as the combined expenditures of the other three candidates. Of that amount, $471,415 was his own money.* He emphasized his eight years of government service and his position as Secretary of the Navy, since defense was a major industry in Virginia. At every turn he stressed his years in the Pentagon, talking about "my personal experience at dealing eyeball to eyeball with the Soviets." He waved the flag, telling people that he had served in the Navy and later in the Marines. He never once appeared in public without wearing a red-white-and-blue tie.

June 1 saw more than 9,700 delegates and alternates assembled in Richmond for what was termed "the largest political state convention in the history of the nation." The biggest spontaneous greeting of the opening day went to Elizabeth when she entered the Coliseum wearing a white sailor cap decorated with a big red W and a blue-and-white-striped blouse emblazoned with the slogan "I'M IN WARNER'S CORNER." Convention business stopped for several minutes as the delegates gave the actress thunderous applause. Warner jumped to his feet and joined the joyous crowd. His wife responded by waving both her hands over her head.

The balloting for the U.S. Senate nomination began at 1:30 P.M. on Saturday, June 3. The conservative delegates reeled through three roll calls before Linwood Holton withdrew, leaving Richard Obenshain ahead with John Warner and State Senator Miller trailing. Warner gave Elizabeth what *The Washington Post* described as his "obligatory public embrace." He then

---

* Warner later said he had had to sell forty acres of his farm near Middleburg to settle the $450,000 loan he took out for his campaign.

threw off his coat, loosened his tie, and headed for some of the undecided delegates. Snapping his suspenders, he grasped shoulders, slapped backs, and whispered in ears as the voting continued. The GOP chairman in Loudoun County refused to change his vote from Obenshain. "Anybody but Warner," vowed Tom Laurence. "That's when I put Eddie Fisher's name in nomination, and Elizabeth got PO'd and walked out."

After two more ballots, Miller dropped out and Warner, convinced of victory, leaped on the table where his staff was working and began leading his own cheers. "Go, go, go," he yelled, urging his delegates on. Flailing his arms wildly, he bobbed and weaved like a prizefighter. By the sixth ballot, at 11:30 P.M., he was no longer cheering. The final tally showed him defeated by 37 votes. But John Warner knew better than to look like a poor loser.

Immediately he stepped to the podium, accompanied by Elizabeth, and with emotion in his voice he asked that the vote for Richard Obenshain be made unanimous. As they were leaving the platform, they stopped to greet the winner and his wife. Warner shook hands with the forty-two-year-old attorney and kissed Mrs. Obenshain. Elizabeth simply shook hands and weakly offered congratulations. Then, arm in arm, she and her husband left the Coliseum for their downtown motel. In the crush of defeat, she left her sailor cap behind next to an empty beer can and a bunch of deflated balloons.

The next day Warner, expressing support for the man who had defeated him, promised to campaign for Obenshain and wrote out a check for $500 which he presented to the candidate, saying, "I'll put my money where my mouth is." Then he announced that he intended to remain active in elective politics. Elizabeth agreed. "We're not quitting," she said. "I don't know what office it will be, but I'm sure something will come up."

CHAPTER 26

NOW THAT THE CONVENTION WAS OVER, Elizabeth was allowed to head for Hollywood to begin work on a television film, "Return Engagement," a ninety-minute *Hallmark Hall of Fame* drama written by James Prideaux. While she no longer commanded her $1-million fee, she was still accorded such star prerogatives as having Sidney Guilaroff style her hair and Edith Head design her costumes. She also demanded complete control over her photographs and insisted that each still be retouched before release. Some of the proofs were returned with heavy black grease-pencil lines running from ear to ear under her chin, like posters of a pretty lady after a graffiti artist had added a beard. The embellishments told the photo lab to delete the bloat and double chins. Other stills were darkened around the arms and midriff. As always, those which Elizabeth did not want used at all were scissored and returned to the photographer in shreds.

"Even fat, Elizabeth's a superstar and she knows it," said playwright Prideaux. "While she would deny this, it's nevertheless true that you must be constantly on in her presence. You have to be up, up, up in case Elizabeth wants something—anything at all—and you have to cater to her, cajole her, and entertain her. She's wearing, exhausting, and so energy-consuming, but I will say this: she never once threw her considerable weight around; nor did she get grand and huffy. She was friendly and very down-to-earth. Earthy, you might say. Very earthy.''

The playwright and the director, Joseph Hardy, were put off at first by Elizabeth's raucous, rib-jabbing humor, but later came to respect her as a consummate professional. She refused to memorize her lines, but could read off cards so well that no one noticed. ''I was especially impressed the day we had to make script changes,'' recalled Prideaux. ''Elizabeth's character was originally written to say something like 'I was always so plain'; but Elizabeth knew the audience would never buy her that way, so she changed all the 'plain' references to 'plump,' knowing the audience would certainly buy Elizabeth Taylor saying, 'I was always so plump.' ''

With a string of box-office flops behind her, the forty-six-year-old actress no longer starred in feature films. She had gratefully accepted $100,000 the year before to play a cameo in *Winter Kills,** in which she did not say a word in any of her scenes. At one point she appeared on the arm of the President of the United States, the on-screen arm being provided by her husband, John Warner.

Television work was a gigantic comedown for the onetime top–box-office movie star in the world. After the reviews of ''Return Engagement,'' even television offers became scarce.

''The general results are not satisfying,'' said the *Los Angeles Times*.

''At best an idle curiosity,'' agreed *The Washington Post*.

Elizabeth looked forward to returning to politics, where she

---

* Elizabeth wore a $10,000 marten fur coat in one scene and told writer-director Bill Richert that she wanted to keep it. ''You can't have it,'' he said. ''It's a prop.'' Elizabeth insisted, ''I want that coat.'' After being told again she couldn't have it, particularly since shooting had to be discontinued when the money ran out, she complained to John Warner; he spoke to Richert, and somehow Elizabeth ended up with the coat. Accustomed to keeping all her costumes, she said she especially wanted the wardrobe from this movie. ''It doesn't matter if the clothes are early-sixties styles,'' she said. ''They'll be great in Virginia to wear to teas and church socials when John and I are campaigning.''

was hailed as the biggest thing to happen to the Republican Party since Dwight D. Eisenhower. Politics was a natural transition for an actress accustomed to lights, camera, action, and Elizabeth made the passage easily. She understood her celebrity value and realized that her glamour was her husband's greatest political asset. Without it the Warners would never have been invited to New Hampshire on August 2, nor would they have drawn one thousand singing, dancing, star-dazzled Republicans into the National Guard Armory in Manchester to raise money for the state's GOP coffers. As they were heading back to their motel with Elizabeth carrying the jug of maple syrup presented to her by New Hampshire's governor, a twin-engined aircraft exploded in a ball of fire and crashed in a wooded area near Richmond. Everyone on board was killed, including Warner's recent rival, Richard D. Obenshain.

Scheduled to address a GOP breakfast meeting the next morning, John Warner had instructed the motel clerk to route all his calls to the room of his assistant so that he would not be disturbed. At 2 A.M., news of Obenshain's death broke in Virginia. Moments later a friend phoned for Warner in New Hampshire. The call was intercepted by Warner's assistant, who decided not to tell him until after he had delivered his breakfast speech. But Warner rose early that morning and heard the news on television.

"John came to the door with an absolutely ashen face," Elizabeth recalled. "He said, 'I just heard on TV that Dick has been killed in a plane crash.' He was shaking. I know I went white. I could just feel the blood leave my face. We found it just too hard to believe. We canceled all our engagements and went back to the farm. We just couldn't get over it."

The next day, Saturday, August 5, the Warners went to Richmond to attend Obenshain's funeral at the Second Presbyterian Church. Warner was solemn-faced as he arrived with Elizabeth clinging tightly to his arm. After the service, she walked over to the family limousine in which Helen Obenshain was sitting with her three children.

"I felt so awful for her," Elizabeth recalled. "She was staring at the floor. Her father touched her and she looked up and saw me. She came out and we just embraced each other."

Elizabeth told reporters after the funeral: "I feel empathy for Helen Obenshain. Having your husband burnt to death beyond recognition is something that gives you nightmares for the rest of your life. I know." *

Political jockeying began within hours of Obenshain's funeral. On Sunday—the day after the service—a group of Obenshain supporters met with John Warner at Atoka. These supporters, some of whom were known within the party as the ABW faction (Anybody but Warner), had already contacted two other people to fill the vacancy and were awaiting their decision. They felt that an immediate announcement by Warner would impede other Republicans' chances. "We knew if we had a fight for the nomination it would impair each person's ability to win," said one man.

Very straightforwardly, Warner told the Obenshain backers that he wanted the GOP nomination. While he preferred a unanimous vote by the party's central committee, he said, he could live without it. He added that he intended to announce his plans soon. Then he brought up Obenshain's $110,000 campaign debt. It was everybody's obligation to help retire the amount, he said, so that it would not become the responsibility of the Obenshain family. He also said he hoped Obenshain's staff would remain intact to help the nominee—whoever he might be—because only three months remained until the general election.

"There was never any discussion or hint of any *quid pro quo,*" insisted one participant.

During the meeting Elizabeth sat across the room and talked to Judy Peachee, Obenshain's campaign director, about setting up a $50,000 educational trust fund for the Obenshain children. "It was just something among ourselves. We were talking as women talk . . . about the loss of Dick and what it meant to all

---

* Elizabeth's direct reference to Mike Todd's death followed news stories months before when the body of the producer was stolen from Waldheim Cemetery in Illinois by grave robbers looking for jewelry.

of us,'' Mrs. Peachee recalled. ''Elizabeth was telling me how she had felt when Mike Todd died in a plane crash. I told her that I was so pleased about the trust fund, because it would cost at least $80,000 or more to educate the children. And she was very sympathetic and leaned forward and said, 'I would like to help.' And I said, 'Thank you. Helen will be grateful to know that.' ''

The meeting lasted three hours, with the Obenshain people offering to keep Warner briefed on the status of the campaign organization and, according to one man, advising ''that it would be wise if he could hold off [the announcement of his candidacy] for a few days . . . to let people settle down. It was only natural. It was a very emotional time.''

Warner's preconvention campaign manager had advised the same thing. ''When I called him in New Hampshire right after the crash, we agreed not to take any action whatsoever to seek the nomination . . . or express any desire or lust for the job,'' said former Congressman Joel T. Broyhill. ''We had to let the initiative come from somewhere else. It was not a question of tactics. It was a matter of taste.''

Four days later, when the last of his potential challengers withdrew, Warner announced his candidacy at a crowded news conference in Richmond's state capitol. ''Dick Obenshain was a good friend, waged a good fight, and gave all he had,'' he said. ''Fate has dictated that someone must step up and assume that responsibility.''

On August 12 Richard Obenshain's widow, Helen, made an emotional appearance before the State Central Committee in which she said, ''I want to help John in every way I can.'' Seconds later the committee made Warner the Senate nominee by acclamation.

The Democratic nominee, Andrew P. Miller, twice-elected attorney general of Virginia, had suspended campaigning after Obenshain's death. With Warner's nomination, Miller resumed his schedule of appearances. He promptly tried to dismiss John Warner's biggest political asset. ''I don't think Mr. Warner intends to campaign against my wife and I don't intend to campaign against his. What Liz may do for John is her affair."*

It was Miller's slim, brown-haired forty-seven-year-old wife, Doris, who made sure that the Elizabeth factor became a major campaign issue. "She's a gorgeous woman and I'm not," Mrs. Miller said. "Compared to Elizabeth I've led a very dull life— with only one husband and three babies." Putting herself forward as Poor Old Doris, the Vassar graduate talked about the first time she had met the glamorous movie star and tried to give her some good advice. " 'You're going to have to learn to change clothes in rest rooms, Elizabeth, if you're going to go campaigning with John,' I said. At the time I was only trying to comfort her because she was so upset at having to change in a gas station before a ball." Stressing her lifelong ties to Virginia, Poor Old Doris pointed out that Elizabeth was a British citizen who couldn't even vote for her sixth husband.

To neutralize her seven marriages, Elizabeth told voters that she was an old-fashioned girl who simply had to marry the men with whom she became involved. "It's nobody's concern, but I think it's fairly obvious why I was married so often," she said. "I was brought up by a very moral, puritanical family and I just couldn't adjust to having affairs. It meant that when I thought I was in love with somebody that it had to more or less lead to the altar. . . . When I met John our kind of love was not conducive to just carrying on a long affair. It turned into the kind of love that spells marriage. . . . And I've never been happier."

This was a reasonable explanation for a constituency of churchgoing women. They wanted to forgive her all those marriages, especially that one to Eddie Fisher, and they felt reas-

---

* The *Richmond Times-Dispatch* polled more than 600 voters, asking, "Do you think Elizabeth Taylor will help John Warner's chances of winning the election or not?" Forty-one percent said yes, 34 percent said no, 23 percent didn't know, and 2 percent gave no answer. Among age groups, the youngest seemed to be the most pro-Taylor and the oldest, the least.

sured when she announced that she didn't believe in psychiatry. "I've never been to a shrink," she told them proudly. Many, like John Warner, wanted to believe that Mike Todd had been the love of Elizabeth's life. The late movie producer was the only one of Elizabeth's previous husbands whom Warner ever acknowledged, although he frequently spoke to Michael Wilding on the phone when Wilding called Elizabeth from England, where he was living with his fourth wife, Margaret Leighton. "You know, her life would have been so different if Mike Todd had not died," Warner told reporters. "She was robbed of that man. She would never have remarried if he had lived."

Sara Taylor agreed with her son-in-law. "If Mike Todd hadn't been killed, there would never have been another husband," she said. "But now John just seems like the perfect thing."

Stumping through Virginia's small towns, Elizabeth campaigned for her husband in synagogues,* churches, hospitals, infirmaries, homes for the aged, and shopping centers. She appeared at barbecues and county fairs, shaking hands, signing autographs, and kissing countless cheeks. Good-naturedly, she hurled gloppy cream pies at party activists, stuffed herself with

---

* There were only 59,360 Jews in Virginia—1.1 percent of the state's population—but Elizabeth endeared herself to each one when Simcha Dinitz, Israel's Ambassador to the United States, revealed that she had offered to go to Uganda in 1976 to negotiate with dictator Idi Amin for the release of 104 Jewish passengers held hostage at Entebbe Airport. "She told me, 'I will try to influence him to release the hostages,' " Dinitz said. "Elizabeth told me, 'I will offer myself as hostage for the people.' " The need for Elizabeth Taylor's intervention was removed when Israeli commandos stormed Entebbe and rescued the hostages. John Warner said: "It was a fact that Elizabeth had no desire whatsoever for the public to learn of. . . . The offer was made in a private conversation. . . . Elizabeth contacted the Ambassador because she was so grieved, so deeply grieved by the whole situation." A spokesman for the Ambassador confirmed the story. "Elizabeth Taylor indeed volunteered her services," he said. "The offer was taken seriously. Of course the Ambassador wouldn't endanger Elizabeth Taylor, but the offer was a serious one. It didn't need to be acted upon because of the action of the Israeli commandos." Later Elizabeth appeared in the television movie *Victory at Entebbe.*

chili hot dogs, and pinned Warner buttons on the Democratic supporters of Andrew Miller. "Every candidate's wife that I've ever met has worked as hard as they possibly can for their husbands," she said. "There is nothing different or unusual about my working for John. I'm doing the natural, the normal thing."

Elizabeth outperformed her husband at every bend, drawing hordes of people from around the state willing to pay money and stand in line for hours merely to look at her. "They come to see my wrinkles and pimples, and I don't disappoint them, do I?" she laughed. "This face has been around a lot of years. People want to see if my eyes really are violet or bloodshot or both. Once they check me out, they can go home and say, 'I saw Liz Taylor and you know what? She ain't so hot!' And you know what? They're right! She ain't."

Elizabeth fared far better with voters than her husband did with reporters. When Warner told a television interviewer that he would do much for Virginia's blacks, the reporter followed with a comment about his record as Navy Secretary: "But Admiral Zumwalt says you slowed his efforts to integrate the Navy. . . ."

"No question about it," said Warner. "I don't deny that."

"You did?"

"I think, let's say, that we had a clash on the subject quite clearly. He wanted to go much faster. But if you look at the track record of achievement during that period of five years, I think that it was a very major step forward. . . . It's a very traditional outfit, and you just don't take a hard right or hard left. You sort of move it along and gradually change it, certainly in peacetime."

One of Warner's grim-lipped aides mentioned the controversial remark after leaving the studio, and within minutes Warner was on the phone to the reporter saying that he had misunderstood the question and wanted the tape corrected. The reporter refused, saying that the station policy forbade editing the videotape of political interviews. He quoted Warner as saying, "I think I've made a terrible mistake. It could cost me the election. It could mean two years down the drain.''

Warner later tried to minimize the incident, saying, "I misunderstood the question. I missed the word 'integrate.' " Rushing to his defense, his aide said that it had been a long, hard, fast-moving day, so the candidate "was not as sharp as he normally is, perhaps." Interestingly, the schedule released to the press showed only one event for that day. Then, compounding his *gaffe*, Warner said that he had really been talking about affirmative-action programs, not integration. The next day Elizabeth, who was publicly associated with trying to raise funds for Botswana, was dispatched to Richmond to attend a black church-group meeting and speak on behalf of her husband.

"I don't talk on the issues," she said. "I leave that up to my John, who does it eloquently and with his heart . . . because he cares about you and about people. . . . He's not a slick politician. He's a dedicated human being who wants to do what he can to make this world a better place for you and your children and your grandchildren."

The executive secretary of the National Association for the Advancement of Colored People, the largest black organization in Virginia, thought otherwise. The NAACP official wrote Warner: "Our theory is that you made the statement intentionally to signal the hard core conservative elements that you are still one of the 'good ol' boys.' " Warner denied the charge, but later refused to go to Richmond to speak to the state convention of the NAACP. Instead he attended an oyster festival in Urbanna.

Andrew Miller immediately cashed in on his opponent's blunder. "I am shocked to have learned of Mr. Warner's statement admitting he had frustrated equal opportunity for men and women in our country's armed forces," Miller said. "Mr. Warner's statement is a most significant development in this race, because his attitude contrasts clearly with my record of complying with the letter and the spirit of the laws assuring equal opportunity for all Americans."

Despite the controversy* stirred by his remarks, John Warner was perceived as an unexciting candidate—"dull," "boring," and "pompous" were the adjectives most often used to describe him.

Even so, he had major advantages. Once solidly Democratic, Virginia now possessed the strongest Republican organization in the South and was the only state in the nation not to have elected a Democratic governor or senator in the last decade. Still, a month before the election, newspaper polls showed the race too close to call, with more than a third of the voters undecided. So the Republicans brought in President Ford, Ronald Reagan, Barry Goldwater, and John Connally to stump for Warner.

Elizabeth continued to accompany her husband on various occasions, but she seemed considerably toned down after Poor Old Doris did a television spot in a wash-and-wear dress, saying that she had been married to the same man for twenty-five years and knew him well. Dressed demurely, with only her wedding band for jewelry, Elizabeth no longer spoke out on the issues as she once had. Formerly a vocal supporter of the Equal Rights Amendment, she now said she would never disagree with her husband publicly. "Besides, there are a lot of women that don't want equal rights," she said. "I just didn't know that last year." She said she was now a Republican, not a Democrat. "I was a convert to Judaism and now I'm a convert to Republicanism." She assured Virginians that since she intended to spend the rest of her life with John on the farm, she had applied for U.S. citizenship again. "But I'm not asking for any special privileges, so it will probably take about three years to come about," she said.

To those who assumed that she and her husband were using

* Fortunately for John Warner, his off-the-cuff comment to a *People* magazine reporter a few years before was never published. "I had interviewed John before he married Elizabeth," recalled the reporter. "Afterwards, we were taking pictures at Atoka and his kids were lined up against the skyline when I commented on how beautiful his daughters were. 'Yeah,' he said. 'I just hope a coon doesn't get 'em.' I filed the comment in my story, but it was later edited out."

the Senate campaign as a stepping-stone to the White House, she said, "No way would I like to see John as President of the United States. No way. No way. No way. John, since he was a little boy, has wanted to be a senator from Virginia, and that's it. I am not politically ambitious. We care about people, and if there is anything we can do to help people, that's why we are in politics."

The public joshing that had gone on between husband and wife disappeared toward the end of the campaign. There were no more jokes by John Warner about "my bride" picking up what she thought was the toothpaste and brushing her teeth with his Head and Shoulders shampoo. No longer did he tell audiences that he and Elizabeth were a real comedy team who had pillow fights at night and laughed together from the time they got up in the morning. Nor did he repeat the story about the time Elizabeth left him at an airport to go to the ladies' room, where she waved to him and he waved back. At the next stop, according to the story, they met the Governor and his wife at the Executive Mansion. Elizabeth's first words were "Hello. Lovely to meet you. May I please use your powder room?"

"But Liz," Warner exclaimed, "you just went at the last airport!"

"Oh, no, you damn fool," she said. "I waved at you for a dime and you didn't bring it."

Warner had joked to his audiences that Elizabeth was stumping for him so that when he got to the United States Senate he could pass a bill making it illegal for airports to charge women for such relief. The men's-room facilities, he pointed out, were free.

The ladies' lounge became a haven for Elizabeth when reception lines got too long and fans too overwhelming. Fleeing to the rest room, she sat sipping her whiskey and munching on chicken wings. When her admirers pressed so close that she could not get out, John Warner broke through to rescue her. Occasionally Warner was so busy backslapping and giving his smacking kisses that he did not notice when his wife crept away. At these times she would collapse and sob uncontrollably until rescued.

By the end of the campaign the candidate's nerves were frayed and his patience thin. He had poured over $800,000 of his own money into the race and still trailed Andrew Miller by 6 percentage points. To catch up, he planned to spend another $200,000 for a media blitz in the last few days. Yet he could not buy his way out of his many *gaffes*. He was asked about contributing money to Richard Nixon's presidential campaigns. He said he had never done that. He retracted his denial days later when newspapers disclosed that he had given over $100,000 to Nixon's various political committees. He said he had forgotten those contributions.

As the political pressures increased, so did the number of Elizabeth's incredible accidents. She was thrown off a horse; she broke two blood vessels in her hand; she wrenched her back; she fell off an electric bike. At a Richmond pizza parlor, she suddenly cried out about a sharp pain "like lightning going through my eye." She was taken to the hospital, where a small sliver was removed and her eye was bathed and bandaged. A few days later at a campaign breakfast in Norfolk, she walked to the head table to join President Ford and caught her heel in the carpet, twisting her ankle, spraining her neck, and breaking the handle on her purse. Warner took her back to their suite and later told reporters, "I felt I had to stay with her for a while. She needed a little love and affection."

Elizabeth's most dramatic accident occurred two weeks before the election in Big Stone Gap, when she and her husband were circulating among GOP guests at a buffet dinner. They were on the way to the kitchen to greet the cooks and waitresses when Warner spotted a tray of fried chicken and grabbed a piece, saying, "That's my favorite dish." Elizabeth opened her mouth wide and he gave her a bite. Seconds later she gagged and clutched her neck with her hands. The chicken bone was lodged in her throat and, barely able to breathe, she could not cough it up. She reached for a handful of hot buttered rolls and started stuffing them down her throat to shove the bone into her stomach. Nothing worked. Warner's campaign aides sped the couple to the Lonesome Pine Hospital. There Elizabeth was sedated and a thoracic surgeon dislodged the bone with an extended plastic tube.

"She's lucky," he said. "She should count her graces. This could have lodged in her larynx and killed her."

The next morning, newspapers headlined Elizabeth's dramatic escape from death. "ACTRESS NEARLY CHOKES AT CAMPAIGN RALLY," blared *The Washington Star*. "HOSPITAL DASH FOR LIZ TAYLOR: SHE CHOKES ON CHICKEN BONE," proclaimed the *New York Post*. One of Andrew Miller's aides, remembering the last time Elizabeth Taylor had almost died, threw down a newspaper in frustration. "She won an Oscar then," he said. "Now she'll probably win the election!"

His concern was legitimate, for Elizabeth's experience with the chicken bone moved the public to sympathy and gave her husband's campaign added momentum. Neither candidate could compete with her for the next two weeks as radio, television, and newspapers reported her daily recuperation from a torn esophagus.

Still, she was missed on the campaign trail. Days before the election, she was released from the hospital and Warner's manager told her, "Elizabeth, if there's a time when the show must go on, this is it." Behind in the polls, Warner agreed. So Elizabeth resumed her tours of American Legion halls, church basements, and country-club luncheons.

"I'm slightly croaky," she told her audiences. "I guess you know the story. I was pretty hungry. I ate a piece of chicken and the bone fell in love with my throat."

As the crowds cheered and shouted, she added, "I guess I'm a fighter and a survivor. Otherwise I wouldn't be here."

On election day, November 7, John Warner went to the polls to vote for himself while his British wife stayed home. Then they went to Richmond with some of their children to eat fried chicken with Governor and Mrs. John Dalton and watch the returns in the Executive Mansion. They remained in the mansion until 1 A.M., when the unofficial count indicated that Warner had squeezed ahead by less than 1 percentage point. Out of 1.2 million ballots cast, he had a margin of 4,721 votes.

A misty rain was falling as their limousines pulled up to the awning-sheltered entrance of the Hotel Jefferson. The Warners and the Daltons pushed their way through a crowd of hundreds yelling, "We want John," "We want Liz." Warner took the microphone and said, "Elizabeth and I—our hearts go out to Andy and Doris Miller. We've come from a point of zero in this campaign last August to hold the lead tonight." Then he paid his respects to the widow of Richard Obenshain and told supporters that the campaign had been the greatest learning experience of his life. Turning to his wife, he said, "Now I want to introduce my partner in this thing, someone who has been at my side throughout."

Elizabeth clutched a dozen American Beauty red roses as the loudest applause of the night went up. With tears in her eyes she told the jubilant celebrators, "I'm just so thrilled because I know you did the right thing. It's going to be so marvelous for all of us." She looked up at her husband's face, closed her eyes, and said, "Thank God. Thank God."

Warner whipped out of his pocket a torn piece of newspaper which he waved to the crowd. It was, he said, his horoscope from the Richmond newspapers that day which predicted he was "a winner."

But it would be three weeks before he could officially claim his victory. He had to wait for a recount by the State Board of Elections, which did not certify his election until November 27. Even then the victory was insecure because Andrew Miller had not yet conceded defeat. Under Virginia law the Democrat, who was less than 1 percentage point behind in the vote, could demand a precinct-by-precinct recount. However, the loser of the recount would have to bear the $125,000 cost—an amount that Miller was having trouble raising. On December 7, Miller announced that he would proceed with a recount. But ten days later Miller was unable to post an $80,000 bond ordered by a court, and he was forced to concede defeat.

Senator William Scott resigned his seat a day early so that John Warner could be sworn in as an interim Senator and get twenty-four hours' extra seniority. The first swearing-in ceremony took place on January 3, 1979, in Virginia's state capitol, where Elizabeth, swaddled in silver fox fur, held the Bible on which her husband vowed to uphold the U.S. Constitution. "I felt such a marvelous sense of relief," she said later. When Governor Dalton introduced John and used the term "Senator" for the first time publicly, she squeezed his arm affectionately.

On January 16 they headed for the United States Capitol in Washington, where the newly elected Senator was to be sworn in by Vice President Mondale. He carried the same Bible that Elizabeth had held in Richmond. This time she wore a bright blue suit with a white fur boa and sat in the family gallery to watch the oath-taking. Accompanying her were her eighty-four-year-old mother, Sara Taylor, who had flown in from Palm Springs; her eighty-two-year-old mother-in-law; and the two black maids who worked for the Warners in Georgetown.

"Do you solemnly swear to support and defend the Constitution of the United States against all enemies foreign and domestic . . . so help you God?" asked the Vice President.

"I do," replied John Warner. Turning to the gallery, he threw back his head and puckered his lips in the direction of his wife. Elizabeth responded by standing up and blowing him back a huge kiss. "I'm so excited and so very proud," she said, her eyes full of tears. Business stopped on the floor of the world's most exclusive club as all eyes looked in her direction. Only one man—a Democrat—remained unimpressed. "Looks like Virginia just elected the three biggest boobs in the country," he said.

CHAPTER 27

THE MONDAY AFTER JOHN WARNER TOOK OFFICE, he opened the morning newspaper to see himself described in Garry Trudeau's *Doonesbury* comic strip as Senator Elizabeth Taylor. He chuckled. On Tuesday the strip defined him as "a dim dilettante who managed to buy, marry, and luck his way into the United States Senate." He shrugged it off. On Wednesday the cartoonist described Elizabeth as "a tad overweight but with violet eyes to die for." Trudeau had her saying: "We had a tough race. But happily the voters of the state of Virginia knew me and they knew what I stood for even when I myself wasn't sure. As those of you who are in politics know, you can't buy that kind of support, although we certainly did our level best. It is thus with great pride that I introduce you to my husband, John Warner." The Senator laughed, saying he could take a joke.

On Thursday he no longer found the comic strip quite so funny. "Remember when the party's original nominee died in that accident?" asked one *Doonesbury* character. "The Warners were so stricken with sympathy that they offered to take on the campaign debt and to set up a trust fund for the family. Guess who was then tapped the next day?"

"Well, they didn't have to offer anything. . . ."

"Can't you just hear him making his case?" continued the character. " 'I'll show you my quid if you show me your quo!' "

The implication that Warner had paid off the campaign debt

and established a trust fund in exchange for the Obenshain family's support of his nomination rankled the new Senator. His press secretary said, "There is no basis in fact for that Obenshain business."

Elizabeth was angered by the *Doonesbury* strip and refused to be polite when reporters asked about it. She was still seething over an editorial-page cartoon by Pat Oliphant that had appeared a few weeks earlier in *The Washington Star*. The cartoonist had drawn Warner in a riding habit astride an extraordinarily fat, bosomy, and besaddled Elizabeth, who was carrying him to victory. The caption read: "TALLY HO—A VIRGINIA HUNT SCENE." Elizabeth said the cartoon was vicious. She hated the jokes at her expense, especially the one told by the politician who was last in a long line of speakers: "Standing here, I feel just like Liz Taylor's seventh husband. I know what I'm supposed to do, but I've got to figure out how to make it interesting."

The *Doonesbury* strip appeared in 450 newspapers throughout the United States, including ten in Virginia. The *Richmond Times-Dispatch* reprinted it with a special explanation to readers that it found "some of the comments in bad taste."

Days later the *Richmond News-Leader* ran an open letter from Helen Obenshain refuting the allegations. She said John Warner had paid $39,000 for her husband's campaign supplies, office space, and equipment, but nothing more. "John Warner did not contribute to paying off the accumulated campaign obligations," she said. "His only contribution to the Obenshain campaign came on the day following the June convention. At that time he wrote a check for $500 and handed it to Dick. . . . Neither he nor his wife had anything whatsoever to do with the establishment of the trust fund. Nor have they, singularly or jointly, made any gift of any kind to it. Mr. Warner has been prudent in perceiving the potential conflicts that could derive from involving himself and/ or his wife in the trust."

Unfortunately, Mrs. Obenshain's denial did not appear in 450 newspapers as did Garry Trudeau's comic strip, and the image of Senator Elizabeth Taylor as a dim but opportunistic dilettante

The Last Star • 381

was firmly established. Aware of the problem, John Warner sat down with his press staff to try to repair the damage. Unlike most freshman senators, he had national identification. In fact, he had so much recognition that he instructed his aides to turn down every interview request from the national media, including the *Today* show, *Good Morning America,* and *Time, Newsweek,* and *People* magazines—the very outlets that most politicians run after. He decided to cooperate solely with the media in Virginia and then only when asked. Press releases were to be kept to an absolute minimum.

Determined to look like a serious, hardworking senator, Warner realized that he had to maintain a low profile. "No more showboating," he told his staff. He said he did not want to be saddled with the sobriquet Senator Elizabeth Taylor the rest of his life, and he no longer wanted to look "flashy" or "Hollywood."

This image change was so important to him that he took the problem home to Elizabeth and reported back to his staff that she was going to cooperate fully. "She took a year's leave of absence from her career so as not to upstage him or to detract from the image he was trying to build," confided one of Warner's Senate staffers.*

The law was laid down to the farmer's wife—no more discotheque parties and no more Studio 54. Socializing had to be strictly limited to politics. "We represent a lot of blue-collar workers in Virginia, so if a labor union invites us to a reception, we have to go," he said. No more outrageous comments to reporters and no more public profanity. "You must play a very low profile," he instructed.†

---

* As part of her effort to tone down the movie star and play up the Senator, Elizabeth insisted that her name be omitted from the advertising for *Winter Kills.*

† In 1980, political columnist Max Lerner reflected on Elizabeth's low profile. "Every time we talked she tried to make a great point of telling me that there was nothing between us. She doesn't want John Warner to find out about our love affair. I'd be a real threat to him because I am a serious man."

During the campaign Warner had promised that he would not take any trips abroad during his first year in office. "I am staying home," he said. He did not want to look like his predecessor, who visited forty foreign countries during his single term. He told Elizabeth that he could not travel with her and that if she wanted to accept President Anwar Sadat's invitation to visit Egypt or to attend the Taiwan Film Festival, she had to go by herself or with her British friend Sharon Hornby.

Having sworn that he would conscientiously make every roll-call vote, even if it meant staying in his Capitol Hill office until midnight, he also told her that he would not always be available to take her out to dinner in the evenings. Elizabeth, not realizing what personal sacrifices would be required, said she understood.

The first big disappointment came the night of her forty-seventh birthday, when they had reservations for dinner at Dominique's, one of Washington's finest French restaurants and Elizabeth's favorite. Warner called at the last minute to say he couldn't make it because the Senate would be in session late and he did not want to miss a roll call. In tears, Elizabeth slammed down the phone, fixed herself a drink, and called Dominique D'Ermo, the restaurateur.

She said that John was on the Hill, and she could not come to the restaurant by herself because people would talk. But she couldn't stand being alone, she said, so would Dominique please come to her house in Georgetown and cook dinner for her there. Dominique, who had first met Elizabeth in Paris in 1963, asked

Although John Warner was unaware of Elizabeth's earlier involvement with Max Lerner, he did know about her relationship with Henry Wynberg, the used-car salesman. In an effort to help extricate her from business dealings with Wynberg, Senator Warner accompanied his wife to California to meet with him. Elizabeth had promised to testify in his behalf in a lawsuit Wynberg had brought against the *National Enquirer*, which had alleged that Elizabeth had presented him with $770,000 in camera equipment and gifts. In exchange for her testimony, Elizabeth demanded the termination of their business dealings in the Elizabeth Taylor Cosmetic Company and the Elizabeth Taylor diamond business. She also insisted that Wynberg never discuss their former relationship with anyone.

what she wanted for dinner. Stone crabs, she said, yellowtail fish, Dom Perignon champagne, and chocolate cake. He gave her menu to his chef, selected some of his finest wines, and drove the birthday dinner to the Warners' $800,000 house on S Street. He stayed with her, sipping wine and talking, until the Senator arrived a few hours later. He left the house that night convinced that Elizabeth Taylor was still very much in love with Richard Burton. But John Warner was not worried.

"It's not easy for any wife to wait late into the evening for her husband to come home," he said. "Candidly, that's been the most difficult adjustment for her. But Elizabeth's number one role is that of wife and homemaker. Number two, I encourage her in her career, in which she has the luxury of stepping in and out of cameo roles that can be done in thirty to sixty days. Third, she wants to be a typical Senate wife. She went to her first bandage-rolling session, only to find that they don't roll bandages anymore." *

The prospect of Elizabeth Taylor as a typical Senate wife, dressed in a blue-striped Red Cross uniform with a badge stitched to her left sleeve saying LADIES OF THE UNITED STATES SENATE, sent photographers racing to the ornate Caucus Room of the Russell Senate Office Building one morning shortly after John Warner took office. Naturally, Elizabeth was the only wife whose picture appeared in the newspapers the next day. On the record, none of the ladies begrudged her the publicity. Privately, a few thought she was "a bit tarted up with all that makeup," but most said she was very nice.

"She probably knows that her picture will be taken wherever she goes, and with all that makeup on she will photograph better," said one Senate wife, trying to rationalize the Cleopatra eye makeup.

"Since Elizabeth is a great friend of Halston, maybe she can

* For many years the Senate wives rolled bandages, but they now make puppets and clothing to be distributed to children in hospitals. They meet every Tuesday while Congress is in session, and the wife of the Vice President presides at the meetings.

get him to create a new Red Cross uniform for us to wear—one with a plunging neckline," joked another.

For her part, Elizabeth publicly professed to like the ladies of the Senate. "I feel very much at ease with them," she said. "They're all a little bit crazy and have a sense of humor. They can laugh at themselves. If you don't have a sense of humor in politics, you're cooked."

In her new role as a U.S. Senator's wife, Elizabeth began a round of official activities, appearing at high school drama festivals in Virginia and sponsoring projects connected with the International Year of the Child. She never gave speeches; she simply appeared and said a few words, which thrilled her audiences. The mere sight of Elizabeth Taylor was enough to send people home happy. They felt privileged to be in her presence, and they were ecstatic when she told them how much more she enjoyed her political incarnation than her life as a movie star.

"In both worlds you are in front of the public and you are constantly on," she said, "but politics is real life and show business is fiction and fantasy. In politics you write your own script. You don't have Tennessee Williams writing for you, and if you make a boo-boo, you can't ask for a retake or blame it on the director. Of course, in show business you're protected. In politics you're not. You can be asked any insulting question and you have to answer."

Even with the campaign over, reporters continued to dog her at every appearance and flashbulbs popped whenever she walked into a room. The questions never stopped, and Elizabeth bristled each time she was asked if she felt diminished in her new role. Did she resent basking in the reflected glory of her husband, rather than being the star herself?

"Listen," she snapped at one reporter, "I've been working since I was ten years old. I haven't gone out to pasture. I haven't given up. I have no problems with my identity and I'm not on an ego trip. I know my own identity, not as a movie star, but as a woman."

She grew increasingly hostile toward the press as she saw herself described in print as "overripe," "matronly," and "Rubenesque." She heard whispers about her drinking—"Well, I'm not so sure it's the cortisone [for her bursitis] and not Jack Daniel's," one woman told *People* magazine. She walked out of a $60-a-plate testimonial dinner in her honor when the comedian joked about the upper slopes of her chest, saying that her bosom sank into her stomach like the sun into the sea. She read innumerable unflattering comments about her immense weight, which were always accompanied by starkly realistic photographs. Finally she refused all interviews. She began going out less and less, preferring to stay home to do her eating and drinking.

"More people worry about my weight," she said. "I don't. I don't even know how much I weigh. My husband doesn't worry about my weight either. He seems to like the way I look."

Actually, John Warner was quite concerned about his wife's weight. He tried to encourage her to diet, while her secretary discreetly checked out various beauty spas where she might go for a few weeks to reduce. Finally her good friend Maury Hopson, a New York hairdresser, recommended The Spa at Palm-Aire in Pompano Beach, Florida.

The $2-million fat farm, located between Miami and Palm Beach, sits in the middle of a leisure-living community surrounded by 2,400 acres of condominiums, apartments, and swimming pools with five golf courses, three clubhouses, and nineteen tennis courts.

"We needed a place that was easily accessible and would provide nice arrangements for privacy," said Hopson. "I went with her because her daughter couldn't go and neither could Chen Sam. And she certainly couldn't go by herself!"

Secretly, arrangements were made for Elizabeth to go to the spa in July for three weeks. The director assured her that July was the least busy time, and she promised private classes so that Elizabeth would not have to exercise with the rest of the ladies. The director also agreed to close the spa facilities to the other guests for a few hours in the afternoon so that Elizabeth could have absolute privacy in the steam room and swimming pool. The $1,800-a-week spa regime consisted of three hours of exercise throughout the day interspersed with sauna and steam baths, massages, and beauty treatments, plus a salt-free diet of 600 calories a day and absolutely no alcohol.

"I flew to Washington and we had a big pig-out," recalled Maury Hopson. "Then we went to the spa. We were so good there. We didn't drink, but we kept two bottles on hand just in case. We said, 'Let's not get ourselves crazy that we can't drink. We'll take it and have it if we need it.' We had a wonderful time at Palm-Aire."

Elizabeth weighed nearly 175 pounds by the time she went to Palm-Aire. She was so self-conscious about her weight that she refused to take off her robe in front of anyone for the first few days.

"Her spirits were not great when she arrived," confided the director. "It obviously bothered her to be overweight, and she had never been to a spa before."

"I felt so sorry for her," said one employee. "She looked like a big violet-eyed balloon when she rolled in here. You could tell she hated herself for being that fat. At first she was so uptight that she didn't speak to any of us, but after a few days on the plan she lost weight and began to relax. Lisa, the director, turned herself inside out to help and even gave her private exercise classes in her room, which is unheard of here, but I guess for Elizabeth Taylor you break all the rules."

Elizabeth took all her meals in her room rather than eat with the rest of the guests in the spa dining room. "She can't just go *shlumping* in someplace," explained Maury Hopson. "She's got to put it all together, and that takes hours. So it was much easier to just eat in the room."

Elizabeth did not want anyone to know that she had signed herself into a reducing resort, especially after a career of forswearing such places, but the news soon leaked, and reporters from around the country flew to Florida.

"Lisa, the spa director, told me she was being hounded by the press and journalists wanted a comment," said Hopson. "I told her to say nothing." *

Over the Fourth of July, John Warner flew to Florida to spend a few days with his wife celebrating their engagement anniversary. He arrived with a gift—three little red, white, and blue bracelets from Cartier. He also brought a front-page article about himself from *The Washington Post* which evaluated his first six months in office. Titled "SURPRISING SENATOR," the piece reported that he had not, as expected, become a regular on the Washington party circuit with his actress wife. "Nor has he been the showboat that angered critics during the campaign. He hasn't done a lot of dumb things."

Some cynics said that John Warner's not acting stupidly was indeed front-page news. But the Senator was convinced that his low-profile plan had paid off, and he waved the article triumphantly. He said he especially liked Elizabeth's quoted comment about how pleased she was that people were beginning to think of her "more as Mrs. John Warner and less as Elizabeth Taylor."

"He was thrilled that there wasn't one thing negative in that article," recalled Hopson. "Just thrilled."

The Senator also was delighted with the progress his wife had made by dieting and exercising every day. By the end of her stay she had lost 20 pounds and looked years younger and happier. "She's prettier than I've ever seen her in the three years since we married," Warner told spa personnel. "She's the Liz I used to know."

---

* Elizabeth presented the spa director with a set of the private photographs that Maury Hopson had been taking of the three of them. Days later several of those pictures appeared in the *National Star,* including two which showed Elizabeth taking a bubble bath. The spa director (no longer associated with the spa) refused to comment on the matter. Senator Warner was so incensed by the invasion of his wife's privacy that he called the chairman of the board of Palm-Aire and complained loudly. He also took the matter to a lawyer. Both the attorney for Palm-Aire and the attorney whom the Warners originally consulted refused to comment on the matter. Despite the apparent dispute, Elizabeth later returned to the spa for several weeks.

"Now I can say 'no' to all those snack foods," she said. "No more chili hot dogs, no more potatoes, French-fries or popcorn. My target is to knock off thirty-five pounds."

Elizabeth's stay at the spa was cut short by a transatlantic call announcing the sudden death of Michael Wilding, her second husband. The sixty-six-year-old British actor, plagued by epilepsy, had died of head injuries after a fall in his home near Chichester, England. Elizabeth made plans to fly with her daughter Liza Todd and her two sons, Michael and Christopher Wilding, to the memorial service. Although divorced for twenty-three years, she and Michael Wilding had shared a touching affection. In fact, he was the only husband with whom she had remained on good terms. The message on her wreath of white roses read: *"Dearest Michael, God bless you. I love you. Elizabeth."*

Unfortunately, her presence overshadowed Wilding's death, and her new weight loss received far more coverage, with before and after pictures appearing in the British press. One headline proclaimed: "LIZ LEAVES LOURDES."

She returned to Washington and continued her supporting role as Mrs. John Warner, wife of Virginia's junior Senator. Together they hosted their annual Republican fund-raising picnic at Atoka for 4,000 people, with some of the proceeds from the $25-a-ticket affair going to pay off Warner's $1.8-million campaign debt. At the party Elizabeth circulated, shook hands with everyone, and do-si-doed with her husband on stage so the crowds could snap them with their Instamatics.

"It's a good thing to focus on the political wife," John Warner told his guests. "After all, she takes the same bumpy rides and has to eat the same chicken as her husband."

But she did not reap the same rewards. Once the election is won, the political wife is left behind while her husband goes to the United States Senate to pass laws that make the world turn.*

---

* John Warner's first piece of legislation was a law banning pay toilets in airport rest rooms. "It's not something to build a career on, and I know there's some humor arising from it," he said. "But in between SALT briefings and FTC regulations, I took a little time to try to help

She is now expected to entertain constituents and quietly make puppets. Try as she did, Elizabeth could not constantly submerge herself in the role. At a Redskins football game in Washington that fall, she was drinking and huddled in conversation with a male reporter. Her husband worried that she might be characteristically frank with the journalist and regret it later, so he kept trying to get her to come back to watch the game with him.

"Fuck him," said Elizabeth. "I'm having fun."

A week later that incident was reported in *The Washington Post,* with the gratuitous observation that "Mrs. Warner's much publicized recent weight loss at that Florida health spa has now been regained." *

In February of 1980 the Senator and his wife attended the GOP's annual Tidewater Conference in Maryland, where John Warner offered a resolution that draft registration be resumed, but only for men.

"Only for men?" snapped Elizabeth. "I'm a lady who likes to fight, and I think women would go into the trenches tomorrow if they could."

"I'm sorry, but you don't have a vote on this issue," he said.

"Well, you invited me here," she said.

"I'm sure that Abe Lincoln, the Great Emancipator, would have taken my same view," said Warner.

"Abe Lincoln? Just how many years do you want to go back?"

Exasperated, John Warner observed again that spouses of

---

some people with a small but real problem." When Congress enacted the law, Warner issued a press release which he later framed for his wife with a note saying: *"Elizabeth, my dear wife and fellow campaigner. I have kept my promise to get this law passed. John."*

* Weeks later Elizabeth was sitting in a restaurant when an ardent fan kept pestering her for autographs, saying, "And just one more for my cousin in Oklahoma." The fourth time, Elizabeth struck back. Instead of giving the woman another autograph, she scribbled a two-word message which was reported in the next day's newspaper. "We can't print the first word in a family newspaper but we can tell you that the second word was 'off,' " stated the story.

390 • ELIZABETH TAYLOR

U.S. senators and congressmen were part of the conference but did not have a vote. Then he said that testimony before the Armed Services Committee indicated that women were volunteering for more jobs than the services had to give them.

"What kind of jobs are those?" asked Elizabeth.

"Well, I'm proud to say that when I was Secretary of the Navy I opened up many more jobs to women than they had ever held before," he said.

"Rosie-the-Riveter jobs," sneered Elizabeth.

At this point Congressman Bud Shuster interrupted to say that excluding women from the registration requirement would discriminate in their favor.

"It all depends on how you look at it," said Elizabeth.

Another congressman jumped in to say that he thought the registration issue should not be confused with the problem of "alleged discrimination" against women.

"Alleged discrimination!" Elizabeth shouted. "Did you say alleged discrimination?"

"Now, Liz, hold on, here," said Warner, waving his hand to silence her.

"Don't you steady me with that all-domineering hand of yours," she said.

"Liz, you'll have to defer to my base of knowledge," he said, citing his background in the Navy and the Marines.

"Yeah, but I've been working since I was ten years old."

"And you've got to get back to work again soon, too," muttered her embattled husband.

People misinterpreted this incident and assumed that the public flare-up indicated trouble in the Warners' marriage. Misreading the signs, they figured that Elizabeth's continual weight gain was symptomatic of her unhappiness with her life in Washington and the role of political wife. Soon the European press published reports that the actress was headed for another divorce. The rumors seemed confirmed after Christmas, when John Warner returned to the United States alone and left his wife in Gstaad at her chalet.

Hotly denying the reports, Elizabeth said, "There is absolutely no truth to any of it. It's those damn European photographers who started the rumors. John left to return to the States to fulfill political commitments and I stayed in Switzerland to spend the New Year with my children. Since John had gone home, the European press started screaming about a fight—which was simply untrue."

Still the rumors of a rift persisted, especially with the news of Elizabeth's plan to revive her movie career. Now even good friends wondered about the Warners' marriage. "I had dinner at Katharine Graham's house and she even asked me if John and I were breaking up," fumed Elizabeth. "Katharine said her newspaper, *The Washington Post,* and her magazine, *Newsweek,* were getting reports of the marriage breakup."

Elizabeth reassured Mrs. Graham that all was well. She then called a reporter to get her point across to the public. "I am really angry about these lies," she said. "Everything is very happy with John and me. There's no separation whatsoever. I'm enjoying all of my life here, and I think I go on getting better at handling it all. I love the life of a senator's wife and being involved in politics. I am happy with my life in Washington—I don't miss the glamorous life of Hollywood. My life did change when I married John and moved here, but I have finally found the basic life I had been looking for all my life."

Senator Warner, who was sitting with his wife at the time, said, "Any politician's wife gets a little tired of the strains here. You get fed up with eating rubber chicken on the road, even when chicken is the meal Liz most loves cooking for me. There have been many nights when she's had to be alone when I've remained at the Senate for a vote.*

"But everything is honestly beautiful between us. It keeps on getting better, too," he said. "It's just a shame that there's an

---

* John Warner was still very proud of his perfect attendance record and sent notice to all his constituents that he had made every roll-call vote in the Senate and had thereby established a record that was unequaled by any Republican senator in nearly a decade.

annual spate of rumors that indicate our marriage is about ready to break apart.''

Having made his mark in the U.S. Senate as a conscientious, hardworking member, John Warner was no longer referred to as Senator Elizabeth Taylor. And to that end, Elizabeth, who insisted on being identified simply as Mrs. John Warner, had given him her lowest possible profile. Now both agreed it was time for her to go back to work. She began making inquiries into possible movie, television, and even theater projects.

"I have never announced a retirement from films," she said. "I have never said I wouldn't make another film again. I've always said that I'd wait patiently for the right project to come along. Making a movie wouldn't take me away from John for much more than six weeks, and I think we can both comfortably survive that. We plan on living our lives together until we die— so a brief return to Hollywood wouldn't hurt us.''

Senator Warner agreed. "I am really encouraging her to do it," he said. "I hope it all works out for her to do a new film.''

John Warner had never seen Elizabeth Taylor in a movie before he married her. Their first argument occurred when she wanted him to stay up one night to see *National Velvet* and he wanted to go to bed. Thumping him with a pillow to keep him awake, she won, forcing him to watch her favorite film.

"He was under pain of death if he didn't see that one," she said. "Afterwards he kept saying we must ride in the hunt together.''

"There are times when Elizabeth will determine that we are going to watch one of her old movies on television," he laughed. "I'm dead tired, because I get up at six fifteen in the morning, but she says, 'We're watching,' and one by one I'm seeing all her movies.''

His favorite was *Who's Afraid of Virginia Woolf?*—"There's no question about it. It's a very dynamic and moving piece.''

Warner even admitted that he'd "always had a secret dream that I'd like to play a bit part in a movie. I tease Liz about it, because it shows the competitiveness of our marriage. . . . She would be the boss and I would be the butler. Even better would be one where I play a gun-slinging cowboy and she is the barmaid. We would have just a red-hot affair.''

Leaving his film fantasy aside, John Warner returned to the U.S. Senate while his wife waited for a movie to come her way. Finally, after Natalie Wood turned it down, Elizabeth was offered a part in *The Mirror Crack'd,* a film version of an Agatha Christie mystery. She signed for $250,000 to play an aging glamour star who clings to the memories of her heyday. The role was that of a fading movie queen who has been out of work for some time and tries for a comeback. In it, she parodied her own career, her vulgar taste in clothes, her ornate hairdos, and her bitchiness. Critics agreed that she played the part splendidly. ''And why not?'' she asked with self-effacing humor. ''The role seemed vaguely familiar.''

CHAPTER 28

"OH, MY GOD!" GASPED ONE WOMAN. "She looks like Ethel Merman."

"She's gorgeous."

"She's so fat. She must have elephantiasis."

"She makes Nancy look anorexic."

Every woman in Detroit's Joe Louis Arena strained to catch a glimpse of Elizabeth Taylor Warner as she made her grand entrance into the Republican National Convention and was escorted to a seat of honor in the balcony.

Beside her sat another former MGM actress, once known as Nancy Davis, who now was Mrs. Ronald Reagan and was on her way to becoming the First Lady of the land. The same conservative tide that had brought John Warner to the U.S. Senate in 1978 was going to elect Ronald Reagan President of the United States in 1980, finally coalescing the glamour of Hollywood and the power of politics. The GOP convention in July was merely a nominating formality, but the appearance of Elizabeth Taylor suddenly enlivened the arena and electrified the crowd. Cameramen, delegates, reporters, and photographers jammed the stairs that led to her seat until the Secret Service roped off the balcony.

Turning to Elizabeth, the future First Lady whispered, "Did you ever think that you and I would be sitting here tonight?" While reporters took notes on Elizabeth's flashy diamonds and Nancy's conservative pearls, the two former Metro girls giggled and chatted through a speech by NAACP Executive Director Benjamin Hooks.

Later the Reagans moved their campaign headquarters to the East Coast and took up residence at Wexford, the secluded country estate built in 1963 by President and Mrs. John F. Kennedy only a mile and a half from Atoka, the Warners' Middleburg property.*

Although Virginia's junior Senator initially backed John Connally for President, he and his wife were now firmly in the Reagan camp and promised to work hard throughout the state for the Republican ticket. They launched the fall campaign in September with their annual $25-a-person party, which had become the largest political gathering in the state. More than 4,600 Republicans arrived at Atoka to devour 5,250 barbecued chickens and meet Ron and Nancy during the John and Liz Show.

Holding a microphone, John Warner pointed to the kitchen in his farmhouse and said, "Tomorrow Liz is going to cook a chicken in that kitchen all by her little old self."

"That's what he thinks!" Liz yelled. "I will open a tin of beans!"

The crowd clapped and cheered as Warner told them about the time he was rehearsing a political speech and cut himself shaving. "Well," quipped Liz, "you ought to have thought about your face and cut your speech."

There was more applause and adulation as John Warner wrapped it up with one last joke about the politician who had approached him at the GOP National Convention and asked about his speaking fee. "I'll come for just my expenses," he replied.

"Ah, and, um, how 'bout Mrs. Warner?"

---

* Named after John Fitzgerald Kennedy's ancestral home in Wexford, Ireland, the home had been built by Mrs. Kennedy as a summer retreat for herself and the President. "It was the only house that Jack and I ever built," Jacqueline said. The Kennedys spent their first weekend in the house in October 1963, less than a month before the President was assassinated. Mrs. Kennedy sold the estate in 1964 with the provision that for the next ten years no reporters or photographers were to be allowed inside to do a story on the house without her written permission.

"Liz comes along for ten thousand," said her husband, grinning.

Having undergone extensive dental surgery, three weeks of hospitalization for a salivary-gland infection, and plastic surgery for the removal of a small facial skin cancer, Elizabeth did not much feel like hitting the campaign trail. She made a few public appearances for Ronald Reagan and then secretly crept off to another fat farm for a week of diet and exercise. She emerged looking much less bloated.

Upon her return she attended the opening of a revival of *Brigadoon* at Washington's National Theater, where she told producer Zev Bufman that she had always wanted to be a stage actress. "We talked about the theater in general," he recalled, "and then I popped the question—would she think about doing a play?—and she said yes. The grain of the idea was pretty well decided upon before the evening was over."

"I've been waiting to do a play for a long time," said Elizabeth, "and now that the election is over this seemed like a perfect time. It was my husband's idea. I've campaigned so much for the Republicans in the last four years. He wanted me to have something of my own."

Not knowing which play she wanted to do, Elizabeth leaned toward *Who's Afraid of Virginia Woolf?*, the last movie in which she had excelled and the one for which she had won her second Oscar. "This time I wouldn't have to gain weight for the part," she said, "or spend three hours in makeup getting wrinkles."

Her husband suggested she try something new so that she would not be compared with her younger movie-star self. He later said, "She already did the movie, and excellence is achieved only once." Elizabeth agreed. "People always remember glowingly things you've done in the past, so why should I compete with myself?" she said. "The challenge of doing something new is more interesting."

She considered several revivals, including Tennessee Williams' *Sweet Bird of Youth* and William Goldman's *The Lion in Winter*. To help her decide, the producer held a series of play readings in New York and called in actors and actresses to read various properties with her. Finally she narrowed down her selection to Noël Coward's *Hay Fever* and Lillian Hellman's *The Little Foxes*. "They're both dynamite plays, but we all seemed to agree that *Little Foxes* was the one," Elizabeth said in announcing her selection.

After Tallulah Bankhead's dazzling performance in 1939, Lillian Hellman had refused to allow other actresses to do *The Little Foxes* on Broadway. But the seventy-six-year-old playwright made an exception for Elizabeth Taylor. "Elizabeth," she said, "is the right person at the right age at the right time."

Since her cinema stock-in-trade had been the bitchy Southern belle, the role of Regina Giddens in *The Little Foxes* seemed most appropriate. "Regina is not just a total icicle and avaricious bitch, as she is usually portrayed," claimed Elizabeth. "I've found so many facets in her. There is also a certain vulnerability in Regina."

Announced in *The New York Times,* the news of Elizabeth Taylor's making her theatrical debut left many people gasping. Some were convinced that it was a joke. Others predicted that she would call it off at the last minute. "You watch," said one man who had worked with her in the past. "She'll never go through with it. She'll get a chicken bone stuck in her throat a week before the opening and have to be hospitalized."

"Why, I can't believe it," said one of her former scriptwriters. "She never memorizes her lines, and that voice—oh, my God, that voice of hers is so thin and reedy it will never carry."

Not everyone consigned the movie star to theatrical failure. "You forget how competitive the woman is," said one of her Hollywood friends. "And you also forget that Richard Burton is now starring on stage in *Camelot*." *

---

* Dried out and face-lifted, Richard Burton opened on Broadway in the summer of 1980 in the twentieth-anniversary revival of his hit musical, *Camelot*. After New York the company moved to Toronto, where the actor's wife, Suzy, made national headlines when she saw a picture of Elizabeth Taylor in the souvenir program and flew into a rage, demanding that the offending photograph be cut out of each one of the ninety thousand booklets.

Elizabeth scheduled rehearsals for the last week in January, so that she could take part in the Reagans' swearing-in festivities and host one of the inaugural balls with her husband. She insisted on opening the play on February 27, the night of her forty-ninth birthday, at the Parker Playhouse in Fort Lauderdale, Florida. That locale was chosen so that she could spend time at the nearby Palm-Aire Spa to lose weight. Only then would she appear in Washington and New York.

"Washington is definite because she lives nearby and her husband likes her to be home as much as possible," said the producer. "New York is a terrific probability. Six weeks on Broadway would be fine with me, but we have not yet come to grips with her commitment to a limited engagement in New York. We saw 42nd Street—the star Tammy Grimes is a friend of hers —and after that, Elizabeth said she is more inclined to come to New York. She is a gutsy lady."

Theater people, surprised that the flamboyant movie star would even consider the stage, asked why she would risk the rough audiences and exacting critics of Broadway. "I've been gambling all my life," Elizabeth said. "I've been rapped enough by movie critics and I can take it. If you're rapped by theater critics, what's the difference?"

Being exposed on stage is a nakedness unknown to movie stars, who are cosseted by expert makeup, soft camera angles, retakes, and skillful editing. But Elizabeth refused to be intimidated. "I always planned to do a play at some point in my career," she said. "Did I think about the risk? For about half an hour. I don't expect to fail. People pay their money and I have a responsibility to give them their money's worth."

Behind the bravado was an intense desire to succeed in acting's toughest arena, to be considered good, to be accepted and applauded as an actress—not just a celebrity. Yet Elizabeth refused to acknowledge her amateur theatrical status, and further confounded people by bragging that she had never had an acting lesson. "I'm an instinctive actress," she said. "I have experience—experience from just working, from observing, from trial and error. But I've never had an acting lesson in my life."

Determined to be a success, she wanted Mike Nichols to direct her, but he was already committed, so Austin Pendleton was assigned the job. Elizabeth wanted to be surrounded by good actors, and she got some of the best the theater had to offer: Maureen Stapleton, Anthony Zerbe, and Joe Panazecki.*

The cast spent six weeks rehearsing the story of a greedy Southern family at the turn of the century. The plot revolves around Regina, a woman whose deadly charm is directed at fulfilling her craving for material wealth. Her two unscrupulous brothers have promised to make her extraordinarily rich if she persuades her husband to put $150,000 into a partnership with a Chicago businessman to build a cotton mill in their hometown, a venture that will produce enormous profits by exploiting the cheap labor of local blacks.

Regina immediately envisions a fortune that will finally pave her way out of the South, and she is determined to get the money from her husband, Horace, who has been hospitalized in Baltimore for five months with a terminal heart ailment. An honest yet wealthy banker, Horace Giddens refuses to go along with the scheme, partly because he disapproves of his brothers-in-law but mainly to salve his bitterness toward his wife.

Under false pretenses Regina manages to get him home, but he still resists giving her the money. Her two brothers realize this and decide to go elsewhere for their funding. At this point Regina's nephew steals $188,000 in bonds from the banker's safe-deposit box, which he gives to his father and uncle. When Horace discovers the theft, he decides to treat it as a loan instead of instituting criminal proceedings, and he tells Regina there is nothing she can do about it as long as he is alive.

Regina tells Horace she despises him for depriving her of potential millions, and her vitriolic contempt triggers a massive

* When told that Maureen Stapleton had been signed to play Aunt Birdie in *The Little Foxes,* Elizabeth responded, "I said I wanted good actors, but not that good."

heart attack. Grasping for his life-saving medicine, Horace accidentally knocks it off the table and begs Regina to help him. She sits silently and watches her husband in his death throes. Her refusal to help becomes an act of murder.

Enveloped in her own evil, Regina now turns on her two brothers and demands 75 percent of the profits of their venture, threatening them with jail if they refuse. They accede to her demand. By the end of the play, having vanquished them and killed her husband, she wearily mounts the stairs to her bedroom. A moment before the final curtain, her daughter, Alexandra, calls after her, "Are you afraid, Mama?"

Elizabeth was aware of the caliber of actresses who had played Regina in the past—Tallulah Bankhead in 1939, Bette Davis in the 1941 movie, Greer Garson in the 1956 *Hallmark Hall of Fame* television production, and Anne Bancroft at Lincoln Center in 1967. Still, she wasn't worried.

"I'm not trying to compete with other Reginas before me," she said. "I want to give her a new dimension. She's a woman who's been pushed in a corner. She's a killer—but she's saying, 'Sorry, fellas, you put me in this position.' "

The publicity generated by her stage debut resulted in sellouts at the Parker Playhouse in Florida weeks in advance of the opening as well as at the forty-seven performances at Washington's Kennedy Center. The night after an ad appeared in *The New York Times* a line began forming outside the Martin Beck Theater in New York. By the end of the week, nearly $1 million worth of tickets had been sold.

"Elizabeth is the hottest draw I've ever seen in my twenty-two years as a producer," marveled Zev Bufman. He now realized that people would go to see Elizabeth Taylor the way they would go to see the Washington Monument.

Bufman hired a Florida policeman to serve as Elizabeth's bodyguard and drive her to the theater every night in a $100,000 Rolls-Royce Silver Shadow. He had her dressing room carpeted in white, papered in lavender, and filled with tanks of the exotic fish that she loved. He also hired a publicist who was instructed to bar any reporter who might write something less than favorable. "No tacky questions," instructed the publicist.*

Having been warned to expect trouble from the always-late, accident-prone star, the producer also protected himself by spending $125,000 for a six-month all-protection insurance contract from Lloyd's of London.

By opening night, excitement ran to a fever pitch. Network newsmen flew to Florida with their camera crews to record Elizabeth's event for national television. After her performance, John Warner bounded on stage and presented her with a birthday bouquet of her favorite lavender roses. The critics were not quite so kind.

"The crowd was on Taylor's side," said *The Miami News*. "It wanted to be thrilled by her and it was, but not by her performance. Her beauty was the magnet that drew every eye to her every move on stage, and she was stunning. But not even the lovely Taylor can conquer the theater overnight on the basis of her beauty and sincere desire to succeed. She could not make the sparks fly, no matter how avidly she desired to do so."

The Miami Herald suggested that the production needed time to settle, "like a new house."

Still, Elizabeth was ecstatic. "I'm on a high," she said. "I have a sense of accomplishment, a feeling of doing something useful in my life. And the applause is wonderful."

By the time the company arrived in Washington, Elizabeth had lost 40 pounds and looked spectacular. So hungry were reporters for a look at the newly slimmed star that the producer was forced to call a press conference the day before the opening.

"This character you're playing, isn't it a departure from your sexier roles?" asked one intrepid journalist.

"Oh, I'm wonderful playing bitches," said Elizabeth.

---

* By this time Elizabeth was incensed by questions about her fluctuating weight. "Does it matter what Maureen Stapleton weighs? Why the hell does it matter what I weigh? It's nobody's damn business what I weigh, but talking about it seems to be a national pastime. And that cheeses me off."

"When they come to write about the great entertainers, what do you want them to write about you?" asked another.

"That I tried—that's it. That's all I can do."

The reporters stood around like puppies with tambourines tied to their tails. They watched in awe as Elizabeth Taylor in a violet silk blouse and gray flannel suit let them know in no uncertain terms that it was she—and not they—who was in control. Even her co-stars stood back like the good supporting players they were and allowed her to shine alone in the spotlight.

"It's amazing how people defer to her," said Dennis Christopher, the young actor who had won acclaim in the movie *Breaking Away* and who played Regina's larcenous nephew. "You listen to these questions. And it's like people are afraid to ask her anything, like it's a first date. . . ."

Tom Aldredge, who played Regina's invalid husband, recognized the unending fascination Elizabeth Taylor exercised over anyone who came into her presence. "I think it must have to do with the paucity of experience in the average person's life," he said. "They try to get it wherever they can."

Opening night in Washington brought the President of the United States and the First Lady to the Eisenhower Theater in the Kennedy Center to see their show-business friend make her stage debut. Even in their elevated Presidential box above the orchestra section the Reagans could hear the audience gasp as Elizabeth made her first entrance on stage. She was wearing a beaded garnet gown and looking once again like the woman whose flawless beauty had set the standard of excellence for twentieth-century America.

Her ripe, opulent looks were perfect for the role of Regina Giddens, whose sweet Southern accent barely camouflaged her coarseness. Her performance itself drew mixed reviews from critics. *The Washington Post*'s James Lardner pronounced her "impressive," saying that she "gave a robust and involving performance as Regina, one of the great scheming women in American drama, pumping life and suspense into many of the critical passages. . . ."

The Washington Star's David Richards disagreed. "For the first act her status as a superstar is probably enough to sustain an audience's interest. We are all creatures of incontinent curiosity, and one of the reasons we're there is to measure the movie goddess against the real person. . . . But mere voyeurism is not enough to keep us going. Sooner or later, the actress must take hold of our imagination and foster new fantasies. That does not happen in the Eisenhower Theater."

It is true that the audience could not forget for a moment that they were watching Elizabeth Taylor on stage; but that was precisely the reason they were there—to see the renascence of the last movie star. They cheered her effort and applauded her audacity and took pleasure in the fact that she finally cared enough about herself to try to look like their ancient fantasies.

And then in the last act, when Regina turns to her dying husband and says, "I'm lucky, Horace. I've always been lucky. I'll be lucky again," members of the audience experienced a sudden blood rush. They heard Elizabeth Taylor say those words, and in an unconscious reverie of her life, they remembered her escapes from death, from suicide attempts, from sickness, from scandal.

They remembered that through it all this woman—plagued by illnesses, injuries, and heartbreaks—refused to succumb. And surviving as she did, she brought a measure of hope to millions, and a great deal of magic. Graced by good fortune, she stood out as the one movie star who had been born beautiful, had become famous, had made millions, and had endured through the years. Despite the personal chaos of so many stormy marriages and bitter divorces, she had never completely abandoned herself. Yes, she was lucky. A beautiful, historic, fateful woman who for more than three decades had drawn the world to her on her own terms, she defied conventional morality and demanded to be judged by the more spacious standards of time.

"I'm lucky . . . I've always been lucky," Elizabeth said on stage. "I'll be lucky again."

ACKNOWLEDGMENTS

President John F. Kennedy once said that what makes journalism so fascinating and biography so interesting is the struggle to answer that single question: "What's he like?"

For the answer to Elizabeth Taylor, I relied on more than four hundred interviews with members of her family, friends, co-workers, employees, former directors, producers, co-stars, and lovers, plus published recollections which are reflected in the bibliography. Because of the confidential nature of some of these interviews, not everyone can be thanked publicly, but I am grateful to all, including Elizabeth Taylor's publicist, Chen Sam of Chen Sam Associates; her good friends Roddy McDowall, Edith Head, and the late Ketti Frings; and her former stand-in, Marjorie Dillon Sink. People in the movie industry were most helpful, and I'm indebted to Pandro S. Berman, Ernest Lehman, Ivan Moffat, Marty Ragaway, Mike Mindlin, Paul Maslansky, Irving Asher, Sheilah Graham, and the late Bosley Crowther.

The research would have been impossible without the help of librarians William Hifner of *The Washington Post,* Sunday Orme of *The New York Times,* Joe Wright of *The Miami News,* Merle Thomason of Fairchild Publications, and John Hodgson of the New York *Daily News.* I am also grateful to Emily Sieger of the Motion Picture Broadcast and Recorded Sound Division of the Library of Congress; Earl Higa of the Academy of Motion Pictures Arts and Sciences in Los Angeles; and the staffs of the American Film Institute in Los Angeles and Washington, D.C., the Theater Collection of New York's Lincoln Center Library of the Performing Arts, and the Oral History department of Columbia University.

My special thanks to the executives of Metro-Goldwyn-Mayer for the unrestricted use of their studio's legal files, and to Mike Boylan of McFadden Publications. For individual research assistance my thanks to Jane Winebrenner, Carol Capra, and Janet Donovan in Washington, D.C., Mervin Block in New York, and Bob Turner in London. I also appreciate the helpfulness of William H. Kling, Press Secretary to Senator John W. Warner.

Writers who were particularly generous with their time and information include Liz Smith, Patricia Bosworth, Richard Epstein, Eleanor

Acknowledgments • 405

Harris Howard, Lester David, Gwen Davis, Robert LaGuardia, Hollis Alpert, Jon Bradshaw, Sidney Michaels, Zef Stuart, John Kobler, Tommy Thompson, Frank Farrell, Donald MacLachlin of the London *Sunday Express,* Roberta Ashley of *Cosmopolitan* magazine, Lenore Hershey of *Ladies' Home Journal,* Wayne Warga and Bettijane Levine of the *Los Angeles Times,* Bob Colacello of *Interview,* Peter Ross Range of *Playboy* magazine, Charles McDowell of the *Richmond Times-Dispatch,* Don Sider and Roland Flamini of *Time* magazine, Garry Clifford of *People* magazine, and David Richards, drama critic of *The Washington Star.*

I am especially grateful for the kindness of dear friends Helyne Landres, Alice Everett, Larry Leamer, Tom Timberman, and Peter Menegas. My thanks also to Sylvia and Irving Wallace, Christine and Joe Laiton, Vanessa Brown and Mark Sandrich, Yvonne and Angelo Sangiacomo, Marylou Luther and Arthur Imperato, Deborah Raffin and Michael Viner, Golda and Nathan Weiss, Pat and Shep McKenney, Julie and Bob Sherman, and Heather and Tom Foley.

For continuing good cheer, my thanks to Al Koblin of The Lion's Head in New York and Mike Reardon, Nick Browne, Joel Oppenheimer, Bernie Kirsch, Vic Ziegel, and David Markson. My thanks also to Josie Aquilino and her wonderful staff at Coolbreeze's in Washington, D.C.

For their help at various points, my thanks to Maggie Ferguson, Ann Straus, Helen Morgan, Michael Maslansky, James Prideaux, Joseph Hardy, Deeanna Wilcox, David Chirichetti, Don Crider, John Treanor, David Gregory, Glenn Davis, Marilyn Hilton, Blaine Waller, Mike Hall, John Prince, Charlie Muise, Gregory Tweed, St. Clair Pugh, Harvey Mann, Jim Mitchell, Tony Manning, Harold Salemson, Melissa Bancroft, Betsy Von Furstenberg, Al Hudes, Way Bandy, Maury Hopson, Paul Neshamkin, Patty Cavin, Scottie Fitzgerald Smith, Patsy Kauffman, Jane Coyne, Karen Fawcett, Jeanne Viner Bell, Sherri Blair, Kate Levy, Joanne Nicholson, Dominique D'Ermo, Alex Sheftell, John and Edith Kunle, Maria DeMartini, Brigette Weiss, Paul Wieck, John and Suzie Groth, Corky and Ted Davidov, Regina Greenspun, Stanley Tretick, Germaine and Dick Swanson, Mari Lyn Henry, and Marvin H. McIntyre, a.k.a. "The Wizard."

Finally, my thanks to my typist, Cosette Saslaw, for grace under pressure; to my editor, Michael Korda; to my agent, Lucianne Goldberg; and to my husband, Michael Edgley.

BIBLIOGRAPHY

Astor, Mary. *A Life on Film*. New York: Delacorte Press, 1967.

Bacon, James. *Hollywood Is a Four Letter Town*. New York: Avon Books, 1977.

———. *Made in Hollywood*. New York: Warner Books, 1977.

Blackwell, Earl, ed. *Celebrity Register*. New York: Simon and Schuster, 1973.

Bosworth, Patricia. *Montgomery Clift: A Biography*. New York: Harcourt Brace Jovanovich, 1978.

Brodsky, Jack, and Weiss, Nathan. *The Cleopatra Papers*. New York: Simon and Schuster, 1963.

Burton, Richard. *Meeting Mrs. Jenkins*. New York: William Morrow & Co., Inc., 1964.

Cohn, Art. *The Nine Lives of Michael Todd: The Story of One of the World's Most Fabulous Showmen*. New York: Random House, Inc., 1958.

Collins, Joan. *Past Imperfect*. Chicago: Coronet Books, 1979.

Cottrell, John, and Cashin, Fergus. *Richard Burton: Very Close Up*. Englewood Cliffs, N.J.: Prentice-Hall, Inc., 1971.

David, Lester, and Robbins, Jhan. *Richard and Elizabeth*. New York: Funk & Wagnalls, Inc., 1977.

Davidson, Bill. *The Real and the Unreal*. New York: Harper & Brothers, 1957.

Dmytryk, Edward. *It's a Hell of a Life but Not a Bad Living*. New York: Times Books, 1978.

Eames, John Douglas. *The MGM Story: The Complete History of Fifty Roaring Years*. New York: Crown Publishers, Inc., 1975.

Flamini, Roland. *Scarlett, Rhett and a Cast of Thousands: The Filming of "Gone with The Wind."* New York: Macmillan Publishing Co., Inc., 1975.

Geist, Kenneth. *Pictures Will Talk*. New York: Charles Scribner's Sons, 1978.

Gelmis, Joseph. *The Film Director as Superstar*. Doubleday & Co., Inc., 1970.

Goodman, Ezra. *The Fifty-Year Decline and Fall of Hollywood*. New York: Simon and Schuster, 1961.

Graham, Sheilah. *The Rest of the Story*. New York: Bantam Books, 1965.

Greene, Myrna. *The Eddie Fisher Story*. Middlebury, Vt.: Paul S. Eriksson, Publisher, 1978.

Griffin, Merv, with Peter Barsocchini. *Merv*. New York: Simon and Schuster, 1980.

Grossinger, Tania. *Growing Up at Grossinger's*. New York: David McKay Co., Inc., 1975.

Gully, Bill, and Reese, Mary Ellen. *Breaking Cover*. New York: Simon and Schuster, 1980.

Harris, Radie. *Radie's World*. New York: G. P. Putnam's Sons, 1975.

Head, Edith, and Ardmore, Jane Kisner. *The Dress Doctor*. Boston: Little, Brown & Co., 1959.

Herndon, Venable. *James Dean: A Short Life*. New York: New American Library, 1974.

Hersh, Burton. *The Mellon Family*. New York: William Morrow & Co., 1978.

Hickey, Des, and Smith, Gus. *The Prince: The Public and Private Life of Laurence Harvey*. London: Leslie Frewin Publishers Ltd., 1975.

Hirsch, Foster. *Elizabeth Taylor*. New York: Pyramid Communications, Inc., 1973.

Holmes, Nancy. *The Dream Boats*. New York: Bantam Books, 1978.

Hotchner, A. E. *Sophia: Living and Loving*. New York: Bantam Books, 1979.

Joseph, Joan. *For Love of Liz*. New York: Manor Books, Inc., 1976.

Keyes, Evelyn. *Scarlett O'Hara's Younger Sister*. New York: Lyle Stuart, Inc., 1977.

Koskoff, David. *The Mellons: The Chronicle of America's Richest Family*. New York: Thomas Y. Crowell Co., 1978.

LaGuardia, Robert. *Monty: The Biography of Montgomery Clift*. Arbor House, 1977.

LeBlanc, Jerry, and LeBlanc, Rena Dictor. *Suddenly Rich*. Englewood Cliffs, N.J.: Prentice-Hall, Inc., 1978

Maddox, Brenda. *Who's Afraid of Elizabeth Taylor?* New York: M. Evans & Co., Inc., 1977.

Miller, Ann, with Browning, Norma Lee. *Miller's High Life*. Garden City, N.Y.: Doubleday & Co., Inc., 1972.

Powdermaker, Hortense. *Hollywood: The Dream Factory*. Little, Brown & Co., 1950.

Reed, Rex. *Valentines and Vitriol*. New York: Delacorte Press, 1977.

Rose, Helen. *Just Make Them Beautiful: The Many Worlds of a Designing Woman*. Santa Monica, Calif.: Dennis-Landman, 1976.

Schary, Dore. *Heyday: An Autobiography*. Boston and Toronto: Little, Brown & Co., 1979.

Sheppard, Dick. *Elizabeth: The Life and Career of Elizabeth Taylor*. Warner Books, 1975.

Stone, Paulene, with Evans, Peter. *One Tear Is Enough*. London: Michael Joseph Ltd., 1975.

Strasberg, Susan. *Bittersweet*. New York: G. P. Putnam's Sons, 1980.

Taylor, Elizabeth. *Elizabeth Taylor*. New York: Harper & Row, 1964.

———. *Nibbles and Me*. New York: Duell, Sloan & Pearce, Inc., 1945.

Thomson, David. *A Biographical Dictionary of Film*. New York: William Morrow & Co., Inc., 1976.

Vermilye, Jerry, and Ricci, Mark. *The Films of Elizabeth Taylor*. Secaucus, N.J.: The Citadel Press, 1976.

Walker, Alexander. *Sex in the Movies*. Pelican Books, 1966.

Wallis, Hal, and Higham, Charles. *Starmaker: The Autobiography of Hal Wallis*. Macmillan Publishing Co., Inc., 1980.

Warhol, Andy, and Colacello, Bob. *Andy Warhol's Exposures*. Andy Warhol Books. New York: Grosset & Dunlap, 1979.

Warhol, Andy, and Hackett, Pat. *Popism: The Warhol '60s*. New York and London: Harcourt Brace Jovanovich, 1980.

Waterbury, Ruth. *Elizabeth Taylor: Her Life, Her Loves, Her Future*. New York: Popular Library, 1964.

———. *Richard Burton: His Intimate Story*. New York: Popular Library, 1965.

Wilcox, Herbert. *Twenty-five Thousand Sunsets: The Autobiography of Herbert Wilcox*. London: 1967.

Wilkie, Jane. *Confessions of an Ex–Fan Magazine Writer*. Doubleday & Co., Inc., 1981.

Wilson, Earl. *Show Business Laid Bare*. New American Library, 1975.

———. *The Show Business Nobody Knows*. Chicago and New York: Cowles Book Co., Inc., 1971.

Winters, Shelley. *Shelley: Also Known as Shirley*. New York: William Morrow & Co., Inc., 1980.

Zec, Donald. *Marvin: The Story of Lee Marvin*. New York: St. Martin's Press, 1980.

FILMOGRAPHY

There's One Born Every Minute (Universal, 1942)
Director: Harold Young. Associate Producer: Ken Goldsmith. Screenplay: Robert B. Hunt, Brenda Weisberg. Original Story: Robert B. Hunt. Cinematography: John W. Boyle. Art Direction: Jack Otterson. Costumes: Vera West. Sound Director: Bernard B. Brown. Music Director: H. J. Salter. Editor: Maurice Wright. Assistant Director: Seward Webb. Running time: 59 minutes.

Lemuel	Hugh Herbert
Helen	Peggy Moran
Jimmy	Tom Brown
Cadwalader	Guy Kibbee
Minerva	Catherine Doucet
Moe Carson	Edgar Kennedy
Lester	Scott Jordan
Quisenberry	Gus Schilling
Gloria	Elizabeth Taylor
Trumbull	Charles Halton
Miss Phipps	Renie Riano
Junior	Alfalfa Switzer

Lassie Come Home (MGM, 1943)
Director: Fred M. Wilcox. Producer: Samuel Marx. Assistant Director: Al Raboch. Screenplay: Hugh Butler. From the novel by Eric Knight. Cinematography: Leonard Smith. Art Direction: Cedric Gibbons, Paul Groesse. Set Decoration: Edwin B. Willis, Mildred Griffiths. Music: Daniele Amfitheatrof. Special Effects: Warren Newcombe. Editor: Ben Lewis. Lassie's Trainer: Rudd Weatherwax. Running Time: 88 minutes.

Joe Carraclough	Roddy McDowall
Sam Carraclough	Donald Crisp
Rowlie	Edmund Gwenn
Dolly	Dame May Whitty

Duke of Rudling	Nigel Bruce
Mrs. Carraclough	Elsa Lanchester
Priscilla	Elizabeth Taylor
Hynes	J. Patrick O'Malley
Dan'l Fadden	Ben Webster
Snickers	Alec Craig
Buckles	John Rogers
Jock	Arthur Shields
Lassie	Pal

Jane Eyre (20th Century–Fox, 1944)

Director: Robert Stevenson. Producer: William Goetz. Screenplay: Aldous Huxley, Robert Stevenson, John Houseman. Cinematography: George Barnes. Art Direction: James Vasevi, Wiard B. Ihnen. Set Decoration: Thomas Little, Ross Dowd. Costumes: René Hubert. Music: Bernard Herrmann. Special Effects: Fred Sersen. Sound: W. D. Flick, Roger Heman. Editor: Walter Thompson. Running time: 96 minutes.

Edward Rochester	Orson Welles
Jane Eyre	Joan Fontaine
Adele Varens	Margaret O'Brien
Jane (as a child)	Peggy Ann Garner
Dr. Rivers	John Sutton
Bessie	Sara Allgood
Brocklehurst	Henry Daniell
Mrs. Reed	Agnes Moorehead
Colonel Dent	Aubrey Mather
Mrs. Fairfax	Edith Barrett
Lady Ingram	Barbara Everest
Blanche Ingram	Hillary Brooke
Grace Poole	Ethel Griffies
Leah	Mae Marsh
Miss Scatcherd	Eily Malyon
Mrs. Eshton	Mary Forbes
Sir George Lynn	Thomas London
Mason	John Abbott
John	Ronald Harris
Auctioneer	Charles Irwin
Helen Burns	Elizabeth Taylor

The White Cliffs of Dover (MGM, 1944)

Director: Clarence Brown. Producer: Sidney Franklin. Screenplay: Claudine West, Jan Lustig, George Froeschel. Based on the poem *The White Cliffs of Dover* by Alice Duer Miller. Additional Poetry: Robert Nathan. Cinematography: George Folsey. Art Direction: Cedric Gibbons. Set Decoration: Edwin B. Willis, Jacques Mesereau. Music: Herbert Stothart. Costumes: Irene. Special Effects: Arnold Gillespie, Warren Newcombe. Editor: Robert J. Kern. Running time: 126 minutes.

Susan Ashwood	Irene Dunne
Sir John Ashwood III	Alan Marshal
Hiram Dunn	Frank Morgan
Nanny	Dame May Whitty
Colonel	C. Aubrey Smith
Lady Jean Ashwood	Gladys Cooper
Mrs. Bancroft	Isobel Elsom
Betsy (age 10)	Elizabeth Taylor
John Ashwood III (as a boy)	Roddy McDowall
John Ashwood III (age 24)	Peter Lawford
Sam Bennett	Van Johnson
Reggie	John Warburton
Rosamund	Jill Esmond
Gwennie	Brenda Forbes
Mrs. Bland	Norma Varden
Betsy (age 18)	June Lockhart

National Velvet (MGM, 1944)
Director: Clarence Brown. Producer: Pandro S. Berman. Screenplay: Theodore Reeves, Helen Deutsch. Based on the novel by Enid Bagnold. Cinematography: Leonard Smith. Art Direction: Cedric Gibbons, Urie McCleary. Set Decoration: Edwin B. Willis, Mildred Griffiths. Costumes: Irene. Special Effects: Warren Newcombe. Music: Herbert Stothart. Editor: Robert J. Kern. Running time: 125 minutes.

Mi	Mickey Rooney
Mr. Brown	Donald Crisp
Velvet Brown	Elizabeth Taylor
Mrs. Brown	Anne Revere
Edwina Brown	Angela Lansbury
Malvolia Brown	Juanita Quigley
Donald Brown	Jack Jenkins
Farmer Ede	Reginald Owen
Ted	Terry Kilburn
Tim	Alec Craig
Mr. Taski	Eugene Loring
Miss Simms	Norma Varden
Mr. Hellam	Arthur Shields
Mr. Greenford	Dennis Hoey
Entry Official	Aubrey Mather
Stewart	Frederick Warlock
Man with Umbrella	Arthur Treacher

Courage of Lassie (MGM, 1946)
Director: Fred Wilcox. Producer: Robert Sisk. Screenplay: Lionel Hauser. Cinematography: Leonard Smith. Codirector of Animal Sequences: Basil Wrangel. Art Direction: Cedric Gibbons, Paul Youngblood. Set Decoration: Edwin B. Willis, Paul Huldschinsky. Music: Scott Bradley, Bronislau Kaper. Costumes: Irene. Editor: Conrad A. Nervig. Running time: 93 minutes.

Kathie Merrick	Elizabeth Taylor
Harry MacBain	Frank Morgan
Sergeant Smitty	Tom Drake
Mrs. Merrick	Selena Royle
Judge Payson	Harry Davenport
Old Man	George Cleveland
Alice Merrick	Catherine McLeod
Farmer Crews	Morris Ankrum
Freddie Crews	Arthur Walsh
Farmer Elson	Mitchell Lewis
Mrs. Elson	Jane Green
Pete Merrick	David Holt
Sergeant	William Lewin
Sheriff Grayson	Minor Watson
Youth	Windy Cook
Charlie	Donald Curtis
Casey	Clancy Cooper
Bill	Lassie

Cynthia (MGM, 1947)
Director: Robert Z. Leonard. Producer: Edwin H. Knopf. Screenplay: Harold Buchman, Charles Kaufman. Based on the play *A Rich Full Life* by Viña Delmar. Cinematography: Charles Schoenbaum. Art Direction: Cedric Gibbons, Edward Carfagno. Set Decoration: Edwin B. Willis, Paul G. Chamberlain. Music: Bronislau Kaper. Musical Numbers: Johnny Green. Costumes: Irene. Editor: Irvine Warburton. Running time: 98 minutes.

Cynthia Bishop	Elizabeth Taylor
Larry Bishop	George Murphy
Prof. Rosenkrantz	S. Z. Sakall
Louise Bishop	Mary Astor
Dr. Fred I. Jannings	Gene Lockhart
Carrie Jannings	Spring Byington
Ricky Latham	James Lydon
Will Parker	Scotty Beckett
Fredonia Jannings	Carol Brannan
Miss Brady	Anna Q. Nilsson
Mr. Phillips	Morris Ankrum

McQuillan	Kathleen Howard
Stella Regan	Shirley Johns
Alice	Barbara Challis
J. M. Dingle	Harlan Briggs
Gus Wood	Will Wright

Life with Father (Warner Bros., 1947)
Director: Michael Curtiz. Producer: Robert Buckner. Screenplay: Donald Ogden Stewart. From the play by Howard Lindsay and Russell Crouse. Cinematography: Peverell Marley, William V. Skall. Art Direction: Robert Haas. Set Decoration: George James Hopkins. Music: Max Steiner. Costumes: Milo Anderson. Editor: George Amy. Sound: C. A. Riggs. Technical Adviser: Mrs. Clarence Day. Running time: 118 minutes.

Father	William Powell
Vinnie	Irene Dunne
Mary	Elizabeth Taylor
Rev. Dr. Lloyd	Edmund Gwenn
Cora	ZaSu Pitts
Clarence	Jimmy Lydon
Margaret	Emma Dunn
Dr. Humphries	Moroni Olsen
Mrs. Whitehead	Elizabeth Risdon
Harlan	Derek Scott
Whitney	Johnny Calkins
John	Martin Milner
Annie	Heather Wilde
Policeman	Monte Blue
Nora	Mary Field
Maggie	Queenie Leonard
Mrs. Wiggins	Clara Blandick
Dr. Somers	Frank Elliott

A Date with Judy (MGM, 1948)
Director: Richard Thorpe. Producer: Joe Pasternak. Screenplay: Dorothy Cooper, Dorothy Kingsley. Based on the characters created by Aleen Leslie. Cinematography: Robert Surtees. Art Direction: Cedric Gibbons, Paul Groesse. Set Decoration: Edwin B. Willis, Richard A. Pefferle. Musical Direction: George Stoll. Music Arrangements: Leo Arnaud, Albert Sondrey, Robert Franklin. Songs: "It's a Most Unusual Day" (McHugh-Adamson), "Judaline" (Raye–De Paul), "I'm Strictly on the Corny Side" (Unger-Templeton), "I've Got a Date with Judy" and "I'm Gonna Meet My Mary" (Katz-Jackson). Dance Direction:

Stanley Donen. Costumes: Helen Rose. Sound: Douglas Shearer. Editor: Harold F. Kress. Running time: 113 minutes.

Melvin R. Foster	Wallace Beery
Judy Foster	Jane Powell
Carol Pringle	Elizabeth Taylor
Rosita Conchellas	Carmen Miranda
Cugat	Xavier Cugat
Stephen Andrews	Robert Stack
Lucien T. Pringle	Leon Ames
Mrs. Foster	Selena Royle
"Oogie" Pringle	Scotty Beckett
Gramps	George Cleveland
Pop Scully	Lloyd Corrigan
Jameson	Clinton Sundberg
Mitzie	Jean McLaren

Julia Misbehaves (MGM, 1948)

Director: Jack Conway. Producer: Everett Riskin. Screenplay: William Ludwig, Harry Ruskin, Arthur Wimperis. Adaptation: Gina Kaus, Monckton Hoffe. Based on the novel *The Nutmeg Tree* by Margery Sharp. Cinematography: Joseph Ruttenberg. Art Direction: Cedric Gibbons, Daniel B. Cathcart. Set Decoration: Edwin B. Willis, Jack D. Moore. Music: Adolph Deutsch. Special Effects: Warren Newcombe. Editor: John Dunning. Running time: 99 minutes.

Julia Packett	Greer Garson
William Packett	Walter Pidgeon
Ritchie Lorgan	Peter Lawford
Susan Packett	Elizabeth Taylor
Fred Ghenoccio	Cesar Romero
Mrs. Packett	Lucile Watson
Col. Willowbrook	Nigel Bruce
Ma Ghenoccio	Mary Boland
Benjamin Hawkins	Reginald Owen
Lord Pennystone	Henry Stephenson
Vicar	Aubrey Mather
Hobson	Ian Wolfe
Pepito	Fritz Feld
Daisy	Phyllis Morris
Louise	Veda Ann Borg

Little Women (MGM, 1949)

Director/Producer: Mervin LeRoy. Screenplay: Andrew Solt, Sarah Y. Mason, Victor Heerman. Based on the novel by Louisa May Alcott. Adaptation: Sally Benson. Cinematography: Robert Planck, Charles

Schoenbaum. Art Direction: Cedric Gibbons, Paul Groesse. Set Decoration: Edwin B. Willis, Jack D. Moore. Music: Adolph Deutsch. Costumes: Walter Plunkett. Special Effects: Warren Newcombe. Editor: Ralph Winters. Running time: 122 minutes.

Jo	June Allyson
Laurie	Peter Lawford
Beth	Margaret O'Brien
Amy	Elizabeth Taylor
Meg	Janet Leigh
Professor Bhaer	Rossano Brazzi
Marmee	Mary Astor
Aunt March	Lucile Watson
Mr. Lawrence	Sir C. Aubrey Smith
Hannah	Elizabeth Patterson
Mr. March	Leon Ames
Dr. Barnes	Harry Davenport
John Brooke	Richard Stapley
Mrs. Kirke	Connie Gilchrist
Sophie	Ellen Corby

Conspirator (MGM, 1950)
Director: Victor Saville. Producer: Arthur Hornblow, Jr. Screenplay: Sally Benson. Adaptation: Sally Benson, Gerard Fairlie. Based on the novel by Humphrey Slater. Cinematography: F. A. Young. Art Direction: Alfred Junge. Music: John Wooldridge. Sound: A. W. Watkins. Editor: Frank Clarke. Running time: 87 minutes.

Major Michael Curragh	Robert Taylor
Melinda Greyton	Elizabeth Taylor
Capt. Hugh Ladholme	Robert Flemyng
Colonel Hammerbrook	Harold Warrender
Joyce Penistone	Honor Blackman
Aunt Jessica	Marjorie Fielding
Broaders	Thora Hird
Lord Penistone	Wilfred Hyde-White
Lady Penistone	Marie Ney
Henry Raglan	Jack Allen
Mrs. Hammerbrook	Cicely Paget-Bowman
Mark Radek	Karel Stepanek
Alek	Nicholas Bruce
Inspector Weldon	Cyril Smith

The Big Hangover (MGM, 1950)
Director/Producer/Screenplay: Norman Krasna. Cinematography: George Folsey. Art Direction: Cedric Gibbons, Paul Groesse. Set Dec-

oration: Edwin B. Willis, Henry W. Grace. Music: Adolph Deutsch. Costumes: Helen Rose. Special Effects: Warren Newcombe. Editor: Frederick Y. Smith. Running time: 82 minutes.

David Maldon	Van Johnson
Mary Belney	Elizabeth Taylor
John Belney	Percy Waram
Martha Belney	Fay Holden
Uncle Fred Mahoney	Edgar Buchanan
Kate Mahoney	Selena Royle
Charles Packford	Gene Lockhart
Carl Bellcap	Leon Ames
Claire Bellcap	Rosemary DeCamp
Dr. Lee	Philip Ahn
Samuel C. Lang	Pierre Watkin
Steve Hughes	Russell Hicks
Williams	Gordon Richards
Mrs. Packford	Kathleen Lockhart

Father of the Bride (MGM, 1950)
Director: Vincente Minnelli. Producer: Pandro S. Berman. Screenplay: Frances Goodrich, Albert Hackett. Based on the novel by Edward Streeter. Cinematography: John Alton. Art Direction: Cedric Gibbons, Leonid Vasian. Set Decoration: Edwin B. Willis, Keogh Gleason. Music: Adolph Deutsch. Costumes: Helen Rose, Walter Plunkett. Makeup: Jack Dawn. Hairstyles: Sidney Guilaroff. Editor: Ferris Webster. Running time: 93 minutes.

Stanley T. Banks	Spencer Tracy
Ellie Banks	Joan Bennett
Kay Banks	Elizabeth Taylor
Buckley Dunstan	Don Taylor
Doris Dunstan	Billie Burke
Mr. Massoula	Leo G. Carroll
Herbert Dunstan	Moroni Olsen
Mr. Tringle	Melville Cooper
Warner	Taylor Holmes
Rev. Galsworthy	Paul Harvey
Joe	Frank Orth
Tommy Banks	Rusty (Russ) Tamblyn
Ben Banks	Tom Irish
Delilah	Marietta Canty
Dixon	Willard Waterman
Fliss	Nancy Valentine
Effie	Mary Jane Smith
Peg	Jacqueline Duval
Miss Bellamy	Fay Baker
Duffy	Frank Hyers

Father's Little Dividend (MGM, 1951)
Director: Vincente Minnelli. Producer: Pandro S. Berman. Screenplay: Albert Hackett, Frances Goodrich. Based on characters created by Edward Streeter in his book *Father of the Bride*. Cinematography: John Alton. Art Direction: Cedric Gibbons, Leonid Vasian. Set Decoration: Edwin B. Willis, Keogh Gleason. Music: Albert Sendrey. Costumes: Helen Rose. Editor: Ferris Webster. Running time: 82 minutes.

Stanley Banks	Spencer Tracy
Ellie Banks	Joan Bennett
Kay Dunstan	Elizabeth Taylor
Buckley Dunstan	Don Taylor
Doris Dunstan	Billie Burke
Herbert Dunstan	Moroni Olsen
Police Sergeant	Richard Rober
Delilah	Marietta Canty
Tommy Banks	Rusty (Russ) Tamblyn
Ben Banks	Tom Irish
Dr. Andrew Nordell	Hayden Rorke
Rev. Galsworthy	Paul Harvey

A Place in the Sun (Paramount, 1951)
Director/Producer: George Stevens. Screenplay: Michael Wilson, Harry Brown. Based on the novel *An American Tragedy* by Theodore Dreiser and the stage adaptation by Patrick Kearney. Cinematography: William C. Mellor. Special Photographic Effects: Gordon Jennings. Process Photography: Farciot Edouart, Loyal Griggs. Art Direction: Hans Dreier, Walter Tyler. Set Decoration: Emile Kuri. Music: Franz Waxman. Costumes: Edith Head. Sound: Gene Merrett, Gene Garvin. Editor: William Hornbeck. Running time: 122 minutes.

George Eastman	Montgomery Clift
Angela Vickers	Elizabeth Taylor
Alice Tripp	Shelley Winters
Hannah Eastman	Anne Revere
Earl Eastman	Keefe Brasselle
Bellows	Fred Clark
Marlowe	Raymond Burr
Charles Eastman	Herbert Heyes
Anthony Vickers	Shepperd Strudwick
Mrs. Vickers	Frieda Inescort
Mrs. Louise Eastman	Kathryn Givney
Jansen	Walter Sande
Judge	Ted de Corsia
Coroner	John Ridgely
Marsha Eastman	Lois Chartrand
Mr. Whiting	William B. Murphy

Boatkeeper	Douglas Spencer
Kelly	Charles Dayton
Rev. Morrison	Paul Frees

Callaway Went Thataway (MGM, 1951)

Director/Producer/Screenwriters: Norman Panama, Melvin Frank. Cinematography: Ray June. Art Direction: Cedric Gibbons, Eddie Imazu. Music: Marlin Skiles. Editor: Cotton Warburton. Running time: 81 minutes.

Mike Frye	Fred MacMurray
Deborah Patterson	Dorothy McGuire
"Smoky" Callaway/	
"Stretch" Barnes	Howard Keel
Georgie Markham	Jesse White
Tom Lorrison	Fay Roope
Martha Lorrison	Natalie Schafer
The Drunk	Douglas Kennedy
Marie	Elisabeth Fraser
Johnny Terrento	Johnny Indrisano
Marvin	Stan Freberg
Director	Don Haggerty
Guest Stars	June Allyson, Clark Gable, Dick Powell, Elizabeth Taylor, Esther Williams

Love Is Better than Ever (MGM, 1952)

Director: Stanley Donen. Producer: William H. Wright. Screenplay: Ruth Brooks Flippen. Cinematography: Harold Rosson. Art Direction: Cedric Gibbons, Gabriel Scognamillo. Music: Lennie Hayton. Editor: George Boemler. Running time: 81 minutes.

Jud Parker	Larry Parks
Anastacia Macaboy	Elizabeth Taylor
Mrs. Macaboy	Josephine Hutchinson
Mr. Macaboy	Tom Tully
Mrs. Levoy	Ann Doran
Pattie Marie Levoy	Elinor Donahue
Mrs. Kahrney	Kathleen Freeman
Albertina	Doreen McCann
Hamlet	Alex Gerry
Smittie	Dick Wessel

Ivanhoe (MGM, 1952)

Director: Richard Thorpe. Producer: Pandro S. Berman. Screenplay: Noel Langley. Adaptation: Aeneas MacKenzie. From the novel by Sir

Walter Scott. Cinematography: F. A. Young. Art Direction: Alfred
Junge. Music: Milos Rozsa. Costumes: Roger Furse. Sound: A. W.
Watkins. Editor: Frank Clarke. Running time: 106 minutes.

Ivanhoe	Robert Taylor
Rebecca	Elizabeth Taylor
Rowena	Joan Fontaine
DeBois-Guilbert	George Sanders
Wamba	Emlyn Williams
Prince John	Guy Rolfe
Sir Hugh de Bracy	Robert Douglas
Cedric	Finlay Currie
Isaac	Felix Aylmer
Austrian Monk	Carl Jaffe
King Richard	Norman Wooland
Waldemar Fitzurse	Basil Sydney
Locksley	Harold Warrender
Philip de Malvoisin	Patrick Holt
Ralph de Vipont	Roderick Lovell
Clerk of Copmanhurst	Sebastian Cabot
Hundebert	John Ruddock
Baldwin	Michael Brennan
Norman Guard	Valentine Dyall
Roger of Bermondsley	Lionel Harris

The Girl Who Had Everything (MGM, 1953)
Director: Richard Thorpe. Producer: Armand Deutsch. Screenplay: Art
Cohn. Based on the novel *A Free Soul* by Adela Rogers St. John.
Cinematography: Paul Vogel. Art Direction: Cedric Gibbons, Randall
Duell. Music: André Previn. Costumes: Helen Rose. Editor: Ben Lewis.
Running time: 69 minutes.

Jean Latimer	Elizabeth Taylor
Victor Y. Ramondi	Fernando Lamas
Steve Latimer	William Powell
Vance Court	Gig Young
"Chico" Menlow	James Whitmore
John Ashmond	Robert Burton
Julian	William Walker

Rhapsody (MGM, 1954)
Director: Charles Vidor. Producer: Lawrence Weingarten. Screenplay:
Fay and Michael Kanin. Adaptation: Ruth and Augustus Goetz. Based
on the novel *Maurice Guest* by Henry Handel Richardson. Cinematog-

raphy: Robert Planck. Art Direction: Cedric Gibbons, Paul Groesse. Set Decoration: Edwin B. Willis, Hugh Hunt. Musical Adaptation: Bronislau Kaper. Conductor: Johnny Green. Piano Solos: Claudio Arrau. Violin Solos: Michael Rabin. Costumes: Helen Rose. Special Effects: A. Arnold Gillespie, Warren Newcombe. Montage: Peter Ball Busch. Editor: John Dunning. Running time: 115 minutes.

Louise Durant	Elizabeth Taylor
Paul Bronte	Vittorio Gassman
James Guest	John Ericson
Nicholas Durant	Louis Calhern
Professor Schuman	Michael Chekhov
Effie Cahill	Barbara Bates
Bruno Fürst	Richard Hageman
Otto Krafft	Richard Lupino
Frau Sigerlist	Celia Lovsky
Dove	Stuart Whitman
Mrs. Cahill	Madge Blake
Edmund Streller	Jack Raine
Madeleine	Birgit Nilsson
Yvonne	Jacqueline Duval
Student Pianist	Norma Nevens

Elephant Walk (Paramount, 1954)

Director: William Dieterle. Producer: Irving Asher. Screenplay: John Lee Mahin. Based on the novel by Robert Standish. Cinematography: Loyal Griggs. Special Photographic Effects: John P. Fulton, Paul Lerpae. Process Photography: Farciot Edouart, Wallace Kelley. Art Direction: Hal Pereira, Joseph McMillan Johnson. Set Decoration: Sam Comer, Grace Gregory. Music: Franz Waxman. Costumes: Edith Head. Sound: Gene Merritt, John Cope. Choreography: Ram Gopal. Editor: George Tomasini. Running time: 103 minutes.

Ruth Wiley	Elizabeth Taylor
Dick Carver	Dana Andrews
John Wiley	Peter Finch
Appuhamy	Abraham Sofaer
Dr. Pereira	Abner Biberman
Planter (Atkinson)	Noel Drayton
Mrs. Lakin	Rosalind Ivan
Planter (Strawson)	Barry Bernard
Planter (Ralph)	Philip Tonge
Planter (Gregory)	Edward Ashley
Planter (Chisholm)	Leo Britt
Rayna	Mylee Haulani
	The Madhyma Lanka
	Mandala Dancers

Beau Brummell (MGM, 1954)
Director: Curtis Bernhardt. Producer: Sam Zimbalist. Screenplay: Karl Tunberg. Based on the play by Clyde Fitch. Cinematography: Oswald Morris. Art Direction: Alfred Junge. Photographic Effects: Tom Howard. Music: Richard Addinsell. Costumes: B. J. Simmons, Walter Plunkett, Elizabeth Haffenden. Editor: Frank Clarke. Running time: 111 minutes.

Beau Brummell	Stewart Granger
Lady Patricia	Elizabeth Taylor
Prince of Wales	Peter Ustinov
King George III	Robert Morley
Lord Edwin Mercer	James Donald
Mortimer	James Hayter
Mrs. Fitzherbert	Rosemary Harris
William Pitt	Paul Rogers
Lord Byron	Noel Willman
Midger	Peter Dyneley
Sir Geoffrey Baker	Charles Carson
Dr. Warren	Ernest Clark
Mr. Fox	Peter Bull
Mr. Burke	Mark Dignam
Colonel	Desmond Roberts
Thurlow	David Horne
Sir Ralph Sidley	Ralph Truman
Mr. Tupp	Elwyn Brook-Jones
Dr. Dubois	George De Warfaz
Dr. Willis	Henry Oscar
Mayor	Harold Kasket

The Last Time I Saw Paris (MGM, 1954)
Director: Richard Brooks. Producer: Jack Cummings. Screenplay: Julius J. and Philip G. Epstein and Richard Brooks. Based on a story by F. Scott Fitzgerald. Cinematography: Joseph Ruttenberg. Art Direction: Cedric Gibbons, Randall Duell. Set Decoration: Edwin B. Willis, Jack D. Moore. Music: Conrad Salinger. Song: "The Last Time I Saw Paris" (Kern-Hammerstein). Special Effects: A. Arnold Gillespie. Costumes: Helen Rose. Editor: John Dunning. Running time: 116 minutes.

Helen Ellswirth	Elizabeth Taylor
Charles Wills	Van Johnson
James Ellswirth	Walter Pidgeon
Marion Ellswirth	Donna Reed
Lorraine Quarl	Eva Gabor
Maurice	Kurt Kasznar
Claude Martine	George Dolenz
Paul	Roger Moore

Vicki	Sandy Descher
Mama	Celia Lovsky
Barney	Peter Leeds
Campbell	John Doucette
Singer	Odetta

Giant (Warner Bros., 1956)
Director: George Stevens. Producers: George Stevens, Henry Ginsberg. Screenplay: Fred Guiol, Ivan Moffat. From the novel by Edna Ferber. Cinematography: William C. Mellor. Second Unit: Edwin DuPar. Production Design: Boris Leven. Set Decoration: Ralph Hurst. Music: Dimitri Tiomkin. Costumes: Marjorie Best, Moss Mabry. Sound: Earl Crain, Sr. Editor: William Hornbeck. Running time: 198 minutes.

Leslie Benedict	Elizabeth Taylor
Bick Benedict	Rock Hudson
Jett Rink	James Dean
Luz Benedict II	Carroll Baker
Vashti Snythe	Jane Withers
Uncle Bawley	Chill Wills
Luz Benedict	Mercedes McCambridge
Angel Obregon III	Sal Mineo
Jordan Benedict III	Dennis Hopper
Mrs. Horace Lynnton	Judith Evelyn
Dr. Horace Lynnton	Paul Fix
Sir David Karfrey	Rod(ney) Taylor
Bob Dace	Earl Holliman
Pinky Snythe	Robert Nichols
Old Polo	Alexander Scourby
Judy Benedict	Fran Bennett
Whitside	Charles Watts
Juana	Elsa Cardenas
Lacey Lynnton	Carolyn Craig
Bale Clinch	Monte Hale

Raintree County (MGM, 1957)
Director: Edward Dmytryk. Producer: David Lewis. Screenplay: Millard Kaufman. Based on the novel by Ross Lockridge, Jr. Cinematography: Robert Surtees. Art Direction: William A. Horning, Urie McCleary. Set Decoration: Edwin B. Willis, Hugh Hunt. Music: Johnny Green. Special Effects: Warren Newcombe. Costumes: Walter Plunkett. Sound: Dr. Wesley C. Miller. Makeup: William Tuttle. Hairstyles: Sidney Guilaroff. Songs by Johnny Green and Paul Francis Webster: "Never Till Now" and "Song of the Raintree" (sung by Nat "King"

Cole). Editor: John Dunning. Filmed in MGM Camera 65 Process. Running time: 166 minutes.

John Shawnessy	Montgomery Clift
Susanna Drake	Elizabeth Taylor
Nell Gaither	Eva Marie Saint
Jerusalem Stiles	Nigel Patrick
"Flash" Perkins	Lee Marvin
Garwood B. Jones	Rod Taylor
Ellen Shawnessy	Agnes Moorehead
T. D. Shawnessy	Walter Abel
Barbara Drake	Jarma Lewis
Bobby Drake	Tom Drake
Ezra Gray	Rhys Williams
Niles Foster	Russell Collins
Southern Officer	DeForrest Kelley

Cat on a Hot Tin Roof (MGM, 1958)
Director: Richard Brooks. Producer: Lawrence Weingarten. Screenplay: Richard Brooks, James Poe. Based on the play by Tennessee Williams. Cinematography: William Daniels. Art Direction: William A. Horning, Urie McCleary. Set Decoration: Henry Grace, Robert Priestley. Special Effects: Lee LeBlanc. Costumes: Helen Rose. Hairstyles: Sidney Guilaroff. Makeup: William Tuttle. Editor: Ferris Webster. Running time: 108 minutes.

Maggie Pollitt	Elizabeth Taylor
Brick Pollitt	Paul Newman
Big Daddy Pollitt	Burl Ives
Gooper Pollitt	Jack Carson
Big Mama Pollitt	Judith Anderson
Mae Pollitt	Madeleine Sherwood
Dr. Baugh	Larry Gates
Deacon Davis	Vaughn Taylor
Dixie	Patty Ann Gerrity
Sonny	Rusty Stevens
Buster	Hugh Corcoran
Trixie	Deborah Miller
Boy	Brian Corcoran
Lacey	Vince Townsend, Jr.
Brightie	Zelda Cleaver

Suddenly, Last Summer (Columbia, 1959)
Director: Joseph L. Mankiewicz. Producer: Sam Spiegel. Screenplay: Gore Vidal, Tennessee Williams. Adapted from the play by Tennessee Williams. Cinematography: Jack Hildyard. Production Design: Oliver

Messel. Art Direction: William Kellner. Set Decoration: Scot Slimon.
Photographic Effects: Tom Howard. Music: Buxton Orr, Malcolm Ar-
nold. Associate Costume Designer: Joan Ellacott. Sound: A. G. Ambler,
John Cox. Editor: Thomas G. Stanford. Filmed at Shepperton Studios,
England, and on the Costa Brava, Spain. Running time: 114 minutes.

Catherine Holly	Elizabeth Taylor
Mrs. Venable	Katharine Hepburn
Dr. Cukrowicz	Montgomery Clift
Dr. Hockstader	Albert Dekker
Mrs. Holly	Mercedes McCambridge
George Holly	Gary Raymond
Miss Foxhill	Mavis Villiers
Nurse Benson	Patricia Marmont
Sister Felicity	Joan Young
Lucy	Maria Britneva
Medical Secretary	Sheila Robbins
Young Blond Intern	David Cameron

Scent of Mystery (Holiday in Spain) (Michael Todd, Jr., 1960)
Director: Jack Cardiff. Producer: Michael Todd, Jr. Screenplay: William
Roos. Based on an original story by Kelley Roos. Associate Producer
and Technical Supervisor: Ned Mann. Cinematography: John Von
Kotze. Production Supervisor and Art Director: Vincent Korda. Special
Effects: Cliff Richardson. Music: Mario Nascimbene, Jordan Ramin,
Harold Adamson. Costumes: Charles Simminger. Editor: James New-
com. Running time: 125 minutes plus intermission. Smell-o-vision.

Oliver Larker	Denholm Elliott
Smiley	Peter Lorre
The Decoy Sally	Beverly Bentley
Baron Saradin	Paul Lukas
Johnny Gin	Liam Redmond
Tommy Kennedy	Leo McKern
Fleming	Peter Arne
Winifred Jordan	Diana Dors
Margharita	Mary Laura Wood
Miss Leonard	Judith Furse
Pepi	Maurice Marsac
Englishman	Michael Trubshawe
Truck Driver	Juan Olaguivel
Constance Walker	Billie Miller
The Real Sally Kennedy	Elizabeth Taylor

Butterfield 8 (MGM, 1960)
Director: Daniel Mann. Producer: Pandro S. Berman. Screenplay:
Charles Schnee, John Michael Hayes. Based on the novel by John

O'Hara. Cinematography: Joseph Ruttenberg, Charles Harten. Art Direction: George W. Davis, Urie McCleary. Set Decoration: Gene Callahan, J. C. Delaney. Music: Bronislau Kaper. Costumes: Helen Rose. Associate Producer: Kathryn Hereford. Assistant Directors: Hank Moonjean, John Clarke Bowman. Sound: Franklin Milton. Editor: Ralph E. Winters. Running time: 109 minutes.

Gloria Wandrous	Elizabeth Taylor
Weston Liggett	Laurence Harvey
Steve Carpenter	Eddie Fisher
Emily Liggett	Dina Merrill
Mrs. Wandrous	Mildred Dunnock
Mrs. Thurber	Betty Field
Bingham Smith	Jeffrey Lynn
Happy	Kay Medford
Norma	Susan Oliver
Dr. Tredman	George Voskovec
Clerk	Virginia Downing
Mrs. Jescott	Carmen Matthews
Anderson	Whitfield Connor

Cleopatra (20th Century–Fox, 1963)

Director: Joseph L. Mankiewicz. Producer: Walter Wanger. Screenplay: Joseph L. Mankiewicz, Ranald MacDougall, Sidney Buchman. Based upon Histories by Plutarch, Suetonius, Appian, Other Ancient Sources, and *The Life and Times of Cleopatra* by C. M. Franzero. Cinematography: Leon Shamroy. Art Direction: John De Cuir, Jack Martin Smith, Hilyard Brown, Herman Blumenthal, Elven Webb, Maurice Pelling, Boris Juraga. Set Decoration: Walter M. Scott, Paul S. Fox, Ray Moyer. Music: Alex North. Costumes: Irene Sharaff, Vittorio Nino Novarese, Renie. Special Effects: L. B. Abbott, Emil Kosa, Jr. Editor: Dorothy Spencer. Todd-AO. Running time: 243 minutes.

Cleopatra	Elizabeth Taylor
Mark Antony	Richard Burton
Julius Caesar	Rex Harrison
High Priestess	Pamela Brown
Flavius	George Cole
Sosigenes	Hume Cronyn
Apollodorus	Cesare Danova
Brutus	Kenneth Haigh
Agrippa	Andrew Keir
Rufio	Martin Landau
Octavius	Roddy McDowall
Germanicus	Robert Stephens
Eiras	Francesca Annis
Pothinus	Grégoire Aslan

Ramos	Martin Benson
Theodotus	Herbert Berghof
Phoebus	John Cairney
Lotos	Jacqui Chan
Charmian	Isabelle Cooley
Achilles	John Doucette
Canidius	Andrew Faulds
Metullus Cimber	Michael Gwynne
Cicero	Michael Hordern
Cassius	John Hoyt
Euphranor	Marne Maitland
Casca	Carroll O'Connor
Ptolemy	Richard O'Sullivan
Calpurnia	Gwen Watford
Decimus	Douglas Wilmer
Titus	Finlay Currie
Queen at Tarsus	Marina Berti
High Priest	John Karlsen
Caesarion, age 4	Loris Loddi
Caesarion, age 7	Del Russell
Caesarion, age 12	Kenneth Nash
Octavia	Jean Marsh
Marcellus	Gin Mart
Mithridates	Furio Meniconi
Valvus	John Valva
Archesilaus	Laurence Naismith
1st Officer	John Alderson
2nd Officer	Peter Forster

The V.I.P.s (MGM, 1963)
Director: Anthony Asquith. Producer: Anatole de Grunwald. Screenplay: Terence Rattigan. Cinematography: Jack Hildyard. Art Direction: William Kellner. Set Decoration: Pamela Cornell. Music: Miklos Rozsa. Wardrobe Supervisor: Felix Evans. Miss Taylor's Wardrobe: Givenchy, Paris. Sound: Bill Creed. Editor: Frank Clarke. Running time: 119 minutes.

Frances Andros	Elizabeth Taylor
Paul Andros	Richard Burton
Marc Champselle	Louis Jourdan
Gloria Gritti	Elsa Martinelli
Duchess of Brighton	Margaret Rutherford
Miss Mead	Maggie Smith
Les Mangrum	Rod Taylor
Max Buda	Orson Welles
Miriam	Linda Christian

Commander Millbank	Dennis Price
Sanders	Richard Wattis
Reporter	David Frost
Joslin	Ronald Fraser
John Coburn	Robert Coote
Airport Director	Michael Hordern
Schwutzbacher	Martin Miller
BOAC Official	Lance Percival
Miss Potter	Joan Benham
Doctor	Peter Sallis
Hotel Waiter	Stringer Davis
Jamaican Passenger	Clifton Jones
Air Hostess	Moyra Fraser

The Sandpiper (MGM, 1965)
Director: Vincente Minnelli. Producer: Martin Ransohoff. Screenplay: Dalton Trumbo, Michael Wilson. Adaptation: Irene and Louis Kamp. Story: Martin Ransohoff. Cinematography: Milton Krasner. Art Direction: George W. Davis, Urie McCleary. Set Decoration: Henry Grace, Keogh Gleason. Music: Johnny Mandel. Song: "The Shadow of Your Smile" (Mandel-Webster). Costumes: Irene Sharaff. Sound: Franklin Milton. Editor: David Bretherton. Running time: 116 minutes.

Laura Reynolds	Elizabeth Taylor
Dr. Edward Hewitt	Richard Burton
Claire Hewitt	Eva Marie Saint
Cos Erickson	Charles Bronson
Ward Hendricks	Robert Webber
Larry Brant	James Edwards
Judge Thompson	Torin Thatcher
Walter Robinson	Tom Drake
Phil Sutcliff	Doug Henderson
Danny Reynolds	Morgan Mason

Who's Afraid of Virginia Woolf? (Warner Bros., 1966)
Director: Mike Nichols. Producer: Ernest Lehman. Screenplay: Ernest Lehman. From the play by Edward Albee. Cinematography: Haskell Wexler. Production Design: Richard Sylbert. Set Decoration: George James Hopkins. Music: Alex North. Costumes: Irene Sharaff. Sound: M. A. Merrick. Editing: Sam O'Steen. Running time: 130 minutes.

Martha	Elizabeth Taylor
George	Richard Burton
Nick	George Segal
Honey	Sandy Dennis

The Taming of the Shrew (Columbia, 1967)
Director: Franco Zeffirelli. Executive Producer: Richard McWhorter. Screenplay: Paul Dehn, Suso Cecchi D'Amico, Franco Zeffirelli (with acknowledgments to William Shakespeare). Cinematography: Oswald Morris. Production Supervisor: Guy Luongo. Art Direction: Elven Webb, Giuseppe Mariani. Set Decoration: Dario Simoni, Luigi Gervasi. Production Design: Renzo Mongiardino, John De Cuir. Music: Nino Rota. Costumes: Irene Sharaff, Danilo Donati. Editor: Peter Taylor. Running time: 122 minutes.

Katherina	Elizabeth Taylor
Petruchio	Richard Burton
Grumio	Cyril Cusack
Baptista	Michael Hordern
Tranio	Alfred Lynch
Gremio	Alan Webb
Hortensio	Victor Spinetti
Biondello	Roy Holder
Vincentio	Mark Dignam
The Widow	Bice Valori
Bianca	Natasha Pyne
Lucentio	Michael York
The Priest	Giancarlo Cobelli
Pedant	Vernon Dobtcheff
Tailor	Ken Parry
Haberdasher	Anthony Gardner

Doctor Faustus (Columbia, 1967) (An Oxford University Screen Production)
Directors: Richard Burton, Nevill Coghill. Producers: Richard Burton, Richard McWhorter. Screen Adaptation: Nevill Coghill. Based on the Play *The Tragicall History of Doctor Faustus* by Christopher Marlowe. Cinematography: Gabor Pogany. Production Designer: John De Cuir. Art Direction: Boris Juraga. Set Decoration: Dario Simoni. Music: Mario Nascimbene. Choreographer: Jacqueline Harvey. Costumes: Peter Hall. Editor: John Shirley. Running time: 93 minutes.

Doctor Faustus	Richard Burton
Helen of Troy	Elizabeth Taylor
Mephistopheles	Andreas Teuber
Empress	Elizabeth O'Donovan
Emperor	Ian Marter
Beelzebub	Jeremy Eccles
Lucifer	David McIntosh
Valdes	Ram Chopra
Cornelius	Richard Carwardine
Pope	Adrian Benjamin
First Scholar	Richard Heffer

Second Scholar	Hugh Williams
Third Scholar/Lechery	Gwydion Thomas
Cardinal/Pride	Nicholas Loukes
Evil Angel/Knight	Richard Durden-Smith
Wagner	Patrick Barwise
Attendant at Court	Jeremy Chandler
Rector Magnificus	Angus McIntosh
First Professor/Avarice	Ambrose Coghill
Second Professor/Envy	Anthony Kaufmann
Third Professor	Julian Wontner
Fourth Professor	Richard Harrison
Fifth Professor	Nevill Coghill
Good Angel	Michael Menaugh
Boy-Turned-into-Hind	John Sandbach
Idiot	Sebastian Walker
Wrath	R. Peverello
Sloth	Maria Aitken
Idleness	Valerie James
Gluttony	Bridget Coghill, Petronella Pulsford, Susan Watson
Dancers	Jacqueline Harvey, Sheila Dawson, Carolyn Bennitt
Nun/Court Lady	Jane Wilford

Reflections in a Golden Eye (Warner Bros.—Seven Arts, 1967)
Director: John Huston. Producer: Ray Stark. Screenplay: Chapman Mortimer, Gladys Hill. Based on the novel by Carson McCullers. Cinematography: Aldo Tonti. Production Designer: Stephen Grimes. Art Direction: Bruno Avesani. Set Decoration: William Kiernan. Costumes: Dorothy Jeakins. Music: Toshiro Mayuzumi. Sound: Basil Fenton-Smith, John Cox. Editor: Russell Lloyd. Hairstyles for Miss Taylor: Alexandre of Paris. Running time: 109 minutes.

Leonora Pendleton	Elizabeth Taylor
Maj. Weldon Penderton	Marlon Brando
Lt. Col. Morris Langdon	Brian Keith
Alison Langdon	Julie Harris
Private Williams	Robert Forster
Anacleto	Zorro David
Stables Sergeant	Gordon Mitchell
Captain Weincheck	Irvin Dugan
Susie	Fay Sparks

The Comedians (MGM, 1967)
Director/Producer: Peter Glenville. Screenplay (from his novel): Graham Greene. Cinematography: Henri Decae. Art Direction: Francois de

Lamothe. Set Decoration: Robert Christides. Music: Laurence Rosenthal. Sound: Cyril Swern. Miss Taylor's Gowns: Tiziani of Rome. Miss Taylor's Hairstyles: Alexandre of Paris. Editor: Françoise Javet. Time: 160 minutes.

Brown	Richard Burton
Martha	Elizabeth Taylor
Jones	Alec Guinness
Ambassador	Peter Ustinov
Smith	Paul Ford
Mrs. Smith	Lillian Gish
Henri Philipot	George Stanford Brown
Pierre	Roscoe Lee Browne
Mrs. Philipot	Gloria Foster
Dr. Magiot	James Earl Jones
Michel	Zaeks Mokae
Joseph	Douta Seck
Concasseur	Raymond St. Jacques
Marie-Thérèse	Cicely Tyson

Boom! (Universal, 1968)

Director: Joseph Losey. Producers: John Heyman, Norman Priggen. Screenplay: Tennessee Williams, based on his play *The Milk Train Doesn't Stop Here Any More*. Cinematography: Douglas Slocombe. Production Design: Richard MacDonald. Music: John Barry. Sound: Leslie Hammon, Gerry Humphreys. Editor: Reginald Beck. Running time: 110 minutes. Gowns: Tiziani of Rome. Hairstyles: Alexandre of Paris.

Flora Goforth	Elizabeth Taylor
Chris Flanders	Richard Burton
Witch of Capri	Noel Coward
Blackie	Joanna Shimkus
Rudy	Michael Dunn
Doctor Lullo	Romolo Valli
Servants	Fernando Piazza, Veronica Wells
Journalist	Howard Taylor

Secret Ceremony (Universal, 1968)

Director: Joseph Losey. Producers: John Heyman, Norman Priggen. Screenplay: George Tabori. Based on a short story by Marco Denevi. Cinematography: Gerald Fisher. Production Design: Richard MacDonald. Art Direction: John Clark. Set Decoration: Jill Oxley. Music: Richard Rodney Bennett. Costumes: Marc Bohan, Christian Dior, Susan Yelland. Miss Taylor's Hairstyles: Alexandre of Paris. Sound: Leslie Hammond. Editor: Reginald Beck. Running time: 109 minutes.

Leonora	Elizabeth Taylor
Cenci	Mia Farrow
Albert	Robert Mitchum
Hannah	Peggy Ashcroft
Hilda	Pamela Brown

The Only Game in Town (20th Century–Fox, 1970)
Director: George Stevens. Producer: Fred Kohlmar. Screenplay: Frank D. Gilroy (based on his play). Cinematography: Henri Decae. Art Direction: Herman Blumenthal, Auguste Capélier. Set Decoration: Walter M. Scott, Jerry Wunderlich. Special Photographic Effects: L. B. Abbott, Art Cruckshank. Music: Maurice Jarre. Costumes: Mia Fonssagrives, Vicki Tiel. Sound: Joe de Bretagne, David Deckendorf. Miss Taylor's Hairstyles: Alexandre of Paris. Editors: John W. Holmes, William Sands, Pat Shade. Running time: 113 minutes.

Frank Walker	Elizabeth Taylor
Joe Grady	Warren Beatty
Lockwood	Charles Braswell
Tony	Hank Henry

Under Milk Wood (Altura Films International, 1972)
Director/Screenplay: Andrew Sinclair. Executive Producers: Jules Buck, Hugh French. Associate Producer: John Comfort. From the verse drama by Dylan Thomas. Cinematography: Bob Huke. Art Direction: Geoffrey Tozer. Sound: Cyril Collick. Music: Brian Gascoigne. Editor: Willy Kemplen. Running time: 90 minutes.

First Voice	Richard Burton
Rosie Probert	Elizabeth Taylor
Captain Cat	Peter O'Toole
Myfanwy Price	Glynis Johns
Mrs. Pugh	Vivien Merchant
Mrs. Ogmore-Pritchard	Sian Phillips
Mog Edwards	Victor Spinetti
Second Voice	Ryan Davies
Gossamer Beynon	Angharad Rees
Mr. Waldo	Ray Smith

Zee & Co. (X, Y & Zee) (Columbia, 1972)
Director: Brian Hutton. Producers: Kastner-Ladd-Kanter. Screenplay: Edna O'Brien. Cinematography: Billy Williams. Art Direction: Peter Mullins. Set Decoration: Arthur Taksen. Costumes: Beatrice Dawson.

Sound: Cyril Swern, Bob Jones. Editor: Jim Clark. Running time: 110 minutes.

Zee Blakeley	Elizabeth Taylor
Robert Blakeley	Michael Caine
Stella	Susannah York
Gladys	Margaret Leighton
Gordon	John Standing
Rita	Mary Larkin
Gavin	Michael Cashman
Headwaiter	Gino Melvazzi
Oscar	Julian West
Shaun	Hilary West

Hammersmith Is Out (J. Cornelius Crean Films, 1972)
Director: Peter Ustinov. Producer: Alex Lucas. Screenplay: Stanford Whitmore. Cinematography: Richard H. Kline. Costumes: Edith Head. Sound: Neil Brummenkant, Jim Bullock, Norman Suffern. Editor: David Blewitt. Running time: 108 minutes.

Jimmie Jean Jackson	Elizabeth Taylor
Hammersmith	Richard Burton
Doctor	Peter Ustinov
Billy Breedlove	Beau Bridges
Gen. Sam Pembroke	Leon Ames
Dr. Krodt	Leon Akin
Henry Joe	John Schuck
Cleopatra	Carl Doun
Guido Scartucci	George Raft
Princess	Marjorie Eaton
Kiddo	Lisa Jak
Miss Quim	Linda Gaye Scott
Fat Man	Mel Berger
Oldham	Anthony Holland
Pete Rutter	Brook Williams
Duke	José Espinoza

Divorce: His/Divorce: Hers (ABC-TV, 1973)
Director: Waris Hussein. Executive Producer: John Heyman. Producers: Terence Baker, Gareth Wigan. Teleplay: John Hopkins. Camera: Ernst Wild, Gabor Pogany. Costumes: Edith Head. Music: Stanley Myers. Editor: John Bloom. Miss Taylor's Hairstyles: Alexandre of Paris. Production Designer: Roy Stannard. Running time: 144 minutes.

Martin Reynolds	Richard Burton
Jane Reynolds	Elizabeth Taylor

Diana Proctor	Carrie Nye
Donald Trenton	Barry Foster
Turi Livechi	Gabriele Ferzetti
Franca	Daniela Surina
Minister	Thomas Baptiste
McIntyre	Ronald Radd
Kaduna	Rudolph Walker
Tommy	Mark Colleano
Peggy	Rosalyn Landor
Judith	Eva Griffith
Gina	Marietta Schupp

Night Watch (Avco Embassy, 1973)
Director: Brian Hutton. Producers: Martin Poll, George W. George, Bernard Strauss. Screenplay: Tony Williamson. Additional Dialogue: Evan Jones. Based on the play by Lucille Fletcher. Cinematography: Billy Williams. Art Direction: Peter Murton. Costumes: Valentino. Music: John Cameron. Song: "The Night Has Many Eyes" (Barrie-Cahn). Sound: Jonathan Bates. Editor: John Jympson. Running time: 99 minutes.

Ellen Wheeler	Elizabeth Taylor
John Wheeler	Laurence Harvey
Sarah Cooke	Billie Whitelaw
Appleby	Robert Lang
Tony	Tony Britton
Inspector Walker	Bill Dean
Sergeant Norris	Michael D. Walker
Dolores	Rosario Serrano
Secretary	Pauline Jameson
Girl in Car	Linda Hayden
Carl	Kevin Colson
Florist	Laon Maybanke

Ash Wednesday (Paramount, 1973)
Director: Larry Peerce. Producer: Dominick Dunne. Screenplay: Jean-Claude Tramont. Cinematography: Ennio Guarnieri. Art Direction: Philip Abramson. Costumes: Edith Head, Valentino. Miss Taylor's Makeup: Alberto De Rossi. Hairstylists: Giancarlo Novelli, Mirella De Rossi. Technical Adviser: Dr. Rodolphe Troques. Sound: Basil Fenton-Smith. Editor: Marion Rothman. Running time: 99 minutes.

Barbara Sawyer	Elizabeth Taylor
Mark Sawyer	Henry Fonda
Erich	Helmut Berger
David Carrington	Keith Baxter

Dr. Lambert	Maurice Teynac
Kate	Margaret Blye
Mario	Dino Mele
Paolo	Carlo Puri
Simone	Jill Pratt
Comte D'Arnoud	Andrea Esterhazy
Silvana del Campo	Irina Wassilchikoff
Tony Gutiérrez	José de Vega
Nurse Ilse	Dina Sassoli
Viet Hartung	Muki Windisch-Graetz
Helga	Nadia Stancioff
Gregory de Rive	Raymond Vignale
American Producer	Jack Repp
Hotel Director	Piero Baccante
Concierge	Gianni Rossi
Mandy	Kathy Heinsieck
Prince von Essen	Rodolfo Lodi
Samantha	Samantha Starr
German Woman	Monique Van Vooren
Bridge Player	Henning Schlüter

That's Entertainment! (MGM, 1974)
Director/Producer/Writer: Jack Haley, Jr. Executive Producer: Daniel Melnick. Cinematography: Gene Polito, Ernest Laszlo, Russell Metty, Ennio Guarnieri, Allan Green. Opticals: Robert Hoag, Jim Liles. Film Librarian: Mort Feinstein. Music Supervision: Jesse Kaye, Henry Mancini. Sound: Hal Watkins, Aaron Rochin, Lyle Burbridge, Harry W. Tetrick, William L. McCaughey. Assistant Directors: Richard Bremerkamp, David Silver, Claude Binyon, Jr. Editors: Bud Friedgen, David E. Blewitt. Running time: 132 minutes.

Narrators	Fred Astaire
	Bing Crosby
	Gene Kelly
	Peter Lawford
	Liza Minnelli
	Donald O'Connor
	Debbie Reynolds
	Mickey Rooney
	Frank Sinatra
	James Stewart
	Elizabeth Taylor

Identikit (The Driver's Seat) (Avco Embassy, 1974)
Director: Giuseppe Patroni-Griffi. Producer: Franco Rossellini. Screenplay: Muriel Spark (from her novella), Raffaele La Capria, Guiseppe

Patroni-Griffi. Cinematography: Vittorio Storaro. Art Direction: Mario Ceroli. Music: Franco Mannino. Costumes: Gabriella Pescucci. Running time: 105 minutes.

Lise	Elizabeth Taylor
Richard	Ian Bannen
Carlo	Guido Mannari
Mrs. Fiedke	Mona Washbourne
Bill	Maxence Mailfort

The Blue Bird (20th Century–Fox, 1976)

Director: George Cukor. Producer: Paul Maslansky. Executive Producer: Edward Lewis. Screenplay: Hugh Whitemore and Alfred Hayes. Based on the play by Maurice Maeterlinck. Russian Version of Screenplay: Alexei Kapler. Cinematographers: Ionas Gritzus, Freddie Young. Composers: Andrei Petrov, Irwin Kostal. Lyrics: Tony Harrison. Art Director: Valery Urkevich. Wardrobe Designers: Marina Azizian and Edith Head. Running time: 99 minutes.

Mother	
Maternal Love	Elizabeth Taylor
Witch	
Light	
Night	Jane Fonda
Cat	Cicely Tyson
Luxury	Ava Gardner
Tyltyl	Todd Lookinland
Mytyl	Patsy Kensit
Grandfather	Will Geer
Grandmother	Mona Washbourne
Father Time	Robert Morley
Oak	Harry Andrews
Dog	James Coco
Bread	Richard Pearson
The Blue Bird	Nadejda Pavlova
Milk	Margareta Terechova
The Clown	Oleg Popov
Sugar	Georgi Vitzin
Father	Leonid Nevedomsky
Water	Valentina Ganilaee Ganibalova
Fire	Yevgeny Scherbakov

Victory at Entebbe (David L. Wolper Production, 1976)

Director: Marvin J. Chomsky. Executive Producer: David L. Wolper. Producer: Robert Guenette. Associate Producer: Albert J. Simon. Teleplay: Ernest Kinoy. Photography: James Kilgore. Music: Charles Fox. Production Design: Edward Stephenson. Editors: Jim McElroy, Mike Gavaldon. Running time: 150 minutes.

German Terrorist	Helmut Berger
Yakov Shlomo	Theodore Bikel
Chana Vilnofsky	Linda Blair
Hershel Vilnofsky	Kirk Douglas
Col. Yonatan Netanyahu	Richard Dreyfuss
Mordecai Gur	Stefan Gierasch
Benjamin Wise	David Groh
President Idi Amin	Julius Harris*
Mrs. Wise	Helen Hayes
Yitzhak Rabin	Anthony Hopkins
Shimon Peres	Burt Lancaster
Captain Dukas	Christian Marquand
Edra Vilnofsky	Elizabeth Taylor
Nomi Haroun	Jessica Walter
Gen. Dan Shomron	Harris Yulin
Natan Haroun	Allan Miller
German Woman	Bibi Besch

A Little Night Music (A New World Picture, 1977)
Director: Harold Prince. Producer: Elliott Kastner. Executive Producer: Heinz Lazek. Screenplay: Hugh Wheeler. Music and Lyrics: Stephen Sondheim. Book: Hugh Wheeler. Suggested by *Smiles of a Summer Night*, a film by Ingmar Bergman. Editor: John Jympson. Photography: Arthur Ibbetson, B.S.C. Costumes: Florence Klotz. Choreographer: Patricia Birch. Running time: 124 minutes.

Désirée Armfeldt	Elizabeth Taylor
Charlotte Mittelheim	Diana Rigg
Frederick Egerman	Len Cariou
Anne Egerman	Lesley-Anne Down
Mme. Armfeldt	Hermione Gingold
Carl-Magnus Mittelheim	Laurence Guittard
Erich Egerman	Christopher Guard
Fredericka Armfeldt	Chloë Franks
Kurt	Heinz Marecek
Petra	Lesley Dunlop
Conductor	Jonathan Tunick
Franz	Hubert Tscheppe
Band Conductor	Rudolf Schrympf

Return Engagement (NBC-TV, November 17, 1978)
Director: Joseph Hardy. Producers: Mike Wise, Franklin R. Levy. Writer: James Prideaux. Associate Director: Mike Stanislavsky. Pro-

---

* He replaced Godfrey Cambridge, who died during production.

duction Designer: Boris Leven. Set Decoration: Ruby Levitt. Music: Arthur B. Rubinstein. Stage Manager: Val Riolo. Costume Designer: Edith Head. Production Assistant: Ellen Halpin. Lighting Director: Tom Schamp. Choreographer: Marty Allen. Miss Taylor's Hairdresser: Sidney Guilaroff. Casting: Ramsey King.

Elizabeth Taylor
Joseph Bottoms
Peter Donat
Allyn Ann McLerie
James Ray

Winter Kills (Avco Embassy, 1979)
Director/Writer: William Richert. Producer: Fred Caruso. Executive Producers: Leonard J. Goldberg and Robert Sterling. Based on a book by Richard Condon. Director of Photography: Vilmos Zsigmond. Costumes: Robert De Mora. Film Editor: David Bretherton. Music: Maurice Jarre. Running time: 97 minutes.

Nick Kegan	Jeff Bridges
Pat Kegan	John Huston
John Cerruti	Anthony Perkins
Joe Diamond	Eli Wallach
Z. K. Dawson	Sterling Hayden
Emma Kegan	Dorothy Malone
Frank Mayo	Tomas Milian
Yvette Malone	Belinda Bauer
Gameboy Baker	Ralph Meeker
Keith	Toshiro Mifune
Keifetz	Richard Boone
Miles Garner	David Spielberg
Captain Heller One	Brad Dexter
Ray Doty	Michael Thoma
Cameo role	Elizabeth Taylor

The Mirror Crack'd (EMI Films Ltd., 1980)
Director: Guy Hamilton. Producers: John Brabourne, Richard Goodwin. Screenplay: Jonathan Hales, Barry Sandler. Based on a book by Agatha Christie. Cinematography: Christopher Challis. Music: John Cameron. Editor: Richard Marden. Running time: 105 minutes.

Miss Marple	Angela Lansbury
Cherry	Wendy Morgan
Mrs. Bantry	Margaret Courtenay
Bates	Charles Gray
Heather Babcock	Maureen Bennett

Miss Giles	Carolyn Pickles
Major	Eric Dodson
Vicar	Charles Lloyd-Pack
Doctor Haydock	Richard Pearson
Mayor	Thick Wilson
Mayoress	Pat Nye
Scoutmaster	Peter Woodthorpe
Ella Zielinsky	Geraldine Chaplin
Marty N. Fenn	Tony Curtis
Inspector Craddock	Edward Fox
Jason Rudd	Rock Hudson
Lola Brewster	Kim Novak
Marina Rudd	Elizabeth Taylor
Margot Bence	Marella Oppenheim

STAGE APPEARANCE

The Little Foxes, a play by Lillian Hellman
Producers: Zev Bufman, Donald C. Carter, and Jon Cutler. Director: Austin Pendleton. Settings: Andrew Jackness. Costumes: Florence Klotz. Lighting: Paul Gallo. Casting: Julie Hughes, Barry Moss. Production Stage Manager: Patrick Horrigan. Hair Designs: Patrik D. Moreton. Music adaptation: Stanley Silverman.

Regina Giddens	Elizabeth Taylor
Birdie Hubbard	Maureen Stapleton
Benjamin Hubbard	Anthony Zerbe
Oscar Hubbard	Joe Ponazecki
Leo Hubbard	Dennis Christopher
Addie	Novella Nelson
Cal	Joe Seneca
William Marshall	Humbert Allen Astredo
Alexandra Giddens	Ann Talman
Horace Giddens	Tom Aldredge

INDEX

(For further information on Miss Taylor's films, their directors, writers, producers, casts, etc., see Filmography, pp. 409–38)

Abzug, Bella, 334
Academy Awards (Oscars), 23, 40, 52, 57, 87–88, 103, 105, 107, 108, 125, 133–34, 138, 140, 147, 156, 167, 183–84, 257, 258–60, 262, 272–73, 328
Adams, Sherman, 155
Aimée, Anouk, 258
Albee, Edward, 244, 249
Aldredge, Tom, 402
Alexandre (hairdresser), 283
All the Brothers Were Valiant (film), 98
Allen, Gracie, 160
Allen, Steve, 136
Allyson, June, 16, 35, 67, 352
Alpert, Hollis, 218
American in Paris, (film), 88
American Tragedy, (Dreiser), 44, 48
Anderson, Judith, 149
Andrews, Dana, 98, 99
Andrews, Julie, 243
Anne of the Thousand Days (film), 261
Ann-Margret, 244
Arnaz, Desi, Jr., 303
Around the World in 80 Days (film), 114–15, 121, 123, 124, 125, 134–36, 138, 149, 240
Asher, Irving, 98
Assassination of Trotsky, (film), 281
Ast, Pat, 328
Astaire, Fred, 67
Astor, Mary, 28

Bacall, Lauren, 233
Bacon, James (Jim), 134, 141, 144, 146, 216, 236–37
Baker, Stanley, 269
Ball, Lucille, 276
Bancroft, Anne, 260, 400
Bankhead, Tallulah, 397, 400
Barcher, Larry, 282–83, 298, 299
Barefoot Contessa, The (film), 105
Barrie, George, 288
Beau Brummell (film), 101, 103
Beaverbrook, Lord, 127
Becket (film), 220, 223, 224, 256
Bell, Jeanne, 313, 314, 315
Bennett, Joan, 43, 67
Bergman, Ingrid, 25, 260
Berman, Pandro S., 19, 20, 23, 38, 84–85, 114, 117, 139, 174, 176
Bettina, 170
Big Hangover, The (film), 42
Blackstone, Milton, 153, 162, 163, 181–82
Blaik, Red, 36
Blanchard, Doc, 34
Blondell, Joan, 123
Bloom, Claire, 197, 243
Bluebeard (film), 281–82, 286
Blue Bird, The (film), 306, 309, 311, 314–15, 320, 329
Bogart, Humphrey, 25
Boom! (film), 261
Bosworth, Patricia, 47, 254
Boyd, Stephen, 177, 179

Bozzachi, Gianni, 239*fn.*
Brando, Marlon, 103, 106, 308
Bridges, Beau, 274
Briskin, Ted, 84
Brisson, Frederick, 67
Brooks, Richard, 83, 103, 104, 139–
 140, 144–45, 149, 160, 186
Brown, Clarence, 23
Brown, Harry, 87
Brownell, Herbert, Jr., 140
Broyhill, Joel T., 368
Bruckel, Arthur, 302, 311, 313, 332,
 344–45
Brynner, Yul, 184
Bufman, Zev, 396, 400
Bujold, Geneviève, 261–62
Bulgari, Gianni, 282
Burns, George, 160
Burns, Lillian, 85
Burton, Jessica, 218, 266*fn.*
Burton, Kate, 266
Burton, Maria (adopted daughter),
 209, 215–16, 224, 226, 227, 235,
 238–39, 240, 266, 310, 316
Burton, Philip, 205, 231, 233
Burton, Richard, 89, 196–99, 201–25,
 227–34, 235–51, 253–70, 271–93
 passim, 296–301, 307, 309–10, 312–
 315, 317–23, 325–27, 331–33, 338,
 342, 343, 346, 356–58, 360, 396
Burton, Susan, 320–21, 323, 327, 332,
 342, 343, 397*fn.*
Burton, Sybil, 197, 201–6 *passim*, 209,
 211, 212, 215, 217, 219, 222, 231,
 256
Butterfield 8 (film), 172, 173–76, 183,
 360

Caine, Michael, 283
Callow, Ridgeway, 119
Camelot (revival), 397
Cancannon, Patrick J., 68, 69, 76
Cantinflas, 129, 131
Cantor, Mr. and Mrs. Eddie, 162
Capote, Truman, 83, 168, 180, 183,
 232
Carter, Jimmy, 334, 339, 346
Casablanca (film), 26
Cat on a Hot Tin Roof (film), 139,
 148–50, 151, 156, 360
Chancellor, John, 297
Channing, Carol, 233
Chapman, Ceil, 64

Christian, Linda, 158
Christopher, Dennis, 402
Christopher, Jordan, 279*fn.*
Churchill, Winston, 310
Clarke, Thurmond, 76
Cleopatra (film), 172, 176, 177–79,
 183, 194–200, 207–11, 215, 217, 223,
 227, 240
Clift, Montgomery, 44, 46–48, 50–51,
 53–55, 57–58, 81–84, 87–90 *passim*,
 99, 101, 109–14, 118, 119, 120, 147,
 164, 165, 166, 187, 210, 233, 252–54,
 296, 324, 359
Coco, James, 314
Cohen, Alexander, 326
Cohn, Art, 114, 141
Cohn, Marta, 114
Cohn, Roy, 188
Collins, Joan, 63, 177
Comedians, The (film), 258, 261, 272
Connally, John, 373, 395
Conspirator, The (film), 37, 38, 85, 127
Conway, Jack, 33
Cooper, Gary, 25, 103, 193
Courage of Lassie (film), 25, 38, 42
Coward, Noel, 124, 397
Crawford, Joan, 15, 100
Crider, Don, 303, 304, 309
Colacello, Bob, 293
Crisp, Donald, 21
Crist, Judith, 223, 242
Cronyn, Hume, 213, 233
Crosby, Bing, 25, 103
Crowther, Bosley, 104, 166
Cukor, George, 85, 308, 309
Curtis, Tony, 79, 136, 160, 196
Curtiz, Michael, 26
Cynthia (film), 27, 28, 32

Dalton, John, 351, 352, 376, 377, 378
Dalton, Mrs. John, 376, 377
Danile, Cesare, 213
Darmanin, Peter, 322–26
Date with Judy, A (film), 31
Davis, Altovise, 303
Davis, Bette, 349, 400
Davis, Glenn, 34, 35–41, 85
Davis, Gwen, 313
Davis, Sammy, Jr., 157, 303, 339, 351
Day, Doris, 26, 244
Dean, James, 106–8
DeHaven, Gloria, 68
de Havilland, Olivia, 260

Delon, Alain, 185
Delon, Nathalie, 282, 286
DeMann, Ronald, 227
Dennis, Sandy, 245, 249, 258
Derby Day (film), 96
D'Ermo, Dominique, 382
De Sica, Vittorio, 297–98
Dietrich, Marlene, 86, 87, 90, 124, 134
Dillon, Marjorie, 34–35, 43, 50, 53, 62, 65, 66–67, 73–75, 77, 82, 85, 103
Dinitz, Simcha, 370*fn.*
Divorce: His/Divorce: Hers (T.V. film), 287
Dmytryk, Edward, 111, 120, 282, 284, 287
Dmytryk, Jean, 111
Doctor Faustus (film), 260, 273
Doctor Faustus (play), 253
Dodson, Derek, 284, 286
Dodson, Mrs. Derek, 284, 286
Donen, Jeanne, 80
Donen, Stanley, 77–80, 82, 84, 86, 92
Donizetti, Heidi, 322
Douglas, Ann, 327
Douglas, Kirk, 141, 327
Dreiser, Theodore, 48, 49
Driver's Seat, The (film), 291, 294, 312
Dunnock, Mildred, 174

East of Eden (film), 106
Eisenhower, Dwight D., 36–37, 147
Eisenhower, Julie Nixon, 306
Ekberg, Anita, 107
Elephant Walk (film), 98, 99
Elizabeth, Princess of Yugoslavia, 269, 309–10, 313, 314
Elizabeth, Queen of England, 335
Elizabeth Taylor (book by E. T.), 251
Elizabeth Taylor in London (T.V. special), 224
Equus (play), 321, 325, 326

Farley, Kevin, 332–33
Farrell, Frank, 35–36, 88–89, 109–10
Father of the Bride (film), 43, 63, 73, 80, 84
Father's Little Dividend (film), 73, 79, 84
Faye, Alice, 67
Feo, Emmanuele, 201, 202
Fiedler, Arthur, 135
Finch, Peter, 98, 99, 177, 179
Fisher, Eddie, 89, 116, 130, 131, 144,

146, 152–56, 157–65, 168–71, 174–184 *passim*, 189, 190, 192, 193, 197, 198, 200–203, 208–14 *passim*, 215, 216–17, 218, 222, 225–27, 239, 243, 307, 311*fn.*, 333, 344, 360, 361, 363, 369
Fisher, Joe, 170–71
Fonda, Henry, 313, 351
Fonda, Jane, 314, 338
Fontaine, Joan, 84
Ford, Gerald, 334, 335, 339, 346, 373, 375
Ford, Glenn, 245
Foreman, Joey, 155, 162
Freeman, Mona, 22–23
Freeman, Pete, 60
Frings, Ketti, 114, 138, 144, 153, 155, 160, 162, 175, 185, 189, 226*fn.*
Frings, Kurt, 114, 138, 141, 144, 155, 160, 162, 172, 185, 190
Frosch, Aaron, 222, 240, 263, 264, 309, 311*fn.*, 327, 334

Gable, Clark, 13, 22, 96
Gabor, Zsa Zsa, 61, 67
Gang, Martin, 162
Garbo, Greta, 15
Gardner, Ava, 29, 33, 105, 224, 315
Garland, Judy, 13, 15, 28, 250
Garner, Peggy Ann, 9, 18
Garson, Greer, 14, 15, 25, 67, 96, 400
Gassman, Vittorio, 99, 116
Gates, Phyllis, 111
Giant (film), 53, 105, 109, 139
Gielgud, John, 230, 273
Girl Who Had Everything, (film), 97
Glenville, Peter, 221, 256, 272
Goetz, Ben, 95
Goetz, Edith, 275
Goldbogen, Avrom Hirsch, *see* Todd, Mike
Goldbogen, David, 145, 146
Goldstone, Jules, 27, 77, 97
Goldwater, Barry, 373
Gone With the Wind (film), 98
Grable, Betty, 15, 25
Grace (Kelly), Princess of Monaco, 100, 108, 269, 283
Grady, Billy, 19
Graham, Katharine, 391
Graham, Sheilah, 17, 18, 68, 86, 211, 265
Granger, Stewart, 86, 90, 197

Grant, Cary, 244
Gray, Colleen, 79
Grayson, Kathryn, 22
Green, Adolph, 233
Griffin, Merv, 88, 89
Griffith, Hugh, 269
Grimes, Tammy, 203, 262, 398
Grossinger, Jennie, 153
Guilaroff, Sidney, 10, 66, 144, 151, 158, 162, 176, 178, 308, 364

Halston, 328, 353, 383–84
Hamlet (play), 220, 227–30, 234
Hammersmith Is Out (film), 274
Hanley, Richard (Dick), 114, 138, 143–46, 151, 153, 162, 164, 175*fn.*, 181, 191, 211, 231, 239*fn.*, 256, 258, 268, 296, 302, 311*fn.*
Hardwicke, Cedric, 136
Hardy, Joseph, 365
Harvey, Laurence, 174, 288, 290, 294–296
Harvey, Paulene, 288, 294–95
Harriman, Averill, 140
Harris, Eleanor, 117
Harris, Phil, 67
Harrison, Rex, 100, 196, 198, 223, 268
Hart, Kitty Carlisle, 233
Hayes, John Michael, 176
Hay Fever (Noel Coward play), 397
Haynes, Brian, 319–20
Hayward, Susan, 105, 177, 178
Hayworth, Rita, 16
Head, Edith, 49, 56–57, 64, 69, 87, 313, 364
Hearst, William Randolph, 60
Heatherton, Joey, 282, 286
Heaven Knows, Mr. Allison (film), 138
Heiress, The (film), 46, 47, 48
Hellman, Lillian, 397
Hendry, Whitey, 66
Hepburn, Katharine, 15, 22, 164–67
Hernandez, Fernando, 129, 131
Heyman, Norma, 345
Hift, Fred, 268
Hilton, Barron, 69, 74
Hilton, Conrad, 59, 60, 61, 64, 67
Hilton, Conrad Nicholson (Nicky), Jr., 58, 59–69, 70–76, 78–79, 81, 84, 91, 92, 93, 131, 182, 208, 222, 286, 301, 307
Hilton, Marilyn, 61, 66, 73, 74
Hine, Al, 87

Holden, William, 103
Holman, Libby, 90
Holton, Linwood, 340, 362
Hooks, Benjamin, 395
Hope, Bob, 25, 260
Hopper, Hedda, 17, 18, 30, 54–55, 68, 69, 89, 92, 100, 154, 155
Hopson, Maury, 385, 386–87
Hornbeck, William, 87
Hornby, Sharon, 382
Hudson, Rock, 107, 108, 109, 111, 113, 160, 244, 308
Hufty, Page Lee, 336
Hughes, Howard, 84, 146
Humphrey, Hubert, 136
Hunt, James, 321, 332
Hunt, Susan, *see* Burton, Susan
Hussey, Olivia, 308, 311
Huston, John, 253
Hutton, Betty, 84
Hyams, Joe, 158

I'll Cry Tomorrow (film), 105
I Love Lucy (T.V. series), 276
Ireland, John, 296
Ivanhoe (film), 84–85, 86, 87
Ives, Burl, 148–49

Jacobson, Dr. Max, 174
Jagger, Bianca, 353
James, Cissie, 231–32
Jane Eyre (film), 9, 18
Janssen, David, 174
Jenkins, Ivor, 284, 296
Jenkins, Richard, *see* Burton, Richard
Jessel, George, 136
Johansson, Ingemar, 170, 188–89, 208
Johnson, Eve, 67
Johnson, Van, 25, 42, 43, 44, 67, 103, 104
Julia Misbehaves (film), 33

Kaminska, Ida, 258
Karl, Harry, 181
Kearns, Doris, 34
Kearns, Hubie, 34
Kelly, Emmett, 136
Kelly, Gene, 67
Kelly, Grace, *see* Grace, Princess
Kenmore, Robert, 264
Kennamer, Dr. Rex, 112, 113, 138, 143, 146, 148, 150, 151, 162, 180, 183, 194, 254, 288, 303

Kennedy, Edward, 336
Kennedy, John F., 174, 230, 338, 360, 395
Kennedy, Robert, 255, 339
Kern, Robert J., 23
Kerr, Deborah, 138, 183, 224
Kerr, Walter, 326
Kerry, Margaret, 22
Keyes, Evelyn, 114–17, 121, 130
Khan, Aly, 136, 170, 171
Kissinger, Henry, 327–28
Kissinger, Nancy, 327
Klansman, The (film), 299
Klotz, Florence, 344
Korda, Vincent, 135
Koverman, Ida, 68
Krupp, Vera, 265

Ladd, Alan, 103
Lady with the Lamp, The (film), 90
Lahr, Bert, 136
Lamarr, Hedy, 22
Landrigan, Ward, 263
Lansbury, Angela, 22
Lantz, Robert, 253, 327
Lardner, James, 402
Lassie Come Home (film), 14, 18
Last Time I Saw Paris, The (film), 103–4, 127
Latin Lovers (film), 100
Laurence, Tom, 363
Lawford, Patricia Kennedy, 160, 233
Lawford, Peter, 82, 160, 288, 294, 296, 303
Leachman, Cloris, 331
Lee, John, 164, 231, 239*fn.*, 311*fn.*
Lehman, Ernest, 244, 250, 257, 258
Leigh, Janet, 35, 67, 79, 136, 160, 352
Leigh, Vivien, 14, 98, 260
Leighton, Margaret, 247, 370
Lemmon, Jack, 244, 245
Lepotouguí, Mario, 130, 131
Lerner, Alan Jay, 174, 233
Lerner, Edna, 188, 189
Lerner, Max, 83, 153, 163–64, 185–90, 191–92, 208, 303, 305, 306, 307, 310, 312, 314, 381*fn.*, 382*fn.*
Lewis, Ed, 315
Lewis, Jerry, 103
Life with Father (film), 26
Lillie, Beatrice, 233
Lisi, Virna, 281, 286
Little Foxes, The (play), 397–403

Little Night Music, A (film), 327, 342, 345, 355–56
Little Women (film), 34, 35
Loew, Arthur, Jr., 67, 84, 151, 152, 170
Loos, Anita, 125, 233
Loren, Sophia, 185, 291, 292, 297, 298–99
Losey, Joseph, 283
Love Is Better than Ever (film), 75, 77
Loy, Myrna, 15, 233, 308
Luchenbill, Gloria, 162
Lynch, Peggy, 16
Lynn, Diana, 79
Lyon, Bill, 143, 144, 147
Lyon, Sue, 224

McCambridge, Mercedes, 108, 164, 165
McCarthy, Glen, 62
McCarthy, Joseph, 96
McCarthy, Kevin, 111, 112, 113
McClory, Kevin, 114, 116
McClure, Gaylen, 31
McDowall, Roddy, 14, 67, 88, 109–10, 197–98, 199, 207, 208*fn.*, 211, 213, 251, 254, 288, 311
MacLaine, Shirley, 179, 244
Magnani, Anna, 138
Mamoulian, Rouben, 177–78
Man for All Seasons, A (film), 260
Mankiewicz, Christopher, 199
Mankiewicz, Joseph, 141, 165, 166, 167, 179, 199, 200, 201, 209, 213, 217
Mann, Daniel, 176
Mannix, Eddie, 144
Manville, Lorraine, 125
March, Fredric, 203
Margaret, Princess of England, 250, 255, 265, 352
Marshall, Betty, 151–52
Martin, Dean, 103, 312
Marvin, Lee, 119, 299, 300
Marx, Sam, 42, 90
Maslansky, Paul, 315
Matthau, Walter, 260
Maxwell, Elsa, 136, 156
Mayer, Louis B., 14–17 *passim*, 23, 25, 26, 33, 96
Meadows, Jayne, 136
Mellon, Catherine, 335, 336, 339
Mellon, Paul, 335, 336, 340
Mellor, William C., 87

Merrill, Dina, 174, 233
Messel, Oliver, 180
Metro-Goldwyn-Mayer (MGM), 9, 11,
    13–18 *passim*, 20–24 *passim*, 27,
    30–31, 33, 35, 38, 40, 44, 61, 63–66
    passim, 68–69, 73, 75–76, 84–85,
    90–91, 96–97, 98, 101, 105, 111,
    113–14, 117–19, 139, 143, 156, 168,
    172–73, 175, 183, 241
Miller, Andrew P., 368–69, 371, 372,
    375, 377
Miller, Ann, 61
Miller, Arthur, 187
Miller, Doris, 369, 373, 377
Miller, Nathan, 362, 363
Milli, Mary Jane, 229, 230
Milli, Robert, 229, 230
Mindlin, Mike, 220
Minnelli, Liza, 303, 311, 328, 351
Minnelli, Vincente, 242
Mirror Crack'd, The (film), 393
Moffat, Ivan, 55, 84
Mondale, Walter F., 378
Monroe, Marilyn, 103, 157, 179, 187,
    306, 306–07*fn.*
Moore, Terry, 40*fn.*, 67
Moorhead, Agnes, 119, 159*fn.*
Morgan, John, 269
Morgan, Reverend Neale, 347–48
Mosley, Leonard, 150
Mrs. Miniver (film), 14
Murphy, George, 67
My Fair Lady (play), 100

National Velvet (book), 19
National Velvet (film), 19–24, 28, 31,
    38, 84, 129, 392
Neagle, Anna, 90, 91, 94, 95, 96
Neal, Patricia, 65
Neshamkin, Paul (tutor), 235–36, 237–
    240, 241, 242, 268, 331
Newcombe, Patricia, 162
Newman, Paul, 148, 150, 151, 244, 352
Nibbles and Me (book by E. T.), 25
Nichols, Mike, 246–47, 249, 250, 251,
    257, 258, 260, 399
Night of the Iguana, The (film), 222,
    224–25, 236, 244
Nine Lives of Mike Todd (book), 141
Niven, David, 283
Nixon, Richard M., 335*fn.*, 338, 339,
    375
Nizer, Louis, 187

Novak, Kim, 16, 179
Nussbaum, Rabbi Max, 151, 157

Obenshain, Helen, 366–67, 368, 377,
    380
Obenshain, Richard, 362, 363, 366–67,
    368
O'Brien, Margaret, 9, 13, 18, 25, 33,
    35, 67, 352
O'Connor, Carroll, 352
O'Hara, John, 172, 173
Olivier, Laurence, 14, 98, 296
Onassis, Aristotle, 265, 287
Onassis, Jacqueline, 247, 287, 294*fn.*,
    395*fn.*
Only Game in Town, The (film), 270
Orkin, Harvey, 204
Orkin, Mrs. Harvey, 256
O'Toole, Peter, 220, 221–22
Owl and the Pussycat, The (film), 252

Pahlavi, Reza, Shah, 330
Panazecki, Joe, 399
Paramount Studios, 44, 46–47, 64, 98
Parsons, Louella O., 17, 18, 41, 68,
    69, 73, 92
Pasternak, Joseph (Joe), 160
Patrick, Nigel, 119
Patterson-Johansson fight, 188–89
Paval, Philip, 67
Pawley, William D., 39, 41–45, 62, 68
Peachee, Judy, 367–68
Pennington, Dr. Richard, 212
Peretti, Elsa, 332
Peters, Susan, 22
Peyton Place (film), 138
Place in the Sun, A (film), 44, 46–55,
    57, 58, 87–88, 255
Ponti, Carlo, 185, 291, 292, 298
Powell, Dick, 67
Powell, Jane, 66, 96
Power, Tyrone, 126
Preminger, Otto, 221
Presley, Elvis, 244
Prideaux, James, 364, 365
Prowse, Juliet, 216

Radziwill, Lee, 294*fn.*
Ragaway, Martin, 79
Rainer, Luise, 260
Rainier, Prince of Monaco, 269
Raintree County (film), 110, 111, 113,
    118–19, 120, 121, 138, 139, 147, 258

Ransohoff, Martin, 257
Reagan, Mara, *see* Taylor, Mara Reagan
Reagan, Nancy (Davis), 160, 394, 395, 398, 402
Reagan, Ronald, 160, 373, 394, 395, 398, 402
Rebel Without a Cause (film), 107
Redford, Robert, 245
Redgrave, Lynn, 258
Redgrave, Vanessa, 258
Reed, Donna, 22
Reed, Rex, 261
Reflections in a Golden Eye (film), 252–53, 261, 324
Remick, Lee, 203, 233
Return Engagement (T.V. film), 364, 365
Revere, Anne, 23
Reynolds, Debbie, 68, 116, 130–31, 144, 146, 152, 153–56, 159–60, 168, 181, 355
Rhapsody (film), 99, 100
Richards, Evan, 266
Richert, Bill, 365
Ritt, Martin, 243
Rivers, Joan, 355
Roberts, Stanley, 79
Robinson, Jackie, 140
Rockefeller, Nelson, 334
Rogers, Ginger, 67, 136
Rogers, Roy, 25
Rooney, Mickey, 13, 19, 20, 25, 96
Roosevelt, Franklin D., 26
Rose, Helen, 10, 47, 61, 63–64, 66, 67, 92, 101, 104, 130, 131, 139, 144, 146, 148, 151, 308
Ross, Frank, 203
Rostova, Mira, 47
Rothschild, Baron and Baroness Guy de, 269
Ruark, Robert, 163
Russell, Rosalind, 67
Rutherford, Margaret, 273, 308
Rutledge, Peggy, 77, 82, 84, 86
Ryan, Mrs. J. A., 66
Ryman, Lucille, 22

Saint, Eva Marie, 119
St. John, Adela Rogers, 17, 18
Salemson, Harold, 164, 166–67
Salinger, J. D., 30

Sam, Chen, 318, 321, 322, 325, 335, 346, 358, 385
Sanders, George, 84
Sandpiper, The (film), 240–41, 242, 246, 257, 276
Scarrone, Lou, 331
Schary, Dore, 96, 118
Schell, Maria, 190
Scofield, Paul, 258, 260
Scott, Vernon, 141, 162
Scott, William, 338, 377
Secret Ceremony (film), 261
Segal, George, 245, 249
Segal, Marian, 249–50
Shaffer, Peter, 321
Sharaff, Irene, 225, 247, 258
Shearer, Norma, 15
Sherwood, Madeleine, 148
Shouse, Kay, 351
Shuster, Bud, 390
Siegel, Sol, 172–73
Simmons, Jean, 90, 197, 203
Simon, Sylvan, 126
Sinatra, Frank, 21*fn.*, 112, 124, 208, 232, 304, 324
Skouras, Spyros, 177, 178, 179, 194, 217
Smith, Jean Kennedy, 233
Smith, Mary Jane, 68
Snowdon, Lord (Anthony Armstrong-Jones), 250
Spiegel, Sam, 164
Spinetti, Victor, 283
Spirit of West Point, The (film), 39
Springer, John, 254, 258
Spy Who Came In from the Cold, The (film), 235, 242–43
Stapleton, Maureen, 399, 401*fn.*
Stark, Ray, 253
Starr, Ringo, 283
Steinem, Gloria, 247
Stevens, Connie, 331
Stevens, George, 44, 48–55 *passim*, 84, 87, 105–8
Stevens, George, Jr., 84
Stewart, James, 103
Stompanato, Johnny, 148
Strasberg, Susan, 197, 262
Straus, Ann, 17, 29, 144
Streetcar Named Desire, A (film), 98
Strickling, Howard, 17
Suddenly Last Summer (film), 162, 164–68, 253

Sujetska (film), 281
Sukarno, Dewi, 305
Sullivan, Barry, 79
Sullivan, Betty, 67, 71–72
Sullivan, Ed, 216, 220, 221–22
Surtes, Bob, 119
Susskind, David, 223
Swan, The (film), 100

Taming of the Shrew, The (film), 253, 260, 269–70, 273
Taylor, Elizabeth Rosamund:
Academy Awards, nominations, 138, 156, 166, 183–84, 259–60, 360; accidents, illnesses, 26–28, 76, 99, 108, 109, 119, 127–28, 137, 175, 176, 179, 180–83, 212, 217, 249, 276–77, 295, 297, 309–10, 313, 319, 320, 347, 351, 359, 375–76, 396; adolescent daydreams, 34–35; beauty, 11, 30, 50, 52, 81–82, 130, 401, 402; childhood, earliest films, 9–18; children (*see* Burton, Maria; Todd, Elizabeth; Wilding, Christopher; Wilding, Michael, Jr.); and Montgomery Clift, 46–58 *passim*, 81–84, 87–90, 99, 109, 110–14, 118–119, 120, 252–54, 359; conversion to Judaism, 157–58, 271; and Peter Darmanin, 322–26; and Glenn Davis, 35–40; and Stanley Donen, 77–80; education, 56; and Entebbe hostages, 370; generosity, 82–83, 252, 254, 255–57; humor, 88–89; jewels, love of, 262–65, 322–23, 328, 358–59; and Max Lerner, 185–192, 303; in *The Little Foxes*, 397–403; marriage, optimistic outlook on, 7–8; marriages (1st, *see* Hilton, Conrad N., Jr.; 2nd, *see* Wilding, Michael; 3rd, *see* Todd, Mike; 4th, *see* Fisher, Eddie; 5th and 6th, *see* Burton, Richard; 7th, *see* Warner, John W.); as "Martha," 244–51; new persona, 260–61; and William Pawley, 39–45, 68; poetry reading by, 233–34; politics, 334, 338–39, 353–54; preoccupation with death, 187, 192–94; as starlet, 19–24, 28–31; weight problems, 97–98, 275, 314, 355–56, 364, 365, 385–90, 394, 398, 401*fn.*; and Henry Wynberg,

see Wynberg, Henry; and Ardeshir Zahedi, 328–31
Taylor, Francis (father), 10–15 *passim*, 21, 27, 30, 36–38, 40, 43, 59, 61, 63, 67, 94, 96, 122, 162, 296
Taylor, Howard (brother), 14, 27, 31, 35, 66, 95, 131, 144, 146, 147, 278, 310
Taylor, Mara Reagan (sister-in-law), 66, 131, 145, 147, 162
Taylor, Robert, 37, 84, 127
Taylor, Rod, 119
Taylor, Sara (mother), 9–15, 17–18, 20–22, 24–32 *passim*, 34, 35, 37–43 *passim*, 45, 47, 51, 54–64 *passim*, 68, 69, 72, 74–78 *passim*, 82, 84, 91–96 *passim*, 102, 122, 127, 158, 162, 182, 308, 310, 378
Temple, Shirley, 13, 33
Thau, Benjamin (Benny), 24, 27, 90–91, 98, 101, 105, 144, 162, 174
There's One Born Every Minute (film), 13
Thomas, Helen, 354
Thompson, Barbara, 67
Thompson, Thomas, 83
Thorpe, Richard, 85
Three Faces of Eve (film), 138
Todd, Bertha, 123
Todd, Elizabeth Frances (Liza) (daughter), 132, 133, 140, 149*fn.*, 158, 191, 224, 226, 227, 235, 236, 238, 266, 310, 311, 345, 388
Todd, Mike, 114–17, 119–42, 159, 161, 164, 169, 187, 191, 193, 208, 211, 222, 227, 236, 243, 244, 292–93, 296, 304, 307, 312, 324–25, 344, 360, 367*fn.*, 368, 370; death, 141–47, 149, 151–52, 155
Todd, Mike, Jr., 126, 131, 145, 146, 148, 149, 151, 153, 162
Torch Song (film), 100
Tracy, Spencer, 22, 43, 44, 67, 73, 96, 164
Trudeau, Garry, 379–80
Truman, Bess, 29
Truman, Harry S, 26
Tunder, Pat, 197
Turner, Cheryl, 148
Turner, Lana, 15, 29, 33, 100, 138, 148
Turner, Tina, 305
20th Century-Fox, 9, 18, 173, 177, 194, 200, 204, 217

Tynan, Kenneth, 219
Tyson, Cicely, 314

Universal Studios, 11, 13
Uribe, Rudy, 302–3, 304, 308, 309,
  311, 313
Ustinov, Peter, 284*fn.*, 290

Valentino (couturier), 332
Valva, John, 198
Vanderbilt, Gloria, 170
Victory at Entebbe (T.V. film), 370*fn.*
Vignale, Raymond, 302, 311, 313
Vidal, Gore, 165
V.I.P.s, The (film), 219, 273
Von Furstenburg, Betsy, 74, 91
Voyage, The (film), 291

Waller, Blaine, 81–82, 210*fn.*
Wallis, Hal, 223–24, 261, 269–70
Walters, Barbara, 335–36, 338, 346,
  354
Wanger, Walter, 67, 168, 176, 177,
  178, 190–91, 210–12, 217, 233
Warhol, Andy, 268, 293, 340*fn.*, 353
Warner, Catherine Mellon, *see*
  Mellon, Catherine
Warner, Jack, 251, 257, 258
Warner, John W., 335–42, 344–48,
  350–57 *passim*, 358–63, 366–83,
  385, 387, 388–93, 395–96
Warner, Mary, 345
Warner Brothers, 26, 105, 106, 244,
  253
Waxman, Franz, 87
Wayne, John, 103, 244
Weingarten, Laurence, 144
Welch, Raquel, 281, 283
Welks, Danny, 153
Wesson, Melissa, 70–71, 81
Westmore, Anne, 15, 66
Wexler, Haskell, 246, 258
White Cliffs of Dover, The (film), 18
Who's Afraid of Virginia Woolf?
  (film), 244–51, 257, 260, 272–73,
  284, 360, 392
Wigg, David, 319
Wilcox, Herbert, 86, 88, 90, 91, 94, 95
Wilding, Beth Clutter (daughter-in-
  law), 278–81

Wilding, Christopher (son), 100, 102,
  110, 184, 191, 224, 235, 236, 238,
  310, 388
Wilding, Leyla (grandchild), 279–81
Wilding, Michael, 85–87, 89–97, 100–
  103, 108, 109–17, 119–21, 126, 128,
  144, 183–84, 190, 197, 208, 222, 278,
  307, 360, 370, 388
Wilding, Michael Howard, Jr. (son),
  97–98, 191, 224, 235, 236, 238, 277–
  281, 283, 285, 345, 388
Wild Is the Wind (film), 138
Williams, Andy, 174
Williams, Brook, 320, 321
Williams, Dick, 55
Williams, Emlyn, 231, 269
Williams, Esther, 67, 96
Williams, Tennessee, 139, 164, 166,
  384
Wilson, Bob, 228, 239*fn.*
Wilson, Mrs. Bob, 256
Wilson, Earl, 161
Wilson, Michael, 87
Windsor, Duke and Duchess of, 70
Winter Kills (film), 365, 381
Winters, Shelley, 44, 48–52 *passim*,
  56, 87, 116, 136
Wood, Natalie, 393
Woodward, Joanne, 138, 147, 151,
  177, 178, 250, 352
Wyler, William, 48
Wyman, Jane, 103
Wynberg, Henry, 294–97, 299, 301–10
  passim, 312, 313, 315–16, 325, 326,
  328, 334, 382*fn.*

York, Susannah, 283
Young, Howard (great-uncle), 10, 35–
  40 *passim*, 64, 78, 109
Young, Terence, 300
Young Bess (film), 98

Zahedi, Ardeshir, 328–31, 345–46
Zahedi, Firooz, 332
Zarak Khan (film), 109
Zee & Co. (film), 280
Zeffirelli, Franco, 290–91
Zerbe, Anthony, 399
Zinnemann, Fred, 246, 260
Zumwalt, Elmo R., Jr., 371